Reflections *on* Fundamental Matters

Not for the Satisfied Mind

JOHN H.T. FRANCIS

Copyright © 2013 John H.T. Francis.

All rights reserved. No part of this book may be reproduced, stored, or transmitted by any means—whether auditory, graphic, mechanical, or electronic—without written permission of both publisher and author, except in the case of brief excerpts used in critical articles and reviews. Unauthorized reproduction of any part of this work is illegal and is punishable by law.

ISBN: 978-1-4834-0235-2 (sc)
ISBN: 978-1-4834-0234-5 (e)

Library of Congress Control Number: 2013912183

Because of the dynamic nature of the Internet, any web addresses or links contained in this book may have changed since publication and may no longer be valid. The views expressed in this work are solely those of the author and do not necessarily reflect the views of the publisher, and the publisher hereby disclaims any responsibility for them.

In the memory of my father

Contents

Preface . . . . *ix*
Putting Things in Context 1
On What Is Around Us and What Is In Us 21
Interaction and Reflexivity 33
On Knowledge and Truth 65
Deeds vs. Thoughts 125
The Absurd 153
Everything Changes (almost) 173
On the Characteristics of Life 195
The Influence of the Environment 223
On Human Contradictions 249
Brief Notes on the Pains of Evolution and Progress 273
On Ethics 285
On Religions 321
On Political and Economic Systems 347
Power: A Key Paradigm of Living Beings 377
The Ingredients of Success 397
Epilogue *429*
Appendix: Objections to the First Premise *433*
Additional Notes and Bibliography *439*
Index *447*

PREFACE

This work is not to provide you with a solution to all of your questions and problems. This work is to provide you with a framework of thought based on a multi-disciplinary approach. In summary, this is a book to make you think and make you, once you finish, get up and re-check most of what it is in it and explore further.

As Immanuel Kant[1] once said, human ignorance is rooted in laziness and cowardice. This book is neither for the lazy nor for the intellectually coward. This book is another brick in the very large wall many have built throughout History to push back these two human characteristics. It will treat subjects of fundamental importance and hopefully provide a certain framework for thinking about important questions of Humanity. This book is a start and not an end in itself.

Maybe some will say that it is sometimes better to be ignorant and comfortable than to know more and suffer from it. After all, knowledge is not a necessary guarantee of happiness; some of the most simple minds or blind-faith believers are the happiest. Indeed, there exists the notion of an over-questioning man getting entangled in his own thinking and ending up worse off in comparison with an individual leading a more simple and peaceful life. This is merely a romanticised description of a reality that possesses no real foundation. If the reader happens to examine

---
1   Eminent German philosopher.

several life experiences of these two opposing notions, she will often find that despite the fact that knowledge is not a necessary guarantee of happiness, resolving to have a simplistic view or blind faith represents a fragile balance, eventually bound to be either openly refuted or suppressed within in some form of denial.

This book may not be a light read, but it is also not a technical or deeply specialised read. It addresses questions of importance that have been thought of and discussed across different times and cultures. Many of these topics a growing child is capable of thinking of and asking questions about. The book aims to minimise any technical, seemingly savvy vocabulary; much can be explained with simple straight words, not simple or simplistic ideas, but a juxtaposition of simple words that we hope the young as much as the old will be able to understand.

The different pieces of this work are organised in what are intended to be autonomous chapters. With the exception of the first two chapters and the first half of the third chapter, which the writer recommends reading them entirely and in their respective order, each piece of the rest of the work can be looked at separately. The second chapter may seem rather technical, but that is unfortunately necessary, and so is its order in the flow. If a chapter or part of a chapter seems too long, too technical, or simply of no personal interest, the reader can skip it or return to it at a later stage without a major loss of flow. Many chapters start with anecdotes and quotations. Naturally, the aim of these is to give a flavour of what is to come and admittedly frame the reader's mind for a particular start. We recommend not to rush in the reading of this book, but rather to provide each chapter the necessary mental desire, even if this means pausing for a while between chapters.

The style of this work may seem peculiar to some. The book is a work of prose; it is flowing; but it is also structured in short paragraphs, propositions, and sub-propositions. The reason behind this is the conception of the book itself: it is a book of ideas; it is a collection of ideas organised in an orderly manner for it to correspond to a story. Every bullet is an idea or a small subset of ideas that can be accepted or rejected. The whole of the propositions fits together in an intended architecture of thought. The writer hopes from this structure to make the reading and understanding of the whole easier. The structure is no doubt inspired by the style of the *Ethics, Tractatus,* and some of Nietzsche's works, but without the deeper mathematical connectivity of the first two works.

The book may refer in few places to authors or thinkers to corroborate certain concepts or oppose certain views without giving full details of the opinions held by the cited authors or thinkers. This may seem obscure to some. In such cases, the references are more intended for the readers who already know about the positions held by such names and can therefore use them as anchoring points. Not knowing beforehand about such opinions does not take away much from the understanding of the book, and this is the reason behind not elaborating further on the opinion of others. This is a compromise the writer took; the other attitude would have been to explain in details the position of every name mentioned in the book, which risks taking us on many digressions and breaks further the flow of the writing.

The reader may be asking herself, "Who is this person saying all of this? What are his qualifications? Why should I listen to him? And why is he writing this anyway?" Allow me to start by saying that I, as a person, am rather irrelevant; many of the notions referred to here have existed, some since a very long time. But to my surprise, as I discovered them, I discovered how little known some of the basics of these notions are to the general public, and how this ignorance has led in History, time and again, to monstrous behaviours in terms of wars, political choices, and personal choices (e.g. career or faith). It is still today everywhere around us. I just happen to be curious and rarely satisfied with the shallow or authoritative answers given at first hand, and that curiosity spans a broad range of scientific and humanistic fields. This book is born from my love for knowledge and this disconnect which I, and likely many of the readers drawn to this book, cannot but observe constantly around us.

I am knowledgeable in many of the fields the book addresses but a specialist in only few of them. Given the scope of the book, it is evident that being a specialist in all the topics that it addresses requires many times a human life before even attempting to start. I have had the privilege of being exposed to many academic and professional fields; different histories and religions; several cultures, countries, and languages; times of peace and war; and multiple different political systems. I simply observed... and hope to have much of that reflected in a way or another in what follows. I have grown with Physics and Mathematics; worked in Business and Finance; developed a great personal taste for Psychology and Evolutionary Biology from simply living, observing, and wondering; and finally could not do without Philosophy, the historical source of them all. But I consider myself above all else a curious citizen of the world, human and natural, of thought and of action.

This book will provide answers, not only open questions; but more important than the answers is the attitude the writer hopes the book will instil in the reader. Maybe the key novelty in this book will be the adjacency of these multi-disciplinary notions to this extent—and that even is not really novel. The writer has endeavoured in this book to keep as much of the philosophical and linguistic integrity as necessary, but as the purpose of it is to be a starting point for any one person, of any background and culture, native or non-native English speakers, and not intended for any particular philosophical or scientific community, I beg pardon for any philosophical trespasses or scientific simplifications made in it. Some words in the book will be capitalised in some parts and not in others, which may seem random and obscure to some readers. Generally, words will be capitalised from time to time if they are important in the context of the chapter we are in (the importance of some words being different from one chapter to the other); if they refer to a general concept or a class, and not to a particular of the concept or of the class (such as *Knowledge* as a concept vs. the *knowledge* of something in particular); or to differentiate the words as references to key concepts in order not to confuse them with their more common daily uses (such as Life as a phenomenon vs. life in the common daily sense(s), or Space as a relation in Philosophy/Physics vs. space in the more common sense(s) of the word).

Finally, in this writing, the reader might find a curious interplay between the uses of the pronouns *we* and *I* where the subject is essentially the same writer[2]. The writer acknowledges a difficulty in using the pronoun *I* when expressing a certain opinion or hypothesis, not from a longing for any ancient form of writing with the *we*, but rather emanating from a large psychological discomfort in attributing such opinions to the writer as an individual, egoistic person. We all have false modesties at some level; however, the dread of the *I* is admittedly quite present in the writer. The writer will therefore use the *I* in the rather pejorative situations, or when it is necessary to use the first pronoun for a better understanding of the intended meaning. The writer also hopes that the reader will come to associate the *I* with the writer as a normal individual, with his faults and weaknesses, and the *we* with the consciousness of the writer thinking about the individual, everything around, and everything within.

The book does not count; the writer does not count; it is the spread of the ideas and their largest remembrance that matter, for in that lies our hope for a different, more universal tomorrow.

---

2   Except when the pronoun *we* refers to more than the writer himself to include a certain group. In such cases, the meaning is hopefully rather evident.

PUTTING THINGS IN CONTEXT

1. Before we attempt to discuss anything of value, it is important to begin with providing a glimpse of the context within which all that is of human importance and interest came to be. It is, we are sure, an imperfect and incomplete glimpse of the history of everything and yet so crucial that it requires us to say something about it, particularly at the beginning of our discussion, in order for the reader to maintain its presence in mind all along the entire work. Almost everything can be comprehended better when addressed in the light of a better understanding of the history of matter, living beings, and human actions and thoughts.

2. The Universe is the set of *all events* in the Physics sense of the word[3]. Matter and energy are essentially a collection of events. With events are required *relations* between events, and these are essentially what we call Space and Time. Hence, the History of the Universe is the sequence of events along the dimension of Time. From what we credibly know, this sequence of events has started some 13.8 *billion* years ago. We are situated on a very very small part of this Universe we call Earth. This very very small piece of the Universe revolves around another piece of the Universe that is more than 333 thousand times bigger we call the Sun. How small is 'very very small'? Well the Sun, which is 333 thousand times

---

3 We shall attempt to explain the term 'event' in the context of Physics in more details in the following chapter.

bigger than our habitat, happens to be a moderate size star[4] of the *billions* of stars that form galaxies, and there are again *billions* of galaxies in the Universe. These billions of billions, to continue the irony, are according to some of the latest estimates, around 5% of the total *current* events of the Universe; 95% is dark energy and dark matter...

3. One of the reasons why the Sun is so special to us is because it emits enormous amounts of energy and light (which is a particular form of energy) on constant basis. By the fact of our Earth rotating around itself and around the Sun, we obtain phases of light, and we receive higher or lower quantities of energy depending on our changing distance to the Sun; this makes our days and nights, which was likely the first intuitive way for us human beings of grasping the notion of Time, cycles and repetitions, seasons, and to some extent cold and hot. These mechanisms of rotation also provide most of the energy needed for Life (e.g. for photosynthesis in flora), as well as for water and wind movements. The functioning system Earth-Sun is around 4.5 *billion* years old, and it has roughly the same amount of time or slightly more still to go if no externality comes to disturb it.

4. For the first billion years of the existence of Earth, interesting things happened but not so much from our subjective human perspective. Life as we describe it in terms of organisms capable of reproducing and using resources from the environment around started 3.5 billion years ago. These organisms were, however, very simple in nature, one cell to start, then some collection of cells, and later on some basic vegetation and animals. More interestingly, slightly less than 3 billion years after the start of Life on Earth, something ignited a material jump in the quality and diversity of Life on our planet—we call it the Cambrian Explosion. The term is slightly misleading; things happened fast in comparison with the mind-bogglingly slow timespans of previous 'meaningful' stages

---

4   Some stars are so much bigger than our Sun that they do not allow anything to revolve around them by simply sucking everything in, even light, if close enough.

Putting Things in Context

of development, but not as fast as an explosion, not even anywhere close. During a period of more than 70-80 *million* years, starting around 580 million years ago, the complexity, number, and types of living organisms witnessed a magnificent multiplication and spread. Trees and reptiles followed millions of years after.

5. Around 330 million years following the Cambrian Explosion, or 66 million years ago, a major externality took place and shook Earth. It is likely to have been an explosion of one or several meteorites on the surface of our planet originating from our solar system and releasing huge amounts of energy all across our future habitat (we did not exist as a species then). This externality constituted a real game changer for Life on Earth, and it can this time be really called an *explosion*. It was an explosion with more destructive consequences for Life than positive ones, but not in what concerns us as humans luckily enough. Much of Life's variety built over billions of years got wiped out rather quickly. Many species went extinct, and dominant species of the times (such as the famous dinosaurs) faced annihilation, literally. But luckily, an important mass of Life endured and survived. Out of this cataclysmic mayhem, a funny set of species we call today mammals (essentially defined by the fact that newborns take their nutrients from their mother's breasts) emerged in a relatively better shape than all the rest. As we said, the family of alpha species of the time, the dinosaurs, was almost entirely wiped out; its main surviving successor today is the more modest (but very elegant) family of species we call birds. These funny mammals went on to spread on Earth and then back again into the sea.

6. Mammal life developed and spread from there on, and without detailing too much, we all know what came out next. Following a series of ape-like species, which developed with time a better mastery of tools, more sophisticated collective mechanisms, and new ways of communication (including language), came out, around 200,000 years ago, a species we call fancily *Homo Sapiens*, the Humans.

7. Before continuing further, it is worth stopping here to contemplate

some of these time, matter, and space dimensions we have mentioned so far. Billions of years; billions of billions of stars that constitute 5% of what is all of the Universe; billions of years of Life; millions of species and many dominant ones that came and went; and then 200,000 years ago, the first glimpse of us in a far from dominant form of any kind. Next time we hop into our 'big' car wearing the best clothes and accessories; listening to the news on our 'high tech' systems, while our smartphone is Bluetooth-connected to our car; planning our day and life; and using our best knowledge and gadgets, we should take a moment and contemplate these dimensions in comparison with what we are and what is our lifespan. Our life and the things around us are very important from our point of view, as they should be, but it seems that this is the extent of it.

With the above, we could consider having enough elements on the history of matter and living things, and we can start building the proper framework for the history of humans, their actions, and their knowledge.

8. Homo Sapiens **are essentially social mammals with developed cognitive capabilities, including complex abstraction[5] and developed memory.** The definition is long, but in it we can find most of the important elements we need. The history of *Homo Sapiens* is ~200,000 years old, but their agricultural development, the birth cause of villages, later cities, and so civilisation, is only ~12,000 years old. Of these 12,000 years, the more recent 5,000 years from the Bronze Age and the Pharaonic civilisation are the more interesting phase. Alphabets were invented and improved between 1900 and 1200 BC; the first code of Law is from 1772 BC; and what we consider today as meaningful development of knowledge and action took place subsequently to that, mostly in the first millennium BC. Most of this human development was at first basic actions and basic knowledge mixed with mythologies, superstitions, and barbarism.

9. The hundred-to-two-hundred-year period from 600 BC constitutes

---

5   Language is considered as one.

an extremely exceptional time for the history of Humanity as we apprehend it today. Through luck or other circumstances we do not fully understand yet, there came to be very important intellectual developments in several human civilisations almost in parallel. The Greek miracle could be said to have started then with Homer's works in their more final form, as well as the flourishing of some Ionian cities. Similarly, Laozi's work, the foundation of Taoism, has also matured during the 4th or 5th century BC. Both Homer and Laozi are historic figures that are likely to have never existed in reality–they essentially stand for the personification of the wisdom and culture of their time. Confucius and Buddha are equally from this period, and most likely Zoroaster. Pythagoras (if he existed as a person), Formal Mathematics, and Deductive Reasoning; Philosophy as a way of life; and schools of philosophy, are all equally from this period. Empedocles and the schools of medicine are from then too. Evidently, all of it did not happen overnight, nor exactly in parallel, but starting 600 BC, the level of intellectual and cultural productivity notably increased, at a pace much faster than in periods prior to that and in many places. The birth of great philosophy, religions, science, and literature started then and there. Many religions that existed before this time firmed up into proper doctrines following 600 BC, including Judaism. Athenian golden age is from the fifth century BC; Alexander is from the fourth century; and the Carthagian and the Roman expansions are from the subsequent centuries.

10. The opening of the world and different civilisations on each other was realised by Alexander the Great (though not necessarily in a premeditated manner). Despite the fact that the Persian Empire had expanded greatly before the coming of Alexander and was dominant for many years, it does not seem to have resulted in the same kind of transfer of knowledge that took place during and after Alexander's conquests, probably to the credit of the Greeks who were capable of producing so much in so little time. The flow of ideas, of culture and goods, of religions and superstitions, and of mythologies and mathematics, was notably catalysed by the destruction of geographic barriers by Alexander–all of it in

ten years only... Greek civilisation spread as a consequence of Alexander's invasions, but it was not a one-way flow; many Persian and Indian influences also travelled west.

11. But to us, it is with the Romans that came the real and effective definition of the civilised world. Although the Greeks were first to consider themselves civilised and called the rest barbarians, they were often incapable of getting together, except when under external threat, mostly from the Persians, or when they had to submit to Alexander. And soon after Alexander died, the Greeks quickly turned again on each other. We affectionately liken them to a bunch of smart frogs held in a pot; as soon as you open the lid, they start jumping in all directions. The Romans were not as sophisticated as the Greeks at the time, but with them came roads, administration, law, a unified army, and peace after Augustus. The combination of Greek intellectual production and Roman organisation is what came to be known as human civilisation to most of us. A notable and *important* exception is China where a parallel civilisation took place.

12. This civilisation could be hardly labelled 'Greek' or 'Roman' from an ethnic point of view; the more accurate term would be 'Mediterranean'. What the Roman Empire and its civilisation came to represent is Mediterranean civilisation, and the Mediterranean Basin, along with Babylonia and Persia, represents the first notable birthplace of great cultures and civilisations. Alexandria was more important in Mathematics than any other Greek city[6]; Zeno was Phoenician and his movement, Stoicism, was as much Roman and Phoenician as Greek; there was *Beritus* and its Roman law school; and Saint Augustine was from Hippo near Carthage.

13. The next material jump in human thought came a century or so after the start of the Renaissance, roughly a thousand years following the fall of Rome. And this coincides with a great discovery in the realm of action–the New World. The period in between the fall of Rome and the Renaissance was full of activity, full of wars, and full of action in general. There was the

---

6 Euclid for example was an Alexandrian.

emergence of Islam and the Muslim Empire without which much of the interest in the Greeks could have disappeared (in addition to proper discoveries in algebra, astronomy, and alchemy). There were the Tang Dynasty and the Chinese cultural flourishing. There was Genghis Khan with another Alexander-like expansion in reach and speed. There were wars, a Holy Roman Empire, and many kingdoms in Europe. There was the stronger establishment of Catholicism in Europe, the schism between Constantinople and Rome, and the stronger establishment of Sunni Islam in the Muslim world, particularly following Saladin and then the Mamluks. There were the Crusades during that period too. But for all the activity, wars, and historical and religious events, the level of intellectual and technological productivity of this period is not equivalent to the period before or the period after.

14. The period from the 16th century onward is very special in its contribution in terms of ideas, technologies, and action from the current point of view from which we observe History. Almost everything we consider meaningful today has been impacted somehow by this period. It was in this period that proper Physics took shape with Galileo and more importantly Newton. From Physics came Technology and Industrialisation, particularly after the advancements made in Thermodynamics. There was Maxwell then Einstein, Quantum Mechanics, Chaos Theory, and the Big Bang Theory. The development of Physics would not have been possible without great advancements in Mathematics; Logic was built on more solid grounds starting the end of the 19th century. There was Darwin who rendered the theory of evolution of species supported experimentally. Medicine advanced in accelerated forms from Da Vinci to Harvey to Pasteur to the Human Genome Project. Freud opened new perspectives in the understanding of human behaviour. There was the Reformation and the wars of religions, but there was also the start of a greater religious tolerance with Liberalism. There was Descartes, Locke, and Kant in Philosophy. Commerce exploded with the discovery of the New World, and new routes to Asia were developed in the process; the growth and sophistication in insurance followed.

There was the proper development of Economics with Adam Smith and much later Keynes and Hayek. The creation of the Company, the stock market, and the market regulator, all took place first in Amsterdam. There was the English Civil War and the Glorious Revolution, the French Revolution, the American Bill of Rights, the Universal Declaration of Human Rights, and many political theories across the spectrum of tendencies. There was Marx, Socialism, the acknowledgement of worker rights, and the invention of the concept of the 'safety net'. There was the gradual abolishment of absolutism and slavery in many countries and the emancipation of women. And there is of course the Internet, the Space Program, and the development of Cognitive Sciences and Psychology.

This is only a highly imperfect and insufficient overview of the contribution to the present state of affairs of the period from the 16th century onwards. Almost all of what we take for granted today has been created or transformed greatly during this period. It is far from being a perfectly good period; a lot of tragedy, sorrow, and injustice have taken place during this period, not unlike any other period in the past, including colonisation, slavery, mass murders, and two world wars. However, the positive was astonishingly more positive than in any preceding period.

15. This is the general context of the evolution of human ideas and culture: *two hundred thousand years for our species, a thousand years of meaningful productivity, a thousand years of quasi stagnation, followed by slightly more than five hundred years of a more meaningful productivity than the first phase, and it is to be continued.*

16. The second phase of development was initiated by European civilisations and in the process resulted in their cultural and economic dominance, from Europe first then the various colonies they established themselves in. It is only in the 20th century that this dominance has started to be challenged:

    a. The Bolshevik revolution and the spread of Communism from there, concurrent with the end of World War II, advanced Russian cultural and economic influences[7]. Russian influences have however materially retrenched with the fall of the Soviet Empire.

b. The rise of Japan and then quite later that of the Asian Tigers disturbed the economic dominance of the West. The global influence of countries in Far East Asia has so far remained in the realm of economy and industrialisation

c. Yet, the most important challenge is still in the making; it is the rise again of ancient great civilisations like China and India, and the greater affirmation of countries with large populations like Indonesia and Brazil. Despite its importance and the fundamental change in the sphere of influence it would result in, we find that many contemporaries tend to overestimate the pace at which this transformation is taking place. There is no denying that a greater equalisation is ultimately inevitable, at least to a partial extent. Whatever competitive advantage gained by the West through scientific and technological discoveries is bound to somewhat come into the hand of other nations, either directly or indirectly, and from there into the wider global economy. However, for our part, we tend to concur with the view that the path towards such a transformation will take more time than what is widely expected. And it is yet to be seen how much of this emerging influence will go beyond the economic sphere into the cultural one; China, for example, has already occupied in the past the rank of the largest economy in the world without it dominating or shaping Western Asia or Europe culturally.

There are certainly many characteristics of this 'fast' evolution of human thought and action; we shall mention some of the more important ones.

---

7   Although these are sometimes very difficult to distinguish from other European influences.

17. The evolution of human thought and action is far from being linear or accelerating. We had periods of explosion of knowledge and action, followed by periods of stagnation, then followed by other periods of productivity. We had even periods of knowledge and civilisation destruction, some of it irrecoverable. The destruction of many indigenous American civilisations (North and South) is an important example. We are *extremely* lucky that the Greek civilisation was not fully wiped out by its enemies, or that the North African heritage was not fully destroyed by the invasions that the region witnessed. A cynic might say that these achievements if they had been lost, would have been re-realised by other cultures eventually. This is probably, at least partially, true, but the course of History would have been very different. Maybe the thousand years of stagnation would have been longer with such destructions of the global knowledge heritage. Credit should be given to the enlightened Muslim Empire that was the greater preserver of ancient knowledge for many centuries.

   a. One might then ask, "Are there any particular conditions that promote productive thought or is it more of a random development?" There is no clear answer to the question to date; however, conditions more conducive for intellectual productivity seem to exist. Among these conditions, there are definitely material ones (indeed a hungry stomach will not care about the revolution of celestial bodies); but also socio-political ones (security, promotion and protection of intellectual activity, a solid education system, or an encouragement of risk taking); as well as of course intellectual ones (e.g. new streams of intellectual influences propagating through a society). It seems to us that although these conditions cannot happen randomly without some collective effort and a certain historical background, the alignment of all them is due to circumstances that are partially subject to randomness or luck.

   b. Some observers use the period of impressive acceleration in Knowledge and Technology acquisition from the

Enlightenment to our days to conclude that the trend will continue stronger till we ultimately reach the limits of possible Knowledge. Some might even think that we are set on a path of ultimate greatness. Some advocate a continued focus solely on Technology because it is the one ultimate source of all our progress, and nothing else, be it Politics, Economics, Art, or other, ultimately counts as much as Technology (cf. the Zeitgeist Movement). This has also been the attitude of many positivists, which, although admirable in many ways, we fundamentally disagree with. There is no denying of the importance of Science and Technology in the last centuries in improving material conditions, reducing mortality rates, and shaping our way of thinking and living. However, we need as well to realise how lucky we are to live today in a social age conducive to Science and Technology. *Socio-economic and political conditions are key enablers as well as disablers of much intellectual productivity.*

c. There is no evidence that the accelerating trend will continue indefinitely as we have seen from the experience of Antiquity. An unexpected change in conditions can result in an impairment of intellectual productivity as it has previously happened. Moreover, we can argue that, in many fields today, there is a deceleration of growth from the 20th century, significant usually of a maturity phase. Deceleration of growth does not mean absence of growth, but it can more easily lead to an intellectual stagnation similar to the one that took place in the Middle Ages in many fields. The attitude of supposing that an accelerating trend in Knowledge and Technology will continue to accelerate further is not dissimilar from the simplistic attitude of supposing that the stock market or the real estate market will continue to grow forever year over year; such an attitude, more often than not, sets up its holder for disappointment and an ultimate revision of belief.

18. Intellectually speaking, there were many more mistakes and errors in human civilisation than truth and progress. We invite the reader to think about all the wrong wars and conflicts; wrong ideologies; religions that disappeared or evolved in doctrine; philosophies that turned out wrong or worse destructive; economic and political theories that are obsolete; scientific speculations that were proven wrong; and finally superstitions and false popular beliefs, some of which still persist till our days. Errors and mistakes eventually die out, and we therefore tend to forget that they ever existed. We prefer to think the world more full of truths than errors and mistakes.

   a. On average, and only on average, there is definitely more truth and less superstition and prejudice in humans today than three thousand years ago, and the trend is likely[8] to continue. Great intellectual men of the past are great, not necessarily because they are greater than many today, but mostly because they were capable of realising progress in a greater sea of mistakes and obstacles.

19. Human societies even when in a state of animosity feed from each other, culturally, intellectually, religiously, commercially, economically, politically, and militarily. Boundaries continuously change, and as such, definitions of identity, culture, and religion groupings are dynamic and somehow subjective. The history of Thought is full of cross-influences.

   a. Acquired Knowledge is always new but rarely that original. Rousseau's *Confessions* were no doubt influenced by Saint Augustine's confessions; Dali's Angelus is a play on Millet's. Adam Smith's idea of a general law[9] originating from the aggregation of selfish behaviour of all individuals is no different from Hobbes' idea of aggregation of selfish desires for preservation, which Hobbes saw as resulting in a Commonwealth (the Leviathan). Maxwell's approach to Thermodynamics and distribution of gas

---

8 Only likely… No certainty here.

9 The famous 'Invisible Hand'.

velocity, a key turning point in Statistical Physics and Physics more broadly, owes credit to Laplace's and Buckle's works on errors in astronomical measurements and social phenomena respectively. Einstein's ideas on Special Relativity would not have been without the works of Maxwell and Poincaré. Borrowing a quote from the opening of Wittgenstein's *Philosophical Investigations* quoting Nestroy we can say: "The trouble about progress is that it always looks much greater than it really is".

b. Intellectual innovations most often have little to do with coming up with something utterly new out of nothing; such a thing rarely exists. No complex innovation can come from nothing without requiring enormous time exceeding one man's life. Intellectual innovation corresponds more to laying stress on a particular point or notion more than what was previously done, rendering such a notion central, and building a system of Thought around it. Innovation is more about a rearrangement of ideas and experiences into something better rather than pure creation[10].

c. One of the most flawed and politically dangerous theories people have continuously fallen for (and some of them are very smart in other respects) are narrow nationalistic and racial ideologies. They show in our view a complete failure to understand long history; they may portray short, narrow history well but not the long one. We are talking about political theories that praise a particular race or nationality as superior to others, and usually in opposition to some other group of races or nationalities. Throughout History, humans intermixed continuously, influenced each other in every way intellectual, religious, philosophical, and political. Conquerors learned as much from the conquered in many situations. Populations migrated sometimes very far from their original homelands. When

---

10 Of course the new arrangement can be considered itself a creation.

a population was conquered, it was not necessarily wiped out; it stayed and changed maybe its language, dress code, or religion. There is no implied naivety in what is asserted here; cultural dynamics can have an enormous impact on the level of intellectual, technological, and political productivity. However, there is no culture that stayed dominant across all of History and across all conditions, no matter how great or productive it was at a particular point in time. In other words, boundaries, not only geographical but also mental, are human creations and subject to change like most things human. This is important to keep in mind when we attribute a particular invention, discovery, or trait to a particular group of people, culture, or country; it is *never exclusive,* and it could have been attributed to different people, culture, or country under different historical circumstances. For those who are fan of national, racial, and/or religious symbols, here are some facts that might be amusing or hurtful depending on how the reader looks at things:

> i. Jesus is a Jew; he was probably on the shorter side with darker skin and curly hair, not green eyes and light brown silky hair. Likely so were all the great men of Christianity before Saint Paul (inclusive). Three out of the four messengers of God in Islam[11] are Jewish. Some, Jews and non-Jews, consider all the Jews to be one 'race'; we fail to understand how are they able to reconcile the wide range of Jews from Ethiopian Jews to Siberian Jews with this theory coherently. The Buddha[12] was an Indian prince likely born in a current day Nepalese city near the border with modern day India whereas Buddhism predominantly exists

---

11 The four being Abraham, Moses, Jesus, and Mohammad; Adam and Noah are also sometimes added to the list.

12 Siddhartha Gautama Buddha.

today in South East Asia, in the Himalayas, and Sri Lanka. The majority of Muslims are not Arabs, and the majority of Semites are not Jewish. Saint Patrick is English. The Franks are German; so is Clovis and Charlemagne; and so are the Lombards. Charlemagne did not speak a word of Latin, and he was the precursor to the Holy Roman Empire. The Anglo-Saxons are Danish and German; the Normans are Scandinavian. Turkey is less Turk than Turkmenistan; it has more Greeks, Kurds, and other Central Asians in it. Saladin is Kurdish not Arab, Muhammad Ali of Egypt is Albanian, Saint Augustine is Algerian, Saint Paul is Syrian, the Huns are Mongols, and the Philistines (the ancestors of the Palestinians) are originally Southern Europeans invading the Middle East from the sea. Alexander the Great was Macedonian though not from what is defined today as Macedonia; nevertheless, Macedonians at the time were quite distinct and more barbarous than Athenian, Spartan, or Ionian Greeks. Napoleon is Corsican and contemplated rising against France in his youth. Germany would probably not have existed today as one country without Napoleon's actions. Richard the Lion Heart barely put foot in England and considered it a cash cow to finance his expansion wars; he also never spoke a word of English and is widely rumoured to have engaged in homosexual relationships. English kings and queens have as much Norman, French, German, Dutch, and Scottish blood in them as English blood. The Arab armies during the height of the Muslim Empire were a mix of Persians, Berbers, and then Turks. The Umayyads were first opposed to Islam and only converted later on out of political calculations. Avicenna is Persian; Averroes is Moor, i.e. Berber or maybe Spanish. Christopher Columbus is Italian but would never have made it to the Americas without the Spanish support. Japanese are originally Chinese, and so are many populations of South East Asia.

We can indeed pursue this for very long. The purpose of these select examples is not to provoke anyone but rather to show the interconnection of human affairs and the subtleties of History in comparison with some of our current day naive prejudices.

20. History has been written most of the time by the dominant civilisation. Cultural and social influences contemporary to the historical writing play a disproportionate role from that point of view. This is important to notice for its weighty corollaries:

   a. Most of what we call great achievers today come from dominant civilisations, and *it is by the fact that they were born or associated with such civilisations that they are who we consider them to be historically*. A discoverer has usually had the good luck of both timing and the society he or she was born in or migrated to. Even more, some of what was produced by less dominant cultures at the time of the historical recording was, in many instances, expropriated and taken credit for by dominant cultures and men.

   b. Great men of action and great political figures are almost always portrayed as inventors or creators when they usually merely take fame for things they did not come up with. Moreover, they are usually portrayed as 'good' or a role model to follow in his/her footsteps; this is bluntly false and outright dangerous in many situations. There is no denying that there are outstanding men in History, but they are sometimes not the ones commonly advertised. Moreover, all of us humans have our goods and our defects; it is not uncommon for historians to only shine the light on the goods while *purposefully* omitting any negatives of their national heroes. We can give many examples of such collective behaviour: the way the French perceive Napoleon, the way the Americans perceive George Washington and the Founding Fathers, the way the English perceive many of their monarchs and their war heroes like Winston Churchill, or the way the Mongolians perceive Genghis Khan.

    c. *History is often written from the end result backwards and not as a personal journal.* The psychology of the writer and the influences of his contemporaries play an important role in the historical writing. Almost all religions portray their history quite differently from what we find when we consider things more objectively. Spinoza's work on the Jewish history is notable, and important critique of Christian history has been realised since the 17th-18th century. It is only when confronted with historical facts that are almost impossible to deny that religious historians adjust their books or change their line on historical interpretations.

    The role of a good historian is to minimise such influences and attempt a greater objective description of events and accompanying human psychology (individual and collective). This is of course much harder, complicated, and subject to uncertainty than outright biased historical writing. Nevertheless, there is a minimum of contemporary influence that can never be taken away, and it is useful to realise this upfront.

21. For all most common definitions of Good and Bad, we find great presence of each in the history of Thought and Action; human history is not necessarily predominantly good or bad. Whether History broadly tends towards the Good rather than the Bad will be a subject of a later discussion. Furthermore, the definitions of Good and Bad have often been subject to historical change; many things that were considered normal in ancient times are

outright condemnable in our days, such as the possession and use of slaves, the attitude towards confiscation of the property of the defeated in war, or the torture of enemies. Even the most admired historical figures often resorted to one of those tactics.

22. Contemplating the magnitudes of Space and Time in the Universe and comparing them to the age of our species, and particularly the productive period of our age, we cannot but notice that there is no *a priori* reason, proof, or indication of anything special in Humans, of course outside our subjective view of our own importance. In other words, the separation between the Universe and humans is artificial and only in our minds[13], as it equally is between the different groups of humans.

23. Some might argue that we are the most dominant species on our planet[14], the ultimate apex predator. This unfortunately can change as it has already happened in the past. Some might point out to our higher level of consciousness in comparison with other species on the planet. Although there is an element of truth in this, having a higher degree of consciousness than other species on Earth does not necessarily imply supremacy or uniqueness in our Universe. Moreover and more importantly, there are billions and billions of other worlds out there in the Universe, not including past and future worlds in the span of billions of years. We could naturally ask what is the chance of no conscious life in *any* of those worlds that we do not know of? Using a bit of 'falsification', the fact that we do not know *yet* of the existence of such conscious life does not signify that it does not exist. As long as no one can *strictly prove* that there is no conscious life out there, a reasonable man cannot hold to any universal uniqueness of Humans based on the observation that we have a high degree of consciousness.

---

13 Probably the same way the separation between the Universe and Ants is in an ant's mind.

14 Are we really? What is the definition of dominant? Viruses and bacteria do not seem to be doing that bad…

Putting Things in Context

The objective observation of History is that there is nothing special about us. And the more we tend to know about History, the more we realise that the barriers are rather mentally in us.

24. Being small or not unique does not necessarily mean that the human species is irrelevant or useless. *Homo Sapiens* is as irrelevant or useless as we like it or not like it to be. If the Universe in its complexity teaches us something, it is that size does not really matter that much when it comes to the value of existence of a particular thing. Almost everything is ultimately small compared to the size of the Universe. Human species does not need to be bigger to survive better[15] or to acquire a greater degree of wisdom, happiness, or harmony with its environment.

25. Observing the Universe helps put things in context. It provides much of the required intellectual modesty and a certain relativeness concerning what counts and what does not in human affairs.

It is with this imperfect brush of History, an open mind, and an attention to our prejudices that we can start our endeavour of seeking elements of answers to key questions.

---

15 In reality, size often plays against preservation and the agility required in Evolution. Furthermore, we are yet to properly define what we mean by 'surviving better'.

On What Is Around Us and What Is In Us

"[...] I may venture to affirm of the rest of mankind, that they are nothing but a bundle or collection of different perceptions, which succeed each other with inconceivable rapidity, and are in a perpetual flux and movement." Hume

"No aboriginal stuff or quality of being, contrasted with that of which material objects are made, out of which our thoughts of them are made [...]" William James

26. Understanding the environment around and being able to benefit from it[16] are some of humans' greatest aspirations. It seems that humans have attempted, across all cultures and ages, to always seek answers to questions of the type, "Why things are the way they are? Why they happen the way they happen? And what is the reason for us being in all of this, individually and collectively?" The more subtle individuals might have also added, "Why we even ask the kinds of questions we ask in the first place?" Many have attempted to answer such questions in very many ways. Various fields of Thought and Belief have

---

16 As well as protect ourselves from its negative effects.

ensued; some died out, some remained and evolved, and some are still on the path of decline.

27. Parallel to this quest, the more practically oriented among us were more interested in devising new ways of simply making our lives materially easier. From the most primitive tools we observe today within the ape world, they have engineered and improved our tool-kit in every possible direction.

28. The abovementioned questions have traditionally been the domain of Religion and Philosophy; the practical interests belonged more to the field of applied sciences[17], such as Engineering, Medicine, Economics, Administration, and Military. With the progress in all domains, the differences between the two camps in approach and in the nature of the findings have become blurrier. Many subjects of Religion and Philosophy (such as cosmogony, revolution of celestial bodies, origins of life, or the nature of consciousness) have been carved out with time and given more solid footing within scientific domains, while practical sciences stumbled upon discoveries that helped answer metaphysical questions. And equally, while we were attempting to find answers to the abovementioned questions, we have unintentionally discovered new imaginative ways of growing and progressing our tool-kit.

29. Answering questions of the first kind understandably remains a key concern. After all, what is the real value of all our tools and refinements if we do not really know what we are eventually using them for? Or whether seeking them is worth the effort or not in the first place? We can indeed say today that, through our attempts to find answers to such questions, we know more than in past times. But we remain far from being satisfied with the elements of answers we have obtained so far. Nevertheless, we are capable today of discerning what is plainly wrong in the answers (and the questions) of the past, and that by itself constitutes a positive and a progress.

---

17   In a broader sense of the word than customary.

A First Premise

30. We shall start first with an important statement inferred from the history of Thought and Action: *there are no several fundamentally different natures in the Universe*; everything is of the same nature; everything is interacting together; everything is a continuous flux of the same nature. What these mystically sounding statements do mean is that fundamentally everything around us, including us, 'All Being', is of the same fundamental property or nature, and everything interacts with everything.

31. The opposite attitude that we negate is likely easier to understand in the light of History. Man throughout History has always attempted to approach and understand the Universe by separating it into fundamentally different natures. Humans historically talked in separating terms and fundamentally different categories, such as the Soul vs. the Body; the Spirit vs. the Matter; the Subject vs. the Object; God, Soul, and Body; us humans vs. the rest; our consciousness vs. our body; the world of Ideas vs. existence as we see it (as mere illusion); the Essence of something vs. the something; the thing-in-itself vs. the perception; or vegetation, animals, and Man. Often, these opposing notions were not considered as just convenient categorisations in order to treat reality in an easier way but, on the contrary, as *fundamentally different* natures, one usually superior to the other. Like water and oil, even if they are mixed together, these substances or natures remained distinct.

32. We shall talk about many of the historical fallacies at a later stage, but it is important to state the following upfront at least succinctly. A lot of ink and blood has been spilled in order to elaborate on such separating notions and reconcile each nature with the other into a whole that makes sense. As human thinking and scientific discoveries progressed, all such separations progressively turned out to be plain wrong. Animals and Humans turned out to be distant cousins; Man and Earth, its habitat, had special conditions for life and consciousness in them, but nothing of a fundamentally different nature or impossible to find somewhere else in the Universe; and we discovered that Earth is not the centre of the

Universe, that stars are not made of Ether, that human thinking can be explained scientifically, and that all matter in the Universe gets recycled and transformed including us. Even Matter and Energy, which were long considered very different, turned out to be substitutable.

Much of this might not surprise many today, but for the quasi-totality of our human history it was its opposite that was thought true; it is fair to say that even in our days, the idea of fundamentally different natures remains culturally predominant. This predominance is a result of a mix of tradition and social conditioning, lack of proper independent education, as well as psychological predispositions that make it hard to believe otherwise, or at least to openly admit to believe otherwise. *It is such an attitude that we reject as false.*

33. Admitting that there are no fundamentally different natures in the Universe, what can we really say about this 'one' nature? What we can say is that the Universe can be broken down into elemental things we choose to call *events*. We can choose to call them something else, but the word *event* makes it easier for us to relate the concept to our common everyday understanding.

    Event[18] is the simplest possible excitation of an all-encompassing field[19]. If the String Theory gets properly finalised and resolved, a String oscillation would be an event. Energy is a bundle of events, for example a certain number of photons. Events also bundle together to form elemental particles, then atoms, and Matter more generally. Taking this view, it is not surprising then that one can pass from Energy to Matter and vice versa. These events interact with each other through Natural Laws, or what we more commonly call the Laws of Physics. Some like to describe events, or bundles of events, as the terms that fill in the equations of Physics alongside mathematical terms. We find this view risky and potentially portraying the Laws of

---

18 Beyond this chapter, we will resume using the word 'event' in its more common everyday meaning in most instances, except in what concerns the Appendix.

19 In the proper Physics definition of a field.

Physics as transcending the events, which we find ourselves in disagreement with[20].

34. Events interact with each other through other events; these events are what we call in Physics the interaction particles like the photon or the graviton. Laws of Physics are simply mathematical ways of describing these interactions.

35. Even when taking the Humean[21] view that refutes the idea of considering one definite set of Natural Laws, and preferring to describe Natural Laws as our ways of comprehending what is around us using the best and most simple models, the description of the Universe as broken down into events can still hold.

36. The central point here is this: **everything around us and in us is of the same fundamental nature or a bundle of that nature** (which we choose to call event and bundle of events) **and everything is interacting according to defined ways** (which we can choose to call Natural Laws or Laws of Physics). There are no 'influences' or 'creations' from 'outside' that come to affect the totality of events and their interactions; the influences and creations (if any) come from *within*. This is indeed a central concept, and what was meant by when we said earlier " [...] is of the same fundamental property or nature, and everything interacts with everything." Whether events affect the Natural Laws, or that Natural Laws can change with time or be different for different universes, is secondary and does not affect the central premise. The central premise can be made to include these notions.

Talking about what is outside this totality of events is therefore meaningless and purely a linguistic illusion. It is similar to debating what comes before the creation of Time; the word 'before' requires Time, and one cannot talk about 'before' without inferring the existence of Time. Although we can form such sentences linguistically and wonder about them, they are in effect meaningless.

---

20 But admittedly, we could be wrong about that.

21 Of the eminent Scottish philosopher David Hume.

The reader can find some of the technical objections to our First Premise in the Appendix. At first read, the reader can choose not to go to the Appendix and proceed to the Second Premise.

A Second Premise

"Believing, with Max Weber, that man is an animal suspended in webs of significance he himself has spun [...]" Clifford Geertz

37. Objectively speaking, conceiving All Being as one nature is *at least* as plausible as that of conceiving All Being as several natures. Moreover, the growing scientific evidence is against a fundamental separation and the existence of many natures. We need therefore to ask ourselves, "Where does our initial attitude of separating into distinct natures come from then? And how did it persist for so long, and why?"

38. The answer is inside us; it is in our mental structures and our psychology.

    Even when we put aside beliefs emanating from egocentric needs, and we focus solely on the more objectively-oriented mental structures and processes in us[22], we still find much of what can explain our misleading towards fundamental separation. This brings us to the second central premise, which is a junior premise to the one above. **Mental structures and processes are essentially bundles of events that have as objective to analyse events, including themselves.** Mental structures are of the same nature as All Being, and they are within this All Being, not outside it or from outside it.

39. We have been given these cognitive tools by Nature through a long evolutionary process; they are not posited into Nature from outside it. In them we can find most of our greatness but also our faults, in Thought and in Action. These tools have valid evolutionary reasons to be the way they are, but this does not mean that they operate efficiently at every instant and in every circumstance, or that they are free of errors or confusions.

---

22 Such as Rationality.

40. We need to admit that there can be other ways of comprehending things, which we do not possess. One of the most powerful tools these mental structures have is the ability to self-critique, spot errors, and sometimes be able to progress beyond them.

41. It is important to realise that we are talking about mental structures in the plural here, not singular. It is rather inaccurate to think of the brain as one unit and our way of thinking as one and consistent. The reality is quite far from it but more on that later.

42. Let us consider Causality as an example of mental processes. Thinking in terms of Causality is a powerful cognitive tool through which a lot of what we observe around us can be better comprehended, reacted against, or better protected from. Finding correlations, distinguishing certain patterns in Nature, or building links between observations, are all at first mostly the result of us using the shortcut of Causality. Even at a very young age, babies are shown to exhibit a clear use of Causality; less than a year-old babies are shown to repeat certain actions with the hope of obtaining the same results, making a link of Causality between one action and a result, such as shaking a toy or rattle to hear a certain noise or certain music. It is easier and quicker to think in terms of Causality than to develop a long list of Natural Laws in order to explain the relation of one observation to the other. Causality is less accurate than scientific methods, but it is more efficient in terms of brain usage, and more importantly, it yields quicker results. In the wild where we used to live, such criteria mattered more in *most* cases.

43. Memory is another essential cognitive tool. Memory is more than just a useful mechanism for registering previous experiences. Memory shapes our perceptions and the way we conceive things. How can we comprehend the notion of Time for example without Memory? There would be no Past, Present, or Future without Memory; we would not be able to think about Time travelling from the Past to the Future without it. We could not talk about 'before' (temporal not spatial) without Memory. The question "What happened before this time or that time?" is not possible without having derived the notion of Past from Memory first.

44. Categorisation and Naming[23] are other essential cognitive tools. The mind operates in an easier manner after having generalised and categorised first, after having named and labelled. Communication and therefore Language are made more possible following Categorisation. Humans have a tendency to categorise, to separate, to bundle, and then to examine the relation of one thing to the other. When we observe an animal moving, we think about it first as one unit or one entity rather than a collection of organs operating in conjunction. We exclude the air the animal breathes from this unit, but we include its paw, its eye, and its hair—even if part of this hair is likely to separate from the animal some minutes later.

    We create concepts, theories, and paradigms from Categorisation. It is the origin of what Kant called Pure Concepts. The notion of the Self, of the Subject, and of the composite & the simple, are not possible without Categorisation. Thinking about the whole or about parts does not in reality change anything fundamentally to what we are addressing. Categorisation is all in the mind so much so as Necessity, Causality, or Memory. ·

45. Categorisation and Naming are subject to change and evolution. Matter and Time are examples of concepts that evolved with knowledge.

    a. In ancient times, the human conception of Matter started by being that which we touch and see. During Antiquity, it then evolved to include air that we do not see[24]. Much later, with the advance of Science, Matter became that which is 'not void', or that which is not of 'mass zero' (admittedly a more difficult and less intuitive concept). Humans later discovered, with more advanced observations and theories, that there is always something in what we thought of as being void despite the property of zero mass. We remain today unclear on what we should

---

23 Some use the term Clustering.

24 The famous experience of the bucket filled with air in water at the time of the Greeks.

oppose Matter to as the concept of Void has been greatly weakened. The human categorisation of Matter has fundamentally changed, and it is not in its final form yet. Talking about the fixed concept of Matter has therefore turned out to be elusive.

b. Similarly, Time started by being associated with sunrise-sunset, with days, and with seasons. Likely under the influence of Memory, History, and then Science, Time was later considered an unchanging line that goes only in one direction. With Relativity, we have realised that Time is not of a very different property than Space, and that it is subject to change. Moreover, we discovered that Space and Time are substitutable somehow. And finally, whether Time can be travelled in the opposite direction or not is still an open question. Can we really consider our categorisation of Time to still be the same as three thousand years ago?

46. It is important to demystify these concepts and categories of the mind. Modern philosophy till quite recently had favoured the view that pure concepts and categories are *a priori*, i.e. preceding any possible experience and even a necessary condition for any experience to take place. The holders of this view believe that, when we are experiencing things, our perceptions are processed through the lens of these *a priori* concepts, and our *understanding* of these experiences and perceptions takes place through the *a priori* concepts.

47. If there is no organism, no brain, or no body, how can there be experience? Naturally the concept of *a priori* is therefore necessary for experiencing and for cognition. Saying that the organs, brain and body, and their structure, are *a priori* is stating the obvious. However, this is not the extent of what is typically meant by those who hold pure concepts and categories to be *a priori*. They usually do not stop here and mean more by their concept of *a priori*; this more is usually some mystification, transcendence, or a 'different nature' of these *a priori*. This additional layer of

belief is unnecessary in our view and can force some unsuitable narrowness. Moreover, it is likely to be as false as the previous idea we discussed of mystifying Natural Laws and considering them to be transcendental to events. It is this that we consider to be too narrow and unnecessary.

48. What is *a priori* is not our pure concepts and categories, it is the mental structures in us through which categories and concepts are developed. The way these mental structures develop such categories and concepts is by incorporating elements of experience. Hence, experience is indispensable. This is how modern linguistic models are generally thought of (Chomsky, Piaget, or more recent); they resemble greenfield *structures* that are manipulated and altered at an early-enough age (by what else than experience…) to then result in what we consider to be proper linguistic cognitive models.

49. *Our categorisations and pure concepts are ultimately anthropological* and are likely to have been quite different if we had perceived the world the way an ant does or a fish in a bowl does. Moreover, the elements of experience include cultural influences through which concepts exhibit some continuity across time within a certain human culture. That is why, for example, old Chinese or Roman numerals are apprehended differently than what we commonly use today as numerals, while all numerals can ultimately realise the same mathematics with varying degrees of difficulty.

50. One of the easier ways of imagining the operation of mental structures resulting in developed categories and pure concepts is to consider the development of an auto-learning artificial intelligence. What we have at the beginning are algorithms of intelligence without any elements of experience incorporated in them yet. In the case of artificial intelligence, the source of these algorithms is another intelligence (human) that produced them. In the case of biological intelligence, the source is natural evolution or, in other words, a very long series of bio-chemical trials and errors. The artificial intelligence at state 0 has no notion yet of 'Redness' or 'Instantaneity' or 'Truth'; it is only when processing elements of experience and trying to aggregate them that such

On What Is Around Us and What Is In Us

categories and pure concepts are found useful to develop. And the way they take hold is through Intuition rather than through Rationality. We can then argue that this process of 'aggregation' of experiences is what is the *a priori*.

51. It is not the idea of the *a priori* that is to be challenged because understanding does require some *a priori*. Even Hume who is portrayed as the chief antagonist to this idea of the *a priori* had to talk about 'habit' and 'custom' from experience through which Causality as a concept comes to be. The attitude of having 'habit' or 'custom' is in this case what could be considered the *a priori*. It is the transcendence, the mystification, as well as a broadening of the scope of the *a priori* that are rejected.

52. What is *a priori* at the individual level might not be at the level of the species or the biological life in general. Our brain is *a priori* to our perceptions but is not *a priori* to Biological Life in general. We indeed receive a piece of biological life through our DNA. Biological life is ultimately what produced the brain and the mental structures through a mixture of utility and randomness.

Everything is of the same fundamental nature, everything has relations to everything; no outside cause or necessity is needed. What seems distinctive, separate, or outside is only a product of our mental structures, which are nothing else than an integral part of this Everything. The mediums of understanding taken for ends are part of a great illusion.

INTERACTION AND REFLEXIVITY

Bosnia-Herzegovina was made part of the Austro-Hungarian Empire in 1878 following the Treaty of Berlin. On the 28th of June 1914, a young Bosnian Serb student seeking the independence of Yugoslavia assassinated the heir to the Austro-Hungarian throne and his wife while on a visit to Sarajevo. Angry Austro-Hungarians believed this accident to represent the right opportunity to end any interference of Serbia in Bosnia-Herzegovina and issued to Serbia a list of demands almost impossible to accept as condition for peace. When Serbia did not accept two of ten demands made by the Austro-Hungarian Empire, the latter declared war on Serbia. Russia, sensitive to its role in the Balkans and its influence in fellow Slavic countries, stepped in to protect Serbia. Only the Austro-Hungarian Empire was in alliance with Germany[25], and the Russian involvement was interpreted by Germany as a declaration of war against the Austro-Hungarians. Russia, on the other hand, was part of the Triple Entente, a tri-party agreement between Britain, France, and Russia. Hence, Germany, France, Britain, Russia, and Austria-Hungary, all found themselves in a full-scale confrontation less than five weeks after the accident in the Balkans (which the Ottoman Empire had no choice but to take part in despite its frail state, and the United States entered almost three years later). The result: World War I, almost forty million dead and wounded, Bolshevik Revolution in Russia, and a

---

25 Italy was also part in that alliance (the Triple Alliance) but did not enter the war on the side of Germany, as Austria-Hungary was the one to initiate the attacks.

Reflections on Fundamental Matters

humiliating Treaty of Versailles to the Germans. The Austro-Hungarian Empire had clearly miscalculated the possible consequences of its war on Serbia as it found its demise during this Great War. And in the ashes of World War I grew the seeds of World War II. Two world wars destroyed Europe economically and politically, saw many of its greatest minds flee or get acquired by greater military powers, and turned the world into a bipolar stage for the subsequent forty-six years. It is not only the Austro-Hungarian Empire that miscalculated the long-term consequences of its actions; in thirty-one years from 1914, through a series of dramatic interactions, European powers—winners and losers alike—turned from being protagonists of global politics to merely second degree players in a world opposing West and East.

This is a story of interactions, of continuous interactions, of multi-step dynamics, and of unintended consequences. It is not limited to politics but has universal reach.

53. Interaction is one of the most important characteristics of Existence. At whichever level we conceptually break-up the Universe (atoms, photons, stars, animals, bacteria, or cars), we find that the different pieces interact together or are influenced somehow by each other. The simplest way of thinking about interaction is to say that it consists of any 'unit'[26] behaving differently than if it is by its complete self (if such a thing is really ever possible) for reasons, at least partially, outside itself.

54. Elemental particles interact, molecules interact, microorganisms interact, animals interact, winds and seas interact, market participants interact, and celestial bodies interact... Moreover, there are different ways of interacting; some interactions are long distance, while others are short; some constitute strong interactions, while others are weak.

55. We can comfortably say that our observation of causality

---

[26] Whatever our definition of a unit is, with the exception of its absolute opposite, which is the Whole.

everywhere around us stems out from this paradigm of interaction. We talk about cause and effect whereas in reality there are many complicated interactions, which when looked at with a more simplified eye, appear *most* of the time as cause and effect.

56. Before going further, let us clarify which cause and effect we mean in relation to interaction.

    a. Mathematical causality is about implication. It is of the type: A > B, B > C implies A > C. This category of implications is in reality not a form of 'causality' in the proper sense of the word. Causality is about a cause and effect where the effect *is not* already somehow included in the cause. An example of causality is to say, "Long sun exposure causes the skin to burn". In the word Sun, there is no real notion of skin burning already included in it. Conversely, mathematical implications of the (A, B, C) type given above consist of one side of the implication already being included in the other; it is what is called an *analytic* relation. In 'A > B, B > C', there is 'A > C' already embedded in it. This is not what is meant by causality or for that matter interaction.

    b. The causality we refer to here is the causality of all Natural Sciences. It is the billiard ball moving at a certain speed hitting another billiard ball and causing it to move and the process continuing. To use our previous terminology, it is the phenomenon of an event(s) resulting from another event(s). Creation is therefore a notion closely related to this type of causality.

57. The results of an interaction are of various kinds. Some are clearly predictable, others are probabilistic, and some remain completely uncertain. In classical physics, the result of *one* interaction is one and well determined; the result of *many* interactions can be deterministic or completely uncertain. Classical physics can result in chaotic systems when we consider a system with many elements.

Let us illustrate with the following two examples:

a. Consider three objects: A, B, and C. A is linked to B with a rubber band and B is linked to C with a similar rubber band. The other ends of A and C are loose, i.e. nothing is linked to them. Let us then consider an externality that comes and pushes A from the opposite side to B. The externality causes A to move, and thanks to the elasticity of the rubber band, this in turn causes B to move and then C[27]. The stronger the externality A is subject to, the stronger the move C witnesses. This is an example of a predictable system of interactions.

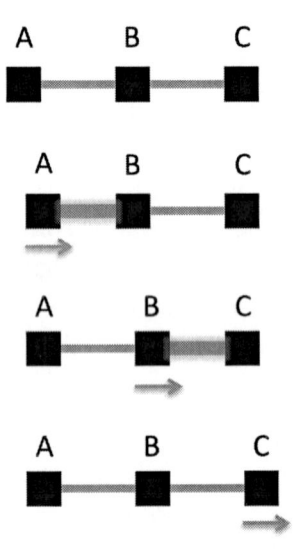

Figure A. Three objects and two elastic rubber bands

b. Now consider the same three objects with one small variation: C is linked back to A through one more rubber band. When A is subject to an externality similar to the one before, A causes B to move which causes C to move which then causes A to move again which causes B to move again and this way indefinitely. In the normal world, various frictions ultimately make the system come

---

[27] Assuming that the rubber band does not shrink back and induce a reactive movement in the opposite direction.

Interaction and Reflexivity

back to rest, but in a world where friction is minimal or other externalities may come to add-up, the movement may propagate indefinitely and the resulting system can become easily unpredictable. This constitutes an example of a non-predictable system of interactions.

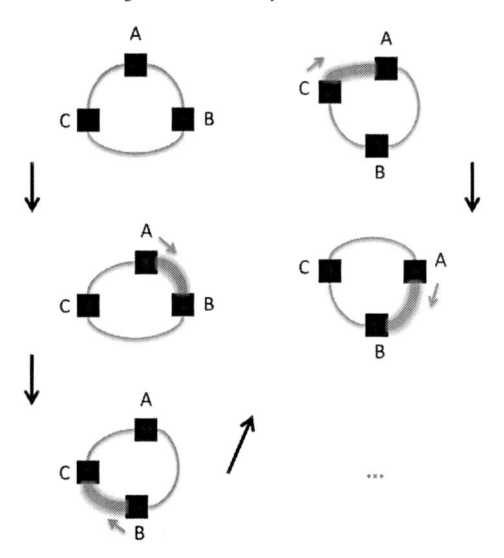

Figure B. Three objects and three elastic rubber bands

58. The second example has a name in social theory; it is called Reflexivity. It is the idea of a series of interactions re-looping back eventually on themselves and causing the system to behave in ways sometimes not easily predictable. Reflexivity is as important to realise as Interaction; it is indeed present everywhere around us. Reflexivity is an important premise of all social interactions and is frequently omitted because of the difficulty in understanding it fully and treating it. It is indispensable in Nature and impossible to forego when trying to predict the weather for example.

59. It is sometimes possible to predict accurately with more simplified models, where the effects of Reflexivity are considered minor, but it is often misleading to ignore Reflexivity altogether.

60. The social world around us constitutes an inter-related system. A simple illustrative model is to imagine a set of billions of small units linked to each other in an enormously complicated fashion.

Each unit acts according to particular rules and incentives, which can be changing with time, and each of these actions from a particular unit has consequences on other units linked to this particular unit. One can then quickly grasp the level of inter-relation and complication in such a system. Worse, the behaviour of one particular unit can be completely random, and through this random behaviour can influence other units all around.

61. Our social world today is actually even more inter-related than in the past. The reason why we say that the system is increasingly inter-related is a consequence of modernity: more links are being added in our societies as we progress. The Internet has added an enormous amount of new links, and so did Globalisation and the easier movement of people and goods.

62. The example of human markets and human exchange mediums is particularly insightful when it comes to Interaction and Reflexivity. The workings of many markets correspond to a complex system of interactions that incorporates exogenous data and noise from outside it but also *creates its realities from inside it* in ways that can also come to influence the outside. There is a strong feedback at play in markets, and events that can start by being purely random can exhibit their own different reality in such interactive systems. In other words, systems of interaction can create their own realities.

63. Naturally, being so prevalent, Interaction has been a subject of Thought for many years. But it is only with the advance of Science that the subject of interactions is starting to be dealt with properly. There are mathematical reasons behind this delay, which we shall describe below.

64. A dominant school of thought in History considers that we are not in a position to fully understand the behaviour or the 'essence' of any one particular unit until we understand all of its interactions with all other units, and consequently all interactions in the Whole of units. Put differently, this school considers that the knowledge of a unit is incomplete and misleading, and it is only through the

knowledge of the Whole that we can acquire any real knowledge. From the overwhelming presence of interactions around us, the thinking of this school may not be as surprising.

This reasoning existed with the mechanistic philosophers such as Descartes, Spinoza, and Leibniz, but of course the chief figure of this school of thought is Hegel. It is Hegel who took the idea to its full logical conclusion. Although at face value, the Hegelian view is logically sound, it constitutes an extreme position, which we disagree with. This view actually stems out from an incomplete understanding of the laws of probability, which were still only at their early levels of development at the time of Hegel; it also lacks to incorporate a proper hierarchy of interactions.

65. The aggregation of interactions follows statistical laws that can make some of this complexity go away. For the mechanical age started by Descartes and fortified by Newton, this was inconceivable. In our days, it is a mainstream view, and Thermodynamics and Chaos Theory have only increased our understanding of such aggregations.

66. Moreover, not all interactions are necessary to understand in order to acquire any knowledge. Some interactions can be negligible at the level we are considering. Otherwise, no knowledge is ever possible, as it requires knowing everything instantaneously. Stating that "we need to know everything in order to know anything" is itself a piece of knowledge that requires this 'know everything' condition, which is blatantly contradictory.

67. Luckily, we do not have to understand the entirety of the units and relations at every moment, as well as the incentives and rules of every unit, in order to form some understanding about the entire system. This is a *very* important observation when it comes to the phenomena of interactions, be it at a particle, a molecule, or a human level. The tools used by Science to analyse such phenomena are not reductionist[28] but rather statistical. The results

---

28 Reductionist means that in order to understand the behaviour of something we are observing, we need to reduce it first to its key constituents and understand the behaviour of all these constituents.

are usually probabilistic[29] rather than deterministic in the classical sense. It is remarkable how much looking at Reality through the statistical lens has enriched our knowledge and application, and in many fields, over roughly the past three centuries. Without this counter-intuitive form of reasoning, Insurance, Investment, Thermodynamics, Socio-Economic Sciences in general, Micro and Nano Physics, Micro Biology, Industrial Engineering, and Traffic Control would have been impossible or grossly crude and inaccurate disciplines.

68. The aggregation of millions and billions of interactions has its own rules, patterns, and behaviour which sometimes has very little to do with one or several particular interactions within this aggregation. It is as if somehow many of the interactions 'nullify' each other, at least partially, and we are left with an aggregate result that can be more continuous and predictable. By the process of interactions nullifying each other, a large part of the randomness and the incomplete information can disappear. In some cases though definitely not all, it goes as far as randomness and/or incomplete information becoming irrelevant for understanding the behaviour of the system at the macro level.

69. An impression of determinism can ensue from purely random and erratic behaviours at the core. Even more surprising, without going into the technical details, the aggregation of billions of interactions and randomness can provide the most valid explanation to such seemingly continuous and predictable phenomena as the increase in entropy or the fact that time travels in one direction and not the other. The Laws of Physics for the most part are completely time-direction agnostic with the exception of what comes out from the aggregation of random and very large number of interactions. It seems that interactions in the Universe are so fundamental that they hone the fabric itself of our Universe and our experience.

As Philip Ball eloquently put it in *Critical Mass:* "Identifying randomness with maximal unpredictability seems intuitively sound, but is not necessarily so [...]".

---

29 I.e. different outcomes or states with different probabilities attached to them.

70. The same idea of obtaining predictable results from the aggregation of interactions has been derived from studying many social phenomena, be it birth rates, death rates, male/female proportions, or trade of goods and services. It constitutes the basis of the philosophy of *laissez-faire*, of the idea of underlying Laws of Probability, which are different and more predictable than the erratic or random behaviour of each individual unit or cell. The idea has also its place in the evolutionary process of species resulting from randomness.

71. Another extreme position has however been taken by others in trying to qualify the results from Interaction. This position considers that everything is ultimately random at the micro level while subject to well-defined laws at the macro level. A corollary to that is the idea that individual behaviour does not matter, only the Laws of Probability do. In Economics, this corollary was extrapolated for example to say that the role of the government does not matter or has little influence over the course of things.

72. This position is in our view as wrong as the reductionist approach of supposing that every single interaction has to be understood for the Whole to be understood. The reality of dynamic systems is that while most of the randomness or interactions can somehow nullify each other, there exist situations where *one* single event (yes one is sufficient) can result in dramatically different consequences for the behaviour of the complete system. It is still very difficult for us to understand which are really all such situations, or the conditions needed for such a bizarre behaviour to take place. This behaviour is however commonly well known as the 'butterfly effect'; the idea that one single micro event can have dramatic consequences at the macro level in a far-away place through a series of interactions. The butterfly effect is a paradoxical idea to the Laws of Probability in some sense.

73. It is important to recognise that both situations can exist. In other words, even though in most situations large elements of micro behaviours can nullify each other, there exist non-negligible

circumstances where even the behaviour of one interactive relation can have dramatic impact on the whole.

74. Even more interestingly, there exist situations where behaviours at the micro level can ultimately impact some social laws. This is an immediate consequence of Reflexivity. We do not mean by this that mathematical laws change, or that a coin toss does not result in a normal distribution any longer. We mean that, through Reflexivity, the behaviour of the individual units can have a changing impact on the dynamics of a system. This consequently results in an observation of a change in the laws measured at the macro level. The easiest example to give of such situations would be in financial markets. Investors who base their investment strategies on analysing market behaviours statistically know well that almost all rules and correlations they discover and use for trades have ultimately a limited shelf-life.

   a. An example of such a strategy would be to buy a certain stock when the stock price breaks out above a certain historical X-day moving average[30]. Such correlations can work extremely well for certain (sometimes long) periods of time only to notably underperform later on. It explains why some algorithmic machines can trade marvellously well in some situations while underperform in others if no adjustments to their parameters are undertaken. This is not about cyclicality of the laws of some sort; it is about fundamental breakdowns of correlations in a system brought from within it. It is usually when such correlations become widely known and used by many market participants that they cease to work effectively. When market participants start to use the correlations more often, they cease to represent valid rules for making money in trading. This shows clearly the reflexive nature of interactions in some situations.

75. Interactions constitute an integral part of Reality at no matter which level we look and in all fields we approach. We can choose to

---

30 X can be 20, 50, 200 days, or any other.

ignore some of the interactions where their effects are negligible; this does not signify that they are not there, or that their effect cannot suddenly acquire a more significant importance in some situations. The universality of interactions goes a great deal into explaining why the same mathematical models can work almost seamlessly between very different fields such as Physics, Biology, or Finance. Units attract or repulse each other, stop or accelerate each other, influence each other to do the same or the opposite, merge into each other, or split into different units etc. Whether the unit is an atom, a bacterium, or a flying bird does not change much to the mathematical similarity, nor does the nature of interaction be it electrical, magnetic, mechanical, or other.

76. Words of caution and an answer to a classical objection here:

    a. Mathematical similarities should not mislead us into thinking that there are few mathematical models that, once known, can help us understand all interactions in the Universe. Despite the similarities we have stated, there remains a great deal of differences in the details, in the parameters of the mathematical models. Moreover, as we mentioned with the example of statistical trading, we are an integral part of the game, and our understanding of any mathematical models can easily alter what we are attempting to understand in the first place.

    b. Some of the statistics we observe at the macro-level are not fundamental in Nature as they might be at the quantum level. "Correlation is not causation" at the macro level. According to my car insurer, I have a certain probability x% of getting into a car accident in a radius of y kms from my domicile. It does *not* mean that an accident will take place with x% probability no matter how I behave, recklessly or attentively. It does not mean either that this probability cannot be minimised by an improvement in road structures or driving regulations. It is in this sense that we mean statistics to not be fundamental (at least most of the time) at the macro-level. Models and paradigms are subject to change and evolution at the macro-level. At the quantum level however, the story seems different[31]. In the quantum world, probabilities are more fundamental, and this results in very dramatic differences[32]. A property of a certain particle (e.g. radioactive break-up or spin) can have a certain value with a certain probability and another value with another probability, *fundamentally*, regardless of the surrounding interactions. Therefore, despite mathematical similarities, there seems to be a difference of fundamentals between the Macro and Nano worlds.

c. Advocates of the human free will almost always object to amalgamating human-related phenomena with inert phenomena. Humans have a free will in making theirs decisions; atoms do not. Atoms obey laws of Physics that are beyond their reckoning. How can we say then that the aggregations of human behaviours and of atomic behaviours share mathematical similarities? This goes against common sense, the claim goes.

The reality is that whenever units or agents have a *limited* number of choices, and part of the choice is driven by a certain interactive phenomenon, mathematical commonalities will ensue independently from what the choices are, or what the nature of interactions is. It matters little whether these choices are made consciously or unconsciously to the mathematical similarity. If a person is standing in a queue, he has a choice between patiently waiting and moving forward towards the cashier when the person in front moves or leaving the line without paying—these constitute a limited number of choices. One rarely sees a person exclaiming that he has free will and therefore wants to push the whole line behind him

---

31 At least based on what we know so far or are capable of knowing generally.

32 The existence of the Universe itself is likely to have come from such a probability play.

Interaction and Reflexivity

backwards or do some other absurd thing. The result is a Poisson law of statistics regardless of our philosophical stand on Free Will.

77. Understanding the behaviour of systems with many interactions is essentially about understanding the configuration of interactions in them, the laws of change of these interactions, as well as the potential external influences to such a configuration. The overall configuration of interactions can be of one kind and then suddenly change to be of a very different kind, sometimes for very obscure or random reasons. This is what is called in Physics a 'Phase Transition'. (*Critical Mass*, the author of which, Philip Ball, we have quoted above, is among the interesting literature on the subject of interactions in simple terms; we refer the reader to it for further development on the subject).

78. Phase transition consists of a change from one configuration of interactions (called in Physics a 'phase') to another. An easy, almost intuitive way of understanding two different phases is to recollect one's daily driving experiences. Any one who drives has come across situations where traffic was congested and other situations where traffic was fluid. Driving in congested traffic is very different from driving in a fluid circulation. High car density and low speed are not necessarily synonymous with congested, bumper-to-bumper, slow, and sequential movement. Fluid circulation is possible with a very large number of cars and at a very low speed. So what causes the difference? The type of traffic we encounter on the roads is actually not only a question of number of cars or speed; the transition from a fluid circulation to a bumper-to-bumper (or vice versa) is what can be called a Phase Transition; the two types of driving states (bumper-to-bumper and fluid movement) are the phases.

79. Phase transitions, or what is also sometimes loosely called 'Tipping Points' or 'Paradigm Shifts', are common phenomena everywhere around us, be it in the change of state from gas to liquid to solid, the magnetism of some metals, fashion trends, the dramatic changes in the velocity of money, or the superfluidity of mercury

at the quantum level. These phase transitions seem to be always there in the laws of Nature; they are simply another reflection of the universality of interactions.

80. The nature of the behaviour of a complex system is driven as much by the architecture and links between the agents as by the rules of behaviours of the agents themselves. The nature of links with the outside and any feedback loops matter greatly. In the case of multiple possible configurations, history also matters[33] in influencing the end state and the type of statistics a system exhibits.

81. Given the complexities of interactions in many situations, our understanding of phenomena related to such systems has to always be moderated by a certain notion of probability and uncertainty. It is not unlike predicting the weather; we can acquire a limited sight into the future, but we need to always temper it with an acknowledgement that our predictions can sometimes turn out to be plainly wrong. Moreover, uncertainty in predicting the behaviour of dynamic systems typically increases with major paradigm shifts, with changes into states that we might not have encountered before.

Human Interactions and Implications

We shall try here to narrow a bit more the discussion to human-related interactions and attempt to derive useful ideas from them. Humans are social animals, and interactions are a key characteristic of social affairs.

82. Human-related collective phenomena are by definition based on interactions between humans. They are therefore reflexive and vulnerable in terms of predictability. Some of the characteristics of human related phenomena include:

    a. Interaction at the human individual level, one human with the other, similarly to the units in a system described above.

---

33 Though not necessarily perceptible at the individual level.

Interaction and Reflexivity

    b. Reflexivity: human behaviour alters the environment (including other humans), and the environment has clear influence on the way humans behave.

    c. Drivers and incentives: human behaviour is driven by inputs the human receives, ways of processing these inputs, as well as changing objectives.

        i. Inputs often correspond to incomplete information.

        ii. Objectives include short-term and longer-term expectations, which can be notably different.

        iii. Ways of processing input can also be very different depending on the situation the individual is in, such as a life-threatening situation vs. meditating on one's sofa on a calm afternoon.

These dynamics result in very interesting and important implications; we choose to detail here seven key implications.

83. Implication 1: Things that happen far or independently from us may have the potential of affecting us, whether we want it or not.

    a. Ducking and denying the reality of Interaction and Reflexivity amounts to adopting an ostrich-like attitude. A dynamic we choose to ignore does not cease to exist for that reason. We have to accept reality and try to understand as much of it as we can in order to make things better and more sustainable. The reality is that even if sometimes everybody is in the best of their behaviour, the combined effect of interaction may lead to completely unintended consequences beyond anyone's control. And the solution is not in trying to destroy interactive links; these links exist because of the general utility they generate most of the time despite the occasional unintended dynamic.

84. Implication 2: We should not declare victory too early as things can come back to bite us later on.

    a. This is the lesson of the war against the Soviets in

Afghanistan for example; some of the armed rebels came to represent one of the most important threats to world security some years later. In the sphere of Economics, we are also realising with pain the economic consequences of lax lending policies that can have wonderful positive economic effects in the short- and medium-term but with more disastrous consequences over the long-term. *Unintended consequences* are one of the key characteristics of a complicated interactive model.

The long-term cautious view of History is notorious of Asian cultures in comparison with the West; when the French asked the Chinese what they think of Napoleon's impact on History, the answer was simply, it was too early to tell. In the Western world, we have the habit of jumping to conclusions minutes after the fact.

b. We are psychologically wired to see continuous trends whenever a trend manifests itself over a long enough period of time. If real estate prices continuously increase over a 30- or 40-year period, we are quick to assume that this is the way of the world, and that things will continue to operate the way they are. If we are on a succeeding streak, we tend to attribute that to something great in us and expect that by continuing to act the way we acted in the past, positive results from the environment around us will continue to come. Dynamic systems do not operate this way; sharp reversals are a common behaviour in dynamic systems. We often fail to realise that our behaviour has consequences on our environment usually beyond our immediate understanding, and some of these consequences can have long-term negative effects. Unfortunately, long-term unintended consequences are often difficult to foresee; but this does *not* mean that they are always difficult to foresee (as in the case of overspending or borrowing irresponsibly). Moreover, positive attitudes usually favour success over failure. If we doubt our actions and ourselves at every step of the way, we are not likely to achieve as much as when we are confident about ourselves. The mirror image of that is that we are not likely to face as many unintended consequences as when we are confident about our actions. This is apparently contradictory as are many of the dynamics of the world we live in…

c. Sometimes doing what seems to be the good at face value can lead to negative unforeseen consequences.

  i. An excess of precaution and protection of the young can actually diminish their natural defence mechanisms and come to hurt them on the long run. Let us take the example of the immune system. A key premise of any immune system is to *interact* with alien bodies in order to develop the required antibodies and fight any eventual intrusion. This is the role a vaccine plays in the body[34]. Worse, no interaction with alien bodies can actually lead the immune system to turn on itself in an auto-destructive manner. While immunising our children from all types of germs seems like the right thing to do, the structural necessity of interaction for the solid development of an immune system is not to be ignored as unintended consequences can result from being 'over-clean'. Naturally, the other extreme is also as damaging: an invasion of germs or one very lethal or dangerous germ in the non-prepared body can be fatal.

  ii. Drawing a parallel from the above, we can ask ourselves the following, admittedly controversial, question, "Does too much peace or too little competition reduce the overall ability and fighting/defending power of a civilisation, making

---

34 An immune system that does not interact with alien bodies is similar to a police force that does not know what a criminal does but has to catch one.

it vulnerable to unexpected challenges? If yes, then what is the least costly way of maintaining this required tension and interaction in order to keep the defence and competitive capabilities ready for the unforeseen?"

   d. The important lesson to retain on the topic of unintended consequences is that success and failure are relative, and success in one instance can result in drastic failures in another instance. The good can lead to the bad unintentionally, the desired to the undesired. Short-term wins can have long-term negative consequences whereas immediate sacrifices can result in larger gains in the future. Modesty and perspective are therefore important when it comes to success and failure, regardless of how the media and the general opinion often like to portray them.

85. Implication 3: Social contradictions do arise from interconnectivity.

   a. Societies hold a relatively large set of values and aspirations. Realising such aspirations causes behaviours which can come back to contradict these same aspirations or a subset of them. Developed societies almost universally preach liberty and civil values to the largest number, even beyond their boundaries, while also highly rate economic comfort. This, through the interacting systems, almost always leads to difficulties and contradictions. The developed man's motto is something as follows: "I preach liberty and civil values, but I also care (often more) about being comfortable." Politics becomes the art of handling such contradictions. Antagonisms in politicians are a reflection of antagonisms in societies more so than antagonisms in the personalities of those who detain political power.

   b. Let us consider an example known to most of us: developed societies and their approach to commodity-rich countries. All societies since the dawn of their development have almost always, at least partially, depended on other societies for some of their resources—this is after all the role international commerce plays in the world. Be it copper, spices, or oil, at every stage of development, societies often find themselves subject to the need of resources beyond their immediate control for their material comfort or progress. In today's world, it is mostly energy (predominantly oil & gas) and basic commodities (such as rare earth, uranium, or nickel). In many countries where these resources lie, political values can be in almost complete opposition to what the societies importing them support. The result is often a foreign policy that turns a blind eye to inadmissible political practices in the name of stability of trade.

    i. Let us assume that a democratic human-rights-preaching society A requires most of its commodities from a society B ruled by a ruthless dictatorship. How is society A supposed to deal with society B? Every one of us has his and her ideas on how to govern this kind of relationship. The reality, however, is that no matter what position we adopt, there are inner social contradictions we cannot fully escape. Worse, let us assume that society A has just witnessed one of the worst financial crises in its history, and any increase in commodity prices will only exacerbate an already precarious situation. Let us assume that at the same time a faction of society B decides to attempt a revolution in order to topple the dictatorship and install in its place political values very similar to the ones society A holds high. A revolution means massive disruption of commodity supplies for long periods of time and a sharp increase in the price of import material, which can be very disruptive to society A. And what if such disruptions in society A result in a form of dangerous populism emanating from large public dissatisfaction similarly to what took place in Germany during the 1930s? The risk to society A from a major disruption in society B can, in *some* instances (of course not all instances!), be as dangerous to the sustainability of democratic political values in society A. How is society A supposed to react to an attempted revolution in society B? Someone who pretends that such social difficulties and contradictions do not exist is holding a very simplistic view about the nature of interactions in societies.

86. Implication 4: When looking at things from a governance angle, it is better to be flexible than ideological with regards to complicated systems.

    a. This implication is in reality closely related to the second implication on unintended consequences and dynamic environments. Almost every governing policy adopted has its negative consequences, and very few policies always work all the time.

    b. Let us illustrate here again with an example from Economics. Since the aftermath of World War I, there has been an almost century-long debate between Keynesianism and Libertarianism on how to handle growth in an economy, particularly in times of economic slowdown.

    The philosophy of the first camp is to say that an economy operates better with state intervention and spending. This spending, while it might increase public deficit over the shorter-term, has the effect of increasing demand and activity within the economy. This has a lasting and multiplying effect, which in turn helps increase revenue the state generates through taxes and offsets the initially incurred deficit. The first camp sees this mechanism as a win-win situation. They add that what the state can do

Interaction and Reflexivity

in terms of stimulus, the central banks can equally do through injecting more money in the economy, putting more money in people's hands, which at first might dilute the value of money, but with time generates the same kind of lasting and multiplying effect as in the case of government spending.

The philosophy of the second camp is in almost complete opposition. It argues that there is no better economic mechanism than a free operating market. Agents in a market know much more what needs to be done than any state government. Market participants do this every day and across all sectors and geographies. This view was tempered with time to say that all that the state needs to do is regulate the market properly but 'thinly', let the central bank properly set the amount of money supply required, and the rest will operate by itself freely and efficiently. The behaviour of the economy might be more volatile than desired at instances, but this in itself is healthy and ensures long-term sustainability and efficiency. It is the idea of *laissez-faire* and the scepticism about government and administrative inefficiencies and greater inertia compared with more active market participants.

The debate between the two camps continues for decades now with no one side clearly winning the argument over the other. Many countries and governments tried one recipe or the other, and no one can really prove today that one approach is better than the other all the time and under all circumstances. Japan has been Keynesian for decades now without managing to turn its economy around yet, and Russia was ruined in the 1990s when it adopted a libertarian view.

c. Being flexible does not mean holding no values or being an opportunist all the time; it means not to be blinded by ideology when it comes to complicated dynamic systems and always recognise that a situation in the future might be different from the past, and what worked then might not work now.

87. Implication 5: The human value chain is increasingly fragmented, and the number of interactions for the same human objective or purpose continues to increase.

   a. We live in a world where the global level of interactions between humans has increased continuously, sometimes in an accelerated manner. Humans rely increasingly on each other for what constitutes the 'benefits of civilisation', such as water, energy, medicine, transportation, communication, protection, and services in general. Humans interact directly or indirectly through the movement of goods and services (commerce), communication, as well as the more accessible movement of people themselves. It is no surprise that the more economies develop, the more the share of what is defined as 'Services' in the Gross Domestic Product increases. This growing interaction coupled with a greater technological complexity continues to result in what we call a fragmentation of the value chain: the breaking into even smaller pieces of the value chain of human activities in which the different pieces could be handled by different agents (humans or machines). It is not that different from a worldwide assembly chain becoming longer and more fragmented. Let us take two examples from our daily life:

      i. For transportation, humans used to use a horse or their feet thousands of years ago. In the case of walking, it is rather clear what is the value chain and who is conducting most of the work in it. With the horse, for the most part, it is a value chain of two to three pieces: taking care of the horses (breed them, train them, groom them), growing food for the horses, and riding the horses. The same person can do all of course; equally, some pieces can be further broken down into a limited number of sub-pieces, as some might prefer.

Let us consider by contrast transportation in our days in mechanical machines, e.g. cars, trains, or planes. Every machine is constituted of hundreds of thousands of pieces; each piece of machinery can have a different origin and can be designed and manufactured in a different location. For the machine to move or transport, it requires a certain infrastructure, a road or a rail for example. This by itself is also constituted of hundreds of pieces coming from different origins, as well as requiring specific skill sets to be put in place. The machine requires energy to produce motion; again, another hundreds of thousands of steps and different agents intervening at each step. We can easily see how in order to realise the objective of transporting, we have moved from a basic value chain to one that is long, fragmented, and dependent on many more agents. There are evident benefits to moving to such a new value chain in terms of speed, reach, cost, and capability; this, however, comes at the cost of a different and more complicated value chain, which we typically take for granted as long as it works.

ii. For breakfast, a human in a gatherer society thousands of years ago used to probably look for the closest fruit bearing tree out there. He used to reach out with his hand or climb the tree to reach for the fruit. He used to then eat it with his bear hands and spit the seeds (if at all). Mission accomplished.

Today, for breakfast, we have cereal with milk (apologies to non-cereal eaters). For the cereal box to land on our table (that is excluding the milk, the spoon, and the bowl), a very large number of activities along a certain value chain have taken place. From the growing, fertilising, and harvesting of the corn[35] and other fruits in the cereal; to the roasting and transportation; to the manufacturing of the packaging; to the transportation of the final product through various geographic barriers and customs; to the marketing of the product for us to know about its existence; to supermarkets and convenient stores from which we buy the cereal... Thousands and millions of pieces along different value chains, pieces that were not existent or relevant in the past, each with possibly different agents controlling it or specialising in performing it.

b. It is ironic that the modern man is more individual in what concerns his philosophical, moral, and political views, less influenced by old institutions than in the past, and at the same time, forced by technology and the fragmentation of the value chain to be more collective in his economic and social activity. It is this form of 'impersonal collectivity' that is the sign of our times. Individualist attitudes were established in theory and thought by Descartes almost four hundred years ago, were spread and confirmed by the Reformation and the individual interpretation of religions, exploded with globalisation and the opening of cultures on each other, and finally have been taken to a whole new level with the invention of the Internet. Individualism started by being within societies, each society by itself, to become more global in the age of global communication and lower barriers to trade and to movement.

c. More fragmented value chains increase the difficulty

---

35 Add genetically modifying the corn.

Interaction and Reflexivity

of governing, be it of a country, company, society, or one's personal finances. It also presents us with difficult career choices. For an individual looking for greater and more sustainable economic benefits[36] in this increasingly technologically fragmented world, three approaches are possible.

i. The first is to develop knowledge and control over one or few pieces of the value chain (which we call in our jargon 'specialisation'). An encryption engineer has a very narrow speciality, so does an astronaut or a brain surgeon. A specialist can enjoy great success if his activity is in demand (e.g. cosmetic surgeon) or very little if his activity has gone out of fashion (e.g. a VHS manufacturer, a portrait painter, or an advanced harpist–these were more lucrative specialisations in past times).

ii. The second approach is to have transferable skill sets that can be used in a number of value chains with minor adjustments or learning. Transferable skill sets tend to be low to moderately advanced in terms of technological know-how, but they can serve in different sectors, industries, and countries. An example of such would be a receptionist, a security guard, or an HR function. In the business jargon, these functions are usually called horizontal (meaning that they cut across many fields). They are present in many value chains, and therefore they contain an attractive element of career hedge; the lower barriers to acquiring them in comparison with very specialised functions make them however usually less lucrative.

---

36 Seeking a job, looking to start or acquire a business, or invest in a particular part of the value chain.

Reflections on Fundamental Matters

      iii. The third is to oversee a larger portion of the value chain without really having a detailed knowledge of every piece of the chain. This is what is called 'management'. A CEO of a large company oversees a large value chain without necessarily having the full expertise in every piece of it. A President can never possess the required skill-set for every part of the governance of a nation of millions of individuals. Management positions are, however, more rare (we do not need as many people to oversee value chains as to work in them) and seldom a career starter.

d. A continuous and increased fragmentation of the value chain presents us individually with a dilemma: increased specialisation is required for a greater tangible value-add; at the same time, being greatly specialised in a field which has lost its allure or importance can represent a dead-end. In an age of increased human interactions and fragmentation of value-add, specialisation becomes a high-risk/high-reward game, and the trend is only accentuating. On the other hand, if we invert the problem, what could have constituted a lethal weakness in an age of lesser exchange and technology could be more easily overcome today. For example, not having a well-developed immune system in a newly born would have been lethal five thousand years ago, while today this kind of 'weakness' could be more easily remedied. The minimal skill set required for survival is in our days lower than in the past.

"[...] Take me as an example", Warren Buffet once said, "I happen to have a talent for allocating capital. But my ability to use that talent is completely dependent on the society I was born into. If I'd been born into a tribe of hunters, this talent of mine would be pretty worthless. I can't run very fast. I'm not particularly strong. I'd probably end up as some wild animal's dinner."

e. In an increasingly interactive and chaotic system, does generalisation seem a better hedge? Should we know a bit about everything and not engage ourselves too much in one direction from fear of changing dynamics and tastes? A society of highly qualified generalists, free from material needs, enjoying a bit of art, a bit of science, and a bit of physical activities, living all in harmony, is a utopia of new and old. It has been the dream of both the Left and the Right of the political spectrum. For Communists and Anarchists, it is the ultimate stage of a stateless society (post-capitalist that is) where all individuals enjoy equally all humanity's productive capacities, are free from all material needs, and spend their time in a general manner at their leisure. It has also been the dream of the aristocratic right, except with a two-tier society, where the upper class enjoys all the benefits of generalisation. European aristocracy held such a view of the world, and so did the Greek aristocracy in Antiquity. Aristotle's political views express this most clearly: education is for virtue and culture more so than usefulness, and each member of a society receives benefits proportional to his or her rank in it. It is a utopia of material freedom but also freedom in terms of intellectual pursuit. Unfortunately, it fails on at least two accounts:

   i. It is a self-defeating strategy: if everybody is a generalist, how are we supposed to really build and maintain the productive infrastructure that provides for all humanity's material need? How do we get there in the first place, and how do we manage to stay there without the specialists? The specialist is someone whom we might not feel her presence every day but is indispensable for most of what we take for granted, particularly in our advanced days.

   ii. Equally important, humans are creatures with self-esteem that is best fulfilled by each beating his own path and achieving his own desires and aspirations as much as possible. Specialisation is (or at least should be) first and foremost a matter of personal predisposition and differentiation in a society rather than a matter of pure economic or rational choice. In other words, the person who chooses to become a jet fighter or an astronaut does so firstly because he realises a certain genuine fulfilment from flying or being in outer space rather than because he analysed accurately the value chain of aerospace or space missions.

The increased interactive fragmentation of the human value chain will no doubt continue to affect the risk/reward profile of specialisation in human societies. Nevertheless, it would be difficult to comprehend a long-term stable and productive society of pure generalists and managers without the existence of specialisation, probably even in a futuristic robot-reliant society.

88. Implication 6: Not all that affects us is humanly intended.

   a. A prevailing populous view when it comes socio-politics and economics is to assume pre-meditation in a lot of what happens around us in terms of economic crises or socio-political conflicts. Many see conspiracy theories everywhere in the social and economic phenomena we do not clearly understand. The reality is that many things can build up randomly and through interaction and result in consequences and behaviours that no one can really predict beforehand objectively. The doomsayers are portrayed after fact as insightful geniuses, whereas in many situations, they do not deserve the intellectual credit they typically get. This is not to say that nothing is predictable or that irresponsible behaviours do not lead to negative consequences. The reality is neither on one extreme nor on the other.

   b. We complain when bad things we do not understand happen to us and look to put the blame on one particular group of people. However, we do not mind when we are picked up by a positive wave (such as the enormous gain in productivity and decrease in price of goods as a consequence of scale effects and globalisation), and we consider the results as granted rights. We are only biased to see conspiracy theories in the negative because we are genetically wired to focus more on that which is negative and threatening to our life and well-being.

c. We touched previously on 'Phase Transitions', and we will detail an aspect of them here. 'Phase Transition' is in reality a name for different types of transitions between a particular phase or interactive configuration and another. There are first-order transitions, second-order transitions, spinodal decompositions, breaking of symmetries, and the list is long. However, there are commonalities even among these different types of transitions. One of the commonalities is the presence of critical points. A critical point is the point of conditions where different 'phases' or 'states' of the system become indistinguishable. For example, for water the critical point is situated at a temperature of 374°C (705°F) and a pressure of around 22 MPa, meaning that above this critical point liquid water is indistinguishable from vapour water (we usually call it supercritical water). Inversely, when we move the conditions below the critical point, i.e. we start with the supercritical water and we try to move back to liquid and/or vapour by cooling the fluid and reducing the pressure, there is no telling which of the two states the system will choose, liquid water or vapour water. *At critical points of matter, the sensitivity to random fluctuations increases greatly in a system;* there is no telling in which of the possible states the system will end up as the aggregation of microbehaviours does not result in the same nullifying effect we talked about earlier close to the critical point. The path the system takes through critical transitions is greatly influenced by what happens close to the critical point, even if randomly. This happens at the critical point and not always[37]; in other words, chance plays a dramatic role in some particular situations and not in others. A whole universe or reality can be defined at these junctions where it could have been distinctly otherwise. The range of correlations between different parts of a system increases dramatically at critical points; butterfly effects can become more prominent in these situations. Something insignificant and random happening very far, which normally would not beg any attention, can, at a critical point, turn to be instrumental. What is even more interesting is that this behaviour is also scale-free; it can happen at a country level, planet level, or universe level!

d. Every time a major financial crisis such as the sub-prime mortgage market collapse and the ensuing economic collapse takes place, we hear a lot of conspiracy theories in both developing and developed countries. They accuse this segment of the population or that country of deliberately orchestrating such a collapse for obscure geopolitical or ideological reasons. With ignorance, conspiracy theories are rife. We are in our current age in a position to know that Phase Transitions and Critical Points are part of the structure of our human interactive world, and they sometimes can take place for a reason or another, unpredictably. The trigger is almost impossible to foresee and becomes only important after fact. We invite the reader to think about the Tunisian street vendor setting himself on fire igniting populous revolutions across the entire Arab World. Much is written about it

---

[37] Critical transitions are not the only situations where small fluctuations can have a dramatic impact on the whole system. Systems in 'metastable state' (i.e. in a state of inferior stability) can be tipped towards a more stable state by a small fluctuation too. However, unlike the case of the critical transition, here we can predict which state the system will be in: it will be the more stable state, and not one of several possible states as in the case of the critical transition (where all these possible states are equally stable).

later but very little before. People who drew attention to the trigger, sometimes out of pure luck, are suddenly seen as wise and with great foresight; they are seen as the predictors and interpreters of a new age.

89. Implication 7: Knowledge of the mathematics of interactions across very different human-related fields counts greatly.

    a. Why some people, companies, movie stars, music singers, and sports men and women can amass fortunes so quickly while others lag tremendously behind? Why a minor event can result in cataclysmic consequences in some instances and not in others? Not every flip of a butterfly wing creates a hurricane somewhere in the world! Why do we witness winner-take-all phenomena? Why do successful businesses grow side-by-side, or the rich become richer while the poor fail to catch-up? How does success bread more success? Why does a superpower lead in science, sport, economy, military, and other fields simultaneously? It is these types of questions that the mathematics of interactions can help answer away from conspiracy theories of all sorts. We will not attempt to answer these questions in detail, as they could easily represent a subject of a book. What we should retain however is that there are specific behaviours and phenomena that result from the way human affairs are structured, regardless of our political or ideological predispositions. And mathematical models are capable of providing several answers to the questions of the human world, more so than any political or economic theories that rely on shallow prejudice.

    b. Many phenomena in nature and the humans could not be understood and acted upon without the mathematical branch we call Statistics. Statistics today is everywhere, in Physics, Biology, Sociology, Economics, Politics, Media, and Advertisement. The role of Statistics is even more prominent in a world of increased human interactions.

    c. Statistics can however be a double-edged sword. It is

a great tool for understanding and acting on human societies, but it is also one of the most perfect candidates for misunderstandings and misinterpretations. We repeat, "Correlation does not imply causation" in Statistics, and two events that seem to be conjoint in some instances do not necessarily cause each other. We should not base our views of Statistics on pure misunderstandings and misinterpretations, and we should not revert back to an extreme view on them similar to Mark Twain's[38] "There are three kinds of lies: lies, damned lies and statistics".

d. An enlightened governance of human societies is not possible today without paying the right attention to Statistics, be it in insurance, traffic management, economics, elections, or mass advertisement. This is one key requirement that is still greatly neglected in many positions of society where it matters the most.

---

38   Twain himself attributed it to Benjamin Disraeli.

On Knowledge and Truth

"Be not astonished at these novelties; for it is well known to you that a thing does not therefore cease to be true because it is not accepted by many." Spinoza

"The fate of our times is characterised by rationalisation and intellectualisation and, above all, by the disenchantment of the world." Max Weber

On a hot summer night, Bouvard and Pécuchet, two French copy-clerks meet each other for the first time in Paris. They quickly discover that they are copycats of each other (except in terms of corpulence): same age, same temperament, and same hunger for knowledge. When Bouvard inherits a large fortune, they move out to Calvados and buy a sizeable property. They set themselves on a journey through knowledge and science. They delve into almost every branch of knowledge looking for intellectual stimulation and fulfilment: agriculture, science, archaeology, literature, politics, love, sport, philosophy, religion, education, music… The result is flounder after flounder. No happiness, no real satisfaction, nothing of meaning comes out from their long ordeal but trouble after trouble. They end up spending Bouvard's fortune, alienating their neighbours in the village, and risk being driven into prison. Disillusioned, traumatised by their experiences, and disgusted with everything, Bouvard and Pécuchet go back to their old occupation of copying…

Reflections on Fundamental Matters

Based on Flaubert's *Bouvard et Pécuchet*.

Knowledge and Truth is a major topic we will detail on. This may be a difficult chapter for some but it is an important one.

90. No approach, theory, philosophy, science, analysis, system, or other of similar scope, can really aim at being valid and comprehensive without dealing with the source of Knowledge and the way through which Knowledge is developed to reach the conclusions, approaches, theories, analyses, and systems it has in mind. One cannot address the material world without a minimal understanding of the nature of matter; similarly, one cannot ground herself in a valid understanding of what she knows or thinks is true without having an idea of the nature of Knowledge. Understanding the nature of Knowledge is extremely essential, and yet, we neglect it in our everyday life, directly or indirectly, when we think the way we think, we choose the way we choose, we act the way we act, and we argue the way we argue. We rarely ask ourselves why we think something is true or not. We go on working hard, making sacrifices, going sometimes to martyrdom, exercising violence on each other, confronting each other in society, and confronting the world, mostly based on some ideas, while we rarely ask ourselves about their irrefutable validity. It is not uncommon to find that the most loyal individuals to particular ideas have not really thought through in details the nature of their ideas and the knowledge they think they possess[39].

91. On Knowledge and Truth is a crucially important subject, possible to grasp much about, but impossible to grasp in totality. The reason behind this is actually simple: Knowledge is about cognition, and understanding the nature of Knowledge is having cognition thinking about cognition (we can call it metacognition), which is obviously circular and consequently can never be completely solved. The irony, as we shall see later, is that such circular

---

[39] For those who are already raising red flags, we will touch on the subject of Belief and Intuition in what follows.

references are everywhere, not only in Knowledge. We teach so much about Knowledge at schools but very rarely about this. Kids grow up conditioned in some sense and never really question the validity of their knowledge until faced with disillusionments, which, we must admit, are far from rare in life. Many great minds have attempted to treat the difficult subject of Knowledge and breakthroughs have been made; but no total comprehension is possible, probably ever.

92. In addition, there are very strong correlations between a trio of concepts, all important and all not fully understood. The trio we are referring to is Knowledge-Consciousness-Language; these three concepts are very difficult to be treated independently from each other, which renders the whole subject of Knowledge terribly difficult, actually impossible in some sense, to be fully treated to satisfaction.

The nature of Knowledge cannot be dissociated from the nature of Consciousness and vice versa, and both are very closely related and influenced by Language in ways we still very little understand but continue to discover more about since the 20th century. We do not ask the questions we ask without Language, and we do not think the way we think without Language. And how can we talk about self-consciousness without the 'I' that we put in front of verbs and manipulate?

93. We should start by drawing three important observations on the topic of Knowledge:

    a. Understanding the nature of Knowledge is extremely crucial and one of the first things to be attentive to in the hierarchy of wants.

    b. Fully understanding the nature of Knowledge is not available today and might never be possible. No one should be surprised or disappointed by that.

    c. This does *not* mean that we cannot qualify the nature of Knowledge to a large extent and be better off than when not paying attention to it.

Reflections on Fundamental Matters

The purpose of this chapter is not to provide the most comprehensive and rigorous treatment of the topic but to offer some of the necessary elements in order to better understand Knowledge and its nature. This chapter will treat among others the following subjects: what we know, what we do not know, what we can know, what we can never know, and the level of certainty of what we know.

94. The history of human beings is as much a history of Thought as it is a history of Deeds. It is a history of Knowledge and evolution of Knowledge as much as a history of Action and evolution of Action. Definitely not all of our actions but a large part of them cannot come to be (by our own nature) without Thought and Knowledge. Humans are born curious and ask questions probably since the dawn of their existence. This very human nature has relations to the trio previously mentioned. Angst takes hold of humans; they are born and grow with many questions, and the world does not provide full clear answers to these questions. However, humans are given tools to address some of this angst in the form of capacity to know, similarly to the limbs they are given for the capacity to act. Capacity to know and capacity to ask questions are one and the same, and it is as if the solution and the problem are one and cannot exist without each other; they continuously create, provoke, and cause each other.

95. Humans realise that Knowledge is convenient at two levels: it helps provide some answers to the questions they ask, but also as important, it facilitates and enhances action, which results in an improved material existence. The effect is therefore both internal and external. However, the path of growing knowledge is far from being straight. The story of Thought is much more dialectical in reality[40], and it is full of assumptions about things that turn out to be wrong or incomplete. And this pattern is likely to continue. Moreover, there are limits to this growth that Knowledge have found impossible to overcome no matter how hard it tries, or what new tools it acquires along the way.

---

40 I.e. we think something then we discover that we are wrong about it then we rectify our thinking and so on and so forth.

Ways of Acquiring Knowledge

Let us first explain some of the ways through which Knowledge can be developed.

96. Acquiring Knowledge is largely synonymous to Problem Solving. The two classical academic ways of developing Knowledge include Deductive and Inductive Reasoning.

97. Deductive Reasoning means starting with a set of axioms and rules assumed to be true and building further knowledge using combinations of these true axioms and rules. No knowledge is simply possible without a set of axioms and rules assumed to be true that we start with. This is the method used in Mathematics, Chess, Analytical Philosophy/Logical Positivism, and to a certain extent Classical Music. The type of Knowledge it leads to is essentially called analytic[41]; Knowledge in this case is fundamentally mostly about complicated identities and negations.

98. Inductive or Empirical Reasoning means (roughly) observing the world around a large enough number of times and inferring from such observations valid knowledge, which cannot be one hundred per cent certain but could be considered as true with varying degrees of certainty. For example, we observe the sun rising every day, and we therefore assume that the sun will rise again tomorrow. This is the method used in all Natural Sciences to develop theories, alongside Deductive Reasoning. Some of the knowledge that is acquired through this method is different from pure deductions and does not concern identities and negations. It is called *synthetic*, in the sense that it can be otherwise without a logical contradiction. With synthetic knowledge, it is only through observation that we can fix ourselves one way or another.

   a. It is worth noting that what is sometimes called Abductive Reasoning falls for us under the umbrella of Inductive Reasoning given its similar dependence on empirical observations. Abduction is essentially about 'guessing'

---

41 Which we have alluded to in the previous chapter.

certain ways of being, patterns, trends, or theories from a particular observation of empirical data points, which might not be complete or fully satisfactory from a classical empirical standard.

99. Induction has been much criticised, especially by Hume and Popper; it remains indispensable nevertheless under some form.

100. The Humean critique (very valid) is an elaborate version of the chicken-and-egg problem. Hume's problem was mainly with Causality. If all knowledge is based on experience, then how can we rely on principles such as 'all knowledge is based on experience' or 'causality', which are necessary principles for us to derive any knowledge from experience? In an observation of 'A causes B', we observe A and we observe B, but we never observe the link between A and B; no matter how often we observe A followed by B, there is nothing in there that cannot be considered conjectural—one instance of A not followed by B is enough to destroy the whole causality.

101. One of the ways Popper attempts to solve this problem is by claiming that Induction is never used in the first place when it comes to scientific inquiry. A detailed discussion of this point requires going into a technical definition of Induction, which is a complicated subject. Popper argues that Induction is actually substituted by several problem-solving tools. The source of scientific theories does not matter; what matters is their predictive power and Falsification.

102. It suffices to say that no matter what is our technical definition of Induction, it is only misleading in our view to substitute it with 'problem-solving tools' or talk about various 'sources' for problem-solving tools and be satisfied. In reality, Popper's epistemology was largely influenced by Einstein's discoveries. Indeed, Einstein, as is the case of the majority of modern theoretical physicists, did not rely as much on Induction as on 'Imagination' as he often liked to name it. "Imagination is more important than knowledge." Einstein famously said.

Others prefer to talk about Intuition[42]. What is the source of this Imagination or Intuition if not an accumulation of experiences and observations?

103. By deliberately ignoring the sources behind imagination and problem-solving techniques, Popper can mislead us into underestimating the role of experience. Experience is not only a tool for validating theories; it is *fundamental* to our cognition directly and indirectly. Our living impacts our thinking structures. Induction cannot therefore be completely ridden off, even if its definition is subject to refinement and change.

104. It might seem that these two sources of Knowledge, Deduction and Induction, are enough to deal with all that surrounds us in a satisfactory manner, especially when we combine both of them. They are the methods used by Science after all, and those who ever liked Science might find themselves drawn to the conclusion that these two methods should be enough. Unfortunately, Reality is much more complicated than that (something of which we shall much see…). Analytical sources of Knowledge are the most solid sources of Knowledge; they allow the practitioner to obtain Knowledge with the highest degrees of certainty, or at least a certainty commensurate with the axioms we start with. However, they remain limited in scope, and they are 'slow' sources of Knowledge development. If we only rely on them, much of what we deal with every day becomes impossible to comprehend, and our action will therefore become limited. If we wait for everything to be demonstrated inductively or deductively, politics, sociology, art, and a large part of Humanities, all become impossible topics to deal with. There is therefore a need for other sources of Knowledge. These include Critical Knowledge and Speculative Knowledge.

---

42 Intuition referred to here is not the instinctive kind (that makes us for example consider ourselves as one entity); it is rather the one that we acquire through repetition or continuous observations, it is this 'gut feel' or '*déjà vu*' emanating from having observed long enough.

105. Critical Knowledge consists of considering all that we know or we think we know, all notions and concepts, regardless of their origins, and subject them to criticism of all sorts in order to determine what is true in them from what is not. It is the dialectic of Zeno of Elea, the reduction to the absurd. It is the dialectical process of Socrates: the process of continuously asking questions without exhaustion in order to highlight potential flaws of reasoning or belief, as well as bring to the surface the real nature of knowledge or belief held.

106. Critical Knowledge is probably the most common method we use. When we are confronted with something, we rarely run statistical experiences to determine the truth or falsehood of what is asserted, or go back to deductively-proven theorems right from the source of Deductive Knowledge to work things out consistently step-by-step from there. We usually fire away all possible critiques and assess the outcome accordingly, relying in the process on other knowledge we consider more 'proven' by our standards. We rely on Rationality in our critique[43], and this is an important point.

    a. Critical Knowledge is what could be qualified as a negative method of acquiring Knowledge; it is more preoccupied with rejecting premises and statements then affirming their certainty. Popper's Falsification, with a bit more formalisation, falls under this category to a large extent. Its starting point is usually Speculation (which we will describe below), and it is rarely able to affirm Knowledge that stands the proof of experience in a satisfactorily scientific manner.

    b. Critical Knowledge has a limited ability to discover new things on its own. One of its negatives is that it often uses crude methods of criticism that can be subject to cognitive biases (such as anchoring or availability bias) or misuse of syntax.

---

43 And so, on some form of Induction or Deduction even if not from original axioms.

107. We can illustrate the contrast between the classical methods abovementioned and the (partial) use of Critical Knowledge with an example from Psychology. When Psychology first started[44], it focused on the individual, on the unit, and on understanding the cause of specific human or animal actions in an experimental manner one-by-one (experiences of the type Pavlov and Wundt undertook). The assumption behind was that, when we understand each and every one of those actions and their root causes, we will be able to combine our findings into a whole that gives a comprehensive behavioural view of the human. This approach is the traditional one in Natural Sciences; it is the *reductionist* approach, which was essentially mathematically set by Galileo and remained predominant until the discovery of new statistical/probabilistic models as well as the use of macro/critical approaches such as the one we are discussing here. As Psychology progressed, psychologists quickly discovered the scope limitation of such methods given the degrees of uncertainty in the experiences, correlations of all sorts, complications arising from combining various findings, as well as simply a set of information that is too large to treat.

Instead of continuing with the traditional methods, some started approaching the whole unit, i.e. the human, as a black box and deriving from that, through critique (Critical Knowledge) and experience (Inductive Knowledge), certain behavioural patterns which turned out to be very insightful; hence, were born functionalism and psychoanalysis, and later the humanist and Gestalt approaches. We are not implying that there are branches of Psychology that are based on Critical Knowledge only; there is a lot of Induction in most of them. However, there is definitely a dialectical element at their birth. Today both methods in Psychology have evolved but remain in use jointly and complement each other: cognitive science, developmental psychology, and differential psychology on the one hand, and social psychology and clinical psychology on the other hand.

---

44 I.e. branching out properly from philosophy into a discipline of its own.

Reflections on Fundamental Matters

108. The history of Economics is not very different from that of Psychology; it has its reductionist and detailed methods of microeconomics, as well as its more simplified and global macroeconomics approach, which can be more qualitative than the micro one.

109. A final method of acquiring Knowledge we shall discuss is Speculative Knowledge. Speculation is simply about generating ideas and the sources of such ideas could be really any. We speculate and then sometimes work to prove whether such speculations are true or not using any of the methods described above. In the development of Natural Sciences, there is an element of Speculation (usually mixed with Abduction) at the initiation of many new theories or insights. The sources of Speculation are usually observations, but also a certain 'feeling' or 'impression' of the type we only experience after having been exposed to a particular problem for a very long time.

    a. When Einstein came up with his theories on Relativity, the source of his work could not have been only Induction. Most of what Relativity deals with at its core is not an easy subject of observation. The source of his ideas was ultimately Speculation based on a certain intuition and meditation about the nature of matter.

    b. But whatever is the method through which an insight in Natural Sciences is posited, it is *never* admitted as true without a rigorous examination and a large number of validations through experience.

110. However, in Speculation, there exist a number of situations where we unfortunately do not even bother to prove the truth or falsehood of our speculation; we usually stop when things become plainly ridiculous or obviously wrong by the current higher thresholds of conviction. In many cases, we do not stop till we reach that point. Worse, if a particular speculation turns out to work in few particular cases, for reasons that may not have to do with our initial premise for coming up with the

idea[45], we consider this as a validation of our speculation and we persevere!

    a. Consider a novice financial speculator who thinks that a certain stock has a great potential to appreciate; he reckons that the company behind the stock is great. The speculator can give all sorts of reasons and feelings for why he thinks it to be the case, all related specifically to the company itself. He consequently invests in the stock of the company. The stock goes up for a week because the market is generally going up, and most stocks happen to be positively correlated. The speculator is jubilant, his account is growing after all, and ultimately after a week, he sells the stock for a gain—he is the king-to-be of Wall Street! The novice speculator goes on telling all the people he knows how great he is at trading, and how he 'managed to beat the market' because of his insights. The speculator now finds another stock and applies the same set of reasons and feelings to conclude that this new stock is even more attractive than the first one. After all, the first one worked, and this one looks even more attractive using the same judgement criteria. The speculator doubles the size of his bet and takes a position in the new stock. Two days later, this new company issues a major earnings warning, discloses pure internal mismanagement issues, and fires the CFO; the stock plummets by 30%. Such a scenario is not uncommon when it comes to Speculation and is far from being present only in the financial space.

111. Speculation is the easiest way of developing what can be later properly called Knowledge, but it is also the method that is most fraught with errors if not subjected to proper validation. The Greeks, and this is one the sources of their greatness and the legacy they left behind, were fantastically speculative. They did not stop at anything; they were not shackled by any state or religious dogma, which allowed them to express original views, at least at

---

45 Through pure luck for example.

the level of the upper Greek social class. There are few ideas the Greeks did not really speculate on at least in some crude form. They talked about empiricism, idealism, positivism, scepticism, cynicism, dialectic approach, analytical philosophy, intentionality, survival of the fittest, evolution of species, origins of the Universe even to include something similar to the multi-verse idea, nature of celestial bodies, historicism and historic finality, intrinsic purpose, materialism, atomism, Brownian movement, determinism/destiny/fate, role of chance, hedonism, utilitarianism, cosmic balance/justice, monism, pluralism, unity in diversity, democracy, aristocracy, plutocracy, morality, tyranny, idea of the gentleman, relativity of motion, deception of the senses, and most of what one finds today in theological doctrines, including body/soul separation, the supra-sensible world, incarnation, reincarnation, trinity, the unmoved mover, eternity and indivisibility of the soul, and fate of souls after death including Heaven, Hell, and Purgatory… to name only a few!

Of course, many of these ideas were very crude, many systems and models were inconsistent, blatantly wrong, and sometimes bizarre. But the key elements were there, and most were only speculative without any necessary validation basis. Much of what subsequent philosophers and men of thought have done is to start with some such models and ideas, elaborate on them, and ground them in more defensible manners. The Greek 'speculative experiment' shows the rapidity of idea generation and the power that can come out from Speculation. And what we know of the Greeks could have existed elsewhere[46].

112. As we discussed, theories in Science can also be speculative. However, they are subject to a more or less drastic validation process through which they become more or less Critical Knowledge or Empirical Knowledge. *Hence, there is nothing wrong with Speculative Knowledge per se; it is the quality of the validation following Speculation that determines the quality of Speculative Knowledge.* Moreover,

---

[46] But we might not have been lucky enough to obtain it or preserve it throughout History.

Speculation can remain as such as long as everybody who uses it is always aware of this fact. Many theories and ideologies in politics and social sciences, religions, and philosophies are mere speculations with no proper validation process behind. Plato's cosmogony and Aristotle's physics are purely speculative, and they did persist for a very long time. Worse, many speculative theories hide behind eloquence in order to provide a certain impression of wisdom that does not exist.

113. It is rather irrelevant how voluminous *Das Kapital* is, or how much complicated language there is in it; there is nowhere in Marx' work a valid demonstration of the inevitable social evolution from Capitalism to Communism as societies develop, or Communism as a guaranteed final model for material optimisation of societies *under all conditions*. A feeling of sympathy towards an abused working force, no matter how legitimate it is, does not constitute a valid demonstration and basis for a complete remaking of the economic model in a particular country; other less drastic ways of remedying against social inequalities are possible. Many countries went down, or were driven towards, the path of communist experiments; generations were destroyed because of such speculations; borders were altered; human rights were abused; and no one stopped and said, "Let us validate such theories before we die or kill for them, before we change all of our social structures for them." Blind theology was substituted by communist ideology with the same disastrous effects.

114. Ages before Marx, Platonic Socrates, despite his remarkable auto-critique on many aspects[47] had equally attempted to fit everything into his mould of the Theory of Ideas. Sometimes he did it clearly, sometimes hypocritically. No matter how complicated the language of Husserl or Heidegger is or how beautiful their speculations are, they remain speculations, and no more, until properly falsified. 'Soft' sciences and humanities are full of such examples. Typically, the worst undemonstrated speculations tend to hide behind some of the greatest eloquence.

---

47 Which is unique for his time.

115. There are naturally commonalities between these four methods of Knowledge acquisition, and they can use many of the same cognitive tools. Logic is an important component of all of them to varying degrees, the highest degree of use of Logic being in Deductive Reasoning. Empirical methods often require mathematical tools, which are based on pure Deduction. However, not all mathematics has its birth in pure love of Deduction and Contemplation. The study of Statistics and Probability was highly driven by empirical reasons, and it is no surprise that it progressed materially only after the Renaissance[48]. Emotionality is often part of Speculative Knowledge alongside Logic. When we address a subject such as Equality or Justice, there is a definite emotional element alongside any logical or purely utilitarian element. As Bergson[49] once said, behind every great philosophy and philosopher lies a central intuition. This observation can be generalised beyond Philosophy.

Historical Disillusionments

Four key disillusionments in Human History are important to know about, not only in order to have a concrete context of what is pure Speculation in opposition to actual Knowledge, but also in order to derive some important lessons about mistakes of thought not to repeat in the future.

116. Of the last two thousand years, a large part of our knowledge, particularly Western knowledge, has been intertwined with Religion. Some of the greatest thinkers were also great religious figures such as Saint Augustine or Saint Thomas Aquinas. Moreover, some of the great religious notions were built on earlier secular knowledge, and in the process, re-biased this knowledge sometimes in a rather unjustified manner towards the doctrine advocated by the religion[50] in place. The reason behind this is rather

---

48 In comparison with geometry, arithmetic, or algebra.

49 Henri Bergson, French philosopher.

50 Think of Christian philosophers and Aristotle for example.

easy to understand: in the tumultuous political times following the fall of Rome and the increased dominion of barbarous kings, religious institutions were the only place where Knowledge was possible. Under the umbrella of Religion, 'Metaphysics', which was essentially a wide spectrum of Knowledge subjects, could develop more easily; however, this did not happen without an influence from Religion. It is mostly at the age of Enlightenment that the two, Metaphysics and Religion, started to take separate distinct roots again.

117. Under the influence of Judaeo-Christian and Islamic religions[51], and likely coupled with the strong psychological human need for feeling and wanting to believe that it is a species of a special kind, it was taken as 'knowledge' that Man and the place it inhabits, Earth, are the *centre of everything*. Man was considered to be a *very special creation*; even some religions went as far as describing Man as the image of God. Man is *fully in control of himself and his decisions*, and he is therefore under some sort of a 'trial period' by God on Earth to do the good. Finally, this existence on Earth is not the last; once Man passes the trial, there is immortality, the ultimate salvation from our mortal condition. *God created the world for our trial*, and once the trial is over, we are recalled back from this world.

Four major concepts of Humanity up until the end of the Middle Ages conditioned and honed generations after generations, four speculations with no duty of proof or validity behind them, and four great historical disillusionments based on speculative reasoning. For the religious readers, the writer begs not to take the below as an affront on all religious belief. It is rather an attack on elaborate speculations taken as irrefutable doctrine without a duty of demonstration. One can very well be religious and not believe in purely false speculations; the Church does not claim any longer that Earth is the centre of the world. No person valuing Rationality and all that has been achieved by Humanity through decent rational effort should have a problem rejecting these false speculations.

---

51 And is concordant with Manichaeism.

118. Consistent with the idea that God created the world with Man specifically in mind, and coupled with human egocentricity, it was easy to assume and indoctrinate that Man and the place it inhabits, Earth, are the centre of a godly creation. Everywhere we look in the sky, things seem to revolve around us; Earth is therefore a special place. God gave us the world to benefit from and to procreate in and expand.

Religious stories are almost by definition only centred on Man as a special species with a special story. This usually comforts us psychologically and may also have evolutionary reasons. Earth indeed is a special place, with rare conditions for Life to develop on, but nothing proves that it is the only such place in the Universe. On the contrary, given the billions and billions of stars and galaxies in the Universe, it is not unlikely statistically to find another place where Life can develop, whether now, in the past, or in the future. The speculation 'Earth and Man centre of all' was assumed knowledge without proof. Anyone who dared to question such 'knowledge' was chased, burned, or put under pressure to deny his/her claims. Even thinkers stumbling on evidence to the contrary had to somehow backtrack in their thinking or auto-censure themselves[52]. We all know how this speculative assertion turned out wrong, and how almost no one today seriously claims anymore that Man and Earth are the centre of everything unless in jest.

119. The bias towards 'uniqueness of Man' was not only reflected in the speculation that Man was the centre of everything. It was also assumed that Man is a special creation, something unique and apart from all what is around it. For Manichaeism, Man is the centre of an eternal fight between Light and Darkness. We are the only species we know of that has a high level of Consciousness, that uses Language, and that can devise advanced ways of using Nature to its advantage. Darwin and his wonderful Evolutionary Theory shed this collective egocentricity into pieces. To be exact, the ideas of Evolution and of the Survival Of the

---

52 Such as Aristarchus of Samos and Copernicus.

Fittest are not Darwin's; the Greeks at the time of Anaximander and Empedocles already speculated about the evolutionary nature of living beings and the survival of the fittest[53]; even Darwin's grandfather was an advocate of Evolution. Darwin has however the full merit of having elaborated a proper scientific theory with experimental demonstrations on the subject, *taking us from Speculation to Knowledge.*

We ultimately turned out to be cousins with animals. Our DNA and that of animals (not only apes and the mammals closest to us) only contain minor differences. We suddenly discovered that there are no special barriers or categorisations between Nature and us; we are part of Nature, and we are a continuum of the animal world. All metaphysical assumptions about us, about our 'Spirit', and about our 'Soul' had to be re-questioned. Observe the social behaviour of elephants, and you will discover that they do not behave that differently from us; even some of their psychological illnesses are ours. We do not seem to be that special; we are a continuum of the environment around us, and we are part of it. A second blow to our speculative arrogance took place.

120. As we started speculating without proof, we ran into logical problems, which to remedy, we found ourselves required to create additional speculative notions that equally turned out to be inaccurate. If God created the Universe, and God is only good, how do we then explain the Bad in the Universe? Man is capable of as much bad as good. It must be that Man can do the bad even if God does not approve of it. Man is therefore free to do either the good or the bad. This works well with the view that this existence is only temporary and a trial—we are free to do the good or the bad, and we are judged afterwards based on our actions (either in another world or in our *karma* when we come back to this world). There is therefore purpose for our existence defined by some entity independent from us. Man is always free and always conscious of all her/his actions. Man enjoys Free Will and is always in control of her/himself.

---

53 However without any proof of such.

The beginnings of the 20th century witnessed a revolution in our perception of this freedom. Freud pointed out to the existence of something else in us than pure, always controlling Consciousness—he called it the Unconscious[54]—and went on establishing relationships and feedback loops between Reality and our Unconscious, between Consciousness and Unconsciousness. One of its main underpinnings is simple: we can sometimes undertake an action not out of our own conscious free will, but out of some unconscious in us that has developed over time and got influenced by our past experiences. In other words, *we are not always one hundred per cent in control.* Today, hearing about the Unconscious does not surprise many. At its inception, this notion and its full phenomenological implications were literally revolutionary, as revolutionary as us and the apes being cousins.

121. In actuality, the Unconscious turned out not to be the only addition to the Conscious and the free rational decision-making process in us; Intuition and Instincts are also there. Instincts are traits we are born with that define certain reactions and attitudes of ours. The word Intuition as commonly used includes innate intuition as well as intuition that we grow and develop with experience. The idea that we use Intuition in decision-making or in art does not surprise many today because we are accustomed to it. In reality, it should surprise us if we are full believers that all that we do is driven by our free will and our rationality. Intuition plays a large role in shaping our tastes, dispositions, and views on the environment around us. Life-changing choices are sometimes made through Intuition.

    a. Some may not see in Intuition an opposition to Free Will, as Intuition can be judged by our rational processes, overcome, or muted. This is true to some extent; however, in situations that require quick decision-making under duress, it is actually the rational, slow processes that are muted, and it is Intuition that is often in control.

---

54 Freud was not the first to use the term 'Unconscious', but he is the first to develop an elaborate theory around.

122. "Fine", says the speculator, "I got ahead of myself. Man and its habitat are not the centre of everything, and we are not a special creation parachuted on Earth from somewhere else. We have special unique traits that we have not found yet in anything else around us, and the majority still believes we have a soul that will continue to exist when the body dies and decomposes. We do not act one hundred per cent based on Free Will although we have freedom to choose in many cases. However, there must be a cause to all of this, one cannot deny that! Causality is a major characteristic of our Universe. Everything interacts with everything, and there is cause-and-effect everywhere. So there must be a first cause for everything around us, and here I am not speculating! I am basing myself on experience! This First Cause is God. Hence, the notion of God is proven and is even necessary. I can hold on to that and be comfortable." And so asserts the speculator…

123. In reality, what the speculator is holding him/herself to is not entirely true. There is a speculative jump from making observations about Causality around us to claiming that there must be a First Cause or a Grand Design behind everything. Here, unfortunately for those who do not have a taste for it, we will have to do a bit of Physics to disprove this particular speculation.

Space and Time as we know them started with the Big Bang, the initial explosion, which in reality is not an explosion but rather an expansion of Space and Time. By definition, talking about 'before' the Big Bang is therefore very tricky and likely meaningless; as we said in the Appendix, the moment there are events, there are relations, and so there is Time, and using a notion of Time (which is what 'before' is) to try to denote something that precedes the sequence of events is nothing more than bad semantics. Let us define the Big Bang at $T=0$. We are starting to know a great deal about what happened some time after $T=0$ but not a single thing about what happened between $T=0$ and roughly $T=5.39 \times 10^{-44}$s (1 Planck unit). "Like I care about this interval!" some might exclaim.

As we said, talking about Causality without the necessity of Time results in problems. We can however have an initial simultaneous Cause-Effect by which Time and Space come to be, and everything develops afterwards from there. And so we can imagine God as the initial simultaneous Cause-Effect. The Universe has constant Energy, and God must be the source of that Energy. Unfortunately, God is not the only plausible answer. This First, this Initial, this Start of Everything including Space, Time, and Energy, could have come from Nothing, yes Nothing, Void, Emptiness; and here we are staying within the realm of Theoretical and Quantum Physics. We should stress the word *could* as we are not in a position (yet) in Physics to affirm it with certainty. However, what is becoming certain is that God as Initial, First, or Start of Everything is *not a necessity*.

Let us try to be concrete and simple in explaining how this could come to be. All the theories about the initial stages of the Universe talk about matter and particles of different types, all interacting with each other all the time according to four different types of interactions, which we suspect that at some point back in the past were actually one common type of interaction. The theories also talk about the Space in between, empty space with nothing in it, in which this matter and these particles are. As the theories progressed, they added anti-matter, which was a curious discovery in the beginning but turned out to be extremely important. Anti-matter is named as such because it turns out that for every class of particles of any kind we are accustomed to, there is a corresponding anti-particle. When a particle of one kind interacts with its anti, the result is annihilation, which results in the disappearance of both particles and the release of energy[55]. The interesting question is where is all this anti-matter today? If it was lying around, nothing of the matter would be left, explosions of energy would be everywhere and annihilation would be the only game in town.

Another major leap came from this empty space in between that

---

55 While the particle and its anti-particle disappear, different types of particles get created through this release of energy; these particles are called force carrier particles such as photons. Some forms of annihilation also result in other different particles of matter in addition to the force carrier particles.

we mentioned. It turns out that this empty space is actually never 'empty', and the whole notion of 'empty' needs to be reviewed. In this emptiness takes place from time to time what we call *quantum fluctuations*. Remember the anti-particles? Well it turns out that this nothing could manifest itself from time to time as a particle and an anti-particle. So the empty or the void could actually be considered as the one and the other neutralising each other; this void has no charge and no momentum. Let us assume that one of the particles contains a positive charge, and its anti contains a negative charge. 0 can be also put as (+1) + (-1). What usually happens is that the 0 manifests itself from time to time, and this is what is meant by quantum fluctuation, as (+1) and (-1), and then goes back to being 0 without any consequences. However, very rarely, due to reasons we do not need to go into here[56], the (+1) can 'break away' from the (-1), and the (-1) can immediately change in nature into something else[57]. We could end up theoretically through this process with a particle and gravity instead of nothing. In other words, out of Nothing, out of zero, can result particle and energy in ways we do not fully understand yet but have only started to put our fingers on. In such a way, from Nothing can come something, and the speculation God must be the initial simultaneous Cause-Effect, the initial Energy, is not necessarily true. For those resting on elaborate dogmas, Science is not likely to stop surprising us.

Speculations and Systems

124. Speculation helps build intellectual systems faster than any other way, and systems are of key importance to Knowledge. Without self-consistent and elaborate systems, no complex Knowledge is possible. Sometimes, Speculation is the only way forward. Almost as much in the field of Natural Science was developed through Speculation as through Induction. Furthermore, there is a large

---

56 Such as the closeness to a black hole.

57 This something else could become gravity force.

gap between what we can know and what we actually know even with the lowest level of certainty. We humans crave for answers and for a 'way of life', for which scientific knowledge seems unable to fully provide; Speculation is what fills this gap. Many forms of human expression (for the lack of a better word) are by nature speculative. Art in all its forms is mostly about Speculation, at least in the non-classical sense of beauty, away from the Ideal, Sublime, and Perfect.

125. Let us ask the following rhetorical question: "Who do you think are the greatest philosophers of all times? Who are the philosophers who influenced most the academic fields of Philosophy, Religion, and Sociology?" The answers, more likely than not, will include Plato and Aristotle for the Antiquity period, and Kant and Hegel for more modern times. It is not surprising that all four of them could be qualified as prime 'system builders'. They all belong to the idealist systematic tradition in some sense. The Atomists, Locke, Hume, and the analytical philosophers are all great but not as influencing as the four names previously cited[58]. Even in non-Western cultures, what transpires from Western philosophy is mostly due to the first type of system builders rather than the second.

126. Humans are greatly interested in finding a one ever-encompassing Truth, and hence, their fascination with systems that are 'total' (i.e. addressing everything) and with those who propose them. Often, the appeal of systems is also aesthetic and political, not only rational: the poor are more favourable to Socialism and Communism, the rich to Conservatism, and the rebellious to Romanticism and Anarchism.

127. Systems can however be equally dangerous in several respects. Creators often fall in love with their systems, particularly when their systems start showing signs of success. Systems become a mould where everything has to fit in, and everything has to be explained by them: Freud and the sexual drive, Marx and

---

[58] Except in their 'home' cultures of Britain and subsequently America for philosophers such as Locke and Hume.

On Knowledge and Truth

materialism/class conflict, or Einstein and determinism. This same love can lead to blindness when systems are failing and can very well result in dogmatism.

128. From Fichte to Schelling to Hegel to Marx and then Heidegger, Philosophy became increasingly affirmative of new systems and ways without temperance or duty of demonstration, while also becoming more and more complicated in words and eloquence (but not necessarily in ideas). Hegel and Marx affirmed how History works (or should work), what it will ultimately lead to, and therefore proclaimed that History has a finality[59]. They created and enforced systems and forced them to be total; all based on pure Speculation and without a duty of demonstration.

129. The excesses of Speculation are not a limited phenomenon to the 19th-20th century or German idealism, far from it. The trap of dogmatising some speculations for no other valid reason than eloquence of the text, historical status of its creator, his/her social influence, or inherited prejudices and 'traditions' plagued the history of Knowledge at all steps of its progress. Plato's theories were beautiful, insightful, and unique for his age; they are an irrefutable building block of Philosophy and Theory of Knowledge. Aristotle's work was also extremely productive in many fields. Plato and Aristotle were both highly speculative; notable exceptions include Aristotle's work on Logic (though not without its flaws). All in all, it took Western and Mediterranean civilisations between 1,200 and 1,800 years[60] to break away from these dogmatised speculations and prove able to move forward in their thinking in a significant manner. It is no surprise then that some political systems from the 19th century onwards also became totalitarian in their approach and took their ideologies from such a totalitarian speculative thinking.

130. This is not to say that the philosophers mentioned above did not make great contributions to human thought and knowledge.

---

59 Inherited from the dialectic of Socrates and likely the sense of purpose of Aristotle.

60 Depending whether we count from Platonism or Neoplatonism.

Philosophy would be missing a lot without the 'negativity' and 'dialectical' approach that Kant had missed and Hegel instated. Marx's contribution to Sociology, among others, is immense. Although many of his conclusions proved to be wrong afterwards, Marx' methods continue to be used and built upon even till today. Karl Marx remains the father of Material Reflexivity. The trouble was that such philosophers speculated and enforced systems, and these systems became almost doctrinal without a burden of proof. And we should not because of their historical status assume them to be superior and not faulty in their philosophy.

131. We do not mean to say that this was the approach of all German philosophers either—Schopenhauer approached things differently, and Nietzsche could be put somewhere in the middle, destroying old wrong beliefs on one side, but speculating on the other.

132. At the end of the 19th century, Philosophy started to witness a revolution against the excessive speculations of the previous two to three centuries, which was largely driven by German idealism and some of what followed it. This speculative affirmation resulted in a revolt, which came mostly from within the same Germanic community of philosophers. A new kind of philosophy emerged, in both the English- and German-speaking worlds. With the influence of Science and Mathematics, it refused to affirm something as true without a duty of demonstration. It took a more rigorous and grounded approach to Philosophy and relied on deductive methods to build its systems. The name of this approach is Analytical Philosophy, which includes logical positivism and language analysis. Its key figures (mostly mathematician-philosophers) include Frege, Peano, Russell, Wittgenstein, Carnap, and Schlick. Karl Popper and his 'falsification' is also a result of this philosophical stream. This new approach to Philosophy was not only a different way of doing things; it was a reaction against excessive speculation generated by previous thinkers when it came to Metaphysics and Philosophy. The story of the Vienna Circle falls under this category.

133. As a rule, systems have limitations that most creators have

difficulty admitting. The dream of one ever-encompassing system has been part of almost all thought disciplines. And in all cases, it has proven to be illusory. If one adventures a bet based on History, it would be that such a system is utopic and is more likely to be replaced by multiple systems, each in its area of expertise, with overlapping boundaries where inconsistencies have to be addressed. Hence, a piecemeal theory is usually more versatile, resilient, and conducive to applications as well as improvements than the dream of the perfect system. The most complete and rigid systems are the most vulnerable; any mistake at any point breaks the entire system.

134. There is an important lesson to be learned from the historical mistakes of Speculation, which goes beyond Science and Philosophy into our daily life and relates to our personal intellectual and emotional integrity. Talk is easy in life; anyone can say anything, think anything, and pretend that anything is true. We should always ask ourselves whether we deserve the right to express our opinion on a particular subject. No one is advocating here a limitation of the freedom of speech; *the restraint should come from within each and every one of us only* when it comes to expressing one's own opinions. And no one is expecting a doctorate level of knowledge in a subject before expressing an opinion on it; what is at mind is a minimal degree of real knowledge and qualification before expressing strong opinions about a particular subject, to leave room for acknowledging possible errors, or at least to temper the opinion with some acknowledged modesty. It is not a question of academic qualifications; it is a question of honest self-restraint in case of lack of sufficient knowledge about a particular subject. Anyone can express an opinion on anything, especially in our days of digital media and the Internet. We can blog, tweet, or email whatever we want. We rarely ask ourselves whether we ought to assert our opinions and spread them. This comes back to intellectual modesty and more on that later.

135. Conscious of being repetitive: there is nothing wrong with Speculation as method for obtaining Knowledge. The problem is when suddenly Speculation is taken for Knowledge and

indoctrinated without a duty of demonstration. Knowledge should always be juxtaposed with a certain level of certainty, and the level of certainty we have about our knowledge should temper our actions. Low level of certainty dictates temperance in action, particularly when action has moral consequences or influences the life of one or many.

> **"[...] not entertaining any proposition with greater assurance than the proofs it is built upon will warrant."** John Locke.

What Is Knowledge? What Is Truth?

Many would have noticed by now that we have gone a long way in talking about Knowledge and some of the ways of acquiring it without really defining what is Knowledge. We all have an intuitive understanding of the word 'Knowledge', and yet defining it in an acceptable manner is actually difficult. This difficulty is the reason for the delay in this text in addressing the definition of Knowledge as some exploratory work leaves this definition easier to deal with. There will be no pretention here that we will offer new ground-breaking insight, but, rather, as in many other places in this book, we will provide some of the key elements to be considered when looking into the definition of Knowledge.

136. First, let us start by saying what Knowledge is different from (this is usually easier): Knowledge is not Belief (I can believe that something is true, and it turns out not to be true), and Knowledge is not Intuition[61]. We also prefer to keep Knowledge separate from Acquaintance[62]. The confusion between Acquaintance and Knowledge in English is purely of a linguistic nature. For a French, there is no need to worry about confusing *Je connais* and *Je*

---

61 Intuition has indeed been proven wrong on many things; Intuition is a type of short-circuited reasoning, and as with any reasoning it can be subject to errors.

62 Bertrand Russell talks about Knowledge by Acquaintance and Knowledge by Description; one could call the first simply Acquaintance and the second Knowledge.

On Knowledge and Truth

sais. Acquaintance corresponds to an immediate experience while Knowledge to a more abstract mental process.

137. Once Acquaintance and Knowledge are separated, Knowledge becomes intimately related to the notion of Truth. The three, Acquaintance, Knowledge, and Truth are of course closely related.

138. Knowing that 'André is a redhead' goes back to meaning that the statement 'André is a redhead' is 'True' (even if something is 'False', its negation is 'True'; hence, having knowledge is about a certain statement being true). Now what do we mean by saying {'André is a redhead' is 'True'}? It can mean (but not only) that whomever gets *acquainted* with André, i.e. whomever gets the experience of meeting André, can establish a one-to-one correspondence between the *hypothetical* relationship between 'André' and 'redhead' and the *actual* relationship between 'André' and 'redhead' being acquainted with. Hence, Knowledge is about a statement being true, and Truth includes (but is not limited to) the accordance of a hypothetical relationship or series of relationships[63] with an actual relationship emanating from Experience or Acquaintance.

    a. When the accordance is not there, we talk about *error*.
    b. When the accordance is not possible to establish one way or the other, we talk about *uncertainty*.

139. Now if Knowledge was only limited to that then it would only concern statements that can be subjected to Experience, which is obviously not the case. In addition to our acquaintances/experiences, we have basic primitive beliefs mostly of the logical kind. When and as we are born and grow, we combine acquaintances/experiences (which by definition are 'True'[64]) with these basic mental tools to create new more Abstract Knowledge, and we continue to do so throughout our life. The result is a hierarchy of Knowledge from the directly subjected to Experience to the very abstract.

    a. Probably the easiest way of thinking about this is how

---

63 Represented by arrows in the mathematical jargon.

64 And here lies one source of trouble.

theories in Science are built. A theory is not considered valid unless it concords with reality; however, not all that is in such theories can be directly tested through Experience element-by-element; actually, the majority is not. How do we know that a theory works? It is through the predictions it makes using assumptions from the theory and logical rules.

140. As we described, there seems to be two key sources of Knowledge: Experience/Acquaintance and Basic Primitive Beliefs or Logical Axioms. The latter is an indispensable source for constructing any Knowledge that moves away from immediate experience or, for that matter, immediate primitive beliefs. The first source (Experience/Acquaintance) is possible but not necessary in some sense. The result is two realms of Knowledge: one involving the first source, i.e. Experience/Acquaintance, the second without it. Let us call the first realm Empirical and the second Purely Deductive.

141. Several things need to be said about these realms and their distinct hierarchies. In the hierarchy of the Empirical realm, Knowledge closest to the source (i.e. to Experience/Acquaintance) is considered the most secure. The more we move away from immediate experiences with rational and scientific rules, the more the Empirical Knowledge loses from its robustness. In other words, the more abstract is the Empirical Knowledge, the more vulnerable it becomes. Moreover, there are (at least) two types of abstract Empirical Knowledge. The simple one consists of basic combinations of immediate experiences and rational tools, while the further abstract one involves theories and Natural Laws. Let us consider an example of each:

   a. Of the first: Assume there are three boys Joe, Philip, and William. Say I compare Joe's height to Philip's height, and I find Joe to be taller than Philip. Following that, I do the same with Philip and William, and I find Philip to be taller than William. From these two experiences, using a simple logical rule, I can state that Joe is taller than William. This is a basic piece of Empirical Knowledge of second degree.

   b. Of the second: Let us consider Linda, a mother who does

not like her son Adam touching any of her cherished ceramics. One day, Linda comes back home to suspect that Adam has been playing with her ceramics. Linda, a big fan of investigations, fingerprints Adam and compares the results to the fingerprints on her ceramics. Linda finds a match in the fingerprints; she therefore concludes that Adam has been playing with her ceramics. This type of Empirical Knowledge is equally of second degree, but of a much weaker form than the first one. From the immediate experience of fingerprinting, Linda is moving into Abstract Knowledge not by using a simple rational rule (like we did with the previous example), but by using a 'Natural Law' of the kind "a particular fingerprint corresponds to one particular person". Natural Laws are the way they are, but nothing logically precludes them from being otherwise; the Laws of Physics are of this kind. We discover these Natural Laws through a long process of Induction, and this is the reason why the second example, although of a similar second degree, is actually more vulnerable than the first one.

    i.   Moreover, some Natural Laws seem more certain than others. The rule "the total sum of energy of an isolated system is constant" is more certain than the rule "nothing can travel at a speed exceeding the speed of light". Physicists continue to attempt to find breaches to the speed of light limit (with no success so far), but no serious attempts are made today to try to negate the rule on Conservation of Energy. This is a sign of a higher certainty—there is a hierarchy, even if not explicit, in the Natural Laws we use[65]. In some cases, we also dispose of a choice between

---

65 Nevertheless, even the strongest of axioms such as the Conservation of Energy is not without its exceptions as is the case with quantum fluctuations, as well as a result of Heisenberg's uncertainty principle. The total amount of Energy can fluctuate even if it is for a very short period of time.

two equally valid and equally incomplete sets of rules, such as in the case of General Relativity and Quantum Mechanics.

142. In the hierarchy of the Purely Deductive realm, the further away one moves from the original axioms and rules, the more abstract Knowledge becomes. However, the parallel with the Empirical realm stops here. The distance from the source in the Purely Deductive realm is not necessarily a sign of a lower security of Knowledge. Indeed, there are higher chances of realising mistakes of Logic when one moves away from the axioms, but this higher chance of mistake is not of the same nature as the insecurity in Empirical Knowledge development.

   a. It is not because a 10th grader has a greater chance of making a mistake in solving a difficult mathematical problem that mathematical knowledge is suddenly less secure.

143. The attentive reader might object to our earlier definition of Truth when it comes to the Purely Deductive realm. If we remember well, when we first attempted to define Truth, we described it as the accordance of a hypothetical statement with Experience/Acquaintance. But by definition, there is no Experience/Acquaintance to measure against in the Purely Deductive realm. The definition of Truth in this realm comes from *within* it, and in a simplified manner we can say that in this realm Truth equals Tautology[66].

144. Suddenly, the reader can realise that the notion of Truth itself is more complicated than originally thought.

145. Let us ask a final question about Truth then, "What is our position in the cases of Empirical Knowledge where a hypothetical statement and an actual statement concord but purely out of luck?" We gave the example of the financial speculator before as an illustration.

---

66 This is not entirely accurate as some logical validities in first-order and second-order logic do not correspond to tautologies; but we shall not say more on that here.

The simple answer is that in some of the empirical situations, it is *necessary* to establish such accordance a large enough number of times in order to be able to validate the Truth. Attention needs to be paid not only to the rules of Logic and Natural Laws, but also to the method of establishing the accordance between hypothesis and experience. This is related to the subject of Induction, which we have chosen not to detail on here. Suffice to say that all of this renders Truth a much more complicated affair than what we normally envisage in our daily life.

146. Defining Truth is not easy; moreover, it is one of those words that are subject to evolution and change of definition as our Knowledge develops. The most resilient definition has an element of pragmatism, or as some would call it *instrumentalism*.

    a. For things immediately verifiable through Experience, Truth is the accordance of a statement with observation.

    b. For things not immediately verifiable, these can be broken down into immediately verifiable things, rules of Logic, and Natural Laws. The first have to be in accordance with observation, the second have to respect the axioms of Deduction, while the third continue to be subject to evolution. Truth has to also ideally also respect the Principle of Parsimony (more on this term later).

        i. The level of certainty of such complex Truth depends on the validity of the rules of Logic and the efficiency of the solution relating to the Natural Laws.

147. Now let us briefly look at Acquaintance/Experience. Acquaintance/Experience is a particular phenomenon of living, and therefore, as anything with living, it depends on particular organisms to take place. We cannot see without well-functioning eyes to see with, or hear without well-functioning ears to hear with, and we cannot do any of the two without a well-functioning brain[67]. Hence,

---

67 At least the necessary parts of the brain that deal with sight and hearing.

Acquaintance is dependent on some organisms in us, which we shall consider as part of our *cognitive models*, particularly when it comes to the brain functions.

148. Acquaintance/Experience is model-dependent. Our senses provide electrical signals to the brain, and the brain interprets those signals based on sensorial models. Internal reflection and metacognition use specific cognitive models; even Intuition uses specific models. It is likely that one day, we will equally discover a model-based reality for our feelings[68] and our Unconscious.

149. Not only Acquaintance/Experience is dependent on cognitive models; we can also say that Abstract Knowledge is also model-dependent. Categorisation, Naming, and Causality are all manifestations of the presence and influence of these specific cognitive models (it is not impossible that they could have been otherwise).

150. It follows that Knowledge, particularly one related to Experience, is model-dependent, and it is therefore entirely subject to the cognitive models our brain uses. Acquaintances/experiences serve as input to the brain and are then interpreted and analysed through our cognitive models.

    a. These models start by being primitive and are genetically inherited, not only from our parents, but the species in general, and this is an important point to stress on. *Whatever precedes Experience at the individual level does not need to precede it at the species level.* Experience alters our cognitive models; they evolve and grow with time.

151. We need to state that not all our cognitive models are interested in Rationality or Knowledge. Feelings, Intuition, and the Unconscious are all cognitive phenomena that we cannot deny. At the same time, we can hardly claim that these phenomena are primarily concerned with Knowledge or Rationality–they are more concerned with direct Survival and living. However, they

---

68 It started with Emotional Intelligence and has to be an integral part of clinical psychology.

do have their influences on Knowledge, such as in the case of emotional biases to the way we tend to view the world.

152. What can we say about our rational mental models? Of course, there is much that we cannot say without being circular. However, we can pinpoint some key characteristics. There seems to be at least five key components of the human mental models:

    a. Memory.

    "[...] the most essential characteristic of mind is memory, using this word in its broadest sense to include every influence of past experience on present reactions." Bertrand Russell, *Portraits from Memory and Other Essays*.

        i. Without Memory, one fails to see how Knowledge would be possible (or much else for that matter). Memory is to be considered in the broadest sense[69], be it short-term or long-term, visual, sensual, olfactory, auditory, internal, or external. Memory is what links us to Acquaintance/Experience, links us to the past, whether immediate or longer-term past, and it is indispensable for synthesis and accumulation of Knowledge.

        ii. Memory for living beings is about remembering successions, and from successions comes the notion of Time as we have mentioned before.

        iii. Memory may seem at first to be an animalistic trait. However, recent experiments have also indicated that some plants can equally exhibit some interesting forms of Memory (with different biological processes than that of the animal world).

        iv. All animals seem to have good short-term memory, and it is not surprising to find animals with better short-term memory than Humans (for example visual memory). What distinguishes

---

69 An amnesic does not lose all of his/her memory.

Humans is first the scope of their memory, which seems to be wider than that of animals (e.g. remembering feelings, previous thought processes, or metacognition), and second, more importantly, a more powerful long-term memory. The process of passing information from short-term memory to long-term memory is a very interesting one and looks to involve sleeping, dreaming, and the Unconscious.

v. Incidentally, Memory and History matter, not only for living beings but also for inert matter. Non-equilibrium states behave in particular ways because of their history; water movement has memory but we need not to go into that here.

vi. Without Memory, Language would not be possible. The language or communication model may still exist independently from Memory but vocabulary acquisition would not be possible without Memory.

b. Language and Symbols.

i. We cannot imagine Knowledge developing to advanced levels without the necessity of Language and Symbols. Human language seems different and/or more elaborate than that of the animals surrounding us[70] (till proof of the contrary), and although Knowledge acquisition and development could be conceived without the specific type of human language we use, it is without a doubt that Knowledge is closely related to our use of Language and Symbols. Many of the questions we ask have their root in Language. Our conception

---

70 Animals do possess communication mediums (e.g. ants, birds, dolphins, or elephants). Some could argue that these types of communication could equally be called 'languages', which takes us back to the definition of Language. Elaborating on these nuances is not necessary here.

of the world and of metaphysical notions is of a linguistic nature to a large extent. We invent words in order to represent, be able to manipulate in writing, and talk about abstract or complicated descriptions more easily; it would be impossible to construct one single phrase efficiently if we are to break down every abstract word in it back to its original description.

ii. Language is not only used for external communication but also for *internal* cognition, which is key.

iii. One of the sources of great fallacies that plague us is taking symbols of descriptions as finalities and start asking questions about these finalities. The meaning of words can be subject to change, and some words can simply lack proper definition. Some words are used as 'gap-fillers' in our logic. Utter ignorance has persisted from the mystification and lack of definition of 'Grand Words' such as Free Will, God, Romantic Love, Justice, Equality, Good, and Bad. In reality, the definitions of these words have often varied through ages, and some were ultimately fully abandoned for lack of anything being left in them[71].

iv. Storytelling constitutes an important part of Knowledge acquisition (for minors and adults), and storytelling would not be possible without some form of Language.

v. Some theories concerning Language consider that *Homo Sapiens* (or most likely our close ancestors) started their language process by uttering meaningless sounds. Subsequently, we started to

---

71 Such as the words Essence or *Nous*.

associate a meaning to these sounds, which was the first step towards a proper language. From there, we took the habit of associating sounds with objects and things, which resulted in short and basic storytelling, and later on in more elaborate stories. Some would even argue that the phenomenon of Consciousness is nothing more than the result of human storytelling; we, as a species, seem to have created our own big story.

c. Logical Models.

   i. Logical models concern the engines of Logic we are born with. What we have in mind when we say Logic is *Formal Logic*. Logic concerns itself with relations between elements of Thought. It is about 'what is' and 'what is not'. Its core engines are not taught but inherited.

   ii. We (and animals) need not to be taught everything, as we do not come as a 'blank sheet'. Some of our basic instincts and reflexes can also be put under this category. Apes with their cognitive capabilities possess rather developed logical models.

   iii. Logical models do not necessarily require a human-type of language or a very developed memory. One can imagine scenarios with no use of Memory at all, but yet with a logical behaviour to a particular set of conditions as with computer processing of certain inputs.

   iv. Logical models are the most fundamental and probably the most mysterious of our cognitive models. Without them, there is not much left in us than mechanical reflexes and feelings. They are so fundamental that understanding them is likely never completely possible. Yet, they are our most powerful construction tools. From very humble starting points, enormous constructions can be made in the realm of Thought, by our own brains or by logical machines such as computers. Things that look mysterious at first can be broken down into simple statements. Reality indeed looks very different through the eyes of Logic[72] and hence the central position of Logic to philosophers like Hegel.

d. Consciousness.

    i. Consciousness is a key characteristic of Human Knowledge. Consciousness is also present in the animal world, but in a more limited manner. Consciousness allows a different kind of knowledge from mechanistic unconscious knowledge. It also adds greatly to the scope of Knowledge.

    ii. All the serious questions we ask would not have been possible without a developed Consciousness. It is difficult to see how we can, in the first place, ask questions about our knowledge and existence without Consciousness.

    iii. Consciousness is not easy to define in a satisfactory manner. The easiest way is to say that Consciousness is about awareness of oneself, actions, thoughts, and feelings. But then how do we define 'awareness' without being circular? Is it some sort of internal reflexivity? We might say that Consciousness is a 'state' or 'result' of other components in our cognition, but what are these components really? More importantly, where does the boundary exactly lie between being conscious and being unconscious?

e. Basic *A Priori* Beliefs.

---

72 Think again about reality through the PC screen.

i. In the same way that we dispose of primitive instincts for self-preservation, reproduction, and parental love, we inherit basic mental beliefs without which there can be no starting point. Some of these beliefs are part of the Logical Models we previously discussed. Others include for example the notion of the I or the Self, and so of Consciousness in a certain way, the necessity of the Good and avoidance of the Bad, the Desirable vs. the Non-Desirable, Existence, or Beauty. Many elements have been added or subtracted from this set of primitive beliefs over time such as God, Natural Rights, Causality, and other Kantian categories. Some of this is debatable and likely wrong. However, the deniability of the fifth component altogether is rather impossible.

There are several important consequences behind this realisation of the model-dependency of Knowledge.

Consequence I

153. Reality, which is dependent on and apprehended by our knowledge and our cognitive models, is consequently model-dependent. Moreover, our models are not unique. Animals equally possess cognitive models and perceive reality through them. Their models can be close to ours, but they differ more and more as the species in question branches away from us on the evolutionary tree. In other words, each type of animals has its own reality, different from our reality, and it is as much of a 'reality' as ours. Reality through the lenses of my cat is different from my reality—I am conscious of that. If I want to understand my cat better, I have to try to change my perception of Reality to move it closer to how cats perceive the world. Surprisingly enough, our brain is capable of adapting to new ways of perceiving in a more flexible manner than what we might originally think. **There is no one Reality, there are multiple realities!**

154. We invite the reader to try to imagine how an ant or a cockroach perceives the world. Kafka's *Metamorphosis* is seminal on the subject. When we stand and give great moving speeches about Life, Knowledge, Progress, and Humanity, all that we are doing is account for a reality perceived through our lenses and models–an ant passing by does not care about our ideas as long as they do not alter its material environment. The ant would likely consider our progress as a mix of good news (less natural predators and better access to food) and bad (human insecticide frenzies from time to time). It is not inconceivable that one day we meet a species that has developed cognitive abilities but through a different perception and through different cognitive models. Such a species could be able to predict celestial movements through a model completely different from Newton's, but more or less as accurate, and it could have its own different mythologies, legends, and allegories… A highly conscious cockroach species is not likely to have in its antiquity a deity called 'Mother Earth' and symbolised by Artemis or Diana[73], and later Virgin Mary (who became 'Mother of God'). Cockroach mother-son relationship is not as intimate as ours by the looks of it, and the concept of virginity is likely irrelevant.

155. Model-dependent Knowledge does not necessarily imply that all Knowledge is subjective in totality, or that everything is true depending on the point of view or the angle we look at things from. This argument was used against Protagoras and the Sophists validly. Protagoras believed that every man is the measure of all things; there is no right or wrong; it all depended on the point of view and perception. He was countered with the example of the fool: if everything is subject to perception, then what guarantees us that what Protagoras says is any better from what a fool says? On which grounds we take Protagoras any more seriously than a fool?

156. No matter what are the sensors and the channels through which information is communicated to the cognitive model, this model has invariably to respect 'things' from outside it or independent

---

73 Symbol of childbirth and virginity.

from it. These 'things' include rules of Logic; moreover, it is a condition *sine qua non* for what is derived from the cognitive model to tie up with subsequent experience to be considered valid. Models are fashioned by the nature of our perception, but they are not fully subjected to them. No matter whether the mind relies on Euclidian or non-Euclidean geometry, it still has to use some geometry.

    a. A fool can perceive the environment around as accurately as any other human being; the difference is that the interpretive models that are used to treat these perceptions are different or flawed. This brings us to the second major consequence.

Consequence II

157. The cognitive models and processes we use to produce Knowledge are subject to errors. These models do not always work the way they are supposed to, i.e. they may sometimes fail at their evolutionary task of facilitating our existence as a species in *some* situations. This is important at several levels. First of all, acknowledging the room for cognitive malfunctions opens the door to the realities of cognitive mistakes and misperceptions. There are two types of malfunctions:

    a. Our sensorial models can malfunction, i.e. our brain interprets the signals from our senses not in the way it is normally supposed to. We sometimes call such malfunctions 'pathologies', 'lesions', or 'agnosia'; the models do not receive the required inputs as they should.

    b. Our abstract processing of acquaintances/experiences, using first basic beliefs and models, and later more complicated ones, is subject to mistakes, which we commonly call logical errors. In other words, the models themselves do not function accurately. For example, our brain's preference to use pattern recognition processes can result in misinterpretations: we see the sun rising every day, all of our life, and we would want to assume from these multiple observations that the sun will rise

On Knowledge and Truth

tomorrow forever. Rationally speaking, this constitutes an error; there is a probability not equal to zero that the sun will not rise tomorrow.

158. It is only since recently that we are aware of such cognitive errors and biases. The idea of cognitive models malfunctioning has two important corollaries:

   a. As we previously detailed, the more our Empirical Knowledge moves away from direct Acquaintance/ Experience, the higher is this risk of cognitive malfunction or error. Moreover, some of the rules we use to move ourselves away from immediate Experience increase the risk of malfunction.

   b. When we say that our cognitive processing misfires or malfunctions, what we are really saying is that the cognitive processing should have been working in a certain specific way, but it has not–similar to an engine that overshoots till we intervene and fix it. By saying so, *we are effectively drawing a one-to-one correspondence between our actual cognitive process and a reference outside this cognitive process,* and we are concluding that the correspondence is not there; thus, there is an error. This "reference outside this cognitive process" is *Mathematics*. In other words, cognitive errors result from the absence of correspondence between the actual cognitive processes we use and Mathematics.

   i. This realisation drives some to say that Mathematics is a 'universal' and 'subsists' outside us and independently from our existence and nature (more on that later). Some go further to postulate that Mathematics exists independently from our universe, in the sense that if the Universe tomorrow ceases to exist or changes in nature (whatever any of this might mean), Mathematics will continue to subsist and remain unchanged. The latter is rather more extreme, but it is likely true that Mathematics subsists in some sense.

Consequence III

159. The third important consequence of model-dependent Knowledge is its implication on the definition of the notion of Existence. Why is this important for Knowledge? Because a large part of validating Knowledge through Acquaintance and Experience consists of stating that X exists or does not exist. Many theories in Science get validated or rejected on the basis of a particular particle, predicted by the devised model, is actually discovered to exist or not, or that a particular phenomenon, predicted in theory, actually takes place or not. So what do we mean when we say that 'X exists'? Actually, we can mean many things, and this confusion of meaning puts us in trouble frequently.

160. The classical scientific definition of existence is to say 'X exists' is equivalent to 'X is in Space-Time', whether X is a tangible or intangible. 'My cat exists' means that my cat is in Space-Time. An imagination of a dragon or a certain image on TV also exists as it is in Space-Time although it is not material. An image in a brain created by chemical and electrical reactions is in Space-Time, in the same way that a piece of software exists for a Personal Computer. However, a dragon does not exist, even if an imagination of a dragon exists.

161. This definition of Existence as in Space-Time is far from perfect on the account of at least two things:

    a. What does the question 'Does Space-Time exist?' mean then? One could relate back Space-Time to Energy, but then one can ask the same question what does 'Does Energy exist?' mean then? These are the difficulties of considering Space and Time as receptacles, and not as a system of relations. If we consider them a system of relations, Existence becomes about interactions with other events. If something interacts with other events then it 'exists'.

    b. Existence becomes a very funny concept at the ultrasmall level. Multiple states can co-exist till observed[74], and a particle can draw several simultaneous histories all at once. The only way to define existence in such a situation becomes whether the thing that exists has its place in the quantum model used, and whether the quantum model predicts accurately. Hence, **Existence becomes also a specific quantum model-based Existence** similarly to Knowledge.

162. Model-based Knowledge has as corollary a model-based Existence with possible distinction between the tangible and intangible, and *Subsistence* beyond the model without which any model would not be possible.

163. What we need to retain from this technical analysis, probably boring for some readers, is that we are born with innate models including our most primitive instinctive beliefs. Work is still to be done on defining and summarising these beliefs. Nevertheless, we are born with some form of *A Priori* Knowledge, Knowledge that does not depend on Experience, and we are equipped with cognitive models, no matter how primitive they are; we ought to accept this. All of our knowledge and perceptions of Reality and Existence are dependent on this *A Priori* Knowledge and on our cognitive models.

164. Some examples of such *A Priori* Knowledge and mental models include basic neonatal reflexes such as grasping and rooting.

    a. Some even go further, claiming that notions such as the Self and Mathematics are all part of our *A Priori* Knowledge, and what Experience does is merely draw our attention to these universals that we already know. The argument they use is as follows: we do not need to undertake a thousand experiences of 2+2=4 to know that '2+2=4'; one acquaintance with an example of 2+2=4 (such as 2 sheep and 2 sheep equals 4 sheep) is enough to open our eyes to the universal '2+2=4' à la Socratic reminiscence.

---

74 As with the famous example of the Schrödinger's cat.

165. Mental models start by being basic, primitive, and resulting from our DNA. They develop and grow with biological growth, influence from the environment around us, and experience. We experience everything around us (and some of what is in us) through our senses, which provide specific electrical signals to the brain. Our brain processes these signals using specific cognitive models. What count for the brain are the inputs it receives and itself.

166. Hypothetically, if the brain is taken out of the body and provided with all that it needs in terms of blood, electricity/neural inputs, right temperature, and the rest, in the same way as it would receive them in the body but this time artificially, it is not inconceivable that it should not 'feel' much of a difference and continue to experience reality in the same way.

167. The brain is an amazing organism; it is capable of metacognition, and of reflecting on its own self, its own operations, and mental models generally. The brain is not one entity; it is composed of different modules.

168. It has been discovered that the human brain is capable of adapting some of the cognitive models to new environmental circumstances in amazing ways[75].

    a. When we look, we see things in 3D. We know from our knowledge of Physics and Biology that what we have in reality are two tubes called eyes through which we capture light and images in 2D. The result is two separate 2D images, moreover inverted, on our retinas. Usually, our brain takes care of the rest and reconstructs a 3D image according to these inputs. Today, this simple basic fact is used to try to develop 3D TV technologies where pictures are shot with cameras mimicking our eyes, transmitted through electrical waves to our TV, and then transmitted to our eyes. Here too, our brain will take care of the rest and build up 3D images for

---

75 Cf. George Stratton's experiments on perceptual adaptation in the 1890s.

us. If we make people wear glasses that invert the light, they start seeing things upside down; but that is only for a while. On our retinas, the images will have the same direction as in reality, which should not be the case. But after a certain time, the brain realises somehow that a permanent change of conditions took place and readjusts its visual model accordingly, and we start to see straight again! Said differently, the brain adapts its visual model to experience. And if we take off the glasses, the brain re-adjusts back again to the old visual model after a while.

169. All our knowledge is human, any thought we make is human, and we judge humanly. It is impossible to comprehend the act of thinking or knowing through an independent 'soul' or entity from our body. Everything we do, and any idea, feeling, memory, lie, and belief we undertake at any point, are all material events at the biological level (electric and chemical events).

170. Knowledge, Reality, and Existence are all model-dependent notions; they are notions entirely subject to the mental models this organism called The Brain constructs and uses. They are not however pure constructions of the mind as some nominalists might assume. The brain still requires the electrical signals that come from Experience in many cases, and these inputs influence the cognitive models of the brain.

Concluding Remarks on Knowledge Models.

171. It could be easily conceived from here that what we call Knowledge model is nothing more than the sum of various cognitive models in addition to Memory, which registers and processes the operations of the cognitive models. The analogy in Physics would be the unifying M-Theory, not as one theory but as a myriad of different theories at different levels and with different scopes. We remain some distance away from understanding the human Knowledge model. However, some qualities seem necessary:

a. We need to start with the most simple axioms and instinctive beliefs possible. And here Belief cannot be overcome; there is a minimum required. By definition, to build Knowledge based on Experience, one has to live and process this experience, and he/she has 'glue' it together into Knowledge somehow. This requires basic mental models, which is another way of saying axioms and instinctive beliefs.

b. Evidently, the model has to work, i.e. it has to be consistent with Experience and be able to predict future experiences accurately. Otherwise it would not be Knowledge; it would just be brain stimulations. **A Theory of Knowledge has to have a proper place for negation and error in it, as testing Knowledge through Experience requires a place for negation.**

c. **The Principle of Parsimony.**

"Plurality should not be assumed without necessity" William of Occam.

    i. Importantly, the model, similarly to what we find in Natural Sciences, should be the simplest possible. From an evolutionary perspective, it has to be what consumes the least energy possible from the brain.

    ii. Let us take a classical example of philosophy and epistemology here. I stand at the door of a room and look inside; I see a chair. Now, I can ask, "Does this chair exist independently from me?" If I walk away from the door, I do not see the chair any longer. I can say that the chair does not exist, as I am not seeing it. I look back into the room, and I see the chair again. Hence, the chair exists again. There are (at least) two models of Existence that can be used here:

(1) The chair exists in something that I call

Space-Time[76] independently from me (or using the relational definition of Space-Time, the chair exhibits relations to other events). When I look in the direction of the object, light waves reflect on the object and enter my eyes, and consequently, I see the chair. When I do not look in the direction of the chair, light waves reflected from the chair cease to enter my eyes, and I do not see the chair any longer although it still occupies the same spatial position; or

(2) The chair is a 'mirage' created by me or somebody else watching me (maybe to amuse itself out of celestial boredom by fooling me). The chair does not exist by itself in the traditional sense; it is like a mirage. When I am looking in the direction of the room, it gets created instantaneously. When I am not, it does not exist.

Both models can account for the particular experience of looking at the chair somehow satisfactorily even if our common sense makes us uneasy with the second one. However, the second model turns out to be incredibly complicated to handle when we juxtapose several experiences together. Consider a dog jumping on the chair, and me looking into the room at one of the instances when it is jumping. I then look away and then look back again to see the chair and the dog tumbling, and I hear noise. Trying to build a story from this that works well and can be reasonably manipulated based on the second model is much more tedious than based on the first model.

iii. From the Relativity point of view and the non-

---

76 We continue to use the classical definition of Existence despite the flaws we have stated in it, as it is admittedly easier to explain with.

existence of a universal reference, Ptolemy is not more wrong or right than Copernicus. Whether the Sun revolves around the Earth or the Earth revolves around the Sun is a question of relativity of reference. Where Copernicus wins over Ptolemy is in the parsimony of the model he uses, and the ease with which a higher number of accurate conclusions one can draw with his model.

The Dream of a New Atlantis

172. Knowledge, especially Conscious Knowledge, i.e. knowledge aware of itself, comes with a dream. The dream of one day understanding everything, having answers to all questions we could possibly ask, whether about the past (History), present, or future (Predictions). We do not to live well with uncertainty, with not having answers to questions, even if these questions are actually false ones. Since the beginning of Knowledge[77], the dream remains the same, and the core difficulties remain intact. The advances of Science during and after the Renaissance, and the technological and material progress witnessed since, have only accentuated the dream of Knowledge[78]. Laplace's demon is a famous illustration of such a dream: the mathematicians and physicists dream to build, explain, and predict the Whole from initial conditions and axioms. History continues to surprise us with the difficulty and impossibility of such a task. From Aristotle's Laws of Thought to *Principia Mathematica* and Hilbert's problems, Humanity made great strides in terms of understanding the required axioms[79] and Hubble (the telescope), space travel, and satellite technologies enhanced dramatically our measures of

---

77 Starting with Religion and Philosophy, and from which different sciences broke out one after the other with time.

78 Particularly in the scientist era of the 17th & 18th century.

79 Evidently, the reason behind these axioms will ever remain a question that these axioms cannot answer.

initial conditions; yet, the cycle of great discoveries and greater questions continues.

173. It seems that Knowledge acquisition and development undertakes a three-step process, both at the collective as well as individual level. Knowledge has its cycles of creation and stagnation, and sometimes destruction. We mentioned some of this behaviour in the first chapter on History.

- a. The first phase is a raw and fast acquisition of Knowledge in large amounts. This knowledge is acquired through a tipping point of discoveries (e.g. discovery of the New World or the Industrial Revolution) or through transmission (e.g. industrialisation of Japan and now of China, offshoring in India, the rise of the Asian tigers, or at the individual level schooling and university).

- b. With this acquisition of Knowledge comes material and technological superiority, certain optimism in the approach to Knowledge, and confidence at the individual and collective level. The result is a second phase of increased speculation and affirmation of one's knowledge. After all, if we have gone so far with our knowledge and intellect, then we must have really figured out everything, or at least, we have proven ourselves superior and capable of understanding everything if not now, probably in the near future. This is the attitude of the scientist period of the 19th century; the complacency of all major empires and civilisations; Wall Street at its peak years; periods of euphoria after revolutionary changes; as well as the 'twenties' of almost every educated or successful male or female[80].

- c. And as we know, complacency and over-confidence ultimately leads to disillusionments with the state of our knowledge and superiority. This is the period of deceptions and tyranny after many great revolutions;

---

80 Where we think that we have understood everything, and that it is our time to take control of the world around us and affirm our knowledge.

the angst following major technological changes; the Greek defeats first by Alexander then by the Romans; the Arab defeats by the Turks and the Mongols; the Great Recession; the realisation that scientific discoveries can lead as much to horrible weapons of war as happiness and comfort; and the 'thirties' crisis at the individual level, where one realises that one's own capabilities are limited, and many things are not under one's control. The period of disillusionment results in a negativist approach to Knowledge[81] and some form of resignation at the individual level. Some of the negativism is accompanied by a form of escapism, a longing for something far from the daily reality; religions and escapist philosophies become more popular.

d. The period of disillusionment is typically the longest. Some form of disorder usually accompanies disillusionment periods, and going from disorder to order requires much more energy than going from order to disorder. In addition, a transition from disillusionment to an innocent optimism and fresh curiosity in Knowledge usually necessitates a generational change, as well as a new 'ignition', or a catalyst of some sort, which does not come frequently and is somehow obscure and circumstantial in nature. The Western world only woke up into the Renaissance after the Byzantine migration West, the discovery of the New World, and then Descartes and Galileo. Germany did not rise to greatness till after the Napoleonic invasion and administration, which gave a necessary sense of unity to the various German populations. China's economic revival necessitated a Deng Xiaoping and an anti-Cultural Revolution policy, likely coupled with demographic considerations. Once the conditions are ripe and the ignition takes place, the transition from stagnation and

---

81 E.g. the Sceptics, the Cynics, the Stoics, the Romantics, Schopenhauer, the Hippie period, Hedonism, and the Anarchists.

disillusionment to creativity and positivism is quick. And the process of Knowledge starts again…

174. Our advances in terms of Knowledge are unequal. In some subjects, such as Mathematics and to a lesser extent Physics, we enjoy a relatively longer history of research and advances, while in others our progress remains quite limited.

    a. Mathematics started with the Greeks and was not constrained by Experience due to its deductive nature. It has therefore progressed greatly, and the important mathematical problems of our days are so abstract and so specialised that only few people in the world can understand them and work on them.

    b. Physics (including Chemistry) has been slower than Mathematics, as Empirical Knowledge has been a focus point only since the Renaissance. However, the advances in Mathematics, which are essential for doing Physics, coupled with the human realisation, especially during the Industrial Revolution, that we can derive technological and material benefits from Physics has led to remarkable advances in the subject.

    c. In Mathematics and Physics, given the level of advance and specialisation currently required, we are witnessing something similar to the phenomenon of diminishing returns: a certain amount of effort results on average with lower return in the progress of Knowledge in such an advanced field. One of the consequences of this phenomenon is the importance of working *collectively* as a community of scientists (mathematicians or physicists) in order to realise meaningful progress. Particularly in Physics, collectivity is today more important than individuality. The days when one genius[82] could come up with a whole theory that changes the world of Physics are less likely than a collectivity of physicists, in some form

---

82 Newton, Maxwell, or Einstein.

of coordination, realising a certain breakthrough in the field. This coincides well with the age of connectivity and the Internet.

d. This does not imply that we are advanced enough in Technology or Industrialism—it is important to make the distinction. We understand very well the physics of solar panels; however, we cannot yet produce solar electricity at a competitive-enough cost (but this can be overcome in a matter of few years).

e. In other fields, we can consider ourselves less advanced. In Human Biology, we are moderately advanced, with the exception of the study of the brain and sleep. In Animal Biology, we are still quite ignorant. The sad irony is that we hurry to eliminate species in the name of progress and civilisation without minimal consideration to this fact. In Psychology and Cognition, we have barely scratched the surface in the writer's view. While we are quite advanced in some forms of Knowledge over our predecessors, we still almost always exhibit the same level of emotionality as the cavemen.

It is the hope of the writer that the above has provided few insights on the terribly complicated nature of Knowledge, which we take for granted every day of our lives, use and abuse, and so easily summon to justify certain actions and opinions.

Where Do We Go From Here?

What we know and what we do not know.

175. Being curious animals, Humans always want to know or pretend to know, as much as they can imagine. Pretending to know gives us a false sense of certainty and control over the world around us. Ironically, the most important Knowledge we can acquire is that of knowing what we do not know. Knowing one's level of ignorance and limitations is one of the greatest forms of Knowledge and

On Knowledge and Truth

Wisdom; it is also a great leadership style. Intellectual modesty dates back to Socrates and is probably more ancient. Socrates is famous for asking each to know oneself. Socrates also persisted in claiming that he knows nothing; he maintained that by knowing that he knows nothing, he is wiser than most men who think that they know more than what they actually do. We always expect from our leaders to know everything about everything. It would be quite something to hear a president or a prime minister honestly say that he has no idea how the economy really works. We are sorry to say that in reality most leaders do not know half of what they claim they know, and it is a form of hypocrisy on our part to want to believe that they can have answers to all sorts of questions.

176. Sometimes it is easier to prove that something is not true than to speculate about what is true. This is a central idea from Popper's Falsification. Based on our daily observations of white swans, we psychologically prefer to claim that all swans are white than to state that it is enough to find one case of a black swan to render all belief and observations about white swans void of conclusions.

    a. We love to think that Humans are very special and unique, or that Earth is unique because we do not find (yet) Life anywhere else we look in outer space. In reality, it is enough to have one occasion of Life anywhere else in the Universe, in the past, in the present, or in the future[83] to render this assumption of specialty of Earth and Humans void of conclusions. We are talking about billions of galaxies including each billions of stars at any which moment of billions of years…

177. Being sceptical or cynical to some extent is not necessarily a gloomy mental view of the world; it is one with more wisdom than a simplistic attitude of wanting to believe only what makes us temporarily feel good.

178. We are bound to continuously encounter events that we fail to

---

83   And if the multiverse theory turns out to be true, in the past, in the present, and/or in the future of all those simultaneous or subsequent universes.

understand, at both the individual and collective levels. With the advance of Science, these are increasingly rare; they continue to take place nevertheless. *We should always have the courage to admit what we do not know and do not understand without resorting to the pretence of full knowledge.*

179. More importantly, we should not allow such situations of ignorance or uncertainty to be taken over by false or misplaced speculations. Some religious and philosophical zealots love situations of intellectual difficulty; they always like to step in to talk about miracles or the supra-natural while offering no comparably beneficial alternative[84]. What we do not know or understand today is not a miracle; it is ignorance or illusion. Chemistry is a pure miracle for the ignorant, and magic is an illusion. Any temporary (or even permanent) intellectual difficulty should not mean a rejection of all Rationality in favour of pure instincts à la Rousseau.

    a. Placebo-like effects have wonderful consequences on us; they can become self-fulfilling prophecies based on psychological wants and needs.

180. *What we know has to always be associated with a certain level of certainty;* we always need to leave room for mistakes. Only a small portion of our knowledge is entirely certain (and that can be even questionable by some, including the writer). Most of our knowledge actually comes with various shades of certainty. Depending on the model of Knowledge-construction used, as well as the distance of statements of Knowledge from direct Experience, it is fundamental for relation between Deeds and Knowledge to mirror the level of certainty of our Knowledge. Being tentative in action and gathering elements of Knowledge back from first experiences rather than falling in love with one's own models helps increase the level of certainty of Knowledge through healthy feedback loops (more on that in the following chapter).

---

84 What better historical example of a waste of genius than Pascal's renunciation to Mathematics?

What we can know and what we cannot know.

181. There is a lot we can know. Some of it we know today, and much of it we do not know yet. Reasons behind why we do not know what we do not know could be many and constitute an interesting subject of discussion (which we will not detail on here). Some of the reasons we can state include lack of possibility of appropriate experiences[85], lack of courage to push the boundaries of Knowledge, laziness, complacency and/or lack of incentives, and lack of technological capabilities[86].

182. Today, in most Natural Sciences and in Mathematics, we could say that the limitation is not necessarily in understanding the major paradigms, but in working out all of the details. For example, gravity, especially in the classical Newtonian sense, is something we understand well, yet we should wish the specialists the best of luck in solving the n-body problem. We understand how DNA works reasonably well, yet we do not know the DNA of most species on Earth. In Psychology and Brain Sciences, we have only started to scratch the surface, and a lot of exciting discoveries are yet to be made. All such cases are of the domain of the feasible; it is Knowledge we can ultimately acquire if we survive long enough, we do not destroy what we have built as Knowledge so far for some arbitrary reason(s), and we are not subject to some dramatic externalities such as a major asteroid attack.

183. There are things that we will *never* get to know no matter how far, long, or fast we run, areas where simply Rationality breaks down. We can call them Singularities of Reason. This is an important truth not known widely enough. The prevailing assumption and the psychologically feel-good wish is that ultimately everything is knowable, eventually. This is the objective of Science in particular; it has always had the ambition of explaining and knowing everything, of providing answers to all questions. In reality, there

---

85 E.g. not being able to travel far into Space or reach some natural habitats in Madagascar to study some rare species.

86 E.g. necessary computing power for some very complicated and tedious calculus.

are things we can never know, and some such problems have been known since long.

184. Some of what we can never know constitutes false problems or false questions resulting from a rather mistaken or random use of words (as for example in the use of the word 'is' for 'existence'). We previously hinted to how descriptions can be taken wrongly for finalities when they should not, resulting in confusions and bad metaphysics.

   a. Let us take the example of the word Dragon. Dragon is a description of a certain animal-like creature with certain properties. In a properly elaborate analytical language, the word Dragon itself would not be used or needed. What would be considered is the detailed description of this animal-like creature. However, in our everyday language, mostly for efficiency reasons, we substitute such large descriptions with the word Dragon itself in order to be able to manipulate Language more easily. The problem is that down the road, we start to forget this original starting point, and we take these descriptions for finalities. We start talking about the 'idea' of a Dragon, and how this idea must exist somewhere. The question "Does a Dragon exist?" suddenly becomes fundamental; people get strongly divided over such a question. The proponents of the Yes say that we can talk and think about the Dragon, so it must exist somewhere. We start going into very complicated ways of treating and explaining such confusions and trying to make consistent systems out of our ideas. The reality is that forgetting the starting point is flawed, and nothing good can come out from such an attitude. The question "Does a Dragon exist?" does not require such convoluted idealistic systems to treat it. What it really stands for is something like this (and we are making it simple): "[description of the animal-like creature] is included in Space-Time[87]?" The answer

---

87 Or again can be phrased in terms of relations to other events.

to this question is "No". But it is not a certain No; it is a likely No. We cannot refute the inclusion of Dragon in Space-Time. We can only say that we have not seen any such animal-like organism with the properties attributed to it ever, nor any other human being we can rely on did. We do not have a proof of the inclusion in Space-Time of such an animal-like creature.

    b. What applies to Dragon also applies to more concrete descriptions. Take the word France. What does the word France mean? What is the description of France? And from there, what do sentences like "Does France exist?" or "France likes apples" mean? And France is a much more complicated word to treat than Dragon. The meaning of the word France is not only more complicated to define and describe; it also changes with time. France for us today is not France of a thousand or five hundred years ago. Bad metaphysics do not only arise from wrongly taking some descriptions for finalities, but also from considering the meaning of some words as unchangeable with time.

185. We sometimes put together words out of context and without respect to the rules of syntax, and we start wondering about the result. This kind of practice has persisted throughout History and continues to trick us. The result is a long series of false problems and meaningless questions. Let us take another example and we will consider it the last. We can easily compose and think that we apprehend a statement such as "The moon is one". However, from a pure syntactical point of view, it is actually a meaningless sentence, and we are wrong to compose it. Moon is an element of the set of satellites of the Earth. This set of satellites is of the size one. The number one applies to a set and not to particular elements of the set. While we think that we understand the meaning of a statement of the kind "The moon is one", it is in reality utter rubbish. What we can really say is that the set of satellites of Earth is of size one, and Moon is an element of this set. Here is what happens if we start confusing a particular with its set: Jupiter has

66 satellites (and counting); Ganymede is a satellite of Jupiter. No one would think to say "The Ganymede is 66" because it is utter rubbish. Well a statement of the kind "The moon is one" is exactly of the same quality! We think we understand it because the set of satellites of Earth is of the size one, but that is actually purely circumstantial.

186. We are still at a rudimentary level in our understanding of the evolution of linguistics and its impact on our psychology and knowledge. Linguistics relates closely to our internal cognitive systems, but it has also a great element of *cultural creation and transmission*. We call an animal a 'dog' because we were taught to call it as such and not to look at it, for example, as two separate but collated organisms, a 'head-dog' and a 'body-dog'. It is a fascinating subject to understand how the human mind works, particularly at a young age, at categorising and defining entities within certain parameters, and wanting to label such entities with a particular name. This is the core reason behind what Philosophy has called for centuries 'essence'. It is well-known that a new born is incapable of distinguishing the limit of its own body from the body of others, and by the same token whether a face and a hand belong to the same body or not. Names such as 'dog' come from cultural influence; some elements may also be elicited by pure direct experience without cultural 'contamination'. However, the categorisation and definition of entities is, for the most part, cognitive in nature. Everything is a continuum of events. Humans have a tendency to separate, build compartments, define categories, and draw perimeters around the events. Though it is useful for our *modus operandi*, it does not constitute a reality by itself.

187. Analytical Philosophy contributed a great deal into demystifying some of what was considered great philosophical questions. Some long-dated questions turned out to be more or less false ones. Then, in the search for a complete system of Knowledge based on mathematical analysis, particularly with Carnap, a severe blow to such ambitions came from the most noble and pure of thought

disciplines; it came from *within*, from Mathematics and Formal Logic, with Gödel's famous uncertainty theorems. Essentially, one of Gödel's findings can be summarised and simplified as follows: no matter what elaborate-enough consistent system we construct, there will always be something true about this system that can never be proven from within the system. If the system is a system of Knowledge (whatever that may be), this theorem could be made to say that there will always be something True that we can never prove as such from within this system of Knowledge, no matter how we end up defining Knowledge.

188. If we previously said that it is wisdom for one to know what he/she does not know, *the greater wisdom is actually in realising what one can never know as well as what constitute false problems* that can never be overcome. Knowing what we cannot know saves a lot of time and energy; it also puts many charlatans, superstitions, and prejudices at bay. Both Analytical Philosophy and Kurt Gödel made important contributions to that.

189. Popper's Falsification was considered as the natural way forward in the Theory of Knowledge following the divisions and some of the failures of the Vienna Circle and its Analytical Philosophy. Unfortunately, formalising Falsification has turned out to be as difficult as the approaches used by Analytical Philosophy. Both methods are immensely helpful, but we still fail to ground any of them in a completely satisfactory mathematical framework. Of course, if this had been achieved, then most Philosophy, particularly when it comes to the Theory of Knowledge, would have been completed, and no more would be required in this domain.

190. For us, the main take away from the Viennese Circle and then Popper's work, their differences, and their unfolding is probably this: **it is often a much easier task to disprove than to prove based on Empiricism, perception, or observation. Imagination/Intuition and Logic are the builders of systems and ideas; Empiricism is the destroyer of the flawed of them**. We imagine infinity of ideas and beliefs, which with intellectual

and technological progress, we only manage to eliminate some of them bit-by-bit. We cannot fail to think about Spinoza's words "All determination is negation" here. If anything, we hope the reader will retain this vision of Knowledge from this chapter.

191. The reader might then ask, "If we accept such a dynamic, we continue eliminating flawed ideas and beliefs in order to end up with what exactly?" For the positivists, we end up with an ultimate Truth, a Unified Science, or a Work Fully Achieved, which we cannot define today, but still believe we will eventually get to. For the negativists or the sceptics, nothing will be left, and we will find ourselves somehow back to the starting point. For the cynics, this quest will never end, as it is an endless maze. Which one of the three attitudes the reader chooses will ultimately depend on her individual predispositions and character.

192. Knowledge is crucial for Humans, and understanding its nature and intricacies is central. But human intellect is not only about Knowledge in the traditional sense. If we limit human beings to Knowledge, the result is an arid world, a somehow mono-colour world. Intellectually, Man is not only capable of producing Knowledge; he is also capable of producing, rather amazingly, other anthropological intellectual phenomena[88], such as Beauty and Comedy. Animals can create beautiful things, but they do not seem to seek Beauty for the sake of Beauty (they may seek it for reproduction). They also can laugh and show laughter, but they do not seem to seek Comedy for the sake of Comedy as we do either. We do both and this is rather wonderful.

---

88 For the lack of a better word.

Deeds vs. Thoughts

"Dans l'attachement de l'homme à sa vie, il y a quelque chose de plus fort que toutes les misères du monde. Le jugement du corps vaut bien celui de l'esprit et le corps recule devant l'anéantissement. Nous prenons l'habitude de vivre avant d'acquérir celle de penser. Dans cette course qui nous précipite tous les jours un peu plus vers la mort, le corps garde cette avance irréparable."[89] *Le Mythe de Sisyphe*, Albert Camus

Imagine an adventure-style video game, some sort of a minecart speed game. The 'player' is a minecart with two passengers in it: a pilot, who is ultimately responsible for all the driving and the decision-making, and a co-pilot, only the co-pilot is at first without any memory and no maps, plans, or scripts to assist the pilot. The game is a multi-step game. At each step, there is a junction with several doors to choose from; rails go through all the doors in a complicated web of directions. Each time the junction is different, and the pilot has no ability to see the rail directions beyond the doors of the junction it is at. At every junction, the pilot has to choose the door to go through and consequently slides down to the

---

[89] In a man's attachment to life there is something stronger than all the ills in the world. The body's judgment is as good as the mind's and the body shrinks from annihilation. We get into the habit of living before acquiring the habit of thinking. In that race which daily hastens us toward death, the body maintains its irreparable lead. (Justin O'Brien's translation)

next step, a new virtual world. At every step, the co-pilot memorises what happens and advises the pilot at subsequent steps taking into account previous encounters. The pilot listens to the co-pilot, but it is ultimately capable of reflecting independently on the situation, itself, and what the co-pilot is telling it. Sometimes the pilot chooses a door after a careful reflection, sometimes for other motives, and sometimes even randomly. In other words, sometimes the pilot makes a conscious choice of the door to go through; sometimes it decides to go through a door for any other reason than a conscious choice; and sometimes even the minecart slides through a door without the pilot paying any serious attention to what is happening.

Whenever the minecart slides through a door, two things happen: (1) A new virtual world with a new junction and a new different choice of doors presents itself (the nature of the new virtual world is partially, but not totally, subject to the choice of door the minecart has gone through); and (2) The pilot and the co-pilot get incrementally 'affected' by this new world, every time a small bit, the pilot in its decision-making tactics and the co-pilot through registering one more experience of a virtual world and of a 'choice'. The minecart can never go back, gravity is pulling it down continuously from one virtual world to the other, and the pilot and the co-pilot are evolving bit-by-bit every time. Finally, the minecart erodes from one virtual world to the other from all the friction and the movement.

Grossly, I am this {minecart + pilot + co-pilot}. The pilot is my decision-making and motor brain functions, as well as the capabilities of my consciousness; the co-pilot is my memory; and the minecart itself is my body. I am never the same after each door. After door N, all three components of 'Me' change, and 'Me' is simply {minecart + pilot + co-pilot} *as it is after having been exposed to the virtual world behind door N*. To be more accurate, 'Me' is the result of the 'pilot after door N' directing its attention to {minecart + pilot + co-pilot} after door N. At the beginning of the game[90], I am grossly {new minecart + very basic pilot + empty memory}. After a thousand doors, I am {used minecart + pilot with a

---

90   That is the game of my life.

1,000 choices and reflections as background + 1,000 episodes of memory processed}. One can then easily comprehend that what defines 'Me' is the doors I take, the deeds I do at every virtual world I take part of, in addition to my very starting condition 'new minecart', 'very basic pilot', and 'empty memory capabilities'. The reader will hopefully indulge some gross simplifications but can also recognise the closeness of what we are saying here to the reality of my being. What matters are the deeds, shapers of us, and contributors to the virtual worlds we encounter. And what we consider as the 'I' or the 'We' is simply the product of a circular reflection on ourselves at any step or at any virtual world we are in.

We Live Before We Think

Even if we might forget this sometimes.

193. Human life is not only about Knowledge and Thought; it is also about Action. In an existence where Knowledge, Thought, and Truth can be hazy and evolving concepts, where information is often incomplete or simply too large to comprehend and process, deeds have a central role to play. It is what makes Existentialism attractive, even if its public reputation is somehow worn-out lately.

194. What matters for the human species is ultimately Action. Where Thought stops and Action starts is not one clear boundary, and naturally the two influence each other greatly. It is difficult to conceive someone thinking something without it influencing its action, at least indirectly.

195. We are social mammals capable of abstract thinking, but we are first social mammals. In situations of great threat, Thought has seldom a place; it is usually taken over by instinct, emotions, and intuition. Complex thought is a slow but more accurate process, and the higher degree of it is what makes us capable of greater progress than the other animals we know. Nevertheless, complex thought is an additional layer of the *living* organism and therefore necessitates life. Even in artificial intelligence, Thought

necessitates certain hardware and a certain amount of energy or electricity to be there. Thought does not exist separately and independently; we are far from the world of Ideas of Plato.

196. We learn to live before we learn to think, and we never think without living. Thinking is a subset of living. Descartes and most Cartesians who followed him have made the very consequential mistake of considering Thought as a separate 'substance' from reality (or from 'Matter') as we see it, and even worse, that this substance does not interact with the reality as we see it. They have conceived Thought as separate, independent, and capable of being by itself. This has been a great delusion since Plato, and Descartes gave it extra zeal.

   a. In order to make this delusion more consistent with observation, the Cartesians went on inventing greater delusions, such as the theory of the two clocks[91].

   b. Other philosophers went to the extreme of saying that everything is Thought; they had in the process to make the definition of Thought more general and diluted from what is typically conceived by it. At least with them, Thought and Living were not considered separate and independent anymore but actually very closely interconnected and essentially the same. We will refrain from criticising this view, as it would take us far from the purpose of this chapter.

197. The origin of the thinking human is a not-so-thinking mammal with all of its genetic baggage. In actuality, some of what we might

---

[91] The separation and independence of Thought and Matter raised the following question: "How does a thought/will correspond to a certain physical movement as we observe it, such as when I decide to lift my arm, if the two substances are distinct and do not interact?" To make the idea of separation of Thought and Matter hold, Geulincx invented the concept of 'pre-established harmony'. Crudely, it states that Thought and Matter are like two synchronised substances at the beginning of time; they move in conjunction but do not really interact with each other. Leibniz illustrated it better by talking about two clocks synchronised by God at the beginning of time.

consider as independent rational thinking may simply turn out to be the result of a lot of 'doing' by our ancestors. The not-so-thinking animal might have stumbled inadvertently on Thought, which turned out to provide distinct advantages, and which was therefore retained.

198. We are not advocates of Action over Thought, but we are also not advocates of Thought independent from Action. The first takes us backwards; the second gives us the illusion of moving forward but makes us miss the reality of living.

   a. Descartes was known to consider animals no different from mechanistic machines. Their squeaks, when we inflict pain on them, were to him an automatic reflex; animals had no thought, they were only matter, the other substance. Their pain and ours were different to him; we have a soul, they do not. No reasonable man with minimum knowledge of Biology can today seriously hold that. It is this kind of crazy conclusions one can start drawing from mistaking Thought as something completely independent from Life and Action.

199. Daniel Kahneman has been famous for drawing a clear distinction in the human thinking process between (1) A first system more intuitive, quick, based on emotions, relying on some *déjà-vus* and experiences, and frequent; and (2) A second system, more calculating, cool, less prone to error, but slower and likely more conscious. The first system is indeed subject to several biases and can 'overshoot' in many instances; it is a source of great flexibility and creative imagination, but it can also be the source of great prejudice. We must admit that the first system seems more like the one we more often use in Action. This is not however necessarily always true; Action can also be based on cool calculated Thought.

200. Have you ever been surprised by someone who you typically consider to be very smart behaving in what seems to be a rather senseless way in real life situations? Have you ever witnessed a person whom you have so far considered composed and wise

being dominated by his nerves and fear, and wonder is it even the same person? In such situations, in such everyday moments, there is something else that is taking over the cool, composed, and conscious Thought. It is the 'living' in us, the 'animal spirit' in us. The living mostly appears in the world of doing, in the world of Action. Many great plans simply fail because the planners do not grasp the reality of Action. Someone, with particular emotions, prejudices, pre-conceptions, and capabilities, has to put such plans into Action, and this by itself is a very different story from the plan as conceived on a dry piece of paper[92]. Thinking and talking are easier than doing.

201. It is probably accurate to state that, intellectually and academically, Thought has usually been considered more worthy of attention than Action, at least when it comes to Western philosophies (including Western Asia). This historical tendency represents a great contrast with the reality of the interconnectivity between our Thought organs and the rest of us including our environment. We could guess at least two root causes to this:

   a. We view ourselves as capable of a greater degree of Thought and as more conscious of our thought, action, and existence generally than other animals. We therefore tend to overemphasise the importance of this type of human activity over Action. We talk about having a soul that is distinct from the animal body. Naturally, it also suits us psychologically that this soul is immortal.

   b. We cannot fail to notice an on-going Platonic and Neoplatonic bias all throughout our history (which largely shares this common source). From the day Plato posited a world of Ideas superior to the world as we see it, the day he laid doubt[93] on our senses and reality as we see it, this bias has been dogmatised. The Stoics aimed at reinstating an empirical approach which existed with the Atomists, and the scientists tried (and succeeded)

---

92 Or more accurately today, a dry piece of software.

93 And Parmenides before him.

for centuries in demonstrating the value of experimental science, but the bias, admittedly less accentuated, still remains. Neoplatonic Trinity and Christian Trinity talk about the Divine Intellect, the *Nous*, the Word, the Logos, and the Son (Word of God), before talking about the Soul[94] author of all living things, the Holy Spirit, and the Church in Action. The chain goes from the One to the Intellect to the Soul. Is it a coincidence? We say no.

202. Thought could not take place without Action; the man of action precedes the intellectual. Intellectualism requires material goods for it to exist and flourish. There is no wrong in admitting this kind of pragmatism. It is rather hypocritical to sit up on the summit of material progress and draw intellectual theories that call for the destruction of this progress. Rousseau, Thoreau, Tolstoy, and all those who invite us to go back to some natural state would not have even had a chance to be known without material progress; Rousseau, in particular, largely depended on a certain social network around him for material benefits.

203. The early Greeks (particularly the Pythagoreans) and many Eastern Asian schools valued Contemplation over everything else. Wisdom was equated with Contemplation and Mystification. More militarily, industriously, or commercially oriented societies valued concrete action (e.g. the Spartans, Venetians, Turks, or Mongols) over everything else. Today, the leading American civilisation can be said to value more Action over Thought, this despite great achievements in the latter. Financial markets and Business typically favour the same view; financial plans are nice, but execution is ultimately what counts and judged against.

We see that civilisations have placed varying weights on Thought vs. Action. As in many things, the middle path is usually the wisest: Action is ultimately what counts, but Action is greater and more effective when influenced and guided by Thought.

204. The world of Thought, whether scientific or philosophico-religious,

---

94 Soul as synonymous with Action of the Divine Intellect and/or of the One (not in the current prevalent use of the word Soul).

is notoriously full of unanswered questions, dead-ends[95], and ambiguous input data coming from real life[96]. Natural Sciences are tentative by nature and require extensive experimental validation.

   a. Let us not leave room for ambiguity here: the world of Thought is likely the most powerful realm at the disposition of humans; unfortunately, its way of operating presents us often with a high threshold of validation which in instances can create practical difficulties. Any person in a position of responsibility knows that ultimately action is needed, and often, a line has to be drawn on the thinking—we are rarely provided with a clear risk-free solution in life… Intuition[97] usually plays a key role in many of these decision-making situations.

   b. When it comes to the environment around us, the greatest amount of Contemplation will not ultimately change it, only Action does. The question we can consequently ask is, "How important is it for humans to be able to change the environment around them or protect themselves from its negatives?" In answering this question, we can better understand the importance of Action because it is only through Action that we can change the environment[98].

205. One of the prime drivers of us humans and our actions, whether individually or as a species, is 'Survival'. We use the word Survival here in a slightly broader sense than the one usually attributed to it. Survival includes survival as an individual physically, as an individual through transmission of one's DNA to his/her descendants, and the physical survival of the species as a whole; but Survival can also include the continuity of one's legacy and

---

95   Whether circular references or simply too large of a quantity of information to be processed.

96   E.g. errors, misunderstandings in input information, grey areas, or incomplete information. •

97   Or automated decision-making processes resulting from past experience.

98   An entire chapter will be dedicated to the Environment and its influences.

parts of her/his individuality beyond one's limited life. The latter is normally considered part of our self-esteem and self-affirmation rather than Survival in the strict evolutionary meaning. In reality, men and women who actually volunteer themselves to die for a certain cause aim, at least partially, for the survival of a certain legacy, a certain idea, or a certain way of living. We all aim at Survival in a way or another. Part of this drive for Survival is in our instinct, and part of it is more conscious.

206. We do not object that there are other drivers of human activity or other aspirations[99], but there are very few as long-lasting and universal as Survival. What is certain is that Survival is there in almost every one of us, to a certain degree and in a certain aspect of it. **Survival is not possible without Action;** it is not a given in this constantly evolving world we live in. Survival is to be *achieved* and therefore, by definition, it requires Action. Survival includes responding to the surrounding environment, taking advantage of its positives, and reducing its negatives.

    a. We are not claiming here that Contemplation or Thought for the sake of Thought has no benefits for Survival. We hold great appreciation of Contemplation; many of its psychological benefits can have an enduring positive and 'balancing' effect on the human psyche, which has definite survival benefits. What we are challenging is the view that Contemplation or Thought is *superior*. Even the philosopher whose claim is to focus on Contemplation only has to recruit disciples around him, communicate, and ensure that he lives to the minimum in order to contemplate; all these require Action.

    b. More so, the survival and continuity of the species requires great Action. Seven billion people spread over the entire planet, economies that work seamlessly, trade, communication, production, innovation, education, and healthcare, none of which can be achieved without Action.

---

99 Some may consider that living a happy life is their ultimate goal, whatever their concept of happiness is.

207. Putting aside whether one is a religious believer or not, if we hold[100] that old religious books correspond allegorically to the wisdom of the time, this is how the Old Testament starts in its first pages: "Be fruitful and increase in number; fill the earth and subdue it. Rule over the fish of the sea and the birds of the air and over every living creature that moves on the ground."[101] Is there a more clear command of Action? It shows the prime importance of Survival for us humans as much as any other species.

208. Beyond surviving, the environment we live in impacts almost all of what we hold to be the objective of our existence. The minecart after a thousand doors is defined by what it has encountered at these doors and how it came to decide about these doors; the tastes, preferences, and aspirations of the pilot and how it comes to see itself are greatly honed by these thousand doors and the virtual worlds it met and lived in at every instance. And how are we to interact or at least to try to make a difference in our environment without Action? No words and no thoughts could have any impact on the environment if not ultimately translated into Action. Ignoring the influences of the environment is no more than holding a myopic view of 'Being'.

209. Living is not only a necessary condition of thinking; thinking is a by-product of living with distinctive benefits for those who enjoy it. The benefits of the thinking are not ultimately intended for the thinking by itself, but rather for the living being who is doing the thinking. Living and thinking are greatly intertwined, and no dichotomy can seriously hold. Living is not possible without Action; Action is the key condition of Survival. If not the action of the individual itself, then definitely the action of many around who ensure the survival of the overall community.

---

100 As the writer does.

101 Genesis 1:28.

What Kind of Action Exactly?

The essential tie between Action and Morality, the purpose of Action, on judging Action, and making decisions based on Action.

210. The statement concerning the importance of Action has an underlying requirement; there is a need for criteria for judging deeds and for accounting them as desirable or not. Otherwise, all types of Action and all deeds would be desirable and constitute an objective, which would be absurd. All Action is important, but not all Action is desirable.

211. If we endeavour to define an objective for Thought, we could say, "Thought seeks Truth", in the broadest sense of the word Truth. If we are then to draw a parallel for Action, what we could say is, "Action seeks the Desirable" or "Action seeks the Good", Good and Desirable being synonymous and taken equally in a broad sense. How can we define the Good or the Desirable? This is only possible through an ethical approach, a system of values, a **Morality**.

212. At face value, we dispose of more objective tools[102] for defining Truth for Thought than the Good or the Desirable for Action. In other words, there can be greater consensus on the definition of Truth than on the definition of Good.

213. Thought can ultimately be judged and criticised through a validation process, and more broadly by proper observation and by logical rules. In the case of deeds, validation is much less clear-cut, and the starting point is usually a system of values rather than methods of validation. There is a need therefore for a certain Morality, certain criteria for judging actions, which of course cannot come to be without Thought, at least at a rudimentary level. Morality however, as we shall see, is not only about pure thinking; it equally involves the more confusing world of emotions.

214. This may therefore give the reader the impression that the world of Thought is easier to judge and classify than the world of Action.

---

102 Even if they remain slightly imperfect.

Reflections on Fundamental Matters

In reality, the starting point in judging the world of Action may be more difficult; however, once a system of values is agreed, a deed is much easier to judge than a thought. In other words, the finish line is much easier in comparison with the world of Thought.

    a. Rational deductive thought is easy to judge, but only by individuals attentive enough to logical rules. But, simple rational deductive thought is not all thought. Most thought is a simplified anthropological view of reality, where exceptions are purposely omitted for the sake of simplification, and where there is uncertainty, either in terms of the models and laws of Thought used or in terms of input information. All correct[103] rational systems of Thought suffer from one major ill: they are always found to be somehow incomplete. It seems easy to use Rationality to judge Thought; it is very difficult to be completely satisfied by it.

    b. On the other hand, judging action requires a Morality. Once Morality is defined, it is usually easier to judge a deed than the thought behind, at least in most situations. Importantly, not all Action emanates from pure Thought. Most actions, in reality, are based on routine, reflexes, emotions, an unconscious, or an intuition. How much of the action is administered by a pure Thought vs. a blend of Thought and Emotion is ultimately very difficult to judge and could be considered less relevant than the value of a particular action according to the Morality held.

215. Morality of course requires some level of rational thought; the difficulties in the search for a rational system are therefore embedded in the search for Morality, which might seem to defeat our original premise that Morality is more difficult to define but more easy to apply than Rationality. In reality, Morality enjoys more leeway than Rationality. If one believes in a fully rational world of Thought, then Rationality and its system need to be both correct and as complete as possible. The trouble is that these two

---

103 I.e. with no logical mistakes in them.

conditions do not live well together. Morality in comparison can more easily escape this dilemma. Because of emotionality and other non-rational elements in it, Morality can afford being either complete and slightly inconsistent on the margin or incomplete and rationally consistent. We realise that this statement about Morality can seem controversial and may raise many eyebrows, but it is reality of Ethics; otherwise a mind like Spinoza would have solved the issue of Morality rationally a long time ago!

216. Morality regulates Action, whether this action is an applied thought or a more instinctive and emotional one. Morality tempers both Action and Thought. History has provided ample examples of intellectual adventures and over-rationalisations that resulted in terrible absurdities: Eugenics, two atomic explosions, human experiments, forced historicism in the form of Marxism or Nationalism, massacres in the name of religious, ethnic purity, or stability, and drone attacks which from afar resemble more video games than the reality of indiscriminate death. Thought and Science can confer modesty and temperance when they confront us with our origins, limitations, and infinitesimal size, but the ensuing technological know-how can also risk providing a misplaced sense of power that can be misused, and a detachment from the real consequences of our actions that usually comes with distance.

217. "What do deeds look to achieve?" We can answer this question now by first saying that deeds should point in the direction of the chosen Morality or ideals and objectives of a society.

    a. This is however on the aggregate level of a society and never fully realised in practice given the continuously changing conditions beyond our control, but also the changing nature of Morality, albeit at a much slower pace. This phenomenon of aggregation represents the normative aspect of deeds, and the general dynamic of this aggregation typically resides in the political sphere. Politics is concerned with defining the aggregate

Morality, as well as the most satisfactory application of Morality given the sometimes-changing conditions of applicability.

> i. Some look to define Morality as the *result* of the aggregation of deeds and not as the *potential* towards which the deeds at the aggregate level tend to point. Whether Morality precedes the aggregation of deeds or vice-versa is for us nothing more than a chicken-and-egg dead-end; Reality is reflexive and there are definite feedback loops between the two.

218. Outside the dynamic of aggregation, deeds are much more complicated and much less normative at the individual level. In addition to individual morality[104], we equally observe an element of randomness, pure instinct, and pure mechanic at the individual level. As we mentioned, not all deed is rational or conscious. Sometimes we even act in a certain way just to express a certain individuality in opposition to the average or a situation we are up against. An individual can act irrationally against society *on purpose*.

> a. An individual deed has society and its morality as well as the aggregation of deeds as background for comparison. Sometimes we act individually in the face of this background and sometimes we collude with the individual deeds of others in society in order to attempt to change this background. Individual deeds are the result of a combination of many body and brain functions, which we have yet to understand and categorise properly.
>
> b. However, despite this opacity, we can still define which of the deeds are the more determining for us individually: it is the conscious free choices we make, the deeds which engage us on a certain path or in a certain way *in full awareness*.

---

104 Which individually can be varying from the aggregate one.

i. The weak point of classical Existentialism was to see all deeds and states of mind as ultimately emanating from clear conscious choices (even if indirectly). Our view is rather a middle ground: not all deeds are based on conscious choices; however, conscious choices are the summit of the hierarchy of deeds. They are the ones that relate us most closely to our individual morality and our freedom.

219. Conscious deeds are central to the relation between Morality and Freedom, a point we shall elaborate on in a bit. Moreover, the perimeter of conscious deeds is not limited or pre-defined; it can be enlarged with a greater conscious life, a greater attention to our decision-making processes, thoughts, feelings, and actions. A conscious, engaged life is not necessarily the only way; it takes a free choice and courage to live life with more awareness.

220. More importantly, we do not find any better way of defining Freedom than through the free choice of action in the face of a situation that requires it, even more so if the situation is imposed on the individual and no full clarity of the consequences exists. A conscious, engaged life counts more towards experience than simple age counting. It does matter that we enlarge the scope of conscious deeds in our individual life rather than behave mostly based on automatisms. A wide and as consistent as possible set of conscious deeds is what ultimately defines our individual identity in the face of all the uncertainty around us; it is a mark of individual courage and integrity.

221. To the question "What do deeds look to achieve?", the answer is therefore twofold: (1) A trend or an averaging towards Morality at the aggregate level; and (2) An expression of individual identity, morality, and freedom through conscious individual deeds. And where is Survival in all of this? There is no valid Morality that does not comprise Survival as a key building component. Morality regulates Action, and Action has the Environment[105] as its field.

---

105 In the broadest sense, including all living being and us.

222. "If deeds are what counts, do we have the right to judge the ideas and thoughts or shall we always wait for the deeds to happen in order to express a proper judgement? Where is judgment applied best: on Deed or on Thought?" A social or political deed is usually preceded by a social or a political thought. Generally, a conscious deed is preceded by a conscious thought. Assuming that the social or political thought is expressed clearly enough before being realised, do we have the right to lay judgment on the thought before seeing the concrete realisation of such a thought? This is the social problem of thought vs. deed we will attempt to talk about now.

   a. The most distinct political and historical example would be the response European major powers chose (particularly France and Britain) to the gradual expansion of Hitler's powers between 1933 and 1937. It was rather clear what were Hitler's ideological thoughts—he has after all written a book about them and did not refrain from expressing his ideas openly. Yes he bluffed by talking about his desire for peace in Europe; yes he signed a maritime agreement with Great Britain in 1935; but he also did not refrain from openly repudiating the Treaty of Versailles, particularly when it came to the remilitarisation of Germany and the reintroduction of conscription. Were Britain and France right in not judging Hitler on his thoughts and some of his initial deeds in the early and mid-thirties and wait for his later major deeds, particularly the invasion of Poland, to act? Western Europe was indeed not considering war or military defence seriously till probably 1938. It is easier to find answers with hindsight, but what interests us mostly here is when we should use expressed thoughts as basis for judgment vs. real concrete actions? And if the basis for judgement is more Deed than Thought, what is the concrete mass of deeds necessary before a judgement can be made? Clearly, one single act can be circumstantial, accidental, or unintended, and not enough to draw major conclusions. Was that the case with Hitler in the 1930s?

223. In the social and political sphere, it is sometimes clear from the thoughts what the deeds will be, and therefore a level of pre-emption in the judgment is not only possible but also necessary. If some faction's only thought is to wage an attack and is clearly expressing it and preparing for it, we need not to wait for the attack to happen in order to attempt to prevent it. If someone is clearly advocating racial murder, we need not to wait for the first murder to take place to start paying attention.

224. The key word here is *pre-emption*. Pre-emption is not necessarily about acting first[106]; it is about foresight and preparation for the *eventuality* of a negative act or deed. Otherwise, all pre-emption would lead to a guaranteed confrontation of judgements and deeds. Pre-emption is about being ready for the possibility of a negative deed; it is also about creating conditions that make the potentially negative deed more costly to realise by the party we fear from.

225. However, it is not often clear from the expressed thought, particularly if it is a general thought, what the deed would be in a specific situation. Deeds are always situation-specific. Thoughts can be either general or situation-specific; they can address a topic in general and abstract ways, or they can be directed towards a very specific situation. In such circumstances, it is sound to decide on a course of action based on the deed rather than a subjective interpretation of the thought. This mostly concerns thought in the realm of social interactions, including political, legal, and ethical thought.

226. Where can we draw the line between the two types of situations is admittedly a difficult question. What we can say nevertheless is that the level of required cautiousness and pre-emption should be commensurate with the magnitude of the consequences of the thought expressed. Someone advocating the thought of a murder or suicide requires more attention and pre-emption than someone advocating the thought of not paying a certain bill on time.

---

106 For example, attacking before being attacked.

227. Broadly, judging what the action would hypothetically be from reading one's mind is not always possible and may give way to misinterpretations. Judging an action is clearer and less subjected to personal interpretations.

228. By inverting the problem, we can also infer other helpful lessons. There are greater possibilities for agreement between two individuals when it comes to Action rather than Thought, and this is important from a political perspective. Pragmatically, a particular situation often presents us with a limited number of options for Action to choose from. In the realm of Thought, the nuances are greater and the boundaries are more fluid. The world of Thought is a world of infinite possibilities, whereas in Action, we are rarely provided with infinite choices.

   a. When a person lays harm on another person, we have two choices: either to catch the perpetrator or let him go free. If someone extends a hand to us, we either extend our hand back or not. If we want to voice our political support, we vote from a limited number of candidates.

   b. When I vote for a president between two candidates, it *almost never* means that I agree in thought with all policies of the candidate I am voting for. The thoughts and contingencies are endless, but the choice of action is between four possibilities[107] only: vote for one candidate, vote for the other, do not vote, or vote blank. Sure one can argue that another option could be to topple the entire political system and prevent the vote from taking place. Assuming that this is even possible, how often do we really do that?

229. And now a final related question: "If it is indeed wiser to wait for the particular deeds to lay judgment, how can we really then choose someone for any social or political position?" Doesn't it amount to saying that we need to see the actions of someone in office before judging her/him, which is clearly the opposite of

---

107 In a presidential election with two candidates.

the concept of voting? Or does it mean we vote only based on judging past actions and never pay attention to the future political agenda? Surely this cannot be a satisfactory way of voting. How can we vote or judge political programs if actions are ultimately what counts, and they are really what shows the true nature of the political thinking?

230. Voting, in our view, is about judging according to several parameters that involve a mixture of Thought and Action:

   a. The past loyalty between promises and actions as a reflection of the general integrity and honesty of the applicant;

   b. The intellectual and moral agreement of the voter with the future social and political agenda expressed by the applicant. This admittedly does not involve any judgement of deeds; and

   c. The *potentiality* of putting such ideas into action given the overall political structure and the personal acumen of the one we are voting for. This relates to the pragmatism of the ideas, and how much really thoughts and future tangible actions may correspond.

The first point concerns past deeds, the second concerns the realm of Thought, and the third is about the intertwining of deeds and thoughts. Hence, we find that two of the three criteria of voting do include deeds.

231. In the context of Free Choice and Existentialism, it was, and may still is, common to portray the world (that is of Action) as a world full of possibilities; this is misleading in our view. In reality, it is the world of Thought that offers the greater possibilities. From a practical perspective, the world of Action is, more often than the world of Thought, the domain of the limited number of options. Consequently, inviting two individuals to agree on a course of action from a limited number of options is more likely than in the case of Thought, where many other speculative theories might

Reflections on Fundamental Matters

be possible. This is central to any political or social agreements between humans.

   a. It is no surprise then that we do observe in social movements different factions with differing ideologies coming together and agreeing a particular course of action. The French resistance included Communists and right wing Gaullists. Because it is more situation-specific, Action opens itself more to compromise than Thought, particularly the type of Thought we need to consider as either fully acceptable or fully unacceptable[108].

232. There are two exceptions in the world of Thought to what we just said. These are situations where in Thought we can encounter limited options.

   a. The most important one is Deductive Reasoning or tautological reasoning. In case of Deductive Reasoning and Formal Logic, the path of agreement is rather clear.

   b. Thought oriented towards purely conscious action. Naturally, if Action presents us with a limited number of options, at least in most situations, the corresponding thought is also about limited number of options. Conscious action corresponds to a thought of the action and its possibilities, and therefore this is only evident. It is rather a technical point to talk about such an exception, but we have to mention it nevertheless.

233. In Natural Sciences, the agreement is rather less easy to realise and is subject to many conditions that, when made clear, can show rather differing views. It may surprise the reader that we refer to Natural Sciences in this way, but let us take an example we alluded to before to clarify. Joan and Sarah both agree that the Earth revolves around the Sun. We might claim that there is an agreement in thought here. But actually, Joan is a believer that the Sun is the centre of the Universe; everything revolves around the

---

[108] An example of such thought would be religious thoughts of the kind "Did Christ rise from the dead or not?" One can with difficulty answer "It depends"…

Sun, and hence, Earth revolves around the Sun. On the other side, Sarah believes that everything is relative; however, considering the Principle of Parsimony, Sarah believes that a model of Earth revolving around the Sun is an easier model to handle than one of the Sun revolving around Earth. Are Joan and Sarah now really in agreement of thought? Or was the agreement rather at one shallow level only? This is an example of what we mean when we say that the world of Thought can often be more difficult to agree in than the world of Action, even in the context of disciplined thought with clearly organised rules.

Deeds for a Better Thought, Deeds for an Identity

234. Interestingly, it is often the transition from thoughts to deeds that makes the thinking more clear. We have a strong interactive relationship between our thinking and our actions.

    a. Deeds influence the environment, and the environment itself is a key contributor to shaping our thought. The influence of the environment is immense, over the immediate term and over the very long-term.

    b. If we admit that Thought is interested in problem solving (the search for Truth being one), many of the problems to solve would not have arisen in the first place without Action. We need to wake up and walk out of our door first in order to stumble upon a large variety of problems and questions.

        i. If we had not mastered long-distance sailing, we would not have discovered the New World or answered without contention that Earth is somehow round.

        ii. If we had not invented lenses, we would not have been able to observe celestial bodies more closely and realise that they are not that different in substance from our planet, or that, for example, there is or there was water on some of them.

      iii. If we have not dug into the Earth, we would not have discovered skeletons of extinct species nor have been able to trace back our origins.

"[...] a large proportion of our positive activities depend on spontaneous optimism rather than mathematical expectation [...] a spontaneous urge to action rather than inaction [...]" Keynes.

Some of these deeds we undertook were intentional with an eye on a particular discovery; others were purely circumstantial. The discoveries of the cosmic background noise, of penicillin, and of radioactivity, were all rather circumstantial. It is highly unlikely that pure Thought or Meditation would have tilted the balance one way or another.

c. Often in cases of confused thinking, taking a step in one direction or the other is what helps best clarify our mind, sheds a light on grey areas and uncertain information, and allows us to move forward. We can rarely wait for perfect information, perfect engineering, or perfect reasoning.

      i. Product piloting is an example of such a trial-and-error process. Rarely a product is developed solely based on Thought. A large amount of doing and redoing is required to obtain the desired product. Very many prototypes of planes had to be tested before the first one worked, with many casualties in the process unfortunately.

Doing and failing is of greater merit than thinking, talking, and doing nothing. With the first, there is a chance of achievement and progress along with a significant amount of failure, whereas with the latter, there is nothing but talk and a touch of cowardice. "[...] he who is deceived is wiser than he who is not deceived" Plutarch.

d. How many times have many of us been daunted by an empty page on which we needed to write our thoughts or attempt to solve a problem? It is rare that we are able to posit all our thinking or a solution to a problem in one try. Most often, starting to write is what clarifies the thinking. Some problems are simply too big for us to think about in their totality without attempting to tackle them piece-by-piece. We can find ourselves in one instance stuck, unimaginative, dry, and then as soon as we start writing, as soon as we start *trying to do* suddenly ideas start to flow, like an open dam, and we find ourselves closer to what we want to achieve than what we had initially thought. Doing can help break the frozen cycle of thinking and unsuccessful problem solving in many situations.

e. Thinking is often a simplified and categorised view of the world. Things are omitted on purpose in order to be able to move the thinking forward. A typical omission is not to account for the psychology of the people executing the plan (including ourselves). Actions and choices play a great role in shaping our subsequent experiences and thinking. Referring to Dostoevsky's great psychological novel *Crime and Punishment*, Porfiry Petrovich exclaimed to Roskolnikov: "You are a man still young, so to say, in your first youth and so you put intellect above everything, like all young people [...] actual fact and a man's temperament, my dear sir, are weighty matters and it's astonishing how they sometimes deceive the sharpest calculation! [...] The temperament reflects everything like a mirror!"

   i. An interesting political example would be the Bolshevik Revolution, or the more fun version to read in George Orwell's *Animal Farm*. Whether Communism as an economic model works or not on a theoretical level is actually not the important consideration. The Bolshevik Revolution is what we can call an ideology-driven revolution. It is a change driven by a certain idea of a different system, a different social contract to be put in place. Whether populations who constituted the real effective force behind the change towards Communism were driven by other considerations[109] does not change from the fact that the core ideology was a certain clear idea of a system. Unfortunately, as it is the case often in History, such an idea of a system, despite being analysed and thought through in detail at some theoretical level, did not take into account the basic psychology of human beings, their power-loving nature, human natural complacencies, and a certain element of corruption which the communist system can naturally incentivise towards. George Orwell beautifully portrays the result; the pigs become yet again another face of corrupt power wrapped in ideological clothes.

235. Collective wisdom is much more interested in providing a way of life and setting up desirable rules for society and species development than in pure thinking.

    a. In reality, the term philosophy is more widely associated (wrongly) with the meaning 'way of life' than with any other of its more accurate definitions[110]. When we ask someone what is her/his philosophy in life, we rarely mean whether the person is an idealist or an empiricist, a nominalist or a realist. We mostly mean, "How do you conduct your life and your everyday affairs, based on which parameters and ideals?" It hence goes back more to applications and deeds than anything else.

    b. History is full of examples where doctrines and thoughts (religious, philosophical, or other) had to be changed, sometimes radically, for the benefit of deeds. No matter how pacifist one is, and no matter how strongly demonstrated is the utility of a pacifist attitude, if a whole

---

109 Material reasons, exasperation with tsarist abuse, or other.

110 Such as 'asking the right questions'.

society is faced with an existential threat from an alien civilisation which we know will not accept anything else than the annihilation of its enemies, what are we to do? Are we to amend our doctrines and thoughts to cater for this particular circumstance or not? It is through such examples that all religions and philosophies (without exception) have been forced to readjust to deeds and to practical considerations.

236. As with the example of the minecart, it is often the choices we make and the actions we take at a particular junction that determine the course of our future life. Whether these choices and actions are emanating from pure Thought, Emotions, or Randomness is rather secondary, not to our internal psychology, but to the actual world consequences. In setting up the scene for the subsequent stages of our life, choices influence the core of our identity more than thinking and meditation. Meditation tends to revolve around these same past choices. It is extremely important to stress that each and every one of us builds her/ his own identity through the life choices she/he makes. What we reflect upon when we think about ourselves, when we say "I", is no more than the living being resulting from all the choices and the doors of life as seen by our own inner awareness. Deeds are the identity-builders, and the 'I' is a concept that is continuously work-in-progress. None of us can change the past, but all of us have distinct choices about the future whether we wish to admit it or not. Surely, many deeds and actions are undertaken without real awareness of the importance of choice and without sufficient awareness of the importance of deeds and their consequences[111]. Increasing the scope of awareness of choice and deed puts us in a virtuous cycle of identity-building, whereas acting in life without really recognising that a substantial part of it is inherently subject to our choice can only lead to a real loss of sight of our own individual identity.

---

111 Not all deeds need to be undertaken in full awareness for deeds to be identity-builders. Even a subset of deeds taken in full awareness contributes greatly to shaping our life trajectory and hence our identity.

Reflections on Fundamental Matters

237. We are often dealt cards of no choice of ours or find ourselves in situations where little we could have done differently would have prevented a difficult outcome from happening; it is only how we behave in these situations that matters. The men who came to be 18 or 20 years old in Europe in early 1940s had little contribution to the situation they found themselves in. They were all faced with a choice, and each made his own. It is difficult situations like these that reveal the real character of a man or a woman many times more than the discourses, speeches, and thoughts he or she may claim. Many preach doctrines, ideologies, and a certain way of thinking only to behave shockingly differently under duress. Thought can be infested with eloquence and back calculation, Deed much less.

Summary of Key Points.

238. The fundamental importance of Action presents itself in many varying ways and in all aspects of Life. In the world of digitisation and desk jobs, the world of automation and greater isolation from Nature, the world of greater share of Services in the world economy, simply the world of greater abstraction, the importance of tangible Action could escape us from time to time. Here is some of what we could state when we attempt to put back Action into its central position:

   a. Action is indispensable to living in any environment. Action is indispensable for Survival.

   b. Once a system of values is agreed, Action is easier to judge than the underlying thought.

   i. Arguably, there is a larger possibility of agreement in Action than in Thought, particularly when it comes to complicated subjects or where information is uncertain.

   c. Thought is a 'manager' of Action. Action is ultimately the key output.

   d. The process of advancing Thought is greatly enhanced

by Action. Action is sometimes required to reduce some of the uncertainty in Thought. New worlds and new alternatives made possible by Action provide lucrative new fields for Thought. The process of doing can be a catalyst to the process of thinking.

e. We are living beings above all; any amount of thought can be dominated by our fear for our life or by instinctive emotions in many situations. We learn to live before we learn how to think.

f. Action does not only change the environment around us; it changes *us* through changing our environment and the process of reflecting on ourselves.

g. Our individual identity and our existence are defined by the choices we make and the actions we take. We are not pre-defined individuals with a sort of magical destiny or fate. Reality is too probabilistic and fundamentally chaotic for that to be possible. We do not get to choose this chaotic background, but we have the possibility of choosing what to do when we are confronted with a choice. We do not choose the menu of possible actions we are presented with, but we can still choose which road to take, knowing consciously about the other possible options.

h. The best way of defining Freedom is through free conscious choice of Action. Not all Action is conscious or free, but the fact that some of it is, and that every action has an impact on our environment and us, is as good of a definition of Freedom as any other. Moreover, we can enlarge the perimeter of conscious free action. There is a clear golden link between Morality, Free Choice, and Conscious Action.

239. Regardless of our personal predispositions, given the pre-eminence of Life and Action over Thought and Detachment, it is imperative to interest ourselves in the human fully as a human, not only as a thinking entity or a thought. We cannot allow a

purely Cartesian or Hegelian view of the world to dominate. With the first, the individual body is portrayed as a mechanical machine; with the second, the individual only counts so far as he contributes to the State—this Hegelian metaphysical entity. Social and political conditions of individuals are not to be ignored out of personal predispositions or because of some illusion that only Technology, Science, Nationalism, or the race for financial wealth matters. Social and political dynamics not only matter on their own account but also can come to define much of everything else we consider a higher priority.

240. At the individual level, when a person is too much absorbed in Thought, all humans are likely to become a hindrance to that Thought or simply a tool used to progress that Thought. We cannot reasonably allow that.

241. Thought and Detachment are not to be ignored, but they should not come to define all human activity either. Some of the most interesting fields of Thought and Detachment are those related to Action or emanating from Action. The realisation of the Absurd (to which we will turn next) could not have come to be without this close interaction between Thought and Action.

The Absurd

"A simple, decent person who respects ordinary common sense can well understand that the absurd exists and that it cannot be understood; fortunately this is hidden from systematic thinkers." Kierkegaard

"Il n'y a qu'un problème philosophique vraiment sérieux: c'est le suicide. Juger que la vie vaut ou ne vaut pas la peine d'être vécue, c'est répondre à la question fondamentale de la philosophie."[112] Albert Camus

There were once two neighbours, a young monkey and a young koala. The monkey was of the curious and restless kind, always looking to know more, to achieve something, to be great. The koala, on the other hand, liked his sleep and comfort; he cherished his 22-hour-a-day habit of 'resting', resting from what no one really knew... Clearly, the koala had little ambitions apart from devising the most effortless ways of living. One day, the young monkey sets himself on a project, that of becoming the 'King of the Jungle'. The monkey calculated it to be an ambitious task indeed but not unachievable given his whit, constant energy, and curiosity. He was in fact a special monkey among his peers, not the least because he came up with such an objective. Unfortunately, the 'King of the Jungle

---

[112] There is but one truly serious philosophical problem, and that is suicide. Judging whether life is or is not worth living amounts to answering the fundamental question of philosophy. (Justin O'Brien's translation)

Manual' was out of stock that day so the young monkey set himself on the laborious task of looking through the wisdom of his ancestors for tips on how to be great, powerful, rich, wise, and all such good things. He figured that, once he got to understand all that is required to have these qualities, becoming the King of the Jungle would just be a matter of simple application. The monkey poured over book after book, all of the wisest and most intelligent of his ancestors. He was surprised to discover that many of these revered ancestors contradicted each other, sometimes even bluntly. Nevertheless, after great pain, he managed to synthesise their knowledge and wisdom, and he detailed accordingly an exact plan of how to conquer the entire jungle and put it under his dominion. He looked boastfully at his poor nonchalant koala neighbour and thought, "Poor thing, he simply does not realise who he has been neighbour with all this time. Once my plan is in motion, this small resting creature will only discover the extent of the opportunity he missed by not seeking my goodwill."

Finally, Day 0 arrived. The monkey embarked on executing his plan only to discover days later how clearly ineffective it was in the first place. He was faced with many surprises along the way; many things did not work out as prescribed by the ancestors. Even some of the prescriptions turned the situation worse than it was before. Not much difference or benefit was achieved. On the contrary, the outcome was on the whole negative when the young monkey took into account all the effort and hard work he had done. "There must be an error of reasoning or calculation in my plan", he thought, "There is no other explanation. It is based on only the best wisdom and knowledge of my ancestors. Maybe it is something I have not accounted for. Maybe it is something I have not understood." The young monkey went back home; he wanted to recheck everything again, take into account all the nasty surprises he came across, and start again. Upon coming home, the young koala woke up and asked, "What did I miss?" The monkey frowned and looked the other way without answering.

A new plan was devised and a new Day 0 was announced. The results some days later were exactly the same: more additional surprises, more additional bewilderment, and more additional questions. Anger set in but not despair; disillusionment with all this declared wisdom of the elderly set in but not despair. The monkey kept on searching for meaning behind it all, for knowledge, and for wisdom. Everybody around him has always highly regarded hard work, the wisdom of the elders, good ethics, and intelligence. There must be a deep meaning and benefit for existence in all of that. Years passed and the monkey did not lose any of his resolve. Plan after plan after plan were made and tested without success. Always new disappointments; always new unanswered questions and problems along the way; always some new *cul-de-sac*; and always a failure and a disillusionment in the face of what was considered a newly found greater knowledge and power. And the worst of it all, this stupid, almost insulting, question the monkey gets from the koala time after time upon his return, "What did I miss?"... I mean this koala did not even try to do anything ever! He did not work hard, he did not think hard, and he did not look for any meaning in Life. He never had any ambition or attempted anything of substance really! And yet, the monkey has tried it all and still to no avail. These were the thoughts that kept running in the monkey's head. The monkey is now older after every trial. He kept on leaving his home with a plan to come back disappointed to the same question from the koala.

The monkey and the koala turned really old. One day, the koala receives a letter. Upon reading it, the koala, with remarkably wide eyes that the monkey had only rarely seen on him, turns towards his neighbour and shouts, "Hey monkey! You will not believe this! One of my far relatives died recently with no one left behind. I just inherited all of his estate. He happens to control an enormous jungle. I am now the King of my own Jungle!" The monkey was barely able to utter the following before completely subsiding, "Do not look for The Way. Do not look for One Meaning. Do not look for One Truth..."

The monkey passed away not long afterwards; he left a son behind. The young son was of the character of his father. The son had a new neighbour of a similar character to the older koala. I guess the greater absurdity of it all is that the new monkey and the new koala went on repeating the same exact behaviour of their predecessors respectively.

We, individually and collectively, keep on going with our lives without knowing why, and we keep on inventing explanations as to the 'whys' to have them continuously reviewed. CAUTION: (Absurdly) This is not a call for a blind and complete despair or doubt; it is rather a call for a major reset of human expectations, at least the majority of them.

242. The idea of the Absurd, and consequently the idea of Existence being absurd, is probably as old as the Human Condition. It is difficult to imagine the rise of Consciousness without leading to the rise of the Absurd in it, at least in a rudimentary way. The Absurd is the result of a fundamental impossibility of reconciling the continuous search and need for a meaning for Existence on one side, and the absence of any clear, objective, and definitive answer to it on the other[113]. It is the realisation of the circularity between the question of meaning and the answer to it, more generally the circularity of life, of thought, and of action–the hand that is drawing is itself the hand that is being drawn[114]. The Absurd is the ensuing feeling from the realisation that the eternal recurrence of this opposition[115] and that this circularity are a *fundamental* part of Reality, fundamental part of our cognition and of our being, deep down, no matter where we look or how we approach things.

243. The Absurd is a fundamental part of our existence and our condition, whether we choose to recognise it and be aware of it or not. We come into existence to realise that our existence is finite, no matter how long it will be; we do not know why we came into existence, why our existence is finite, and why we are even asking these questions. We walk through life planning and amassing experience, memories, power, and wealth, while knowing that we will have to give it all away at the end. We work towards precise

---

113 For those who consider that there is an objective meaning in Religion, the answer will hopefully become clearer as we progress through the chapter.

114 To use a classical example.

115 Between the need for a definitive meaning and the impossibility of one.

The Absurd

objectives, which, when we draw close to, we often discover them to be less fixed and meaningful than we thought from afar.

244. The very young among us discern the Absurd and ask questions about it; the older ones listen to the questions, may smile, then answer something and pretend surety in their answers, when any sensible human knows that there is no ultimate and full surety in what is said. We come up with religions and philosophies to explain the Absurd without real honest satisfaction, without complete answers to our questions and wonderings. Religions and philosophies look more like a temporary patch against the Absurd that works on some of us but not the others. Through Time and History, we evolve, we change the way we eat and dress, we master new technologies, we inhabit or travel to new places, we alter environments, and we acquire further knowledge; we push further away the boundaries of the Absurd but without really eliminating it. We immerse ourselves in entertainment or in mundane activities in order not to think about all of this. We shop, we drive nice cars, and we come up with all sorts of artificialities. But it remains there, always there... the absurdity of it all.

245. It is absurd that some of the most shrewd and driven individuals among us can go a great deal through life without fully realising or acknowledging (that is to themselves) the Absurd. It is absurd that we consider such individuals role models of success, power, and wisdom. It is equally absurd that those who fully realise the Absurd and have it constantly to their mind keep on with their lives with little change, no different from spending great time and effort building a house while knowing from the first instance that it will eventually be confiscated from you or taken credit for by someone else. The reason for this puzzling counter-intuitive behaviour might (at least partially) be evolutionary. It may rather be more convenient and less energy intensive for survival not to factor in the Absurd on very frequent basis, or to imitate those who do not constantly factor in the Absurd, especially when one is not well-equipped mentally and psychologically to deal with it or analyse it.

246. Of course, the Absurd has been addressed in great detail throughout History, sometimes giving it different names or approaching it from varying points of view. Many have discerned it clearly and addressed it under its various forms. The Absurd is found in Art, Literature, Philosophy, Religion, Science, and Politics. We can conceive it as located at the centre of the sphere of our existence; no matter what is our starting point, we eventually find it when we try to dig deep. It is ultimately one and the same. Parmenides and his disciple Zeno, Flaubert, Dostoevsky, Hume, Kierkegaard, Nietzsche, Kafka, Herman Hesse, and the existentialists, they have all dealt with the Absurd in one way or another; but the chief analysis is traditionally attributed to Albert Camus who represents a culmination of the idea of the Absurd.

247. The Absurd is an intrinsic part of our human existence. It is not a mere fact of Life that we sometimes stumble upon; it is not an idea or a situation that may happen or may not; it is not case-dependent or time-dependent; it is *always* there and under various forms. The only difference is whether we have it present to our mind or not, whether we see it or not.

248. The goal here is not to drive anyone into any form of gloominess or depression. It is not necessarily a call for pure nihilism either. On the contrary, we consider that being fully aware of the notion of the Absurd prevents us from falling into the classical trap of disillusionment (be it intellectual, religious, or emotional). In actuality, it is this disillusionment, the shock between expectations and reality whenever we are confronted with the Absurd and we attempt to deny it, that is likely the largest contributor to the individual loss of meaning and purpose, resulting in anger, angst, and/or depression. On the contrary, being continuously aware of the Absurd offers many advantages:

    a. Immunity against absolutism and false beliefs. Immunity against falling for totalitarian[116] expectations, be it moral, political, or material, to discover later on that they do not correspond to the subtleties of reality and its mode of functioning.

---

116 In the intellectual sense, not only the political one.

b. Immunity against the loss of individuality and personal identity. Indeed, the realisation of the Absurd forces each and every one of us to make her/his choices. One cannot realise this opposition between the want for meaning and the inexistence of one, and not be forced to make a conscious decision on how to deal with it. By dealing with the Absurd, a large part of the personal identity is built.

c. Waking up to the Absurd might lead many to change courses in their lives and might help avoid regrets of never having attempted to do this or that and/or of having lied to oneself for so long. The earlier is the discovery of the Absurd, the lower is the switching cost, and the easier is its acceptance. Many invest their entire life on rigid, wrong ideas and ideologies; by the time the awakening happens, they are too old to openly acknowledge their mistake or admit that they have invested their life on an illusory rigidity—when so much has already been invested, too much pain, shame, or rejection is triggered with the slightest private realisation of the Absurd.

d. Most importantly, the realisation of the Absurd provides a fundamental modesty, intellectual and emotional, in the face of our existence. We too often forget this modesty, especially when things are going in our favour. There may be evolutionary reasons in thinking ourselves great and knowledgeable when we receive validation from the outside world. It is the condition of the successful: a snowball of being in the right, a snowball of validation, ending with a flagrant wrong in the face of self-certainty. The Absurd strips us of our human arrogance and keeps us more in touch with reality.

249. CAUTION: if at the heart lies the Absurd, it does not necessarily mean that everything is absurd, or that we cannot think or act even with the existence of the Absurd. As we shall see in the case of Morality later on, incorporating the necessary absurdist or perspectivist view in our individuality should not constitute an

excuse for those emotionally predisposed to reject everything to claim validation or proof. Realising a difficulty in a theory that has its merits should not become a basis for admitting another opposing, more false on the whole theory. Realising the Absurd forces the question of how to think and act based on a personal choice—it does not eliminate thinking or acting; it is in any case impossible not to think or act, as even the choice of not thinking or acting involves (absurdly) an act of thinking or acting.

Without falling into too much philosophical discourse or too many epistemological technicalities, the aim of the following is to illustrate the Absurd through various examples in order to increase awareness of it. Admittedly, some of these examples do not purely correspond to the philosophical notion of the Absurd; they remain valid nevertheless as an image of this divide between the search for meaning and the nature of Reality.

250. We mentioned the Absurd arising from the opposition between our own mortal condition and our individual behaviour. All sacrifice and effort towards achievements contain an element of selflessness and thanklessness in light of the Absurd. Since we do not really know why we live, and since there is no objective definitive meaning for it all, then what is the reason that drives us to excel and to make sacrifices for our loved ones, for our creations, for art, and for the benefit of the community or society? Why do we keep on living, thriving, and seeking a different or better world since we do not seem ever capable of satisfying the question of meaning? We know that we will have to give it all away at the end, and we know that we might die suddenly and not even have the chance of reflecting satisfactorily over a life well lived. And yet, we keep on doing it. Even the ones who realise the Absurd most keep on doing it. In actuality, many of them are even far more goal-oriented and industrious than the average. But why? Is it something in us that is greater than the realisation of the Absurd? Is it a counter-reaction to the realisation of the Absurd that pushes us to live life fully? Or is it simply a genetic love of life embedded in all living beings? It is not only the opposition

between the desire for meaning and the absence of one that is absurd; it is also the beautiful stubbornness of living and hoping even while admitting this opposition.

251. The role of luck in success and failure may render many of our experiences totally absurd. Someone may play things by the book, work hard, and behave rightly to find herself worse-off than others who behaved less so. We can comfortably guess that this has happened to many of the readers; no matter which 'book' or 'morality' we follow, there are almost always such cases of disillusionment. Experiences of this kind can cause some to question many of the generally desired values, such as working hard or behaving right. When we go through such situations, we may exclaim, "Life is unfair!"

    a. In reality, luck plays a role in all outcomes, and although, for a statistical average, good behaviour and hard work pay off, it might not be the case on any one individual level. Individuality and the average are very different things, and a large aspect of the Absurd arises from that.

    b. Tomorrow if a meteorite of large-enough size hits the Earth, a large part of our human civilisation, probably almost all, with all of its 'progress' and 'achievements' over thousands of years will be annihilated in a matter of days without anyone else in the Universe really caring.

    c. You can work hard, make sacrifices, or believe blindly in your country, community, or political party to wake up one day and find the latter bankrupt or ruined for reasons not of your own making (ask any regular tax-paying Greek), or what you have invested in or believed to be immune and a legacy to the following generations impaired forever.

    d. You can accumulate money diligently and methodically all of your life to have inflation wiping it out because of behaviours or circumstances not of your own.

252. Absurd events can manifest themselves in too-quick-of-a-way for us to even realise them.

253. The notion of Free Will by itself contains the Absurd. Whether we believe in Free Will unconditionally or in a more limited manner, the fact of having Free Will means that we are not free to not have it: a circular reference that corresponds to the Absurd. It is admittedly difficult to think of oneself without thinking that we have at least a partial free will. Yet, even the slightest indication of free will creates the absurd situation of not being free of not wanting that free will.

   a. The belief in Free Will goes with the notion that we are free to choose our life and how we want it to be. But how can that be the case if we are already parachuted into a certain life, with a certain body, in a certain environment, and with a certain attribute called 'freedom' not of our own making?

254. As we have seen before, Causality, one of the most widely used paradigms in Thought, whether one believes in it or not, also contains one of the strongest forms of the Absurd. It is probably one of the subjects on which the largest amount of philosophical breath has been lost. We find ourselves forced to break the cycle of Causality in order to release ourselves from it. And yet, it is one of the key paradigms of our daily life. Causality comes as naturally to us as the notion of Free Will. Some choose to break out from Causality through a 'leap of faith' into an initial cause outside it, others by questioning the entire paradigm of Causality. On the first side we have Kierkegaard, and on the other we have Hume[117].

255. More generally than Causality, our knowledge is limited, as we have also seen before. Not limited for a mechanical reason because of our computing or analysis capacity; not limited because of some discoveries we have not yet made; not limited because we always have to start with some dogmas and/or instinctive beliefs; but limited because even with all of that, we continue to have incompleteness in our knowledge as Gödel demonstrated. We can

---

[117] For honest disclosure, the writer happens to be of the second opinion and considers Causality as a form of cognitive shortcut that has its uses but cannot be applied universally.

acquire some knowledge when we need to and try hard enough, and yet for all the trying and needing, we do not seem to be able to reach the bottom of Knowledge. All answers to questions seem to come with new questions until ultimately reaching the Absurd. We seem to be able to enlarge the scope of our knowledge, but at a certain depth we seem to always hit an obstacle that we cannot breach through. We can chase away many of the clouds of questioning and uncertainty but to see the wall of the Absurd more clearly; we can push further away the limits of ignorance but cannot eradicate the Absurd entirely.

256. Quantum Physics probably presents us with some of the most beautiful examples of the Absurd in comparison with our general acquaintance with the world around us. A particle can be in different states at the same time till observed. Heisenberg's uncertainty principle is another example of the limitation and absurdity of our knowledge and cognition. It states that we can *never* know the position and velocity of any particle simultaneously beyond a certain level of accuracy. This principle may seem absurd in comparison with what we are accustomed to; but for all of its counter-intuitive aspect, Heisenberg's principle seems to be a building block of Nature and hence of us. In the quantum world, things can happen for no reason whatsoever, without a cause whatsoever. Something can spring out of nothing. Much of our intuition breaks down at the quantum level. And the ultimate irony is that in order to address the question of the origin of the Universe, we cannot but rely on this theory with its absurdist concepts.

257. Survival of the species and of our own individual genes as a key driver and purpose of Life is an absurdist, yet true, concept. We are told that Survival is the prime purpose of Life in its various forms. As we have seen in the previous chapter, there are three different ways of surviving: the physical survival, i.e. the survival of the body, the survival of a historical legacy in a way or another, and the survival through DNA transmission, which constitutes the basis of Evolution. Physical survival is only limited and temporary; the other two are rather impersonal and absurd.

a. Personal legacy corresponds to a contemporary view of someone's existence, which often does not correspond to the past reality of the person. For all the information we have about Julius Cesar, his legacy is rather a contemporary limited interpretation of the man he was. We can even adventure to say that it is an almost different person from what the real Julius Cesar likely was. The legacy of Julius Cesar is impersonal; it is only the combination of what we know of Julius Cesar, what Julius Cesar wanted us to think about him, and the place we conveniently attribute to Julius Cesar in our collective historical psyche. It is in this sense that we mean the legacy of Julius Cesar to correspond to a different man from what Julius Cesar really was. It not uncommon to continuously discover new evidence about historical characters that alter substantially a certain romanticised view we have about them. Moreover, what real benefit can the deceased Julius Cesar derive really from his legacy, even the most accurate one or the closest one to what he wished it to be? The greatest or worst of legacies will not result in any physical difference to the deceased, only to the surviving ones related to her/him.

b. DNA transmission is as impersonal as historical legacy. Transmitting certain DNA traits and having long-term repercussions out of it is a game only meaningful in large numbers and not individually. It is a statistical game, a play between a large number of transmissible traits and externalities. Whether a certain DNA trait represents an advantage and makes it through the dynamics of Evolution is rather impersonal to me. How will me, the individual once deceased, benefit from it in any way? Even in the short-term while having a child could bring great joy *while I am living*, this joy will not last beyond the moment of my death. And in a generation or two, all my transmitted DNA traits will become mixed up in the sea of other traits to become even more impersonal.

258. If physical survival is limited and temporary, while historical legacy and DNA transmission are impersonal, why is Survival then central to Life since its inception? What benefit does Life derive from Survival and from perpetuating itself? The Will to Survive is not without its element of the Absurd; the purpose of Life, even biologically, is not without its element of the Absurd. The purpose of Life seems personal and subjective, not definitive and objective.

259. If we attempt to define the Absurd more strictly, we can describe it as the manifestation of what we already called Singularities of Reason. Singularities of Reason are breakdown points in our rational processes, and what we mean by 'rational breakdown' here is rather very well defined.

   a. It does not consist of errors of Rationality that can ultimately be corrected; these could be referred to as biases or heuristics. It does not correspond either to empirical limitations which can be of three sorts:

       i. Too much information we are incapable of processing with the tools at our current disposal;

       ii. Incomplete information making the problem unsolvable at this stage; and

       iii. Impossibility of conducting the required empirical measurement to solve the problem[118].

   b. It is not the situation of trying to apply Rationality to a problem where clearly pure Rationality is not applicable—in other words, applying Rationality to the wrong scope. An example of this would be to try to use pure reason to determine whether a painting of Dali is greater than a painting of Picasso or vice versa.

---

118 For example, measuring the smallest possible quantum distance or time empirically, as measurement requires by definition an interactive matter, which, also by definition, occupies a rather larger space than the one being targeted for measurement.

c. Rational breakdowns are dead-ends of the rational processes despite an errorless conduct all along the rational process, an accurately defined scope, and the availability and capability of processing the required information. It is the point beyond which Rationality can go no more, no matter what we do.

  i. The incompleteness of any non-trivial axiomatic systems of certain strength (in the case of arithmetic) cannot be overcome as Gödel proved.

d. A rational breakdown resembles a mathematical singularity (such as 1 divided by 0, the Dirac delta function, or the limit of certain series[119]) or an endless circular reference that can never be broken.

260. Being exposed to the Absurd corresponds to the situation where one has been relying during her entire journey through the maze of life on a system of signs that has proven to be the most helpful and reliable of any systems ever tried, to eventually arrive to a complete dead-end where no more is possible. Anyone who has lived the Absurd must have experienced this puzzling feeling in a way or another.

261. The writer has evidently no answer to the Absurd. Naturally, if he had one, you would have heard about him for quite some time now. However, the mere recognition and continuous awareness of the Absurd leads in our opinion, and contrary to the general belief, to living life truly as it should be lived. The popular wisdom holds in many places that once we take out religious explanations and face the Absurd without a religious story behind to soothe it, we can become dangerously nihilistic and destructive, or worse amoral or bad. According to this view, losing the compass of Religion is commensurate with losing all discipline. The reality cannot be more far from it. We do not see atheists jumping off balconies, living melancholically all their life, or leading lives of

---

119 Although not all infinity corresponds necessarily to rational breakdowns as demonstrated by Cantor's theory of infinite sets.

criminality just because they dare to admit and talk about the Absurd without relying on religious panacea. One can admit the Absurd, be religious, and be happy; one can admit the Absurd, be atheist, and be happy. One who does not admit the Absurd, whether religious or not, is ultimately subject to disillusionments. Whether one changes her/his life following the admission of the Absurd is not the important question; it is rather realising the Absurd that allows for a better awareness in life and the way it should be, even if nothing else of our major life choices changes at first—this awareness does however ultimately affect our life even if in subtle manners.

262. Admitting the Absurd and not having an answer to it should not result in a resurgence of any sort of suicidal tendencies as some might want to think, either implicitly or explicitly. Inventing false stories in order to answer questions about the nature of our existence is in reality worse than admitting the Absurd. If anything, suicidal and disorienting tendencies are more favoured by believing certain fictitious stories to have them revoked later on.

    a. This is very similar to the problem of dogmatising Morality; having Morality later revoked because some underlying assumptions become evidently wrong, or a Morality not emanating from a conscious and enlightened free choice, results in more grave consequences to ethical integrity than acknowledging the Absurd[120]. Dogmatising is a way for some to stop the cycle of questions, especially when they are at the top of the social hierarchy. Dogmas are axioms, and anyone who knows Logic knows that axioms are necessary; however, the needed axioms are rather simple and do not resemble the detailed fictitious stories and theories sometimes taken as dogmas. A whole theory cannot be posited as a starting axiom based on personal predispositions.

---

120 This is what Nietzsche meant when he referred to traditional moralities and beliefs as being nihilistic.

263. Admitting the existence of the Absurd should not be seen as some sort of a victory of the irrational over the rational. It should not invite us to start favouring sentimental or irrational biases over Rationality in the name of the existence of the Absurd.

   a. This was tried before in History with disastrous consequences. It is the failures of rationality in the 17th and 18th centuries (although in ways that turned out later to be correctable, not of the absurdist type) that led down the road to excesses in romanticism, nationalism, fanaticism, and cult of the hero. Those who are predisposed to hate Rationality, more so for psychological reasons or out of political aspirations, are always on the lookout for any signs of difficulty in Rationality in order to jump on the wagon and attempt to bring down the whole edifice of Knowledge. The trouble is that they have yet to offer anything remotely as beneficial to the overall human progress as Rationality.

   b. There is naturally a place for the emotional and other non-rational side of human beings in the overall paradigm of Thought and Action, but it is not at the expense of or in total leadership over Rationality.

264. We are more ready today to admit and accept the Absurd than at any other point in our past. We are more equipped intellectually, psychologically, and with historical information of Thought and Action than at anytime in the past. Admittedly, it is rather very puzzling and difficult psychologically to make peace with the existence of the Absurd without a minimal level of intellectual and informational development.

   a. However, we do not infer in any way that great intellect is a sufficient condition for admitting the Absurd. This is what Kierkegaard had in mind when he talked about the Absurd being absent from the mind of some systematic thinkers (cf. quote at the beginning of the chapter).

265. The past is full of tricks and ways to mask the Absurd or go around it; much has been tried in order not to face it. The most common

The Absurd

defence against the Absurd has been totalitarian philosophies and systems—the know-it-all type of theories which all turned out to be blatantly wrong—as well as pure and simple voluntary individual or collective amnesia.

266. We human beings are genetically wired to want answers, to seek clarity, and to abhor uncertainty. From an evolutionary perspective, it makes perfect sense as the more we know about the environment around us, the less likely we are to fall in traps or walk into some other predator's territory.

   a. Curiosity, both intellectual and practical, asking questions and attempting hard to find answers to them, is a central driver of progress and a great weapon against blind and rigid dogmatism. History has been on the side of curiosity, and we have managed so far to find great answers to many questions, beyond some of our wildest dreams. We may have become in some sense spoiled by our capacity of eventually finding answers to some of the toughest questions that the idea of admitting that some questions we will never have answers to, no matter how hard we try, might seem ludicrous to some. The combination of being genetically predisposed to want to ask questions and find answers and the historical success of this practice undeniably creates a psychological barrier against any one of us facing the Absurd.

   b. In situations of greater anxiety and uncertainty, there is often a greater human need to ask questions, soothe bewilderments, and expect answers. It is very difficult to admit the Absurd in such situations, and it is no surprise that intellectual charlatans of all kind love to feast on such situations. The reality is that there are no answers in the face of the Absurd regardless of our wants and needs.

267. Not all encounters with the Absurd must necessarily be accompanied with psychological distress. The realisation of the Absurd can provide a much-needed long-term immunity in the

face of the vagaries of life, as well as the opportunity for building a much better identity. The first encounters with the Absurd, the awakenings from the slumber of the know-it-all ideal, are usually the most disorienting. But ultimately, we are indeed creatures of habit, and the habit of incorporating the Absurd into our daily cognition and action prevails.

    a. The discovery that Santa Claus does not exist is surely disorienting for many little children at first; does that justify perpetuating the lie? Or are the children better off and less naive on the longer term without believing in Santa Claus? The dynamics of discovering the Absurd are not so different.

268. Naturally, when we discover that Santa Claus does not exist, we are stronger on the long run and less subject to disillusionment. But we must also admit that we lose an element of happiness that always comes with the idea of Santa Claus. The consequent question becomes, "How can one achieve genuine happiness in the light of the existence of the Absurd?" Candidly, we can think of at least two ways:

    a. Naivety.

        Yes ignorance is sometimes bliss for human's internal psychology. We are all naive and ignorant at some level; it is usually a question of degrees. However, those who have not come to a proper realisation of the Absurd, those who may have touched upon it but not grasped it fully have a temporary chance to realise a sort of happiness that is ignorant of the Absurd.

        i. The kind of happiness which has greater naivety at its centre is however a precarious and shallow happiness; its stability is in danger of collapsing at any point. We can be naive, but we are also curious animals, and through this curiosity, we sometimes stumble on surprising things, of which naturally is the Absurd. The Absurd often manifests itself more clearly at some point

The Absurd

in anyone's life, and for the more naive, it risks jeopardising the old balance of happiness as long as the individual pays enough attention to it.

b. Conscious choice in full acknowledgment of the Absurd.

Once the door to the full realisation of the Absurd is open, it can rarely be shut or ignored. Those who deal with it by hiding it in the depth of their memory and pretending to forget about it are only realising a momentary escape. But once the door to the Absurd is open, we are not necessarily bound to either continuously contemplate it unhappily or commit an internal hypocrisy.

> i. Some invite us to derive happiness from the Absurd itself. Since we are not able to escape the Absurd once we discover it, we might as well take advantage of it. Albert Camus held this view. While the rationale is practical and may have great merits, the writer finds this approach to be slightly convoluted, and contrary to how we are programmed genetically. It is indeed difficult to oppose one's natural genes and pretend to have reached a deep internal happiness—there is an amount of evolutionary biology in us that we cannot constantly fight or think irrelevant.
>
> ii. The best solution we find is to freely choose to put one's happiness in certain subjective desires (such as family, love of growing things, or public service) while continuously acknowledging the permanence of the Absurd. Happiness becomes a *subjective free choice* and not the result of misconceptions and false beliefs. We shall see later on how choosing a morality also invites us to a very similar freedom of choice. It is only natural then that the balance of internal happiness is fortified when the subjective choice of the elements of

happiness coincides with the subjective choice of one's morality. The counterweight to this free choice is the continuous realisation of the Absurd without which such free choices become themselves naiveties.

269. As for the final word on the subject of the Absurd, Laughter remains in the writer's opinion the best defence of men against the Absurd. Laughter is not necessarily synonymous with genuine happiness, but in the capacity for laughter lies a great potential. Laughter does not stand for naive happiness either. Laughter is a denouement, a reaction of relief at the resolution of a conflict between intuition and reason, a reaction of relief at the passing of a certain danger, difficulty, or uncertainty without harming us[121]. And what is the realisation of the Absurd other than an answer to the conflict between an intuition towards knowing more and a reason that tells us that we are at a dead-end? Laughter is known for its soothing effects. It helps release the psychological tension that is bound to accumulate from the opposition of what we want and what is possible. Laughter has even therapeutic effects; it decreases stress levels and increases immunity and the general well-being by releasing the right 'feel-good' hormones. And of course most importantly, Laughter is a social tool and is greatly contagious.

---

[121] Even in Superiority Theory where Laughter is considered as a way of expressing superiority over the misfortunes of others, it can be interpreted as an evolutionary reaction of relief (though to be condemned morally) to the fact that the danger has passed and affected others rather than the person laughing.

Everything Changes (almost)

"Change alone is unchanging." Heraclitus

"Spiritual unhealthiness and misfortunes can generally be traced to excessive love of something which is subject to many variations." Spinoza

"I am weary of seeing the shore in each successive mirage, and I often ask myself whether the *terra firma* we are seeking does really exist, and whether we are not doomed to rove upon the seas for ever." Alexis de Tocqueville

"We must all obey the great law of change. It is the most powerful law of nature, and the means perhaps of its conservation." Edmund Burke

> The following two bullets will seem to antagonise each other, but that is on purpose. The reader has seen enough of this necessary conflict in this work so far to be really surprised.
> 270. For all practical purposes, in almost all that concerns and interests us, as human beings and our civilisation, everything changes and is bound to change. Nothing is final or certain. This does not only concern our life, but it also concerns our civilisation and species as a whole. It concerns all our matter, our living, and

Reflections on Fundamental Matters

non-living environment. Change is everywhere, whether we like it or not. Civilisations grow and decay; species grow and decay; cultural norms continuously change; relationships change[122]; climate changes[123]; stars and planetary systems form, grow, and decay; religions grow and decay; tastes and art change; businesses and companies grow and decay; knowledge changes; political boundaries change; languages change; demographics change; the Universe changes.

271. From a purely consistent and logical standpoint, if one affirms that everything changes then she is being self-contradictory. If 'Everything changes' is always true, then 'Everything changes' does not itself change, and therefore 'Everything changes' cannot apply to itself. So what are the exceptions? The answer is that they are mostly things that rather interest a thought person (e.g. a scientist or a philosopher) than a practical one. It is also *very* tricky to affirm what never changes, as one is setting himself up for big trouble and potential mockery sooner or later, as many things were assumed never to change till we acquired sufficient knowledge in the light of which such assumptions seemed utterly ridiculous. Using a similar logic to how we started here, what can be said is that some things *must* not change although the set of these is itself subject to change[124]. Here are some examples: mathematical and logical assertions and rules do not change, that is if they are proven correctly, such as '1+1=2'; tautologies and contradictions do not change[125]; the total quantity of Energy in the Universe does not change[126]; the continuous increase in Entropy in the Universe does not change.

---

122 Even if they do not crumble, they do change.

123 Not from one season to the other but more fundamentally, e.g. the Palaeogene Period vs. today.

124 From an instrumentalist point of view.

125 Such as 'A=A' is true and 'A≠A' is false.

126 Here we might, just might, be setting ourselves up for some potential trouble in the future.

272. But what is really Change? And how can we best describe it? Change is a *process or phenomenon* of which we have a clearer intuition than what we are usually capable of describing.

   a. Change is typically described as the process of becoming different, of an entity N being in one state at one point in time T0, and in a different state at another point in time T1. This is indeed seemingly quite simple to understand; the trouble is that there are many hidden questions underlying such a definition.

      i. How can we define the entity N, whatever N is? If everything changes indeed, then how are we to define N? What is N really in an ever-changing Universe? This difficulty made some assume that nothing actually changes. Luckily, Leibniz[127] and Hume found an answer to this question. There is no substance, essence, or 'thing-in-itself' that defines N really; N is but a linguistic definition associated with certain characteristics generally exhibited by what we are pointing towards, *despite the process of Change.*

      ii. How can we really talk about time and about points T0 and T1 without the concept of Change itself? Isn't talking about "T0 and then T1" a process of Change by itself? Doesn't Time *by definition* change?

   We can therefore see that this seemingly simple definition of Change uses in itself at least two notions that circularly refer back to what is being defined. Change is indeed so central and fundamental that a satisfactory definition of it is extremely difficult; it is more of a starting point or an intuition than a logical development of cognition.

273. Nevertheless, we shall attempt a definition of Change that intellectually ties it to what we have previously explained about

---

127 Gottfried Wilhelm von Leibniz, German philosopher and mathematician.

the nature of things[128]. According to Special Relativity, Time is not an absolute; what is absolute is rather the observability of events. Regardless of the reference point or the speed at which one is observing, the events are themselves observed, in the same sequence, and that does not seem to change. The speed or nature of the sequence of such events can itself change; this speed or nature of the sequence is nothing else but Time itself. Time is not absolute, and Time has been demonstrated to change; it slows down for an observer travelling at a fast enough speed, and it is very different for two observers at different velocities. Now, we can say from what we have previously seen:

    a. What is this observability of events other than a particular phenomenon of interaction? Observation is nothing else than the result of a photon emitted or projected being captured by the observer[129].

    b. What is this sequence of events, which we observe all through interaction, other than Change itself?

    c. And what is this speed or nature of the sequence other than Time?

274. **Change could be described as the psychological output we 'feel'[130] when we observe a sequence of events.** If All Being is the pair *events-interactions*, then it follows from the above that we perceive All Being psychologically as Change as long as we look at things through the definition of events and interactions. In this resides the natural basis to all philosophies centred on Change, from Heraclitus onwards.

275. Many important concepts of our cognition and understanding are only a particular facet of Change:

    a. Time: We understand Time through Change. How could we really conceive the notion of Time without Change

---

128 Second and third chapters in particular.

129 In natural observation, it would be captured by our naked eye.

130 And hence, have an intuition of.

and the notion of Change without Time? In Past, Present, and Future there is nothing but an accounting of Change, of sequences of events. Time and Change are highly interlinked, and we could conceive both as concepts of internal psychological reactions to one and the same phenomenon, that is the observation of sequences of events. For the nature of the sequences of events we observe, we attribute the word Time, whereas for the overall phenomenon of sequences of events we attribute the word Change.

b. Life: We understand our Life and that of all other living beings through Change. The Human Condition is tied to Change. We are born, we grow, we change, and ultimately we die. We see Change in us and around us, physically, psychologically, and intellectually. When we live, we continuously change, and there is nothing we can do to stop it. When we stop changing cognitively as a living being, we simply stop living. Life seen through this angle is nothing more than a particular type of change patterns with their certain distinct characteristics, such as reproducing, eating, and growing. Could there be a form of Life that does not change? Intellectually, that is easy to imagine; in reality however, it corresponds to a belief in the Eternal (more on that few points below).

c. Evolution: What is Evolution but Change in the fundamental building blocks of Life? Life is not a defined set of change patterns of living forms; there are also changes that occur on these particular change patterns themselves, and this is what we call Evolution. With Evolution, there are several ways of reproducing, growing, and eating. The way a mono-cell organism reproduces, grows, and eats is different from that of a tree, which is different from that of a mammal. Evolution is an on-going process of Change to the building blocks of Life driven by Life from within, but also catalysed by changes from outside Life, from the non-living environment. The goal of such an on-going process is greater resilience and optimisation of Life.

d. Entropy: Entropy in Physics is a measurement of disorder and chaos of a particular system of particles. The Second Law of Thermodynamics states that the change in Entropy of an isolated system is always positive. In other words, Entropy always increases or stays constant for an isolated system. This is the one and rare instance in Physics where a law of Physics points in only one direction of Time rather than being time-agnostic. The Entropy of an isolated system *cannot* decrease as Time progresses. Variation in Entropy is the formalisation of Change in Physics. In Physics, everything that exists is in constant change, be it particles or fields[131]. Matter more generally seems to undergo an on-going process of Change towards more disorder, which counter-intuitively results in more uniformity of the Universe. We invite the reader to think about what happens when we open the door between a warm room and a cooler one; ultimately, the difference in temperature between the two rooms disappears, and they become more homogenous—this is an increase in Entropy at play.

e. The theory of Perpetual Flux: ancient Greeks, for the most part, had an admiration for the static and liked to perceive everything through the lens of the unchangeable. Greeks talked about the unchanging essence of things and about eternal gods in the Olympus; they admired contemplation and perfect forms. There was however one major exception (at least): Heraclitus, the father of the theory of Perpetual Flux. Heraclitus conceived everything as in a constant state of change, like a river where new

---

131 Of course, the laws of Physics themselves are not assumed to change by mainstream Physics, but the laws of Physics are not in the scope of Physics itself; they are rather in the scope of the Philosophy of Science. Physics concerns itself with Matter, whereas the Philosophy of Science concerns itself, among others, with the laws of Physics and their permanence.

water constantly flows. Nothing is static, nothing is ever the same again, and the only thing that is not changing is Change itself. Human affairs are also in constant change, and strife and war are integral parts of human affairs through which things come to pass. Despite some of its limitations, Heraclitus' theory was radically different for his time and served as first historical basis for any subsequent philosophical theory where Change plays a central role. The idea of everything being a constant flux of events, never the same, always new, finds its roots back in Heraclitus and his theory of Perpetual Flux.

f. *Anicca*: Impermanence is the first of the three marks of existence in Buddhism. *Anicca* is a form of Change. For Buddhism, our common existence is about continuous change. Change is what is in the middle between the idea of the Eternal, the existing and never-changing, and Nothingness, the non-existing and never-changing. Hence, we find ourselves, through this Buddhist concept, defining Change differently, by stating what it is not, although this again will not be without its dose of circularity. The concept of the Eternal is derived in opposition to the concept of Change, and the intuitive concept we have of Life[132].

g. Bergson's *Elan Vital*[133]: the combination of Evolution, Entropy, Heraclitus, and Posidonius find themselves in Bergson's notion of *Elan Vital* or Vital Impulse. Bergson is known for his metaphors, strong intuition, and visual representations. He conceived existing things in two kinds: inert and living. The living has its special characteristics including a continuous impulse towards Life cutting

---

132 The second mark ('*Dukkha*') is also, but only partially, due to a continuous state of inner dissatisfaction from trying to cling to fixed things in an ever-changing world. *Dukkha* is the expression of our psychological discomfort with *Anicca*. Spinoza's quote at the beginning of this chapter is also of the same idea.

133 Vital impulse.

through the inert around, an impulse that drives Life to continuously move forward, self-organise, and grow in more complex and creative manners. Life *flows* through the inert in a continuous manner and cannot be looked at as just a juxtaposition of static states one next to the other; Life continuously changes and evolves. Whether Bergson's descriptions are taken literally or metaphorically, or whether they can be proven scientifically or not, is a subject of debate and varies from one subject matter to the other. However, we can nevertheless learn a lot from the metaphors of the *Elan Vital* and the visual intuitive approach of Bergson. It is well-known today that many social and economic affairs are self-organising[134], and many fields of study of human affairs find fascinating how a society organises itself organically, be it in trade, traffic, or other. We continue to be amazed how Life develops in some of the most hostile places on Earth, how it organises itself organically in efficient manners, and how it can sometimes adapt to changes in faster ways than we initially envisage. How can we not see in this some of what Bergson had in mind?

    i. The Vital Impulse is an enriching notion as the Perpetual Flux of Heraclitus, and we are yet to understand where it strictly applies. One thing is sure—Bergson's distinction between the Inert and the Living as two different substances is to be rejected. However, the Vital Impulse itself is present in a certain way, in both what we consider Living and Inert. The Vital Impulse is about Change, a change of a certain type—adaptation. Life has in it an intrinsic characteristic of being able to change, and Bergson is a key figure in highlighting that.

276. Does Change really exist independently from us? Or is it rather

---

134 Complexity theories.

an intuition or a psychological feeling we develop from observing what we consider to be sequences of events? These two questions are very difficult to answer. The only way we could think of Change as existing only in us as a consequence of our observation, and not independently from us, is through conceiving all reality or the entire Universe as One, as a single total Event; all seeming variations, changes, interactions, and events within this One would then correspond to a subjective interpretation of our observing mind, and not an objective reality by itself. How is it better to consider the whole of the Universe as One or as an infinite number of separate events is far from clear to us.

277. Ultimately, what is important to note is that whether Change is inherent to our observation of the world, or rather a more objective characteristic of Existence, does not alter the fact that Change is central to our cognition. We do not seem to be able to do without the concept of Change, the same way we do not seem to be able to do without Space and Time when thinking, feeling, or having an intuition.

"[...] un absolu ne saurait être donné que dans une intuition, tandis que tout le reste relève de l'analyse."[135] Henri Bergson

278. Some sceptics might argue that in practical life[136] not everything changes. Some things such as Love, Belief, or Truth never change. Others might say that although human affairs seem to always vary and evolve, they always tend to repeat themselves somehow. There are always good people and bad people; corrupt people and righteous people; greedy people and generous people. No matter when and where we live, these human characteristics are always there. The saying goes, "History repeats itself."

279. Such objections bring us to the second important element of Change to address: its timeframe. The timeframe of Change is

---

135 An absolute can only reveal itself through an intuition, while all the rest has to do with analysis. (John H.T. Francis translation)

136 Not only in the world of Thought where we have already given examples.

central. Some things may appear constant at some level while they are in reality changing at a different, slower timescale. We humans are prone to what is called 'availability bias', i.e. we like to draw conclusions from what we commonly observe, even if it is but a very limited view of Reality. It is not because we do not perceive the change of something at the scale of our lifetime or our generation that Change does not take place. Some of the most instructive fields to study concern long spans of History, beyond Man and his relatively short three thousand years of development[137]; that usually helps us put things into perspective.

280. The timeframe of Change can be very different for different subject matters; it can go from the ultra-short to the ultra-long. Entire lifespans, cycles, and periods of change can come to be in a matter of fractions of seconds, while others are quantified in terms of billions of years. We choose to illustrate here with some select examples, drawing on a correlation between speed of Change and lifecycles:

   a. At the shorter end of the timeframe of Change, we find the quantum world with its incessantly moving particles and waves, with their infinite configurations, speeds, and positions. The pace of Change at the quantum level is so quick that millions of configurations can be achieved in a split of a second. It is indeed worth mentioning that the initial inflation of the Universe (i.e. several of the first phases of what is commonly called the Big Bang) took only a fraction of a second, and we are talking here about the entire Universe!

   b. Very short but less dramatic, and more imaginable to the common sense than the quantum world, is the lifecycle of microorganisms and cells. Bacteria and cells have varying lifespans and reproduction cycles; some can be on the very short side. The changes a bacterium or a cell can go through in a matter of minutes or hours can be

---

137 The reader can replace three thousand by five, seven, or two hundred thousand as she wishes.

dramatic. Some bacterial colonies can double in size in fifteen minutes; some bacteria live for twenty minutes or a couple of hours only before dying. This is the timeframe of some of the micro-living species, although not all microorganisms have short lifespans; some cells such as bone cells can live for thirty years.

c. We can then consider the lifespan of insects, smaller animals, and small flora. Mayflies are famous for having a lifespan of maximum a day. Some ants live for a few weeks only, whereas *Arabidopsis Thaliana* (a flowering plant) has a lifecycle of around six weeks, and so is the case of many ephemeral, seasonal flowers and plants.

d. Larger animals, including us humans, as well as medium-sized flora, tend to have a longer lifespan, and hence, a slower process of biological (as well as generational) change. Mammals can have a lifespan of 4-10 years or as long as 60-120 years in the case of humans. Some tortoise species, especially giant tortoises, can live more than 200 years with an average lifespan of around 150 years.

e. Human affairs (social, political, economical, and lately epistemological) span multiple generations of humans and therefore usually exhibit timeframes of Change that correspond to multiples of human lifespans. The timeframes are however very different depending on which category of human affairs we choose to consider, but also on the stage of development societies find themselves in—we will discuss later the notion of change in the timeframe of Change itself.

  i. The transition from hunter-gatherer societies to agricultural-based societies took thousands of years, and so did the transition from Agriculture to Industry and Services, albeit at a faster rate than the former.

  ii. Women emancipation took thousands of years

and is still an on-going process, whereas fashion norms[138] can dramatically change in a matter of some generations.

    iii. Medium and large-sized organisations, companies, and political parties are created, grow, and eventually die, get merged, or metamorphose; the cycle can be as short as a few years or as long as hundreds of years, but the process of Change is there. So is the case of any associated brands: the most famous brands 150 years ago were not American, and what will the most famous brands 150 years from now look like is anybody's guess.

f. The biology of some large-size flora is on average slower than that of human affairs, and hence, we observe Change more slowly on larger trees. Redwoods and Cedars are notorious for their long lifespans. There are cases of old trees found to have survived almost five thousand years[139]. What happens at the scale of Redwoods is very different from that of humans, except when humans themselves step over the environment of such long-life trees and alter it.

g. Climatology, Geology, and Species Evolution have timeframes in the range of millions of years. Changes to our global weather patterns and to the movement of the land we live on happen only extremely slowly. Continents drift only by some millimetres a year, and species can take millions of years to evolve. Dry land on Earth continues to evolve and change; mountains have their growth, stagnation, and death cycles. Volcanoes come and go in the span of millions of years. Climate patterns also evolve in cycles of millions of years; there are also cycles within

---

138 Such as men wearing skirts vs. women doing so.

139 Others however, especially fruit trees, have a shorter lifespan, crudely between ten and fifty years.

the cycles[140]. For example, climate on Earth has been of a similar pattern of behaviour for the last 2.6 million years[141] with the potential exception of the latest human-induced climate change.

    h. Slower than the timeframe of the geology or the climate of our planet is that of the solar system we live in, as well as the stars and planets we observe in the sky. The timeframe at this level is quantified in the billions of years. Yes the sun will rise again tomorrow, but only for some other five billion years–too long but not absolute and unchanging. When we observe something fixed in the sky for years, it never means that it is not moving, but, rather, that it is moving at a relatively low speed accentuated by the enormous distance between us and the object we are observing. Galaxies take billions of years to form and grow, and in them grow stars, planetary systems, and the planets themselves. All the significant constituents of the Universe (e.g. galaxies, black holes) have their processes of Change, and they operate in the billions of years.

    i. And finally, globally, the Universe itself has its own timeframe of Change. It is around fourteen billion years old, and its life may come to an end one day[142].

281. The main factor of importance is not whether Change happens or not, but what is the *speed* at which a particular change is realised.

282. The timeframe of Change itself can change; in other words, a particular process of Change can accelerate and decelerate through not much else than Change itself. Change is the ultimate thing responsible for the variation in conditions, and through this variation, the speed of the Change itself can be circularly impacted. Picture a wind tunnel in the shape of hollow loudspeaker with one

---

140 We are not referring here to seasonal changes but cyclical changes that can be compared year-over-year.

141 The Quaternary Period.

142 In the sense that Space-Time might implode.

side wider than the other; fluid is blowing from the wider side into the tunnel and coming out from the narrower side.

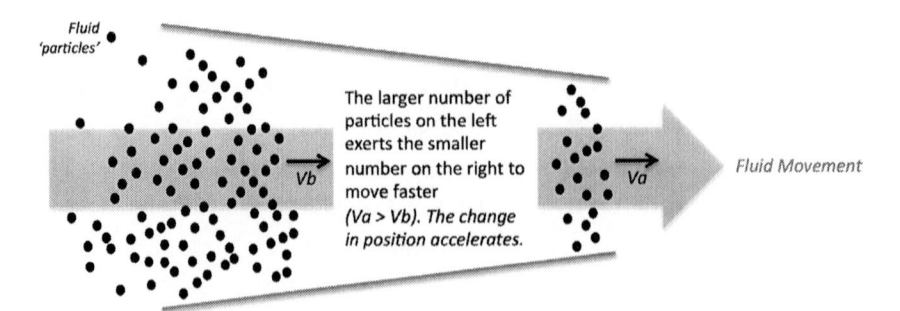

Figure 3. Accelerated change through a fluid tunnel

If we were capable of observing the average movement of fluid particles through this tunnel, we would see that the speed at which the particles are changing positions accelerates the more the particles make their way through the tunnel. The phenomenon is relatively easy to understand: the larger number of particles in the larger side of the wind tunnel exerts more pressure on the particles in the narrower section and forces them to move quicker in order to make way for the particles in the larger section to move too[143]. We have all experienced being in a large crowd where everybody is trying to exit orderly from one door; the closer we are to the exit, the more fluid the movement of people becomes[144]. The speed of Change in the tunnel varies, and that is due to the combination of Change itself, which moves the particles from the larger section to the narrower one, and the shape of the wind tunnel.

283. We can therefore see how seemingly stable rates of Change can vary with varying conditions that are, partially or totally, due to Change exerting its consequences.

---

143 Scientifically, there are other criteria that may also come into play, such as the incompressibility of the fluid or no addition of energy; however, in the simplest case, the velocity of fluid is indeed inversely proportional to the diameter of the section the fluid is at.

144 Up to a certain level of 'crowdedness' after which it actually becomes more difficult to exit.

a. Weather behaviour presents interesting illustrations of how Change can ultimately effect a bigger or smaller Change through simply being: normal wind and sea movements can turn into monstrous tornados or hurricanes by no other fact than Change operating and exerting its consequences.

b. Financial bubbles can accelerate as they gather more momentum, that is until they peak and then burst.

284. The acceleration and deceleration of the speed of Change has a fundamental importance. While it is very difficult to dissociate Change from Time, as one requires the other, the variation in the speed of Change itself offers opportunities to see the two as different despite their association. The speed of Change accelerating or decelerating means that a particular change pattern[145] varying its behaviour in Time, *when Time itself is not changing*. Of course, Time itself can also change as both Special and General Relativity describe–and hence, we find ourselves falling again into the ultimate irony of circularity, here between Time and Change.

285. Before going further, we would like to elaborate on an important historical notion we have alluded to before, but that might seem discredited by the above. Given its importance, it should be restored and given its right place in the judgment-making sphere. When one is interested in History, be it that of individual men (biographies), politics and nations, science, economics, corporations, or institutions generally, one cannot fail to notice similarities in human behaviour and general human-related dynamics. Humans continue to come in all forms; clothes change, technologies change, and some social norms may change, but the classical tragedies continue to unfold much in the same way across ages and geographies. Humans seem to do the same mistakes and pay similar prices. They learn sometimes from their mistakes or that of others, but also sometimes forget, become complacent, and run into the same traps.

---

145 E.g. a particle movement, cell aging, tectonic plate movements, or a star nuclear burning.

a. When someone calls his nation or all the members of his community constantly 'good' or 'doing the right thing', we suggest being highly suspicious.

286. The saying goes, "Nothing is new under the sun." Dynamics repeat themselves, they may get reshuffled, but similarities are often there. So how do we reconcile this important historical observation with the statement "Everything changes"? The answer is two-fold:

   a. Time-frame: as we have detailed, our human time-frame is too short for many things we observe; thousands of years is too short in comparison with the history of the Universe. We shall not say more on that.

   b. We mentioned at the beginning of the chapter two seemingly contradictory statements. We said everything changes *(almost)*. What does not typically change as we have said is usually the underlying material and logical rules. A human by definition is a complex organism with certain properties, and as long as a human is as such, these properties (biology, instincts, cognitive model and its biases, feelings, psychology, and the rest) will result in similar mathematical dynamics, the same way very different interactive systems exhibit the same mathematics (cf. Interaction and Reflexivity). As long as a human is, these properties are, and a large part of the historical dynamics is and will continue to be. What *is not* is that the human is not always likely to be exactly the same, and some of his/her characteristics are subject to very slow change.

      i. The manifestation of Change is limited by the mathematical reality of what it is we are observing. In the case of repetitions, having continuously different permutations of some similar underlying behaviour continues to be Change, even if the permutations are likely to repeat themselves from time to time.

287. Change is a central concept of Existence; it exerts itself at very different speeds depending on the reference point and the subject matter, and it is also circularly subject to changing speeds as a consequence of exerting itself. **What we need to anchor in our mind is that Change, Speed of Change, and Change in the Speed of Change are three characteristics of Reality.**

288. Depending on personal predispositions and preferences, we either like Change and equate it with Progress or we abhor it and equate it with Destruction. In the political sphere, crudely, Liberals tend to hold the first view, whereas Conservatives revolve around the second. Indeed everything changes, but Change itself is neither good nor bad.

    a. In Change, there is building and there is destruction, there is optimisation of purpose but also destructive paradigm shifts.

    b. We hate Change, but it also excites us—the alternative of no Change can be comforting and reassuring, but it is bound to become frustrating and boring. Change is a source of happiness but also of sadness and worry.

289. For the lovers of Change, we say beware the tendency to want to change for the sake of Change, or worse out of boredom of a not fast-enough Change. It is usually a terrible idea to force a change within an inadequate timeframe for it. Those who are frustrated with a current situation or the current view they have of themselves and their identity usually tend to favour a change that allows for a breakaway; that is natural. However, what is unhealthy is to push for a change without a clear or well-examined view of where one is heading, especially when one is dragging many others with him/her in the process.

290. For the lovers of constancy and stability, we can say that permanent infinite stability is an illusion, and Change happens in a way or another. The choice we make is to either be part of that change and influence it or be marginalised by it. Those who define themselves or their identity through a particular role they play would naturally

tend to object to any change that undermines that role, and this is only a natural emotional behaviour. For some, Change can come to represent a loss of identity that is very difficult to accept; the error lies in the false expectation that our identity and our social, political, or economic role is fixed and not bound to change.

291. Any systems of Thought and rules oriented towards Action, be it political, ethical, or financial that do not have at their core a clear and pragmatic way of dealing with unforeseen change are bound to become obsolete and ineffective. Change will happen whether the system takes it into account or not. Some in governance attempt to fight and push away Change; often they may temporarily seem to be capable of fending off Change only to eventually be overwhelmed by it. It seems that a system either factors in Change effectively on a regular basis or opposes it blindly with eventually more dramatic and destructive consequences to everybody.

292. The above is not merely a theoretical dissertation. It has important implications, many of which are very practical in nature. We often take decisions ignoring Change to be disillusioned later on:

    a. We trust that some institutions will never go bankrupt, no matter what happens in the future; we put our life's savings in them, we believe in these 'AAA's (to use a financial jargon), and we feel good sleeping at night. And here we are not talking about wrongly calculated or rated 'AAA' securities such as a collection of subprime debt but rather the most accurately rated 'AAA's, the best one could think of. Consider the greatest historic institutions, the 'ever-lasting' empires in History (the Roman Empire, the British Empire where the sun never sets with all of its rich colonies), weren't they 'AAA's at their time? Consider then their subsequent history; Britain's financial status was in complete disarray in the 1970s. "Real estate will always go up" was the motto of most Anglo-Saxon countries before 2007. Similarly, most French and Japanese consider that their state will always be there and capable of providing and intervening when the going gets tough.

b. Japan's 2011 earthquake and tsunami that resulted in the Fukushima disaster is a recent illustration of what is called 'tail risk'[146] manifesting itself in ways we often fail to imagine. And this happened to the Japanese, one of the best current cultures in terms of forethought and organisation. It is not that Japan was not ready; Japan was ready, but the size of the disaster was so large that all of its defences broke, and a series of very low probability scenarios took place one after the other resulting in the loss of control of a portion of the nuclear power plant. If the magnitude of the earthquake or the nature of the tsunami were marginally worse, it is likely that some more dramatic irreversible consequences could have ensued. If the same thing happens today over the shores of Seattle or California (which are also on a well-known fault line), they would not stand a chance in comparison with the Japanese coast. And yet, very large populations live, multiply, and invest very near fault lines today all over the globe.

c. Who would have thought in Antiquity that horses would become irrelevant one day when it comes to transportation? Or that papyrus would not be needed anymore because we will eventually all carry electronic tablets? Or that women would wear what men used to wear in the past and vice versa?

293. **A 'Penny wise, pound foolish' story.** Here is the story of a decent woman. Mrs G. is a middle-class hard-working disciplined woman. She leads her life in the exemplary fashion of what we consider the best of the middle class. She works hard and well, never absents herself from work, and takes only what she is allowed as vacation time. She pays her taxes and bills on time and never abuses the system. She earns a decent salary, spends a portion of it, and saves the rest. Every month Mrs G. puts aside part of her income in one of the country's most reputed pension funds which

---

146 I.e. very high impact and very low probability negative risk.

in turn invests it in some of the most reputed companies in the country. Mrs G. is frugal, attentive to what she spends, and she meets very specific goals in terms of monthly saving. She only shops where she can save, and she sometimes skips a night-out or two in order to meet her goals. The trouble is that Mrs G. does not know that her savings are invested in Citigroup and Bank of America pre-2007. Over the span of a year, Mrs G. sees most of her life savings almost evaporate from no fault of her own. Mrs G. has been in the middle of an unexpected change that no one has described to her before. She has been saving pennies all of her life, to find her pounds being swept away in one year. This is a tragic story of Change, this is the Absurd…

294. The reality of our affairs is that nothing is certain, and everything is bound to change. Some of what we know will change steadily, while the other will change in very abrupt and unexpected manners. Carefulness and preparation will definitely help protect against some of the negative change, but no amount of preparation can render our living riskless, no matter what politicians like to claim. This poses a genuine difficulty in terms of proper, balanced policy-making and risk management in light of uncertainty and the changing nature of things. Most people in positions of power know it; yet very few admit it openly. Admitting it is equated with weakness, and uncertainty is to be chased away at all cost, even if it requires lying.

295. Human relationships change, and it can be overwhelming. Relationships at work continue to change; neighbourly relationships have their ups and downs; and friendships get created and disappear. Most of our friends from school or college will not continue to be our friends; we lose touch with most of our colleagues from previous jobs or our neighbours from a previous domicile. Most of us do not feel good about such relationships changing, especially when relationships of trust, friendship, or love change for the worse. But many still assume that most human relationships will stay the way they are indefinitely. In fact, we adventure to say that many suicidal tendencies are often largely driven by the change of relationships in one's life and its corresponding disillusionments.

Everything Changes (almost)

We all exhibit a feeling of loneliness or nakedness without the comfort of enduring relationships.

    a. Parental relationships are very important because they particularly are of the most enduring kind. Our parents will love us regardless of what happens, and there is something greatly comforting about that. Most of us retrieve a feeling of security when thinking about home, about our parents, especially after having been exposed to a series of changes and disturbances. This can be extended from parents to the broader family, and somehow a small community, although with distance the certainty of the non-parental relationships enduring usually decreases.

    b. Although it can endure, Romantic Love clearly changes with time as several psychological studies show. The level of passion in the beginning of a love relationship is normally the highest, while the level of trust and intimacy are lower. The evolution of a successful and enduring romantic relationship brings, on average, passion to a lower level and trust and intimacy to a higher one with time; Love changes even if it remains.

296. We find comfort in what we consider unchanging (which in reality changes at a very low speed), a testimony to the burden Change can bring to our psyche.

    a. Humans are known for creating their own routines and deriving comfort from repetitiveness in opposition to the change all around us.

    b. Many humans like animals for companionship, but also for the loyalty and consistency of the relationship they experience with a pet. Some feel that in pets loyalty is more constant and less subject to change than in humans; this may be one of the key reasons why some prefer Nature to the human world.

    c. Some people even love cooking or baking because of the certainty it provides; some like to go to the same restaurant for similar reasons. Many, not only humans but also animals more generally, do find psychological comfort in their routine and its predictable consequences.

Of course, as the reader knows by now, all such examples are subject to certain conditions and timeframes, and they do not really constitute absolute certainties or phenomena that do not absolutely change.

297. Social and political relationships change. Enemies can become friends and friends enemies. Germans and French moved from being the greatest foes in the 19th and first half of the 20th century to becoming great allies. Britain and France buried the hatchet of a long tradition of warring with the *Entente Cordiale*. Jews found refuge with the Muslims when persecuted by the European Christians during the Middle Ages and the Renaissance[147]; in reality, Muslims have been historically more kind and respectful of the Jews than Christians. This may seem impossible in comparison with the current rhetoric coming from the Middle East... Vietnam looks at the USA today as a possible protector against Chinese territorial hegemony; who would have thought that in the 1960s?

Change is a key characteristic of Reality, living and inert. From it we turn to other characteristics of the living, to the amazing phenomenon of Life in general.

---

147 For example following the recapture of south of Spain by the Christians.

On the Characteristics of Life

"[...] the main intention of nature, which willeth the increase of mankind, and the continuation of the species in the highest perfection [...]" Locke

"No virtue can be conceived as prior to this endeavour to preserve one's own being." Spinoza

We will concern ourselves in this chapter with Life and attempt to say something meaningful, although incomplete, about it. Life is the general phenomenon of existence of living beings; it is the general phenomenon of beings that we say about them to be 'living' as opposed to 'inert' or 'not living', that is in the past, present, and future, on this Earth and potentially beyond. This last sentence is a description of what is generally referred to as Life and is not a definition (as it would be circular in this case).

The characteristics of Life in this chapter do not only concern mechanical and biological common characteristics of the living beings; they also include metaphysical and ethical characteristics of that particular phenomenon of Existence. We will therefore not only ask what characterises Life from a biological and physical point of view but also enlarge the scope to other questions.

298. Here are some of the questions we can ask about this curious phenomenon of Life:

Reflections on Fundamental Matters

a. How can we most accurately define Life (essentially as opposed to non-Life)? What is Life really?

b. What are the origins of Life? A question already addressed in the chapter on History[148], and we shall not go back to here.

c. Does Life have a purpose? Why is it there, and what is it heading towards?

d. What philosophical and ethical adjectives and characteristics can we attribute to Life? Is Life Good or Bad? Beautiful or Ugly? Clean or Disgusting?

What Is Life Really?

299. How can we define Life to include everything from bacteria to fungus to planktons to flora to animals and humans? What should we look for in a being in order to be able to label it as living or not living? And is the defining boundary between the living and non-living clear and final, not subject to changes and grey areas[149]?

300. Indeed, the definition of Life itself has evolved with our knowledge as much as everything else. As far back as we can go, it is likely that Life has always included in its definition us, animals, and vegetation; however, the perimeter of Life has been subject to variation with the evolution of our knowledge. With time, Life has come to include microscopic organisms, such as bacteria, unicellular life, planktons, and fungi. The invisible world to our naked eye turned out to contain the crushing majority of Life. We discovered beings that we came to consider as part of Life in volcanoes, in the deepest oceans, and in some of the most desolated places on our planet. We even had to face the reality that what we perceive to be our individual is actually not fully human; that we, animals, and plants actually serve as habitats to

---

148 Putting Things in Context.

149 Whether viruses are a form of Life or not is an example of the difficulties at the boundary of the definition of Life.

many forms of Life; and that actually human cells, for example, are a *small minority* of the cells we actually carry.

301. The question of how best to define Life became with our growing knowledge and technology more important and more difficult to define. Confusion ensued with medical progress: Is a foetus part of Life or not yet? At which stage should it be considered part of Life? Is a patient who can only be 'kept alive' through outside machines and pumps still living or not? How about cloning? Is it a new form of reproduction of Life introduced by humans or is it an ethical abomination? These are the sorts of difficult questions about Life that provoke in us many emotions.

302. In Science, there is still no full agreement today on the necessary and sufficient list of characteristics of Life. There are key attributes of Life all scientists agree on, but the key difficulty remains in defining satisfactorily and in a final manner the key denominators of Life.

303. From a physical and biological perspective, we choose to discuss the following two key attributes of Life—we note that they are not final and are not necessarily the only ones that scientists can consider when characterising Life.

    a. **Life is a self-organising phenomenon.**

        i. Life is a phenomenon of Existence that organises itself by itself. It is what can be called in Physics a negative entropy generating system. As we have previously discussed, the entropy in the Universe as a whole is bound to continuously increase; the Universe is bound to become less orderly with time and more homogeneous. Life precisely goes against that; Life is about organisation, about boundaries between what is considered living and non-living. Life organises matter along this fault line of the living and the non-living. A cell has a boundary, and what is in it is considered to be part of Life, and what is not in it is not part of Life. Moreover,

Life organises itself by itself; it does not need continuous outside intervention to organise itself, to grow, to reproduce, and to spread. A cell will divide itself by itself.

ii. Naturally, Life requires energy to continuously organise itself. Hence, Life uses energy from outside it[150] to order and organise itself. This is what is called in Biology a metabolism. Life consumes energy from outside to generate negative entropy and create an organisation in a universe where the general trend should be towards homogeneity and disorder.

iii. Units of Life (cells) come together in an organised manner to form more complex forms of Life. Cells interact with each other not randomly but rather with a certain purpose (which is self-perpetuation that we will come to). From this organisation, many varying forms of Life can take existence, and changes to the organisation of life units are what we call 'adaptation'. Life adapts and changes its organisation by itself in order to better cope with changing conditions. This is what we commonly call 'Evolution', and that is what Bergson probably meant when he described the living as cutting its way through the non-living.

iv. Not all self-organising phenomena are living ones, but self-organisation is an essential trait of Life. Many dynamic systems are self-organising; financial markets are self-organising; trade routes are self-organising and adapt to change in trade conditions; urban development is self-organising; and planets are self-organising. Complexity

---

150 We absorb nutrients of all sorts from our environment such as food, air/oxygen, and sunrays.

Theory interests itself with such multi-agent self-organising and adapting systems.

b. **Life is a self-perpetuating phenomenon.**

Life primarily concerns itself with self-perpetuating, directly or indirectly. It perpetuates itself as a global phenomenon, but equally each individual class of forms of Life, which we call species, does so by itself.

   i. Life looks to continuously grow and expand; the only limitations to its growth are outside adverse effects or other competing forms of Life at the individual species levels.

   ii. Life reproduces continuously as a way of perpetuating itself.

   iii. As we have previously mentioned in self-organisation, Life adapts to the outside world in order to enhance its long-term chances of perpetuation.

   iv. Life consumes energy from the outside in order to persevere and perpetuate.

   v. Life interacts with the outside world on continuous basis and in so many different ways in order to persevere and perpetuate.

   vi. The search for a human legacy is a higher form of self-perpetuation.

   vii. Different forms of Life have engineered varying ways of promoting self-perpetuation; from electrical, mechanical, and chemical signalling to many ways of reproducing and duplicating, Life has devised a large arsenal of methods for self-perpetuation.

304. A living being ceases to be living when it stops to self-organise and self-perpetuate in all forms and ways. The combination of self-organisation and self-perpetuation for long periods of time

goes a long way into understanding what Life is fundamentally about. There is nothing else of which we know around us that self-organises and self-perpetuates as much as Life.

    a. A planet self-organises but does not self-perpetuate, at least not to the level of Life as we commonly define it.

    b. A virus, although not cellular, enjoys the two characteristics of self-organisation and self-perpetuation, and we therefore consider it as part of Life.

305. We note here that we purposely did not include any particular chemical characteristics in our general description of Life. We did not talk about anabolism and catabolism, we did not make life cells as fundamentally determining of Life, and most importantly we did not talk about organic chemistry and the role of the carbon element in general in Life. Indeed, the predominance of the carbon atoms, and generally the type of chemistry we commonly call 'organic', are central to all forms of Life we currently know of on our planet. Moreover, our search for Life outside our planet currently centres on the search for this particular type of organic chemistry in the Universe beyond Earth and the Solar System. Most space projects that have as purpose to attempt to detect Life outside Earth look for conditions beyond our planet that favour the same kind of organic development of Life as on our planet, including the existence of water as key ingredient of Life[151], optimal temperature ranges, right level of atmospheric pressure, and other conditions in distant planetary systems for the development of the organic compounds of Life (including DNA, RNA, and protein structures). This is indeed natural and practical as most of our knowledge about Life and its chemistry comes from Earth; we know best how to detect Life similar to the one we have on our planet as we have spent hundreds of years studying carbon chemistry on our planet and devising technologies adapted to it. Carbon is a central atom composing Life on our planet and enjoys important characteristics, the key of which is its stability

---

151 Water contains hydrogen and oxygen which both attach quite well to carbon in more and more complex configurations (that we call molecules).

and its ability to 'connect' to four other atoms[152] or have four electro-magnetic connections; it is also the simplest atom to be able to do so. From these properties, a large diversity of molecular structures can be formed with carbon atoms, to include hydrogen, oxygen, and nitrogen atoms. These structures in turn constitute the key building blocks of Life on our planet.

306. However, this needs not theoretically to be necessarily so with all forms of Life, and this is important to recognise. It is precisely for this reason that the role of carbon and elements of organic chemistry have not been mentioned in the above characterisation of Life. Carbon centricity does not necessarily need to have monopoly over Life; self-organisation and self-perpetuation do not necessitate carbon centricity. It is indeed not theoretically impossible to have a functioning similar to some of the living forms we know of on Earth without the carbon centricity. Carbon is in fact the most simple of the atoms with the four electro-magnetic connections that allow for complex molecular formations, but it is not the only one. Silicon (Si) is also capable of such formations[153], some of which we likely do not know the chemistry, as silicon chemistry is not as prevalent on our planet as carbon chemistry (despite silicon being the second most abudant element in Earth's crust). It is therefore fair to say that when we mention today that we are looking for the existence of extra-terrestrial Life, what we usually mean is that we are actually looking for Life outside our planet with similar carbon chemistry as the one we know of on Earth.

307. There are definite negative repercussions to dissociating Life from carbon chemistry.

    a. First of all, it makes it more difficult to define Life. Adding organic compound and carbon chemistry considerations to the conditions of self-organisation and self-perpetuation makes for a more solid and naturally

---

152 Or in other words takes place in the fourth column of the old Mendeleev periodic table.

153 And happens to be the second least complex atom in the same 'column' as carbon.

narrower definition of Life; in other words, we reduce the number of grey areas by doing so. However, the writer finds this approach to somehow open the door to potentially unexpected surprises; again there is nothing theoretically that forbids a phenomenon or being that cunningly behaves like some forms of Life on Earth but based on silicon (or other atom) instead of carbon, and with units of organisation that look different from living cells we know on Earth. What are we to do should we one day discover such a phenomenon? Should we label it as inert or not living? If we do so, wouldn't we be saying then that Life is nothing but a subset of carbon chemistry?

b. Second, limiting ourselves to self-organisation and self-perpetuation alone is not enough to accurately define what we intuitively consider to be living. Let us take an example of something that self-organises and self-perpetuates, but we find intuitively difficult to admit it to be living: computational algorithms. Many sophisticated algorithms today can be made in such a way to have in them on-going optimisation capabilities (which leads to self-organisation) as well as continuous perpetuation capabilities. Algorithms can be made to reproduce and adapt. Moreover, the digital world is by construction based on units or is cellular in nature. The combination of all this can give an uncanny resemblance to the behaviour of Life as we observe it in bacteria or other microorganisms. Indeed, such algorithms are used to simulate living microorganisms as an alternative to real experiments in some situations. We may call such simulations and algorithms 'Artificial Life' (in the logic of Artificial Intelligence), but admitting it to be simply Life draws fervent intuitive objections from most.

   i. For those who would try to object that Artificial Life is not matter will find themselves to be in the wrong; the digital world is about photons and particles, and these are as much matter as what we touch and feel, in an animal or a tree, irrespective of our intuition.

308. Hence, self-organisation and self-perpetuation seem to be necessary characteristics of Life but likely not sufficient. Organic chemistry is not a necessary characteristic in our view, and the requirement of divisibility of Life into cells is too loose if we consider them as another way of saying units; the latter is also somehow included in self-organisation. It is evident that we cannot also purely rely on our intuition to define Life, as planktons are as abstract and counter-intuitive as sand particles. What is (are) the missing characteristic(s) is yet to be discovered.

    a. The writer suspects a major revision in our notion of Life and the living with further discoveries and increased knowledge.

We shall stop here with the biological and physical characterisations of Life to move to more philosophical and ethical considerations.

309. Each one of us hears people express their views almost every day about Life: "Life is good"; "Life is bad"; or "Life is boring". Mostly people draw their conclusions from subjective, and probably immediate, experiences to the overall phenomenon of Life irrespective of its scope, history, and overall behaviour.

310. The question of Life is obviously one of the first metaphysical questions. Most people think that the question remains completely mysterious, with the exception of religious interpretations. In reality, the advances of human knowledge in various fields (including Physics, Biology, and Psychology), in addition to our increased maturity in Philosophy have provided sufficient elements for qualifying Life properly. In other words, at least in our humble opinion, the question of Life is today more easily addressable than other questions such as the nature of Consciousness, albeit many of these questions are inter-related.

311. Life is part of Existence; it is a particular phenomenon or set of

processes of Existence[154]. We shall not talk about the metaphysical characteristics of Existence here; we shall only limit ourselves to those particularly related to Life. It is however worth noting that the two are sometimes wrongly amalgamated (that is Existence and Life). Life is only a subset of Existence; it is naturally the subset that may interest us the most as we are living beings.

312. Our thesis about Life is simple: what can be said about Life metaphysically is very little. Objectively, it is indeed very little. Life is neither good nor bad; it does not look to be a test or an experiment; it is not necessarily a unique one-off phenomenon[155]; there is no proof that Life heads towards anything definite apart from its self-perpetuation in a very broad sense; and the origins of Life could have been completely random or a product of special circumstances. Life can be produced, reproduced, replicated, and cloned by other living beings or by material circumstances[156].

313. *Life simply is*. Life is more of an intuitive concept than an analytical one; we have more of an intuition of Life than what we are capable of describing with satisfaction. If we force ourselves to add some additional adjectives to Life, we may say, based on the above, that Life self-organises and self-perpetuates.

314. Another way of describing self-perpetuation is to say that Life is 'sticky': once it takes place, biological Life sticks to an environment as hard as it can.

    a. Indeed, we have since long observed that among the most powerful instincts of any living being is the survival instinct. Resilience of Life in the face of all possible adversities and inhospitable environments is a by-product of this stickiness. *Life has a great will to exist*. Life is a particular type of Existence that has a great will to be.

---

154 The defining treatment of Existence can itself be found in the second chapter.

155 I.e. it can likely be repeated or it could exist elsewhere (either in the past, present, future, or, more esoterically, in a potential parallel universe).

156 The classical example of that is the 1952 Miller-Urey experiment.

On the Characteristics of Life

b. Has the reader ever asked herself why some animals or vegetation bother living in some greatly inhospitable environments? We find Life in the mouth of volcanoes, at the bottom of the deepest and darkest oceans, and in some of the coldest places on Earth. Even mammals that are not originally equipped to very harsh environments are found to live in hot and cold deserts, or in environments where food is very difficult to come by. Some animals go through great pains to live in very adverse situations, and they keep at it: Emperor Penguins in Antarctica, Snub-Nosed Monkeys in the cold mountains of Asia (instead of the warm forests and tropical jungles where monkeys are supposed to live), Tardigrade in the Himalayas and in hot springs, and flowers growing in earth cracks of some of the driest deserts in the world. Has the reader ever wondered why living beings in such environments do not just pack bags and leave to easier places? The threat of being eaten in a more moderate environment is nothing in comparison with the daily pain of survival that some of these living beings go through. It seems that whenever Life finds a new home, it keeps at it as much as it can regardless of the adversities of this new habitat[157]. Life is indeed a very stubborn phenomenon.

315. What more can we say about Life? The numerous qualifications we like to give to Life every day, drawn from our personal experiences, seem to be simple reflections of our inner nature and psychology.

    a. Putting aside how we define Good and Bad, when we say Life is good or Life is bad, or even Life is both good and bad, all that we are really saying is that there are phenomena

---

[157] We do not mean by this that there are no migratory forms of Life that try to take the best from a particular environment then move to the next one. But even such forms of Life have their own kind of stubbornness and stickiness; their home that they stick to is usually their pack or group.

in Life that concord with our definition of Good and our definition of Bad, whatever these definitions are.

b. Moreover, the notions of Good and Bad do not seem to be consistent notions in all living forms. We shall talk about that in details shortly afterwards. What is good or bad for one species is very different from that of another. There are very few universal good things and universal bad things across all forms of Life apart from self-organisation and self-perpetuation. Even those two can be judged based on the specific actions taken to self-organise and self-perpetuate, and they have to be considered in context. For example, ensuring one's survival is good but not necessarily at the cost of the survival of the pack.

In other words, most qualifications and adjectives concerning Life look to be nothing more than personal selective projections on living reality.

316. Life is an utterly complicated and diversified phenomenon. What we observe of Life today has been developed and expanded over the course of billions of years, and in many different circumstances and environments. Through the dual drive of self-organising and self-perpetuating in varying conditions and habitats, Life has developed a wide and rich arsenal of processes and behaviours through an extensive process of trial-and-error over long periods of time. We find in Life many different processes that help it self-organise, acquire energy, duplicate, reproduce, signal, self-preserve, and move. We should therefore exercise great caution in attributing definite characteristics and descriptions to Life. Life is rich; we find in it the good and the bad, the beautiful and the ugly, the immaculate and the disgusting, the sublime and the absurd, the joyful and the sad, love and hate, wonderful affection and loyalty as well as surprising brutality and treachery.

a. Many Mediterranean, Persian, and Western ancient[158] and

---

158 Which are now considered mythologies.

On the Characteristics of Life

new religions have had a terrible starting point in assuming that living beings, whether humans or godly, are either just good or just bad. Some have considered (and still do) humans and certain living beings to be inherently good or at least aspiring towards some particular pre-defined good. Probably, the culmination of such notions is embodied in the optimistic philosophies of the eighteenth century (Leibniz et al.). Other living beings, such as snakes, were generally considered to be bad.

    b. In contrast, important Asian philosophies (including Hinduism, Buddhism, and Taoism) and to some extent Greek mythologies have somehow grasped the concept of plurality of living beings, with natural focus on human beings, for a very long time. Their gods, heroes, and mythologies are full of dualities and even pluralities. It is only in the last three centuries that Western thought has started to seriously admit the plurality and complexity of living beings again. A certain class of German thinkers helped spread these pluralistic interpretations inspired by the East, including Schopenhauer and Hesse.

317. Today, plurality and complexity of living beings as well as plurality and complexity of every individual living being with enough developed cognition are widely accepted in Science and Psychology. The complexity and diversity of Life is reflected in its different species but also *within* many developed forms of Life.

318. Humanity has long been plagued by an egocentric and simplistic view of Life. This view may be suitable to some part of our collective psychology and might have been beneficial to hold at some particular stage of our collective development. However, cracks in the wall of our initial simplistic convictions about Life are starting to become increasingly visible. We are indeed today collectively less naive and more knowledgeable than in previous times. We have observed ourselves and other forms of Life, and we have documented the history of these observations for a long-enough period of time, which helped us dispose of some of this

naivety. Listening to Life around us objectively, without our inner egocentricity and prejudiced agenda, can only render it more objective and in the process more awe-inspiring.

Utopias of Living Nature. Good and Bad in Life

319. Observing and reflecting on the animal world (ex-human) and comparing it with our human world is an amazingly instructive exercise from an ethical point of view.

320. There exists a prevailing view that the animal world is 'innocent' or that Nature is intrinsically good. A common misconception is that an animal, no matter how ferocious it is, will only kill another animal if it is hungry or in defence of home or family; will only hunt to the measure of its needs and not more; and will generally behave according to natural instincts and in moderate ways if left alone. We think that animals could be easily understood from that perspective, and there is no 'excess' *per se* in the animal world. This is true of some only but not all.

321. The notion of simplicity of the animal world is usually developed in opposition to the rather Machiavellian view we have of human societies, with their insatiable greediness and corruption. This is a self-serving delusion created by some.

    a. There are, in the animal world, behaviours that we would qualify as 'bad' under almost all human moralities. A crocodile will eat her children not necessarily out of hunger; a male polar bear, a charismatic animal that is often used as a symbol of conservation, cuddliness, or humour/joy, can hunt a little cub and his mother for miles in order simply to feed on the cub; a male lion taking over a new pride will kill all the young cubs if they are not its own.

    b. Rape, violence, torture, and the will to dominate and control all exist in the animal world.

    c. Tricking and trapping are common for feeding or reproduction in both fauna and flora.

On the Characteristics of Life

    d. Obesity, illnesses, and psychological troubles are more than common in living organisms with complex cognition.

    e. Sexual monogamy is rather rare in the animal world and so is loyalty in relationships. Monogamy does however exist in Nature. Nature has both monogamy and polygamy in it, and our ethical position on the subject should not be based on Nature. Equally, Nature has bisexuality and homosexuality in it.

    f. Many organisms, such as parasites and viruses, can multiply and expand far more than necessary, destroying and consuming everything around them, not dissimilar to what we humans sometimes appear to be doing with the environment and resources around us.

322. We should feel great difficulty drawing any ethical conclusions from Nature or the animal world. Any such conclusions are only a misinformed, selective view of living beings and what is called 'natural behaviour'. Nature is greatly diverse that almost all that we find in the human world, good and bad, can be somehow also found within the animal world. There are very few common denominators across all living beings with the exception of self-organisation and self-perpetuation. There are no 'Natural Laws' when it comes to relationships, family dynamics, social etiquette, competition, feeding, and fighting; they come and exist in many forms in Nature. Almost all ethical theories and philosophies based on Nature or what seems to be the norm in Nature are nothing but biased observations.

323. Almost all that we call 'natural' in the ethical world should rather be relabelled 'intuitive' instead. When we feel that something ought to be good, such as protecting one's own children, what we are experiencing is rather an intuitive confirmation based on a long historical evolution of our species. It is an intuition genetically wired in us; it is not an objective judgement of Nature and how it behaves. 'Natural' as predominant in Nature and intuitively right are often mixed up in the ethical world.

324. We have long suffered from the utopia of the good Nature with

its natural blessed state. Many ancient books like to refer to an old age of bliss, where patriarchs lived wisely and simply, in full concordance with Nature and its laws. Grotius and Locke particularly fortified this bias through their work on political theory and Natural Laws[159]. Humans are often nostalgic, and it is common that they hold a better image of the past in comparison with what they find in their present. A nostalgic, romanticised view of the past is one of the ways we humans attempt to escape current reality and its difficulties.

325. The greatest historical contribution to the biased idea about Nature lies with the Romantic Movement. Romantics commonly held Nature as the Good and the desirable state of affairs, and Rousseau made of this attitude an escapist political theory. Human civilisation is widely portrayed by the Romantics as corruptive; there is always an invitation with them to go back to the past, to more simple and wiser times. This nostalgia remains very strong today and is usually inversely proportional to the frustrations with some of the negative aspects of our current state of civilisation. Most of us suffer or have suffered from an escapist longing for innocence and simplicity in Nature.

   a. Tolkien's writings were developed somehow in opposition to the growing British and European industrial age, and it is no surprise to find in them wise Elves living in harmony and respect of the virtuous Nature in opposition to devilish civilisations destroying and burning forests. Tolkien loathed industrialisation and the European military machinery of his age and believed them to be perverting of the natural balance of things, in line with the romantic bias.

326. In reality, there is great fear, sadness, and tragedy in Nature without humans even intervening. Not seeing the emotions on the face of animals is not synonymous with simplicity, innocence,

---

[159] It is important to note that not all attitudes towards 'Natural Laws' or 'state of nature' are positive and idealistic. For example, Saint Paul, Thomas Aquinas, and Hobbes all hold a different view on such natural states.

virtue, or joy; it is but an ignorant human illusion. The road to addressing the difficult questions of our current human condition is not in turning backwards to what we mistakenly think to be more innocent and virtuous; the road is rather forward. We can learn a lot from the animal world, but the conclusions are not likely to be the ones we like to assume at first.

327. Emotions exist in most animals as part of their survival and perpetuation kit. It corresponds to neurochemical processes honed by Evolution to the benefit of living beings, for them to survive and thrive. The negative type of Emotions seeks to protect; the positive one corresponds to an effort-reward mechanism. Positive emotions include love and happiness, whereas negative emotions include disgust, fear, sadness, anger, and surprise. Negative emotions look from this perspective to be more frequent and present than positive ones; it seems that Life and Nature, through Evolution, rely more frequently on the stick than the carrot for survival.

    a. Sometimes the stick is too strong to the point of being destructive: sadness and depression resulting in self-termination and fear or surprise resulting in sudden heart attacks. Ironically, more rarely but not impossible, sometimes too strong of a carrot can also carry destructive results: an overwhelming happiness in an old person can trigger heart problems, even death. Both examples present us with a rare overshooting of survival mechanisms which most of the time operate to the benefit of survival.

328. Nature has been structured not to be good or bad but to be about chasing or being chased, eating or being eaten. All forms of Life in Nature seek to persevere and propagate. Social structures in the living world have their root in protecting the community better against being chased. Reproduction is about leaving a legacy before being chased. Life is far from being structured to be a friendly encounter between animals despite the occasions of mutually beneficial co-living among animals. We do not mean that we cannot try to change some of that, but we always need to keep in mind what has been the original starting point.

329. Not all historical interpretations of living Nature are romanticised and blissful. We equally find in History the opposite extreme who considers Nature as simply a tool we should take advantage of and/or a threat that risks destroying us should we not protect ourselves from it. All human colonisation has been based more or less on such doctrines: evangelisation of indigenous tribes, imposition of Mosaic Laws over Natural Laws, or imposition of civility over 'barbarism'. The Industrial Revolution has greatly based itself on similar views: Nature for the industrial world is simply a tool and a receptacle for human industrialisation and development. For Hobbes, the Natural State is a state of constant infighting and brutishness.

330. The point here is this: most humans are binary about Nature and its status—they position themselves either at one extreme or the other of the spectrum. Some idealise Nature in the name of innocence, wisdom, and the natural good, while others only see it as a source of material benefit in a narrow sense. The middle path is seldom walked. Nature is far from being simple or innocent: *everything* complex in us has its source in Nature, and all our cognition and emotions have their source in it. On the other hand, we form an integral part of Nature, we depend on it for many of our benefits, but it can also be a great source of harm if we misinterpret it or take it lightly; we cannot therefore hold for long a pure colonising view of Nature without ultimately jeopardising our own existence in the process.

331. What approach should we then hold vis-à-vis Nature? We shall address this more in a bit, but for now it is enough to say that a wise and effective human morality can help bring to Nature more balance, the same way it does for humans more narrowly. It is an anthropological balance and can alarm many, but we do have a choice here to attenuate some of the brutality and sorrow in Nature. Indeed, the overwhelming view is that we humans should not intervene; we should let things take their normal course and only observe. The writer finds this attitude simplistic. *We have no choice but to intervene by the fact of living.* By the fact of

On the Characteristics of Life

breathing, eating, and moving we intervene in Nature. The only thing really under our control is to decide what level and the type of intervention we choose to apply.

332. A valid morality needs not therefore to only concern itself with the Humans but also with Nature more broadly. We, humans, have a role to play in Nature, and it is up to us to choose what role we occupy.

    a. We are capable of helping an animal in distress or protecting a species from extinction[160]. This is part of the beautiful emotional side of Morality. Some see in this a silly anthropomorphism, others a concordance with our social feelings towards other living companions. To the cynical who only sees in this misfired instincts, allow us to say that the neurochemical reactions of help towards an animal in distress are not very different from those that bring the urge to help other human beings in catastrophic situations (e.g. a tsunami or an earthquake), even if we do not know the human beings affected personally and have not encountered them before. It is rather bizarre to call the first silly anthropomorphism and the second encouraged empathy.

333. The idea that Life, here or somewhere else, ought to be fully good, and that God (whether a separate entity or in the pantheist definition) ought to be good have led time and again to trouble in both metaphysics and ethics. This bias towards the Good has long been predominant from Plato, to Christian Theology, to even the mechanistic philosophies like Spinoza's[161]. Good is a human invention; it is related but not equated to what the majority desires,

---

160 It is worth noting that species extinction is the rule rather than the exception in Nature. Most species are bound to become extinct. Human intervention can accelerate and bias such extinction pattern but can also help provide a break from it, that is as long as humans themselves do not become extinct.

161 Although Spinoza's definition of the Good can be quite different from what is commonly conceived.

and Good, as desires, is subject to change of definition and scope with time and societies. Good should not however be equated with all human desires. Human desires can be contradictory even at the aggregate level; Good is a subset of such desires, which are usually of a long-term nature.

334. One would be emotionally crushed if he/she attempts to internalise all the pain and sorrow that has happened in the world. From the pain and sorrow humans feel today, every day; to the pain and sorrow of past much darker ages; to the pain and sorrow of animals and living beings we so ignore. Pain and sorrow seem to be the constant in Life, the real manifestation of the survival game of life. One would wish that Evolution could do one day without it.

335. There is no evidence that Life came from a source of Good or a source of Bad; there is no evidence either that at least some of it might have come from a source of Good or a source of Bad; there is no evidence that Life is a constant fight between a pre-defined unchanging Good and Bad[162]; and there is no evidence that Life ought to tend towards a pre-defined Good or a pre-defined Bad. We reject this form of historical finality in the name of the large evidence of statistical and chaotic behaviour of Life and Existence in general. We do not mean that nothing is predictable in Life, or that there are no more likely outcomes; what we mean is that there is no rigid determinism in Life given the essential role randomness and chaos play in it. **Good and Bad are not** a priori **shapers of Life; they are notions Life builds and effects.**

336. The existence of the Universe as a whole can come to be from randomness; the same goes for Life as a subset of Existence. In fact, it is rather incoherent to assume the Universe coming out of randomness while the causes of Life in it intended beforehand through some sort of intelligent design, unless we naturally

---

162 Indeed different forms of Life are in a continuous struggle to achieve what is desired and eliminate what is not desired, but these do not seem to be unchanging desires pre-defined at the dawn of time.

assume that this intelligent design itself is a result of the randomly created Universe.

- a. This last hypothesis is not entirely implausible although unlikely given what we know of the highly iterative nature of the evolution of Life.

337. We find in Life both the Good and the Bad, sometimes in unequal proportions, for a very wide range of definitions of the Good and the Bad. Luckily, proportions of Good and Bad change with time and are partially subject to our actions. Seeing Life as essentially good or bad comes down to each individual's biases and emotional predispositions. The latter are greatly honed by the environment we live in and our own personal experiences. Hence, some build their ethical systems on the premise that everything is essentially bad in the underline (like Schopenhauer, Nietzsche, the Greek Cynics, and to a certain extent the Sophists), while others go to the other extreme (like Leibniz and the best of all worlds). Schopenhauer and Nietzsche have clearly frustrated psychologies, which, not surprisingly, lead them to a negatively biased position.

338. On the subject of the Good and the Bad, we personally choose to stand on the side of curiosity, industriousness, courage to seek a better tomorrow, sympathy, and compassion in our attitude towards Life. Not because Life is intrinsically good, and not because the writer is a saint, but because it is the free choice I make and try to stick to. I have no illusion about my own selfishness and the selfishness of everyone around me; the love of self of each one of us; the fascination with the purely material; and the long list of human cruelties and hypocrisies throughout History. I also recognise that in the majority of cases, there are no selfless deeds, and hence, the pretension of sympathy may psychologically contain a mark of hypocrisy in many cases. I also admit to have found it very difficult to feel compassionate all the time when bombarded with all of Life's negativities.

Despite all of that, we choose the push for positive action.

We consider that holding the notion that there are no purely sympathetic attitudes in humans is as flawed as holding a notion of blind optimism in everything; they are both extreme and holistic in their approach.

339. And there is a cherry on top of the cake: Life is reflexive and actions reverberate. In other words, positive action creates more positive action, and hence, sometimes partially positive attitudes (even with an element of egoism) can result in more purely positive attitudes as time goes by. It is known in Psychology that if one forces herself to smile, even if she does not experience real joy deep down at first, eventually a positive attitude ensues; and so is with a lot of positive attitudes. We can all become more positive when we are surrounded with positive attitudes.

    a. Yes we can be conditioned to be positive, and there is nothing wrong with that. Aren't we conditioned to stand in a queue? Stop at a red light? Seek justice rather than personal vendetta when injured? Even the most cynic and negative of people have been conditioned no matter how much they think they have escaped it. One can escape some of the conditioning but never all—not much would be left otherwise.

We Ought to Respect Life Nevertheless

340. Life is an amazing phenomenon; we ought to respect it. We ought to respect that which is more intricate, sophisticated, diverse, and subtle than us. We are only a part of Life, and no matter which position we choose to give to ourselves in it, we should always temper our views on it.

341. Life is the greatest opposition; Life is a sacred phenomenon that stands in the face of billions of adverse conditions to its existence; Life is rich and diverse; Life is in many ways wise and efficient for having tried many permutations and possibilities over billions of years. There is no more proud and stubborn than Life. Life fights every moment of every day for its place in the Universe; Life

On the Characteristics of Life

did not win its place in existence through outside grace. *It fought constantly to be.* Whether its origins are purely random or favoured by some outside intervention is not as important of a realisation as understanding that Life deserved its place through billions of years of trying and optimising. There is no need for the existence and perpetuation of Life, and yet it is there regardless; there is no need for its diversity, and yet it does not cease to devise new ways. We cannot but be humbled by this stubbornness. The resurrection of Life from the ashes of adversity is deep and moving as with many of our legends and stories:

    a. The Phoenix spreading its beautiful wings of fire out of the ashes of adversity.

    b. Jesus rising after so much destruction to his body.

Some of our most sublime stories and emotions are related to Life, its pride, and its stubbornness in being.

342. Life not being necessarily fundamentally good does not justify the doctrine of enslaving all of Nature and the environment to the pure benefit of mankind. *Homo Sapiens* woke up to the world realising that it is a harsh environment for survival, and they are not necessarily the strongest and most resilient of animals. They found strength in collectivity and in mastering and inventing tools, and from there they managed to break further the bond of hardship, generation after generation. Along the way, many religions came to enforce and give more ideological grounds to this attitude of making full use of the environment around. Most doctrines go something like this: God created us into this world, we are his most refined creation, and God gave us this Earth for our benefit, so we can pro-create and fill it. What is quite noticeable in these doctrines is the pure Will to Exist of the human species, wrapped up in religious doctrines, and this is not surprising given how strong is the survival instinct in us.

Then came the Renaissance period, the discovery of the New World, and following that the Industrial Revolution. The marriage of this way of thinking and technology resulted in an explosion of material utility for humans, improvements in our way of living, protection from most hardships, acceleration of discoveries in a more beneficial environment for humans, increase in human lifespan, and population explosion. But all of those achievements came at a cost, as it is almost always the case. As we explode in numbers and our needs continue to grow, biodiversity dwindles. Many species have become extinct or are on the verge of being so, without us having scratched the surface of understanding them. And here is the irony: we derive our utility from mastering the environment, and now we are, in many cases, irrevocably depleting some of these environmental resources before even getting to fully understand them.

343. The reader has for sure heard this story of environmental threats many times before, but it is a story worth mentioning. We are also quite certain that most readers have already their views set on the subject one way or another. Typically, we find four different attitudes to this problem:

    a. An ostrich-like attitude where people choose to hide their head in the sand, prefer not to recognise the problem, shun the details, and defer to other people in society to take a decision on the subject on their behalf.

        i. People too consumed by their daily problems and feeling helpless can also fall under this category.

    b. People who consider global environmental threats as the single biggest challenge to face Humanity and feel a great sense of urgency towards it. People with this attitude may have different reasons for doing so: genuine love for Nature, an enlightened long-term utilitarian perspective, political reasons (such as reducing geopolitical dependence on oil), or romantic ideals of going back to Nature and living as in older times (à la Rousseau).

    c. There are those who look at the problem with great cynicism, see a conspiracy behind it, and a Trojan horse

On the Characteristics of Life

for somebody's leftist political agenda. They either base themselves on:

   i. Historical argumentation of the type, "We have always benefited from this way of doing, so there is no reason to stop now. Technology will figure out some new way of solving these environmental issues";

   ii. Some form of religious interpretation, "It is God's will that we take advantage as much as we can from this Earth, God created it for our use";

   iii. A hedonistic attitude, "All I care about is my immediate happiness"; or

   iv. Some pseudo and false scientific reasoning of the type, "CO_2 remains a small fraction of the total atmosphere composition, so what is the big deal?"

   d. And finally, people who consider it as a problem that would be nice to solve but not a top priority. If there were a cheap way of remedying the environmental destruction, people who fall under this category would not mind. However, should it require some change in the lifestyle or giving up some social acquisitions for it, then they would oppose it vehemently. Their attitude towards solving the problem is going half the mile only.

344. We must admit that not all who are opposed to any changes in the way of doing in the name of environmental protection have bad intentions. Some of the arguments they advance are worth considering.

   a. Technology did remedy many of the problems we previously had, so why not this one? This argument can cut both ways, granted.

   b. The Paleocene-Eocene Junction[163] did witness an

---

163 55 million years ago.

explosion of CO_2 emissions into the atmosphere and Nature survived it[164], so this is not a first-time event.

c. Dynamics in the science of weather (Climatology) and cycles of the Earth are awfully complicated, and we do not fully understand them; even scientists refrain from ascertaining some projections as inevitable.

345. However, and here is the most important point on the subject that is often missed, **human impact on the environment is not, and should not be, reduced to global warming, far from it.** The problem today is that global warming is taking such a central stage in local and global politics that almost everybody has become deadlocked on the subject, and all other environmental problems are relegated to the back. This political polarisation is very damaging to the entire attitude towards Life. Human impact on the environment includes *equally* important problems such as extermination of species, destruction of natural habitats or corridors, acidification of the oceans and its impact on marine habitats, contamination of air and water generally, pollution in cities, agricultural industrialisation of key tropical forests, municipal and industrial waste mismanagement, and large amounts of garbage orbiting Earth's space and threatening humans, satellites, and stations operating in it.

a. We are not advocates of bureaucracy and taxation, but it is important for societies to find ways of internalising such negative consequences into their economic functioning. This is not political doctrine; this is basic sense.

346. The reason why we choose to elaborate on the topic of the human impact on the environment at the end of this chapter on Life is because we view this human impact to ultimately be an impact on Life itself and all living forms. Global environmental impact is a crucial topic that our generations are only starting to appreciate. In a more crowded, more connected, and greater consuming world, we cannot but be faced with the consequences of our behaviour

---

164 Albeit Nature changed in composition and the rate of increase in CO_2 emissions was notably slower than in our modern times.

on almost all living beings. Life is to be respected, and that respect has to be put in action. We possess great power today over Life on our planet. Should we not generally give Life its required status in our ethics, we can find ourselves, inadvertently or purposely, irreversibly altering Life. Altering blindly a 3.5 billion-year-old phenomenon on our planet in a matter of hundreds of years or even thousands of years is outright silly. We cannot foresee the consequences of all of our actions, but that should not constitute an excuse to condone clearly destructive actions we can do something about if not because of laziness, complacency, and short-sightedness.

347. Respecting and preserving Life should be an integral part of our Morality. Several reasons could be given for that:

   a. A long-term utilitarian advantage: we have benefited from understanding and utilising Life and Nature, and our knowledge of it remains limited. We should not destroy what we do not fully understand as we might benefit from it further. All forms of Life are intricately inter-related, and our actions may have consequences that play against us in the long run, so let us at least exercise some caution in our actions.

      i. Any engineer can tell us how elegant and efficient is the flight of a bird, or how great are a cat's 'suspensions'.

   b. Life includes great beauty. This beauty always moves something in us and is a source of great inspiration to many. Nature is often grand, and this induces a feeling of necessary modesty in us. Nature is complicated yet elegant, giving us a snapshot of how complicated is all this Existence we take for granted. As Schiller says: "Only through Beauty's morning-gate, dost thou penetrate the land of knowledge."

   c. The third, and the writer's favourite, is more purely moral. We shall talk in later chapters about key moral values, and one of them is Modesty. Modesty is not only meant in the traditional sense of bowing down to human peers at every instance, but more so as intellectual and existential modesty. We ought to be modest in the face of Life and Nature, and one who really attempts to practice such a modesty cannot but express respect and appreciation for Life, all Life, no matter what other judgments or feelings it can provoke in us.

We will move now from Life, its characteristics, and the threats it faces to the subject of the human environment, not necessarily from an ecological point of view but more from a historical and psychological point of view, both individually and collectively.

•

The Influence of the Environment

"[...] understand that men are the subjects and not the rulers of their accidents." Herodotus

"The emerging field of epigenetics considers what happens to our personal genetic code when it meets the real world. It explains why nature/nurture is not a divide but, rather, an endless feedback loop." Barbara Natterson-Horowitz & Kathryn Bowers

Here is the story of Albert. Albert is a German engineer. He is in his mid-thirties and works for a prominent electrical automation company in a large city in Germany. Albert has never lived outside Germany before. He is a convinced ecologist; he is a member of the green party in his country and has long participated in environmental related activities. He regularly takes part in green party demonstrations and was a key advocate of nuclear power elimination in Germany. He vehemently criticises people who are irresponsible ecologically and cannot but think people in many other countries to be all corrupt and complacent when it comes to the environment. Albert lives his daily life in careful ways to minimise the environmental footprint of his activities. He rides a bicycle to work, installed solar panels on his rooftop to take advantage of the government tax break on solar energy and reduce some of his household electricity consumption, uses heat pumps to climate-condition his home, divides his waste carefully for recycling, takes public transportation when going on long distances, and in case he is forcefully required to rent a car, he always rents a small-engine hybrid car, even if at a higher daily rate than other available cars. Albert's line of work is consistent with his way of life; automation concerns itself with efficiency, and Albert feels good about how his work helps reduce global energy consumption.

One day, Albert's seniors approach him with an opportunity; they offer him the chance to lead their newly formed office overseas. Albert has always been on the lookout for career growth, and this opportunity looks like the right one. Albert will head his company's office in a major location in the Arabian Gulf, where investments in power infrastructure and related activities are exploding. Albert accepts and moves to the Gulf. He rents out a small one-bedroom apartment; given how restrained is the real estate supply, the closest he can find is an apartment ten kilometres away from his work location. All apartments in the Gulf come with a strong central cooling system, without which life would be unbearable in the 40-50°C summer. Albert tries to ride a bike to work but quickly finds road safety to be a major issue. Besides, there is no sense in riding a bike in the summer, or even walking for that matter, as a couple of feet in the sun and humidity would cause anyone to massively transpire. Albert has to buy a car. After careful considerations of what is available in the market, the only thing he can opt for is a small-engine normal fuel car—there are no hybrids where he lives now. The new car is indeed efficient, but the amount of driving Albert has to do for work with the car's air conditioning system in full mode forces him to fill his tank sometimes twice a week. Albert is leading a new business that requires him to market his company and their solutions on an intensive basis. His customers prefer to have their presentations printed, and this requires him and his staff to use heavy printing. Albert tries to find ways for recycling all the paper they consume, but where he lives all trash gets mixed up together and sent to the nearest waste dumpster. Albert has to use water to live and drink; most water in the Gulf is desalinated at a high-energy cost. Power generation in the Gulf is also inefficient, as it relies more on oil than natural gas, oil being more readily available and cheaper in these countries. Albert likes to eat fruits, vegetables, and dairy products; many of these get either shipped from far-away places at a high carbon footprint cost or are produced locally with water from natural aquifers which are depleting. Of no fault of his own, and not from the lack of trying, Albert suddenly finds himself with a bigger environmental footprint than some of the biggest polluting individuals in his native Germany.

The Inescapable Environment

348. All living beings reside in a certain environment that influences them; no one can escape being in an environment or being influenced by a particular environment. The influence of the environment is determining to all living beings in almost all aspects, physical and cognitive. All living forms grow in a certain way, behave in a certain way, and react in a certain way based on a continuous exposure to the environment they live in. The influence of the environment on living forms is impossible to eradicate. The question becomes that of the degree of influence rather than reality of the influence itself.

349. We mean by environment everything around a living being that can potentially interact with it over the course of its life. The environment is the physical and cognitive receptacle the living being resides in during its life.

    a. It is the air, the water, the nutrients, the soil, the magnetic field, the light, the temperature, and all other fields a living being lives in.

    b. It includes members of its own species, and the societal dynamics and structure of the species.

    c. It also includes other beings, whether visible to the naked eye or microscopic, whether detached from the body of the living being or living in it as some form of parasite.

    d. And finally, it is also the physical and cognitive threats and incentives surrounding the living being.

350. We, human beings in particular, are in a constant rich and varying

interaction with our environment. The typical prevailing view we have of ourselves is more static than reality. What we mean by this is that we tend to think of our person and our consciousness as independent entities reacting to the environment around us at any point in time but always keeping total integrity and independence while doing so. This is a wrong conception.

351. As we have seen with the chapter on Deeds, we are work-in-progress as much as anything else around us. The I each one of us calls him/herself is as much of a moving target, an evolving entity, as the wind, and throughout this process of evolving, we remain continuously influenced by experiences and events around us, over which we have only little control. In other words, we are in constant formation; our consciousness is in constant formation; and an environment that we do not entirely control substantially drives this formation. "L'existence précède l'essence"[165] (Sartre).

352. It is very difficult to dissociate personal views and attitudes from the influences of the environment around, even for the most wise among us. As Bertrand Russell noted, an intelligent human might be capable of discounting personal events of his/her life, but it is notably more difficult to discount everything that happens around us—not much would be left for the mind to grab to otherwise. Knowing History is one of the ways of breaking away from the current environment into different times and conditions; another could be travelling to remotely foreign lands to gain a notably different perspective. The latter is however becoming less effective given the increased inter-connectivity of the world, as well as globalisation and normalisation.

353. We usually have less difficulty observing and admitting the influence of environment on the younger among us. We can observe the rate of change and influence more clearly on the young ones, and we assume it to be a natural phase of human development to grow, change, and learn from the environment. However, the reality is that the environment continues to shape

---

[165] Existence precedes Essence. Jean-Paul Sartre, French existentialist philosopher.

The Influence of the Environment

us at every age and in every circumstance even if sometimes it is more difficult to discern.

- a. The idea of finality of knowledge, wisdom, or opinions, of finality of some psychological state we are in; the idea of a static inner balance or a final happiness ("and they lived happily ever after" utopia) after a certain age, a certain level of education, or a certain amount of experiences, are all an illusion. As long as we live, we continue to be a work-in-progress. Balance, happiness, knowledge, wisdom, and maturity get worked on every day; they are not a permanent state independent from outside factors.

- b. When we choose to undertake a certain endeavour, create something, or relocate somewhere new, we usually tend to consider our current state of knowledge and our current psychology, and we imagine how with them we would deal with such an endeavour, work, or challenge. What we often fail to realise is that at every step of the way, we are likely to be changed as much as the change we are making, and that our initial views and opinions can be revised along the way. It is not surprising to see the starting assumptions of an individual re-questioned after a couple of steps.

- c. The right way of approaching such an endeavour or work is to think carefully about a question of the sort, "What taking this particular path will do to me *along the way*, and how will that affect me and affect the path I am taking?"

    - i. A creation changes the creator as much as the creator changes the creation.
    - ii. It is no surprise that, more often than not, initial objectives and goals are forgotten, and people succumb to the daily way of doing, forgetting the reason for which they have started their entire endeavour in the first place. Nietzsche's statement on this topic is harsh but somehow true: "During

the journey we commonly forget its goal. Almost every profession is chosen and commenced as a means to an end but continued as an end in itself. Forgetting our objectives is the most frequent of all acts of stupidity."

    iii. A useful tip taught in the world of Organisational Behaviour and Business is for one to write his own thoughts and declare his own objectives openly and loudly. It turns out that doing so in front of other people actually serves as a deterrent against forgetting initial objectives and contradicting them along the way. Having made these objectives declared and available, coupled with personal pride, usually makes it more difficult for the one who is declaring them to genuinely forget them or attempt to contradict them along the way; not fulfilling declared objectives usually plays against a person's psyche. This is not a guaranteed recipe for behavioural change in the face of a changing environment, but it has shown its merits in many situations and with many people.

  d. Different dynamics in separate environments are part of the reason why people who stay away from each other a long-enough time (whether friends, family, or husband/wife) grow apart. It also explains the higher level of effort required to maintain relationships when distance is continuously involved.

354. The influence of the environment explains how otherwise enlightened people of the 17th to 19th centuries could take a stand against democracy for example, something that might seem surprising to us today from such widely respected political thinkers. In the 17th to 19th centuries, for purely historical circumstances, Democracy was equated in many situations with populism and wild anarchy, to which those intellectuals favoured a monopoly of power and stability. These centuries were a time of tragedies and

religious wars following the Reformation and the social break-up of Europe, the Thirty Years Wars in which a quarter of German populations are thought to have found their death, *La Terreur* in France following the Revolution and the call for Democracy, and the Napoleonic adventures in Europe... Even for some of the greatest minds, it was difficult to escape the disastrous memories of populism of that time, and not somehow (wrongly) equate Democracy with death and peril. Even in our days, such a mix-up continues to exist in some parts of the world; the rise to power of xenophobic political movements is often not totally undemocratic, and many democratic and independence-seeking revolutions in several countries subsequently result in bloodshed, dictatorships, and long civil wars rather than an outright improvement of social conditions.

    a. These situations should not serve as an argument against Democracy but, rather, be accounted for within democratic systems through the necessary safeguards.

355. Our political views, our artistic tastes, our creations, and our psychology, are all largely a fruit of our experiences, and so of the environment we witnessed and reacted to during such times. This does not necessarily mean that we can predict somebody's temperament or opinions solely based on the environment, as different people may react differently to the same conditions (and here is where our innate part plays a role).

    a. Under tyranny, some people might choose to go along, while others revolt fully aware of the harsh consequences of such an insubordination; others might submit for a while then change their mind and revolt. And any such decisions take the individual in a certain direction, and the events he/she witnesses re-loop back on the person and change him/her. The rebellious at first instance may end up reconverting to the general dogma, while the submissive may end up revolting eventually–this is the real nature of human behaviour that can sometimes shock us.

356. Whenever you feel like eating something in particular, or whenever you desire a certain dish or type of fast food, it is almost never because of Free Will. It is either because your body needs particular nutrients in the food; the microorganisms in your body are craving something in particular; your brain has been teased by a marketing message or some peer influence to want a particular food; or your body has lost touch with some of its equilibrium, which makes it crave certain ingredients in particular for relief or energy. Where is the Free Will in that? We see more an influence of the environment.

357. Not only can microorganisms in the body influence our eating behaviour; also pathogens can favour behaviours that ultimately benefit them. Some Sexually Transmitted Diseases (STDs) are known to cause a higher-than-average sexual activity in the carrier as a way of increasing the likelihood of them spreading around. It is rather amazing the depth and scope of tactics little organisms, such as bacteria and viruses, have developed over the course of Evolution in order to favour their survival, well-being, and reproduction. Some of these tactics include influencing the behaviour, taste, and choice of the body they inhabit in ways we still do not fully understand.

358. Social behaviour, or behaviour of the masses, is largely driven by the incentives created by the environment; that is why policy setting is so important. People might look as behaving badly (e.g. Americans and their high level of gas consumption) when it has little to do with what the majority of the population is intrinsically like, and more to do with the incentives put in place.

359. If a policymaker is serious about seeking a change for the better, the environment and its incentives are to be tackled first, then the people. We can be surprised to find many people actually changing their behaviour for the better with the change in environmental incentives. We are not holding a simplistic view; some people may have too much at stake to really change. Those can be tackled later once the environment is fixed; they are also easier to discern with the change of environmental incentives.

The Influence of the Environment

360. Harsh environments can help bring the truth more in people. You know more about the quality of a team, society, or country in situations where you have a limited pie that has to be shared than in the case of a continuously growing pie where everyone can find plenty to eat from.

361. The environment possesses the power to influence our behaviour in ways that sometimes lead us to be contradictory or to become someone we did not originally intend to be. This is an important realisation when it comes to policy making, fighting crime, administering justice effectively, planning to relocate or change jobs, raising a child or sending her/him to a certain school, or simply criticising someone's behaviour.

    a. Very few fancied as a child to become obese, to commit a crime, or to develop mental problems. We are not advocating no personal responsibility in acts people undertake, but equally keeping a blind eye to the environment a human is living in is both poor judgment of the past and poor planning for the future.

362. An interesting dynamic often occurs between the individual and the environment: when we are in an environment for a certain specific purpose (e.g. being in finance to make money "for a certain period of time" as many often claim), and we happen to be confronted with values that contradict our initial internal set of values, we tend to bend our values to conform more with our environment's values[166] in order to preserve some integrity of our ideas. Moreover, we tend to rationalise why our initial values and the new values we live by are not that contradictory in order to preserve some self-esteem. This is a well-known cognitive phenomenon called *cognitive dissonance*.

363. The environment can make of you something that you really hate. The combination of the environment and a particular character matters greatly; judging a character on its own is meaningless. The cautious can appear coward, the courageous foolish, and the

---

[166] If they are not clearly problematic such as murder for example.

idealist naive. There are also environments that turn most people into something they wish they were not.

364. The environment is not only an impersonal receptacle we live in, and it is not only a society or a corporate culture we face on daily basis; the environment is also our human relationships at the personal level. Points of character are not only brought out by material and emotional incentives; points of character also find their way out in our personal interactions with other people. People come in many varying traits, and some of these traits are incompatible with each other. In the same way that an impersonal environment has good and bad influences on our behaviour and identity-building, people we interact with on a very regular basis (partner, close family members, relatives, friends, colleagues at work, and neighbours) play a great role in influencing our behaviour, often unintentionally.

365. It is not only work incentives that can lure us or push us to act in ways we generally disapprove of; the interaction between particular character traits in two individuals has the potential for dramatic behavioural change. It is important not to forget that the environment is also the people we choose to surround ourselves with on a regular basis. "Tell me who your friends are, and I will tell you who you are" has some degree of truth in this context.

366. Nature vs. Nurture has been a great subject of interest in Psychology for decades. The simple question psychologists continue to ask is: "What influences the human cognitive development from early age: genes they inherit ('Nature') or the environment they live in ('Nurture')?" The subject has long been explored and debated.

367. For the sake of making it simple, we could say that the answer is different depending on which level we look (e.g. language development, ethical values, or intelligence), and how we position the problem. What is however clear is that *both* genes and the environment are greatly influential, and the behavioural output that ultimately interests us is a result of the *combination and interaction*

The Influence of the Environment

of Nature/Genes and Nurture/Environment. In other words, the environment is central for human development, but everyone can react differently to the same environment depending on the genetic baggage he or she is born with. This does not only go for the cognitive development but naturally for the physical development also, and the two are seldom detached.

    a. It is well documented that more well-off populations with higher intake of protein are taller on average than populations with more limited access to the right type of food. Europeans today are notably taller and bigger than their ancestors, and the Chinese are walking down this path with the increased economic prosperity they are witnessing.

The environment shapes us to the bone and from a very early age. Dismissing its importance in our individual and collective behaviour is foolish and short-sighted.

368. Not only the environment we join has the potential of influencing our behaviour and our identity. The environment can also be partly created by us, and hence, we can find ourselves creating a certain culture that will come to influence us, its creator, unintentionally. This is only natural from the interactive nature of things.

    a. Lie long enough about something, or live in an environment where a lie is perpetuated and taken for truth for a long time and by many people, and you will start truly believing your own lies. Assuming the lie to be true becomes a natural reflex even if at the beginning one knows it clearly to be a lie.

    b. Talk openly about beliefs that you may not really hold deep down as if they are your own, and you will start believing your own pretensions after a while, particularly if they receive a favourable reaction or confirmation from the environment around.

    c. Tell yourself that you are great all the time, or be in an environment where everybody around tells you how great you are, and this belief becomes unshakeable in you even if you commit mistakes. After all, wasn't this really one of the purposes of royal courts?

The environment has indeed a very powerful effect on the functioning of the mind. Altering the environment unintentionally is one of the ways in which intermediary objectives start to be taken for final ones.

Emotions and the Environment

369. An interesting and complicated dynamic in the field of decision-making is that of the inter-play between conscious decisions and emotions; we see in this a particular corollary to the influence of the environment. In fact, few can deny the role emotions play in influencing the result of our decision-making process. We possess different types of decision-making processes: some are more intuitive and quick, while others are considered more rational, detached, and balanced. Definitely, emotions have more power over the first type of processes; however, we cannot completely rule them out even in the more purely rational processes.

370. Whenever we are subjected to a high degree of emotional instability, our decision-making is impacted for a certain period of time. The question is that of degree and length of time of the emotional influence, which can vary from one person and situation to the other. In the jargon of the field, we say that we become 'compromised' in our decision-making capabilities. Napoleon is famously quoted to have said: "[...] un homme, véritablement homme, ne hait point; sa colère et sa mauvaise humeur ne vont point au-delà de la minute [...]"[167]. The writer wonders how closely did Napoleon follow his own suggestion.

371. Some might believe that, at some conscious or unconscious level, we 'choose' to put ourselves in certain emotional states, and in a certain way we are actually in control of our emotions as

---

[167] A man, a true man, never hates. His rages and his bad moods never last beyond the present moment. (John H.T. Francis translation)

they emanate from a choice. This is the point of view that some existentialists like Sartre took or that of some psychiatrists and psychologists.

- a. This nuance is rather irrelevant here as the point is not about the choice of emotions or not; it is about the nature and results of the decision-making, which are clearly influenced by the emotional state we are in, at least partially, and at least in some situations.
- b. We personally disagree with the view that Emotions can come from a conscious choice. The most modern studies of Emotions put them in the category of neurochemical processes that have defined biological purposes, mostly centred on Survival. Hence, it is difficult to attribute an emotion to a voluntary choice when it is a product of a long evolutionary process, the entire purpose of which was to develop such emotional processes as a way of improving the overall survival of the species.

372. Why the topic of Emotions is important in our context of the environment? It is important as environmental reverberations are commonly internalised through the emotional states we go through. A smile; an insult; a betrayal; someone talking badly about us; an act of generosity or chivalry; a sudden accident we witness; peer success or failure; lack of care from people around us; the death of someone we love; constant obstacles on the road; and all such daily environmental factors have impact on our overall emotional state. And many emotional states impact us in apparent and subtle manners. It can be in our decision-making directly; it can be in our overall state of health, which subsequently impacts our decision-making; or it can be in our unconscious behaviour.

373. The reality of Emotions is that too much of anything can make us eventually numb, no matter how horrible it is. Too much negativity can make negativity become the norm; too much injustice can make injustice look to be normal in the world we live in, and too much death can make it less eventful eventually. This

is sad and horrible, but true. Images from worn-torn places create indignation in the first weeks of the event but become a reality viewers are less sensitive to as the tragedy endures. With the habit of tragedy, the sacred value of Life becomes compromised. These are some of the numbing effects of a negatively monotone environment.

374. The reality of Emotions also is that they can be manipulated, silenced, or redirected by the environment or particular events. Daily politicking makes of mass emotional manipulation a craft. There is no one who knows more about the power of the prevailing environment than politicians and marketers.

    a. Fear is used to advance particular political agendas.

    b. Instinctive family values are evoked in the bid for a certain social reform. A certain product is marketed "for the protection of your kids".

    c. A politician assassinated can suddenly become an untouched martyr regardless of his/her past behaviour because of the drama that goes with the assassination.

    d. Common prejudices are used against intelligence to promote a certain product or a certain policy.

    e. Religious feelings are used masterfully and in greatly misplaced manners. It becomes indeed very difficult to stand for what is right and what is wrong in front of an angry mob or a charismatic authoritative figure.

375. The famous Milgram experiment is one of the most interesting illustrations on the subject of emotional manipulation and numbness. In a series of experiments, an authority figure (the experimenter) gave a teacher a series of word-pairs to teach a learner. The experimenter also asked the teacher to induce what was believed to be painful electric shocks to the learner if he/she provides a wrong answer to a pair of words he/she had been taught. In reality, the electric shocks were fake ones, the learner was actually an accomplice, and the effects of the pain were only simulations. The electric shocks could be administered in

increasing voltage with every wrong answer, the highest being 450V. The incremental increase in voltage was there in order to slowly condition the teacher to an increased degree of pain infliction. At moments of hesitation by the teacher in the face of the learner's pain, the experimenter would step in to prod the teacher to continue; the experimenter would however only intervene four times with increased insistence every time; after four refusals to continue, the experiment was halted. The aim of the experiments was to understand how many teachers were willing to follow the order of the authority figure, despite hearing the effect of their action, and particularly, how many were willing to reach the maximum voltage of 450V. The results of the experiment were very surprising: a majority of the individuals who took part in the experiment followed orders, inflicting up to the maximum shock of 450V, even while questioning the experiment or exhibiting clear signs of discomfort in doing so. The experiments showed that under certain environmental conditions, the teachers, who were normal volunteers with no particular background in violence, turned out to be capable of behaving in surprising ways and followed orders even if they were uncomfortable with them. This is indeed a shocking illustration of the power of the environment.

376. A frog swimming in a pot of water will remain in it if fire under the pot is gradually increased, even up to its own death, while a frog thrown into a hot pot will immediately jump out. The dynamics of emotional conditioning are not very different from that of the frog and heating water.

377. Important questions can be asked here to which the writer does not have satisfactory answers. As we have already mentioned, Emotions are biological processes we have in common with the animal world. We exhibit similar neurochemical processes in situations of fear, fight, flight, social bonding with fellow living beings, and angst as many species in the animal world do. And this is not only restricted to mammals; the whole animal world from insects to reptiles to birds is shown to exhibit some form of emotional behaviour. Animals and Humans exhibit Emotions.

Humans, on the other hand, can reflect on their emotions, or at least be more aware of them; most animals do not seem to exhibit this kind of awareness from our *current* point of observation, at least not to the same level. The question hence becomes: What does this difference in awareness really result in? Are we really less subject to our emotions than animals? And in which circumstances? Can we eventually alter these neurochemical processes more so than animals because we are able to reflect on them? In the answers to these questions lie some of the limits of the influence of Emotions on our behaviour.

Contemporary Challenges and Environmental Considerations

In our current times, the world around us abounds with examples of environmental influences and challenges to the way of living. We shall mention some in this section.

378. The problem of obesity has a great environmental component. It is not from a lack of education or self-control only that one becomes overweight or obese. There are fat doctors, and there are overweight both in the richest and most sophisticated countries, as well as some of the poorer countries. Obesity is becoming an important social development of our present times, and we remain far from understanding all the environmental factors leading to it. There is what we could almost call an obesity and overweight-epidemic in North America; Europe, which has long resisted this trend, is starting to get impacted; and the greater development and availability of high-calorie food in China is resulting in a new generation of obese kids.

    a. With modernity, we have managed to devise many technologies that contribute to life longevity and resilience. But we have also altered the nature of the food we eat and its availability. Some of the cheaper and most available food has become the worst to consume on regular basis. In some places, it has become indeed a struggle to find a cheap-enough salad to buy. Suddenly, green uncooked

The Influence of the Environment

vegetables, the simplest of Nature, have become a symbol of expensive food and restaurants!

b. Daily stress and availability of high-carb food, which our body naturally craves in states of stress or fear, represent a dangerous combination. We have less need for physical effort today, and our economies are more and more automated. A greater proportion of us lives today in urban environments where working out can be a difficult thing to do; running in the streets puts us at the mercy of driving cars and pollution—not talking about congestion—and many of the enticing indoor workout places command a certain price that not everybody can afford.

379. Obesity is greatly environmental; it spreads like a disease in a society, and its long-term consequences in terms of healthcare costs and general well-being are not fully measured. We seem to have replaced death through relatively benign diseases in the past ages, with obesity-related health issues in our days[168].

380. "Join them or stay away from them" is how the experience of doing business in many emerging markets can be described. How can someone marry a desire for prosperity and personal ethics in countries where corruption is the main way of doing business? What does one do in the face of complete public dysfunction where the only way around is through bribing? These are some of the very hard daily realities of the business environment in many developing countries. Should one respect the stated rules when everyone else is not? And if no, then where is the limit to going around the stated rules? Should someone stand in a line when everyone else is not? Sometimes there is not even a line to stand in even if someone wishes so! And what will playing by the local code of doing, by the local rules of the environment, eventually do to one's personal ethics? And how will we perceive ourselves

---

168 In addition to cancer, which remains one of the primary causes of natural death.

after a certain time of playing by the local rules against one's personal ethical code?

381. There is a clear trade-off in such compromised social and business environments no matter what our personal opinion on the environment is: either one does things by the local way of doing to a certain extent or decides to leave the environment for something better. We do not imagine a situation where someone goes into an administrative building in a developing country with archaic administration for some paperwork, starts giving grand speeches about rule of law and anti-corruption, and expects to obtain what he/she is seeking easily. The sad reality of these types of environments is that if one needs to obtain meaningful results, he/she has to somehow play by the rules of the environment, or at least draw some sort of a blind eye on what is going on. It is a reality that is not politically correct to say out loud for many, but it remains a fact nevertheless to all who have had to experience such environments.

382. There are two consequent difficult questions to playing by the local rules to a certain extent:

    a. Where does one draw the line? Each one of us has a limit to how far one can allow him/herself to go, and that limit is different from one person to the other; and

    b. What will one become after a long time of playing by local rules that he/she rejects deep down? What will become of self-esteem and personal ethics? Will one become something he/she will later reject?

383. The dynamic that unfolds in a social or business environment in a country with a certain level of corruption and social dysfunction also applies in a particular company or industry environment. The culture of a company or an industry plays a central role in shaping people's behaviour and work ethics, regardless of what were the initial personal ethics of the people joining the enterprise or the industry. There is a clear correlation between work incentives and the potential for employee's unethical behaviour. We can find this reality with some types of sport athletes, defence contractors, or tobacco executives. We are astonished how people with great

credentials can act unethically, and how barons of industry or sport can actually hide behind corrupt or gruesome practices. The reader should blame the culture and the environment of Wall Street for the financial calamities of the last years as much as the people themselves. Bringing some of the responsible people to justice will serve as a lesson, but the more important and greatly more difficult fix is rather a radical change of the environment and incentive structure of the industry[169].

384. Wise but admittedly difficult questions to ask before joining a certain company or industry are, "What will taking this job or joining this company or culture do to my person over the long run? Will I find myself in inner agreement with that which I will become?" We often ask different questions than this, "How much will the job pay? What will my career path be like if I take this job? How far up can I go? Or does it work out well with my lifestyle or family constraints?"

385. **Every one of us has his/her weak points of character and ought to stay away from environmental incentives that help make these weaknesses dominant.**

Paying enough attention to the environment we are creating can lead to better long-term policies and positive sustainable cultures. We will finish this chapter with two themes that illustrate well some of the positive environmental repercussions we could create to the benefit of all. We chose these two themes in particular as we think them to be some of the most difficult and problematic challenges of our age. They are often subject of political tension and disagreement internationally: Energy Security and Conservation of Natural Habitats. For each theme, we will first state what we consider to be our wishful scenario, and then we will compare it to the current situation, in order to illustrate how things can be different (hopefully better) from what they are today just by the fact of a better choice of incentives and policies.

---

169 Even Warren Buffet, with his public stature and while serving on the board of directors, could not get Salomon Brothers to change its pay and incentive structure.

386. Energy should be as much of a universal right as Light and Air. **Energy for everyone at the lowest cost and in the cleanest way to the environment possible.** Not Energy as a political and economic tool, but Energy as a universal as much as Light and Air are. Air is considered to be an essential human need; Energy should acquire the same status, and we have the means globally to make it as such.

387. We live in an age of greater development than thousands of years ago. Water and Air should not be the only essentials any longer; Energy, particularly Electric Energy, needs to be added to the list. Electric Energy occupies a great portion of our daily lives and of our economies. It is the backbone of our economic lives wherever we are on this planet[170], and we ought to make it universally available. The demands for Electric Energy are bound to continuously grow, and more so as countries with large populations, such as China, India, or Indonesia, develop. A very large number of the problems resulting from development and industrialisation are likely to be solved by ruthlessly and continuously devising the cheapest and cleanest ways of producing Energy and transporting it to *all*.

388. Most emerging countries suffer from chronic electricity problems in the form electricity shortage or too high of an electricity generation cost. Most developed countries commit geopolitical or environmental blunders in order to secure electricity generation and transmission at the lowest cost possible. The global geopolitical map is as much that of Energy as anything else. And the key driving component of this energy game is not oil; it is electricity. With abundant and cheap electricity, oil would not be as strategic as it is today.

389. It is abundantly clear the role Energy Security has played in the world's geopolitics for at least the past hundred years. Wars have been fought, dictatorships have been protected, and regimes have been toppled, mostly for one simple reason: the developed world is hungry for Energy at the cheapest cost possible, and many

---

170 With the exception of very small pockets of indigenous populations in some parts of the world.

The Influence of the Environment

sources of Energy are present in developing countries. To be exact, developed nations do not lack the Energy sources they need; what they lack is the motivation and economic incentive to move away from gasoline into other Unconventional Energy sources, such as clean coal or renewables.

> a. There are countries today that partially broke the bondage of oil addiction. France, for example, produces most of its electricity from nuclear energy.

390. The political calculation developed nations made in the 20th century is simple: it is economically easier to wage wars and intervene politically and militarily in order to secure the continuous cheap supply of oil than to change the built-in infrastructure and move away from oil. At the core of this infrastructure is one particular element: the car. This modern version of the horse if it was reliant on something else than oil, how things would have played out differently in the past hundred years!

391. The first reason for hunger and world famine is not lack of availability of food; it is logistics. Transportation of food at low cost is a difficult issue in places like Africa and India. Cheap clean energy to all helps greatly reduce food transportation costs and is a massive step towards eradicating world famine.

392. Similarly to food transportation, water can be supplied at lower cost to regions badly in need of it if Energy is more available and cheap. Seawater can be desalinated at lower cost if Energy is available and cheap. If we think, as some people like to, that World War III is likely to be about water shortage, then the remedy is actually, again, cheap universal Energy.

393. A global coordinated effort towards cheap abundant Energy is not naive wishful thinking. The economical calculation of developed and energy-hungry countries in the 20th century might have made sense when other means of producing Energy at large scale were unknown or unfeasible. Today, we live in a different situation; these technologies are within our reach; they are only not mature enough yet to be as cost competitive, but with the right coordinated focus they can be. The sun, the

wind, and the oceans produce more energy than what we can ever dream of using. We have managed to lower the technology cost of harvesting food; we are capable of doing the same for harvesting Energy.

394. What is lacking is the political will to do so in a coordinated fashion and at the international level. Every country is so focused on maximising its share of the existing global energy pie or devising ways of taxing each other for emitting CO_2 in an unrealistic and complicated manner, that they all miss the broader picture of the abundance of Energy on Earth. If a fraction of the geopolitical effort most capable countries spend on acquiring conventional energy[171], or trying to negotiate byzantine mechanisms for taxing carbon emission, is redirected towards maturing unconventional ways of producing new forms of Energy, then the global problem of Energy Security could be largely addressed within a matter of a generation or two.

   a. A system of reward-and-punishment like the Kyoto protocol is very difficult to implement properly as it has the potential of becoming an exercise of accounting and financial treachery at a global scale.

   b. We are creating an environment where all nations fight each other over a smaller pie, while a bigger pie can be created to the benefit of all. Give Industry and Science the right support, and they will achieve this objective of extracting unconventional energy more cheaply in a matter of years. Wasn't it the case with the Space Program in the 1960s? Or isn't that what happened with the shale gas revolution in the United States recently?

395. We are not naive about the global political game when it comes to Energy Security, but another alternative is indeed possible and accessible. Unfortunately, it took us two world wars to put together

---

171 Budget of corporations operating in conventional energy sectors such as coal or oil + defence spending to secure energy sources and routes + the un-quantified cost of corruption and intervention in politically fragile but conventional energy resource rich countries etc.

an international governance system, and it is far from perfect. Some might say this is how human beings operate—we only come together under the pressure of major threats or disasters. In the meantime, we focus on taking from each other more so than creating a bigger pie to all.

396. **We ought to recognise the importance of preserving natural habitats (whether on land or in water) away from human influence, and we ought to create 'human-free' land and water areas.**

397. Without explicitly recognising and respecting this categorisation (human free vs. not), the problem of species destruction is not likely to be properly resolved. We humans will always poach on the weak, in this case natural habitats, when circumstances change or when we have economic reasons to do so. By using the excuse of weak economic conditions, too many mouths to feed, or rarity of some resource, we will continue to slowly poach on natural habitats till nothing is left of them and in the process irrevocably destroy different forms of Life.

    a. The examples of regions where natural habitats are destroyed at alarming rates today are abundant: Central Africa, Madagascar, Amazon forests, Indonesia, and soon enough Alaska and the Arctic Circle.

398. Through not clearly defining and implementing strict international Natural Reserves in land and in sea, threats of extinctions will continue to rise. The economic environment influences the natural environment, and natural habitats are among of the primary sufferers of economic mishaps, even more so than people themselves.

399. Current Natural Reserves are defined at a country level, country by country, respecting the sovereignty of each country, but also through a great amount of international lobbying and subsidising of some sort. It is indeed central to respect countries' territorial sovereignty, but the reality is that the current delineations are often the subject of continuous political dealings. At every change

of regime, variation in international subsidies, or sharp change in commodity prices, the integrity of Natural Reserves is put back into question.

    a. Some countries even perceive natural habitats as effective ways of obtaining much needed international help; others pretend conserving habitats while in reality they let local populations poach slowly but surely.

    b. To be fair, some countries do not lack the will but, rather, the means to enforce the required habitat preservation.

400. In the current system, Natural Reserves may often seem as just a tool for political and economic negotiation in many places around the world. We have again a global environment with the wrong types of incentives in place.

401. A more comprehensive solution for preserving natural habitats in a sustainable manner is required and possible. Sceptics might say that this is wishful thinking too. Some might say that territorial integrity makes it an impossible problem to address; others might think that it is already too late to solve the problem, and we will lose ourselves in international politics if we attempt to do so. The writer dares to differ at the risk of sounding foolish. Case in point: Antarctica. Antarctica is a successful example of an internationally negotiated 'Natural Reserve'. The international agreement on Antarctica works, and works well. We have the right conduits to initiate this process and agree on common sense grounds through the United Nations. And we can start with what is easier: Marine Natural Reserves. Marine habitats should be less controversial to agree on, as they do not neighbour human habitations as closely. Moreover, the percentage of marine habitat that is preserved today is notably lower than that on dry land—the marine world is more neglected simply because it is further away from the sight of many.

402. Ultimately, satisfying basic human needs will draw the pressure away from taking advantage of Natural Reserves. The problem is indeed mainly economical, and the economic and technological environment will continue to impact the natural one. There is no

worse than hungry humans at the proximity of easily accessible Nature; it is admittedly an impossible mission to police them properly. However, satisfying growing human needs will require time, and preservation of essential natural habitats in the meantime is indispensable if we are to leave a meaningful variety of Life to future generations. Nothing short of the clear demarcation of human-free habitat, with continuous monitoring by a neutral international organisation similar to the United Nations, will be effective.

ON HUMAN CONTRADICTIONS

"Plusieurs choses certaines sont contredites: plusieurs passent sans contradiction. Ny la contradiction n'est marque de fausseté; ny l'incontradiction n'est marque de vérité."[172] Blaise Pascal

Seneca is one of the chief figures of the Roman stoicism. He was born in Cordoba to an influential and cultivated father (also named Seneca), studied in Rome, and pursued a political career while there. His career was as volatile as Roman politics of the time: he became a Roman magistrate, got close to emperors and their wives, taught their children, but eventually alienated them, was exiled to Corsica, became Nero's teacher and advisor, and paid the price for it following the plot of AD 65 against the emperor, for which Nero (wrongly) blamed Seneca (amongst others), and ordered him to commit suicide. Seneca was a magistrate, an educated man, and a businessman. He lent money at exorbitant rates to Britain, amassed a fortune[173], and was even portrayed as the chief figure of a ruthless capitalism in his days.

Seneca was also a man of letter, a leading Stoic; he openly despised riches,

---

[172] Many things certain are contradictory while many things are without contradiction. Neither contradiction is a sign of falsity, nor lack thereof is a sign of truth. (John H.T. Francis translation)

[173] Thought to be in the hundreds of millions of dollars in today's money.

is thought to have corresponded with Saint Paul, and was considered even a martyr by some early Christians. Hypocrisy? Double personality? Human contradiction? Or genuine detachment from materiality even while amassing it? Seneca faced the emperor's decision of his death with a typical stoicism. His famous last words[174] were: "Never mind, I leave you what is of far more value than earthly riches, the example of a virtuous life".

403. We have innate contradictions we have to be aware of. It seems that we are genetically wired from an evolutionary perspective to think that we are rational beings, consistent, and with one opinion, where in fact we are self-contradictory in many ways. Although we may be aware of some of these inner contradictions at some level, we are rarely willing to admit them openly. The ancients talked about the sensitive soul vs. the intellectual soul in part to reflect inner conflicting forces and the modularity of the mind. We are all contradictory individuals, and human societies are highly contradictory. The difference between various individuals or between societies is that of degree only.

404. Many human contradictions have innate psychological reasons. As Herman Hesse put it in one of his best existentialist novels *Steppenwolf*, human beings are inside not one, not even two, but a multitude of entities fighting for dominion. This is surprisingly consistent with the latest scientific findings and behavioural theories: Psychology talks about the hierarchy of needs, modularity of the brain[175], different cognitive abilities (rational, intuitive, emotional, subconscious), in addition to various cognitive biases and primitive reflexes that we have carried since the days where our species lived in the jungle.

405. Human contradictions do not only come with civilisation, maturity, or education. They seem to be always there, even if the

---

174 According to Bertrand Russell in *History of Western Philosophy*.

175 Think of the brain not as one entity but as multiple units that can go against each other before (and even after) an output is determined.

individual committing them is not aware of them. Children are not without their contradictions, nor are animals; they are much less simple and much less innocent than we like to imagine them to be at first. The dream of reaching back to innocence and peace in childhood is no more than a misplaced popular nostalgia. All examination of living beings with developed cognition shows an amount of contradiction in behaviour and decision-making, far from simple innocence.

406. It is important to realise that many of the human contradictions are innate and bound to happen. Our biology is work-in-progress as much as everything else around, albeit at a very slow rate[176]. Work-in-progress means conflicts between different trends and attributes in us, with certain traits eventually prevailing over others. Looked at this way, it seems that these contradictions are, at least partially, part of the evolutionary selection process.

407. We are genetically predisposed, as a result of billions of years of evolution, to fear and to worry about our survival; about finding enough food and water; about leaving the largest legacy possible; about fending off predators and competing peers; and about avoiding surprises and unknowns that might threaten our existence. We have managed with progress to create a more secure environment to ourselves; yet, the genetic wirings are still there to no avail. Something that was created over billions of years cannot be modified easily in hundreds of years of technology and knowledge progress. The result is that we still worry, probably much more than we should.

    a. We replace competition for survival with the more silly office politics, or the more sinister human wars; the worry about hoarding food[177] by hoarding a certain figure in our bank account which may sometimes seem quite detached from reality; the worry about leaving a genetic legacy with being more famous or more attractive; and

---

176 The rate of change is in the thousands or millions of years.

177 Unfortunately some do still need to really worry about hoarding food in some parts of the world.

the worry about surprises and unknowns in the jungle that may threaten our life with more intellectual and psychological surprises and unknowns. Our wirings are still there; they are for the most part redirected towards other purposes, which may result in misplaced perceptions and contradictions.

408. Progress requires difficulties and contradictions; Progress is about overcoming them. Contradictions are as essential to Progress, as the problem is essential to the solution. Through contradictions, we learn to prioritise, to optimise, and to make choices, provided that we are aware of these contradictions.

409. But are all contradictions necessary and beneficial for Progress? We are inclined to say no… Are we aware of all our contradictions? Naturally not, but that has the potential to change…

410. The Absurd is part of the human contradictions. We did consider having both chapters merged, but the importance and oddity of the Absurd made us opt for a separate treatment. Still, realising the Absurd and dealing with it is not without its inescapable contradictions.

411. We human beings are both concrete and abstract at the same time. We look far, and we worry about the near. We desire a lot, but we want to have most things without any effort if we can manage it. We want to sit idle, but we find ourselves quickly bored with idleness. We set objectives for ourselves, to only create new ones once the prior ones are achieved. We seek happiness without agreeing on what happiness really is. We blame others when the faults are really our own. We talk about grand ideas, when petty matters can influence us greatly. We make resolutions but often do nothing about them.

412. Humans have been described in a narrow sense as purely materialistic individuals only driven by material desires and biological needs. This description is clearly not satisfactory. Self-esteem, the need for some form of Morality, existential questions, Honour, Art, and Curiosity, are all urgent needs in us that cannot be explained by simple materiality. Some humans are found to

On Human Contradictions

reject materiality or to sacrifice themselves to something else other than materiality. Human societies do exist where materiality is not the key to the social fabric.

413. Humans have been considered to have a 'Soul' or a 'Spirit' temporarily inhabiting the body on this Earth. We were later surprised to discover how powerful can this body and its needs be, and how much in control it really is in many situations. Whatever is our definition of the Soul, we find great difficulty dissociating it from the influence of the body and basic biological processes. Even the most ascetic and spiritually or intellectually inclined among us have indispensable bodily needs that, if ignored, will ultimately lead to contradictions that can indeed shock us.

414. Galileo[178] decided not to stand firm for his discoveries and scientific beliefs for practical and material reasons. Brecht in his play *Life of Galileo* put it nicely. A philosopher, seeker of the truth above all else, was shocked by Galileo's final submission to the Church's pressure:

> "GALILEO: I submit that as scientists we have no business asking what the truth may lead to.
>
> THE PHILOSOPHER (in wild alarm): Mr. Galilei, the truth can lead to all sorts of things!
>
> GALILEO: Your Highness. In these nights telescopes are being directed at the sky all over Italy. The moons of Jupiter don't lower the price of milk."[179]

The moons of Jupiter do not indeed lower the price of milk; any scientist has to eat first.

415. So we are material but not fully; we are spiritual or intellectual but not fully; we are rational but not fully; we are conscious but not fully.

---

178 Galileo is the founder of the mathematical approach to Nature, and thus his contribution to Science and Physics cannot be exaggerated. Galileo's scientific foundation was necessary basis for Newton and his mechanical laws.

179 The Wolfgang Sauerlander and Ralph Manheim translation.

416. We mostly live in societies where the more we develop and progress, the more animals we kill, and the more sensitive we become about watching animals beings killed and knowing the details of how it happens. We cry no for bullfighting, but we say yes to burger chains. We cry no to animal torture, but we say yes to *foie gras*[180]. We say we love animals, we seek to have some of them as pets, and we build zoos and parks to take our kids to and watch them, but our collective behaviour is the biggest threat to the survival of most living species on our planet. We want a nice juicy steak regularly, or we think tuna to be great for our diet. We want to help animals on one side, but we need to eat them, kill them with pesticide, or chase them away to make more comfortable space for us.

417. We want to preserve and spread human rights, workers rights, and female rights. But we also want to buy as much as possible at the least cost possible, fully aware of the long series of infringements to our values of which some of the cheap products we buy have been the result. These two attitudes are irreconcilable to a large extent.

   a. Some might argue that it is not the role of the consumer to be the moral judge on such issues; it is the role of the regulator or the government that allows such imports to make their way into the market. This is a valid reasoning. Nevertheless, the point on human contradictions remains.

   b. All we are saying here is that, left to themselves, market participants can behave in contradictory manners that require a watchful eye[181].

418. Moral vs. material contradictions have always existed. Times change, technologies change, our clothing changes, but such contradictions remain. These contradictions may become more hidden or subtle, but they remain. A substantial part of our

---

180 The stuffing of ducks far beyond what their body requires is essential to producing *foie gras*.

181 Usually we name that watchful eye a regulator.

imported oil and minerals hide behind a tragedy more subtle but not that different from the one imported sugar to Europe used to hide behind at the time of Voltaire. When hearing about the real cost of producing sugar for cheap from a dismembered slave, Candide finally renounces to his all-encompassing optimism.

"Quand nous travaillons aux sucreries, et que la meule nous attrape le doigt, on nous coupe la main ; quand nous voulons nous enfuir, on nous coupe la jambe: je me suis trouvé dans les deux cas. C'est à ce prix que vous mangez du sucre en Europe."[182] *Candide, ou l'Optimisme,* Voltaire (1759).

419. We reject torture and admit an inalienable right for every person to obtain fair judgment. We definitely would not want to find ourselves in a situation where we are threatened by torture or receiving punishment without due process. Yet, we know that our governments do operate a form of torture and legal mistreatment, even in some of the countries known best for their freedom, rule of law, and human rights. We prefer not to know about such details; we prefer to mind our own business and leave it to a small number of people to do the dirty work for us. When we are scared, when fear takes hold of us, we allow even more of such actions to take place. And the greater hypocrisy is that we feign shock, and we feign to be greatly indignant when such practices come out to the surface.

420. We pretend that all humans are equal, or at least should have equal defined rights and duties, but our news machinery and our government act every day in ways that point to the contrary, *and we know it*. A lost life in a developed country is reported as a greater tragedy than a life lost in a poorer country, or when the victims are remote or from a different culture. We equate few dead on one side, with thousands dead on the other side.

421. We know that our governments do back dictators, or at least turn

---

[182] When we work at the sugar mill, and the mill snatches a finger, they cut off the hand; when we attempt to run away, they cut off the leg: I found myself in both situations. This is the price at which you eat sugar in Europe. (John H.T. Francis translation)

a blind eye on many of their unacceptable doings, but we prefer not to talk about it. We pretend that it is the fault of a corrupt and unchangeable class of politicians, while we actually elect these politicians to office. In summary, we claim to stand for something, while we actually do something else.

422. **We have different needs and wants, and these can lead to contradicting consequences. We choose to prioritise between them on the basis of closeness, familiarity, materiality, or simply laziness, regardless of the ultimate weight of the consequences.**

423. Humans by nature do not notice the good years and the good events as much as the lean years and the times of reckoning. We are genetically inclined to have the negative weighing more on our psychology than the positive; this helped us survive better in the jungle by focusing more on the threats. We take the good times for granted, and we react much more strongly and with surprise during bad times. Here are two stories from our recent economic times to illustrate this:

   a. The US and the Credit Bubble.

   A lot has been said about the credit collapse in the US from 2007 to 2009, and all the financial and economic consequences of it. Fingers have been pointed to the greedy bankers and their reckless behaviour, to Wall Street, which was opposed to Main Street. Much has been reported in the news about the sad economic repercussions of such greedy behaviour of the few at the cost of many hard-working middle class families. While much of what has been said is valid and worthy of consideration, the reality is different from what the media generally reported or continues to report. The essential ingredients of the Credit Bubble, low interest rates and deregulation, have been in the making for *decades* in the US, and almost everybody has been a part of it or took advantage[183] of it directly or indirectly. The truth

---

[183] It is definitely important to note that not everybody took advantage of it to the same extent; there was indeed inequality of benefits.

is that the US would not have grown at the rate at which it grew in 1990s and the 2000s, up to 2007, without the 'credit push' into the economy. Fewer jobs would have been found, and fewer houses would have been bought without lower interest rates and deregulation. Bankers were just the executors in a paradigm that was set in the United States politics across political parties probably since the time of the Great Depression. Home Ownership is a sacred topic politically in the US, and much has been done across the aisle to bolster it. The credit collapse is in large part a result of all these political and regulatory efforts. We talk a lot about the difficult years from 2007 onwards, without really saying that the general level of home ownership and prosperity in the US would have been different for decades without some of such policies. Let us be clear: we are not defending all such policies blindly; however, we also reject a one-sided naive view of economic history. The same could be said about the ballooning budget deficit and national debt in the US. The US government did indeed spend beyond its means for years but also reduced taxes dramatically for a long time allowing for more wealth creation across society. We see the lean years, but we do not notice as much the easy ones.

b. The Germans, the Greeks, and the Euro.

As we are writing these lines, the Euro break-up or non-break-up saga continues to unravel. A lot of talk has taken place since 2009 about how the Germans will have to subsidize the rest of the so-called 'lazy' Southern Europe. Britain is threatening again of walking out of the European Union and requesting a rewriting of its pact with it, a repeat of the Thatcher days. The parallel with La Fontaine's fable of the ant and the grasshopper is aesthetically attractive; the news media thinks the Greeks, the Portuguese, the Irish, the Spanish, and the Italians as the grasshoppers that will ultimately have to be bailed out by the hard-working ants, the Germans. The reality here again is subtler regardless of populous feelings; it represents another example of how human nature tends to ignore the positive while considering the negative in greater focus. The Germans would not have done as well since the 1990s without Europe, especially 'emerging' Europe, to the east and the south. Germany has benefited from both low-cost locations for production at its doorsteps and emerging economies with increased purchasing power and appetite for high-quality German products with no import duty. Even more importantly, if Germany had remained using its Deutsch Mark in the current money-printing environment for currencies, its currency would have appreciated so greatly (similarly to what the Swiss Frank has gone through) with direct impact on German exports, the key growth engine of the German economy. The reality is that the troubles in Europe ironically keep the Euro lower and help sustain the growth of German exports to outside Europe, particularly Asia.

Many countries in Europe have been fiscally irresponsible and have to undertake deep reforms, which only the pressure they are currently under can hope to deliver. The Germans have been more responsible fiscally and have already undertaken many labour market reforms. They are also known for their high rate of savings. The German industrial acumen and quality & innovation advantages are there and real. Nevertheless, the story of the ants and the grasshoppers is not the accurate description of the situation in Europe. Germany would have suffered more economically in a continent with barriers to trade and investment, and it would have suffered more with a currency that is much more valued. The Germans, the Dutch, the French, and many Nordic countries did benefit from some of more developing Europe's appetite and later problems, and they therefore cannot simply wash their hands and blame them for all the world's problems when the days of reckoning take place. To be fair to the Germans, the loudest voices against helping European countries in difficulty are coming more from the financial community, particularly across the Atlantic, than from the Germans themselves. The bashing of the European Union is indeed a popular topic in some of these circles.

424. Humanity has achieved great progress through increased social interaction and globalisation. The world is more and more integrated; we are more and more reliant on each other, and we have achieved in the process many positive synergies in our societies. Industrialisation, Commerce, and even Science require today a social knit and greater interactions between humans, which goes against individualism. A single man today is much less capable of surviving alone than a single man a thousand years ago; he knows much less about the food he eats or the clothes he wears than in previous ages. In parallel, human emancipation from dogmatism, particularly with the spread of liberal values, a freer movement of people and thoughts, and the (almost) lack of geographic boundaries over the Internet, have all contributed to growth in individuality and individual morality over a morality inherited from society. The Religious Institutions, the Government, and the Parties do not command today the moral weight they used to have in the past. Ethics are becoming more individual, and individuals are finding that they have a choice in their morality. In summary, we seem to have on the one side, greater social, technical, and commercial inter-relation, and on the other, greater individual liberty. A split of the individual and further contradictions and difficulties arise from such opposing trends.

   a. We do not necessarily care to befriend everybody in our community anymore or share their ethical values, but we can enjoy definite synergies from being in a community.

   b. We do not need to socialise as much in Church anymore, but we sure benefit from having a large network of business acquaintances.

   c. We do not sometimes care enough about the problems of the ones close to us, but we find ourselves rushing to aid victims of disasters in faraway places.

> d. We interact with a larger network of people than a thousand years ago, but our relationships are shallower even in-between family members.

425. One of our favourite types of contradictions concerns social comparison. We tend to judge our personal human affairs in comparison with our neighbours and immediate acquaintances, and not in absolute terms. Our self-image is shaped in parts by the social circle we are in, and not necessarily purely by our achievements, our progress, or our hard work. We are psychologically wired to feel good when we are faring better than our neighbours even if all of us are actually regressing. Equally, we are wired to feel bad when we fare worse than our neighbours even if all of us are actually progressing.

"Our envy always lasts longer than the happiness of those we envy" Heraclitus

> a. Our immediate neighbours and friends, and their social status, have actually important psychological influence on us. Sometimes it is enough to change social circle to start feeling differently about oneself and personal situation. In the land of the rich, a middle-class man prone to judge by materiality is more likely to lose self-esteem or spend his time envying everybody, while this same man would have a very different image of himself in the land of the poor.
>
> b. In a group of individuals, it is not uncommon to find people arguing about how to split the pie to their best individual interest before there is even any meaningful pie to split, or, more absurdly, at the cost of growing any pie... Many groups do not manage to grow the pie because of such comparison dynamics.
>
> c. Most people in developed countries today enjoy a better quality of life than a Rockefeller or a Medici, and a great number of people in the world definitely enjoy a better quality of life than the greatest of the Egyptian pharaohs. Yet, our happiness remains largely driven by peer comparison than absolute progress.

426. Humans also exhibit great contradictions in the perception of the Good and the Bad.

  a. Human views on Ethics are sometimes contradictory from one age to the other, and even sometimes within one particular period.

   i. How can euthanasia be considered legal in some countries and murder in others? The differences in the treatment of euthanasia across different countries today are not ones of small degrees; they can be as opposite as black and white.

   ii. How can a drone attack in one case be labelled 'Act of War', while in another go unnoticed under the same international law?

  Our approach to capital punishment, to slavery, or to torture have dramatically changed with time from being acceptable to being right in the middle of the square of the Bad. What can be said to have been Good in the past is not the same as in the present.

  b. The combination of (1) The mechanics of why things happen the way they happen, all that our rational capabilities have led us to discover so far on the one hand; and (2) A need for a human system of values on the other, *is nothing but a great contradiction of essence.* How can we simplistically label an action or a thought good or bad, desirable or undesirable, when all that our cognitive capabilities continuously point to is that everything is somehow linked? Good can lead to the Bad and the Bad to the Good even when not intended. A particular act on its own can be considered good from a certain point of view, or under certain circumstances, and bad in others. Even personal intentions and psychologies have their mechanistic causes or at least inducers, from which one cannot escape. **Nothing is hanging out there on its own to be really judged on its own without some sort of intellectual compromise.**

c. Humans are biased towards stories and storytelling, particularly the ending of the stories. This even influences our ethical perception in a contradictory manner. Between a story full of Bad but with a good nice ending, even if a very brief one, and a story full of Good but with one tragic bad ending, experiments often show that people judge the first story to be better than the second one. In other words, we like our fairy tales. Consider two stories with the same amount of Good and Bad; is it fair to consider one better than the other if its ending is good for random reasons?

   i. We are likely to judge the one with a good ending to be a more positive story. And what if one day we discover that Time sequence can be manipulated, what would happen to the primacy of the story-ending? We are indeed selective and biased in our judgment of what ought to be a good life or a bad life, a good behaviour and a bad behaviour.

   ii. Religions preach avoiding sin, but most of them consider a great sinner repenting at the last moment before death likely to receive salvation, while one who has been virtuous all of his life but managed to succumb in his last days to sins out of circumstantial weaknesses without a final pardon as likely to pay for his sins[184].

427. The contradictions are not only in our social behaviour. They are also in our biology and our psychology.

428. The points of disgust in our bodies are the same as the sexual points; they are the source of much fascination and attention but also disgust. It is no wonder that Sex is present high in the hierarchy of both our interest and our guilt. Sex can be the source of great pleasure but also of great pain, and it can be a great taboo. Sex is the

---

184 Religions will argue that God is wiser than this and sees through things, but the reality is that religions and their judgment systems do act in contradictory manners.

source of Life for many living forms and is instrumental in Love, but it can equally be a source of shame, guilt, and negativity.

429. Our body can secrete the same chemicals for situations that we consider contradictory. Let us take the example of endorphin. Our body secretes endorphin to cope with physical pain. Endorphin helps alleviate some of the pain and allows us to keep on going. But endorphin is also responsible for the feeling of relief we enjoy after exercise or sexual activity. In other words, the feeling of blissfulness after a long run or making love is due to the same chemical secreted by our body in situations of bodily pain. It is no wonder then that the notions of pleasure and pain can get mixed up in some people, in contrast with the average behaviour. Situations of confusion between pleasure and pain are far from being uncommon.

430. We like to think that we are fully rational and conscious of what we do. We blame and critique what seems to us an irrational or idiotic behaviour, especially when it emanates from the smarter or more powerful among us. We amaze ourselves at the mistakes of leaders of industry, politics, or religions. We ask, "How could they be so greedy? How could they preach something for so long and act contrary to it?" The combination of the environment and multiple contradicting aspirations in every one of us can put people in situations where they behave in contradiction with loudly claimed values. We can find corrupt cops, sinning priests, politicians betraying their country or their constituency, bankers breaching their fiduciary duty, and doctors breaching their Hippocratic oath.

431. We think our great men and women, our great leaders, and our saints as superhumans with little of our basic human needs. We force their image to be as such, while we know from our everyday experience that we are all humans with faults, and we are prone to committing mistakes. Our beloved leaders, great men and women, our saints are not capable of mistakes, do not have any weaknesses, and if someone dares to put such a claim on them, we vehemently reject it. Our presidents cannot have extra-marital affairs, our high clergy cannot be corrupt, our most intelligent people cannot be wrong, our great champions cannot be doping, and our great

generals and war heroes cannot be war criminals or capable of some of the worst desecrations to human dignity... We project a blind idealistic image on some of the key symbols in our societies, and we force it to be as such in complete contradiction with the subtleties of our everyday life and what we know about humans. Worse, we take collective offence at any proof of the contrary or at any rational discussion of the actions and decisions of such leaders.

432. Humans have difficulty deciding their way on monogamy vs. polygamy. In our societies, throughout our history, cultures, and religions, we find both monogamy and polygamy to be institutionalised and practised.

   a. In Nature, we find all forms of relationships systemised: lifetime monogamy, serial monogamy, polygyny, and polyandry. Hence, once more, we cannot anchor our ethical norms in natural observations only.

   b. From a purely economic and social coherence standpoint, both monogamy and polygamy can be found to make sense as a structuring basis of social units depending on many factors such as male and female income distribution, which tend to be different across times and societies[185].

433. In our days, a greater part of human societies have what we can call a monogamous culture; in these societies, polygamy is frowned

---

[185] The key-driving factor in family structures from a purely economic point of view is the financial capability of the parents to take care of the needs of their children in a satisfactory manner. Many children born to very destitute parents are likely to become a cost on society in one way or another if their progenitors do not have the means of properly caring to their needs. The rich have greater financial capability of rearing more children. Moreover, in a system where the rich rear more children than the poor, a heredity system based on equal distribution of wealth between siblings ultimately goes a long way into normalising wealth distribution in the overall society. On the other hand, a greater share of partners being monopolised by the more well-off part of society can be unstable on the long run. The two opposing dynamics play against each other in a way that can come to define under which conditions polygamy can be preferred to monogamy and vice versa. These are again only purely economic considerations that do not take into account a necessary ethical code.

upon, at least in public. Historically, the trend is definitely towards monogamy, whether for life or in a serial manner. However, there exist many societies still where polygamy is normal, natural, and approved of by the religion the society follows. Contradictions do exist in both types of societies nevertheless.

    a. In many monogamous societies, monogamy is more of a social pretence than a real social code people strongly abide by. In our days, having extra-marital affairs is considered as an inevitable part of the married life in many social circles. It is one of those things assumed to happen; humans are considered to be weak and will hence succumb to temptation at some point in their married life. It is these same societies that point the finger at polygamous societies with disdain.

        i. If human nature is so weak, then why instate monogamy in the first place?

        ii. If marriage only serves the purpose of providing a suitable legal status to possible children coming out of a relationship, there can be other ways of providing such status without making the institution of marriage so strict on the surface and breached in practice. Less sophisticated hunter-gatherer societies have already figured it out, and so we also can if the entire cusp of the matter is with regard to children.

    b. On the other hand, many polygamous societies do not really practice polygamy in a widespread manner even if it is sanctioned. Polygyny is allowed in Islam yet, in many Muslim countries, a large part, even a majority, of couples today are monogamous. Polygyny is allowed by religion, but some circles of society may frown on it.

We indeed find contradictions on both sides of the spectrum. The preachers of monogamy sometimes apply it less in practice than the polygamous. We dare to say that our societies today remain confused in their practice of monogamy and polygamy.

434. Human beings put much more weight on expectations, even if flawed, over present reality. It is one of the consequences of forethought. We care more about the future, over which we have limited control, than the present. While such an attitude is valid most of the time, it can result in contradictions and mistakes in many instances:

> a. When expectations are synonymous with false hopes or too much hope.
>
> We all have experienced the pain of having been too optimistic or having spent too much time and effort on what turns out to be a waste of energy instead of taking advantage of the present.
>
> b. When we fail to understand the key drivers of what we are really expecting.
>
> By electing their favourite candidate to office, many do believe, for example, that their future will be much brighter and different from their difficult present. More often than not, such human expectations turn quickly into bitter disappointments.
>
> c. When we become unhappy because our future contains uncertainty while our present is good.
>
> Consumers spend based on expectations and confidence about the future more so than their current financial situation. One can have much of what she has always wished for but remain miserable if she feels her future to be clouded or with risk, sometimes unjustly.

435. The power of expectations is that it can control our present in such a dominant manner. People with the same present, and the same positive and negative possibilities for the future, can experience dramatically different outcomes depending on whether they focus on the half-empty or the half-full part of the glass. We do appear contradictory if we have achieved great goals in our present, but we continue to be controlled by the negative narrative about the future.

436. The search for the one model that accurately explains the human behaviour has always interested Science. Till now, nothing of what has been provided constitutes a satisfactory solution. It is unlikely that a satisfactory model that predicts human behaviour at the individual level[186] will ever be found. Part of the reason is that whatever model for individual human behaviour is posited, humans themselves are likely to react to it out of self-esteem and undermine it in the process. There exist clear human traits that are widely shared, but there is no one holistic model that engulfs them in a consistent manner.

437. Human nature has been put into many 'moulds'. The more famous of these are in what follows without respect to chronology.

　　a. Schopenhauer talked about the Will to Exist, the will of the individual to survive as the key driving force of any human being. Survival instincts are without a question strong impulses within us. However, History is full of martyrdom and heroic deaths. For various and contradicting causes, many individuals did not hesitate to give their life freely for ideas that they would not even benefit from. The Will to Exist fails in front of such situations. The will to exist though a legacy can be more encompassing, but it is not complete either.

　　b. Some could argue that those who give their life away for an idea or ideal believe in some benefit obtained from their action in another life. Hence, it is metaphysical belief that constitutes the key drive of human nature. This contradicts Schopenhauer's point above (and others), which remains valid in many instances. Galileo's choice of sparing his own life and giving up his discoveries is a valid example of a situation where the Will to Exist supersedes Ideals.

　　c. Many idealists, especially German idealists (and at the top of them Hegel), attempted to explain all of History through the lens of ideality. They talked about the Mind

---

[186] As opposed to the collective level where more progress has been made.

or the Spirit, in continuous movement and manifestation in everything around us and in us[187]. Hegel argued that the Spirit manifests itself in everything, and that Spirit will lead History to its finality through the dialectical process. Such ideas remain popular with some, under slightly different forms, e.g. Fukuyama and the End of History.

There are many ways, some easier than others, to refute this mould. Our preferred way is based on purely scientific grounds and Chaos Theory, which we do not need to detail on here. Suffice to mention a historical counter-argument. One of Hegel's greatest critiques was Marx, who, rightly so to some extent, pointed out to the materialistic nature of humans and societies, and everything really around us. Wars are indeed fought as much (if not more) for material gain than ideas and ideals.

d. Marx replaced Hegel's Spirit by the Material, but, unfortunately, he also went too far in trying to mould everything in human nature according to the Material. We again find many examples in History of individuals giving up the material, and this while they are still living. The Material is not always the greatest or only driver of human behaviour[188]. Again, the Material is important, but not everything can be solely explained by it. Otherwise, how could we explain the life of Saint Anthony, Saint Francis, or Ludwig Wittgenstein?

e. Darwinism (or Evolutionary Theory) is of one the greatest paradigms of Nature and probably the closest of the moulds to fit human nature for particular timespans. We are after all as much of a living being as any animal or vegetation, and we are the product of this theory.

---

187 An analogy would be how the Christians perceive the Holy Spirit and its ongoing work in the Church, i.e. the community of Christians.

188 Although this might be more difficult to remember in our current times, given the chase for money we often put our lives in.

Darwin demonstrated that the key (mostly unconscious) driver of any species, and of an individual within that species, is the survival of the species in its best forms possible, and hence, he highlighted the importance of gene transmission and selection and its impact on the evolution of species. Unfortunately, there is no place in Darwinism for explaining the everyday behaviour of an individual, and hence, it does not constitute an applicable holistic mould. Darwinism represents more of a 'passive' paradigm, a structure within the human nature, but with no practical implications for explaining everyday behaviour of individuals.

f. Closely related to pro-creation and gene transmission is the Freudian mould of sexual drive. Freud tried to explain all human behaviour through the lens of Sexuality and the Unconscious. He made advances into the subject, but as attested by the role Freudian approach currently plays in the overall practice of Psychology, influences of this approach have greatly diminished over the past half a century, and many of its aspects are considered today either of no practical use or simply wrong.

g. Nietzsche and Russell are very different philosophers, both in terms of character and approach, and we find their points of view opposed on many things. They however seem to agree on at least one element: the importance of Power and its influence on human behaviour. Hence, Power is our next candidate in the look for the perfect mould. Power is a great driver of human behaviour and can be defined in a general enough way to cover some of the moulds previously discussed. Power includes material power as well as the power of ideas, the power of influence, even the power of the gene. Traditionally, different forms of Power include: (1) Raw physical power (military, police); (2) Material power (the wealthy, business owners, money providers); (3) Power of influence (fame, media, church); (4) Intellectual power (scientific community, philosophers)[189]; and (5) Political power (executive, legislative, judicial). Individuals seek to maximise Power; they equally get together in order to gain collective power. This mould is unfortunately not without counter-examples. History contains examples of individuals leaving power not to obtain another form of Power, not under subjugation or pressure, but for pure personal motives that are not related to Power. Many leave positions of Power for family reasons, and some out of need for peace or balance. Some do not even attempt to gain real power in societies; many saints and hermits fall under this category. Even some politicians have given up power for surprising motives. We invite the reader to think about Edward VIII giving up his kingdom for a relationship. De Gaulle gave up power despite the aura and popularity he gained after World War II, probably out of self-esteem more than anything, and did not take part in the 4th French Republic[190].

h. Finally, individuality and individual expression could be considered as a powerful mould.

"Man needs one thing—his own *independent* desire, whatever this independence might cost and wherever it might lead." Dostoevsky, *Notes From Underground*.

Or also from the same author and the same piece:

"[...] people knowingly, that is, possessing full knowledge of their own true interests, have relegated them to the background and rushed down a different path, that of risk and chance [...] merely as if they didn't want to follow the beaten track."

We do many things for our self-esteem and our

---

189 Their power has unfortunately diminished greatly in the last century despite the great advances of Science.

190 He came back to politics few years later and again gave up power in 1969 when he realised that he was not as popular with the people anymore.

individuality, sometimes even irrational things. Force us to do something, and we may end up doing the opposite just because… Teens are probably the best at this game. However, we are also social creatures. When we combine, when we get together, we lose some of this individuality, but we gain a lot in terms of knowledge and materiality. Some of us, especially when faced with threat to existence or in cases of extreme uncertainty, choose deliberately to mute our individuality for long periods of time. But here again, individuality is not a mould or a method for describing general behaviour; if anything, individuality is an antagonist of the behavioural mould.

438. Human behaviour is comprised of a complicated and mixed bag of drivers and cognitive models and modules. It is almost always a bad idea to speculate one particular nature or paradigm and force all the human behaviour to fit in it under all circumstances.

In summary, let us hold off on blaming the others or the environment for all the negatives, and let us look deeper into our nature and our innate contradictions. Disillusionments about human affairs are often a reflection of our inner contradictory aspirations and changing priorities more than anything else.

Brief Notes on the Pains of Evolution and Progress

Is our species still in change, at the DNA level that is? Does Cultural Evolution, which is much faster, impact Darwinian Evolution? What impacts DNA evolution most? And what traits are more important or likely to stick? These are the types of questions we will attempt to discuss here. We do not pretend to hold any out-of-the-ordinary expertise in Evolutionary Biology; nevertheless, we hope to say something interesting about it without raising major objections.

439. Despite the continued denial of the majority[191], we are a product of a trial-and-error process specific to living forms we call Evolution. We are not unlike any other species on Earth present or extinct, and the difference between species is only a matter of degrees, not of anything fundamentally different.

440. There are several ways of elaborating on the process of Evolution. It is after all one of the most central paradigms that humans managed to discover. We like to perceive it as follows: it is the

---

191 From the latest available statistics, the majority of world population still does not realise or fails to accept that our species is a product of the evolution of life forms, as is the case of all living beings on this planet, making us all related and fundamentally not that different. Creationism and theistic evolutionary beliefs are still dominant within the general public.

result of a continuous conflict, a conflict between the force of Life, Life wanting to persist and expand as much as possible on the one hand, and adversarial effects of the environment[192], be it non-living or living, working to limit or eliminate this Life and its expansion on the other. From this continuous conflict, organic functions are tested and re-tested, under varying conditions. Many are dropped, but some are retained and promulgated. More and more complex building blocks are added as they provide a certain advantage for Life.

441. The process of Evolution is not linear, and its output does not follow a constant speed or pattern. Worse, Life can temporarily *regress* in Evolution before progressing again, as is the case with documented periods of mass extinctions. It is not unlike restarting from a cleaner, though not entirely blank, sheet. The environment itself is chaotic, continuously changing, shifting in paradigms, and capable of being influenced by many unforeseen drivers. Hence, the results of Evolution are not necessarily predictable, as much as the evolution of the environment and its adversarial effects are not easily predictable either. Sitting at the cusp of the Dinosaur extinction, one could not have foreseen this cataclysmic event and a complete revision of evolutionary development. *Things could have been otherwise.*

We can note three common false beliefs when it comes to Evolution.

442. First False Belief: Everything in living beings is coming out of Evolution and should therefore have a clear purpose, even if we do not understand it. Everything Evolution produces is the most efficient way possible.

    a. Evolution is a continuous process. There is no reason to believe that anything in it is final. Many of the biological functions developed through Evolution are biological wonders beyond the capacity of any engineering we have.

---

[192] Not all that is in the environment is adversarial and against Life. Otherwise, Life would not have come to be in the first place.

However, not everything in our body, or the body of other species, is perfect and final, and not everything is of *current* usability. Examples abound in humans (e.g. appendices or hair growth on the genitals) and other animals (e.g. small leg bones in whales). Moreover, some biological functions might have been helpful in a different time and age, but not today.

    b. Some traits coming out of Evolution may still represent weaknesses; they are therefore possible candidates for extinction by the same evolutionary process (e.g. sinus problems). **By definition, if everything is perfect and as best as it could be, then there would be no need for any further evolution, and we should then agree that the process is fully achieved. Evolution is about a certain conflict, about trial-and-error, and it is an on-going work.**

443. Second False Belief: Evolution is fast or can be shortcut by human intervention. We humans can confidently understand Evolution and manage it to our taste. This is the most dangerous of the false beliefs and does not date back only to the post-Darwinian era of Galton and Eugenics. Talk about race superiority and weeding out the weak through warfare has been documented since Antiquity. Some of what Churchill expressed in terms of superiority through warfare and greater progress of civilisations when they are in a state of war is almost exactly what Heraclitus had expressed ~2,500 years before.

    a. Evolution is a process that works over a span of millions of years. If we compare this with the entire length of human civilisation, we see how futile and misplaced is this belief. What might seem as a correlate between a certain group of people and a certain performance may be temporary and subject to change with the change in general conditions. We naturally do not mean that there is no relation between physical or cognitive power and DNA transmission. What we mean is that *it is impossible for* us to predict with certainty which human traits or civilizational traits will provide a long-term advantage to the species, or a sub-set of that species. To use again the example of Dinosaurs: they were bigger, faster, and more ferocious than mammals. Did this allow them any long-term superiority? The environment is changing and unpredictable, and so are its adversarial effects. Hence, the process of Evolution is not easy to imagine accurately under all circumstances. **What we think matters might not be, and some elements that we overlook might be instrumental for the next step of our evolution. We can develop knowledge about the drivers of Evolution, but this knowledge should <u>always</u> be checked by modesty.**

b. As with following the story:

There were two brothers, Alan and Fred. Alan was the elder; he was the bigger and the stronger since his young age. Alan was the pride of his parents. He grew up exercising his muscles every day, building his strength continuously, and was the talk of town, for he was among the most handsome and the fittest–Alan was indeed the local boxing champion. Fred on the other hand was the younger and has always been small and frail. Fred never cared much about building his strength and spent most of his time as a little kid running around. Fred had a dog with which he used to love sprinting. No one cared much about Fred; he was small, thin, and with a shy and recluse personality. Fred used to always walk in the shadow of Alan. Growing up, Alan and Fred developed a taste for hiking in the misty mountains. Their routine was to go on full-day hiking trips once every week or two. Alan used to always tease Fred whenever they came across a difficult path or something hard to climb. Fred used to love Alan and take it with a sense of humour; Alan naturally also loved his brother and thought of himself as a great care taker of his frail brother. One day while hiking, Alan and Fred, turning a corner, came face to face with a big bear. What do you think the outcome of such an encounter is? Will Alan with his great muscle strength, tall figure, and outstanding boxing capabilities defeat the grizzly bear? Or will the quick small Fred with his greater ability to escape survive the encounter? We suspect that Fred is more likely to make it out alive. It is this type of unexpected encounter that usually defines the outcome of Survival; few would have considered Fred to be superior up until this unexpected encounter.

444. Third False Belief: There is some sort of finality in Evolution, or that the human species is a finality in Evolution.

   a. This false belief has a great commonality with the first two and can be answered using very similar arguments. What is important to note is that **there is no scientific evidence that we are any final product, any ultimate finality;** we are just another step in the evolutionary process. We should also admit, borrowing elements from the above, that we do not really understand the dynamics of Evolution well enough to be able to ascertain which attributes of the living beings are more important than others or are likely to 'stick' from one generation to the other and come to define a whole species.

These elements of evolutionary theory are not the subject here but serve as necessary background to what follows and for addressing the questions we laid out.

445. To the question, "Is our species still in change, at the DNA level that is?" the answer is, "Yes, there is no evidence of any finality of Evolution. However, we fail to satisfactorily understand the speed at which this is happening *in a lasting manner.*"

446. To the question, "Can Cultural Evolution impact Darwinian Evolution?" the answer is, "Most likely yes although (again) we fail to fully grasp (yet) how do such processes operate."

Here some further detailing is required. Cultural Evolution is a

Reflections on Fundamental Matters

broad term that refers to human kind's evolution from a civilisation and society perspective[193]. It is the evolution of the *Homo Sapiens* from a hunter-gatherer way of living to what we are today with all aspects of our civilisation, our newly created environments, our mastery of technology, and our evolution of language, thought, and knowledge. The question here then signifies, "Is it possible for the evolution of *Homo Sapiens* in terms of civilisation, culture, and way of living to ultimately impact the species DNA evolution?" and the answer is, "Most likely yes." "Will this impact 'stick'?" The answer is, "We don't know. We do not know with certainty what will impact DNA evolution."

447. If we admit that Darwinian Evolution is the result of a continuous conflict between Life wanting to thrive and expand on one side, and environmental conditions on the other; if we also admit that *Homo Sapiens* has developed an ability to change the environment around it in a dramatic and lasting manner; then it is only a matter of logical inference to admit that should the changes realised by *Homo Sapiens* and its civilisation persist for a period long-enough from an evolutionary perspective, then a notable effect on the average DNA of the species can take place from the actions of *Homo Sapiens*. In other words, we adventure to speculate that, through a dynamic we do not fully understand yet, *we are potentially not only changing the environment around us but also changing us*, not only from an existential or psychological perspective as we have largely discussed before, but also in terms of trait selection at our DNA level. Whether a trait selection lasts or not is a more difficult question to address.

448. DNA filtering and selection need not to take place only through random mutations, as it is the case with Darwinian Evolution, but could also be accelerated by Cultural Evolution as long as the newly created conditions, and so the drivers of this acceleration, remain. We however remain ignorant of the details and should therefore exercise modesty.

449. We are altering ourselves through Reflexivity.

---

[193] Or from a broad anthropologist perspective.

Brief Notes on the Pains of Evolution and Progress

    a. Example: Generation 1 invents a paradigm changer[194]. It mostly grapples with the implications of such an invention. Generation 2 pushes all possible applications of such an invention[195] and expands its use further. Generation 3 is born within a new environment altered by the widespread availability and use of this invention, where some of the old human ways of doing have disappeared. Generation 3 takes things for granted, forgets about the old ways and the origins of things, and in the process changes its way of living irremediably.

    b. Caution: change in the species takes time, and the environmental conditions for this change have to exist for a long time and be greatly dramatic before natural selection can take effect.

450. We realise that such an acknowledgement can ultimately result in wide protest and surprise. How can we envisage that we potentially can change ourselves as a species in a recursive manner? Changing the species can only be done by its ultimate creator, God.

451. Yet again, Reflexivity seems to be a very common theme in the world around us as we have seen multiple times. The weather, the environment more generally, financial markets, the economy more broadly, or even societies at the greater level, are all just some of the examples of clear feedback loops. Would it be that surprising then that Reflexivity makes its way internally, into our DNA? Indeed, an extrapolation of the sort should not constitute a satisfying argument but rather the beginnings of a hunch. As we have stated, we have yet to understand many of the detailed mechanics and effective drivers of Evolution. Without attempting to argue over this hunch further, we can illustrate what we mean with a less controversial and more widely accepted example from the human-animal interaction: Domestication.

---

[194] How to make fire, the invention of the car, how to fly, the computer, or the Internet.

[195] We say the technology matures.

452. With their increased civilisation, humans have 'produced' new species out of nature we all identify today as 'pets'. The two common species are of course Cats (*Felis Catus*) and Dogs (*Canis Lupus Familiaris*). Through a process in which humans played a central role, which is of domestication, Cats have resulted from a wildcat version (likely *Felis Silvestris*) and Dogs from Wolves (*Canis Lupus*). Cats and Dogs both stand today as proper species (or sub-species) not only from a convenient human naming perspective but also from a phylogenetic perspective. In other words, *Homo Sapiens* behaviour and interaction with its environment have resulted in (at least) two distinct species, *Felis Catus* and *Canis Lupus Familiaris*. This fact is rather widely accepted.

453. What is striking in the process of Domestication is at least two features: (1) The process of Domestication has started only tens of thousands of years ago, which from an evolutionary perspective is considered a *very* short timespan; and (2) This was done without great requirements in terms of technology, only through careful mating of some particular ancestors with specific traits. The result is a Chihuahua, which with difficulty we can liken to the Siberian wolf.

454. More so, Cats and Dogs are not two purely circumstantial events in the evolutionary history emanating from human specific needs[196]. Recent experiments, the most notable of which is the process of fox domestication during the Soviet era, point to the possibility of producing new sub-species, sometimes, astonishingly, in a matter of some generations. It seems that what has been done with the Wolf can be replicated with the Fox.

455. We do not mean to say that Domestication is always possible and with all species. There seem to be particular social traits in animals that are necessary to start with and cannot be found in all species. Evolution is about trait selection; the trait is therefore the starting point. What is important to retain nevertheless is that the result, where Domestication is possible, can come to be something quite remarkably different from the ancestor we started with, and more

---

196 Getting rid of scavengers and insects around food inventory in the case of cats; protecting, hunting, and sniffing abilities in the case of dogs.

importantly stick as proto-sub-species and multiply to ultimately become its own proper line on the evolutionary tree.

456. Given what can astonishingly be done with animals, without any advanced genetic engineering, would it be that difficult to conceive that we could indirectly and unintentionally also somehow alter ourselves generation after generation with the change we effect on our environment and the way of living? If we compare our situation to one hundred thousands years ago, we do not source our food the same way anymore, nor necessarily eat the same food; we do not protect ourselves from the environment around us in the same manner; we do not migrate or change habitat in the same fashion; and we definitely do not die from the same causes anymore. Many of the fatal weaknesses of ancient times have been replaced by new types of weaknesses, all through our ability to change our environment. And the faster the pace of this change is, the greater are the surprises likely to be.

457. When we consider the human contradictions we have developed on previously through this new lens, we could think of two external environmental factors that exacerbate such contradictions: (1) Us changing or being capable of changing our environment to something much more complicated; and (2) Continuous higher degree of abstraction and corresponding discoveries. With these two dynamics, some of our ways of doing and our assumptions and 'beliefs' become obsolete or proven wrong. The greater the abstraction, the more difficult it is for intuition to follow, and the more likely it is for ultimate surprises to emerge.

458. Humans do not usually live psychologically well with dramatic revisions of beliefs that have been anchored in society for long periods of time. Our evolution, both in terms of altering the environment or greater abstraction and discovery, puts us in psychological pain in front of the destruction of long established collective naivety and worshipped false beliefs. The psychological pain emanates from an emotional attachment to such beliefs. Some things we discover or we invent do not sit well with our

instincts and innate abilities—they do not feel 'natural' or disturb our natural intuition, disturb the 'self-evident'. We hence know in our rational part that these beliefs are wrong but have at the same time great difficulty taking the full measure of our rationality. In other words, we try to negotiate with the rational, go around it with excuses, in order to appease our troubled emotional side. Through this process, many human contradictions do arise.

459. There are several ways of defining the term 'human civilisation', and what makes a civilisation more advanced than another. Our preferred way is to link civilisation to the proportion of the environment humans live in that is the direct or indirect product of human actions. In other words, if 2% of the environment around me (including habitat, food, air, and the rest) is man-influenced, I live in a less advanced civilisation than another man who lives in an environment in which 10% of the environment is man-influenced. Obviously the question then becomes, how can we really measure this percentage? And what do we do if two civilisations have the same percentage? Which one is more advanced? Aside from the difficulty of measuring this proportion, which has to be somehow taken qualitatively, there is an additional attribute that needs to come into play: sustainability. If civilisation A has a high man-influenced percentage but destroys itself after a couple of years, what would really be the use of this civilisation? Rights of Man, Civil Rights, Law, and Morality, all come under the umbrella of enhancing this sustainability through strengthening the cohesion of a society. Efficiency, including natural resource efficiency, also comes under sustainability. If we deplete all that is around us faster in order to increase this percentage of man-influenced environment, then we risk bringing down the whole edifice of civilisation we are trying to improve.

460. Civilisation and Progress are about altering the environment we live in, including ourselves. Those who think that we are "playing God" may be missing a point or have misplaced romanticism. Every time we take a pill against headache we play God; every time we light a fire to warm up we play God; and every time we come up with a new variation of dogs or trees we play God.

461. Rationality and consciousness played a great role in altering the environment around us. A natural corollary to Progress and 'civilising' of the environment is a reduced scope for impulsivity in terms of human behaviour. The animal world ex-human behaves more impulsively than the human world, and the human world today behaves less impulsively than the human world five thousand years ago. Altering our environment rationally increases the benefits of behaving in a more calculating and balanced manner rather than in an impulsive one, *most* of the time. Hence, greater civilisation correlates well with one of its most observed reflections: less impulsive societies on average. But we are also naturally made to have an impulsive side, to laugh out loud, to experience sexual arousal, and to express hatred or disgust without minding what the others think... Civilisation mutes some of that and can create frustrations and difficulties in the process.

462. Final words on the subject. Having high cognition and consciousness does not always guarantee survival. Progress can be self-destructive. Our abstraction and capacity for metacognition and synthesis based on past mistakes are largely what have made us who we are. However, many things are a matter of context. If not used in the right context, what made us progress can equally destroy us or be detrimental.

    a. Complacency and loss of survival focus can corrupt progress from inside. The highly literate Rome got sacked several times, and its empire was broken apart by more basic barbarian tribes. Turkish warring tribes coming from the East dominated the more sophisticated and educated Arabs in the Muslim empire from the 11th century onwards[197].

    b. Mathematical equations will not help you survive a lion attack, but your instincts will.

    c. Nuclear power is a great achievement, but also remains a great threat to our existence today.

---

[197] Some of these Turkish tribes went on, many centuries later, to develop a greater, more productive civilisation than the Arabs, and became the centre of the Muslim world.

On Ethics

"We are building a dictatorship of relativism that does not recognize anything as definitive and whose ultimate goal consists solely of one's own ego and desires." Benedictus XVI

"The most important human endeavour is the striving for morality in our actions. Our inner balance and even our very existence depend on it. Only morality in our actions can give beauty and dignity to life. [...] The foundation of morality should not be made dependent on myth nor tied to any authority lest doubt about the myth or about the legitimacy of the authority imperil the foundation of sound judgment and action." Albert Einstein

There is no topic more important for a society of humans than Ethics. And for this same reason, there is no more difficult to address. We shall not make full justice to Ethics here, but we will attempt to provide necessary insights as well as some personal preferences on the subject.

463. We have no meaning without Ethics; our knowledge is nothing without Ethics; and our actions are pointless without it. Having an ethical system is what defines us as a human race, whether individually or collectively. Ethics is the basis of our societies; it is the compass of our legal and political actions. Ethics is the light

we look towards in the darkness of uncertainty and confusion. Ethics is the reason why we do what we do beyond necessity and instinct. In Ethics lies the crux of our liberty and our humanity. Kant was accused of being a fanatic of Ethics, to have made Ethics supreme. We are willing to stand on his side in the face of such an accusation[198].

464. If Action is central for our humanity as we have seen, then Ethics is that against which Action is to be judged. If we cannot but interact with our environment, then it is Ethics that can guide us in some of this interaction. If we have any Free Will, any real liberty and independence, and if we are really *sapiens*[199], then it is through Ethics that these attributes are mostly expressed. Ethics are central in our religions and social life, and no philosopher or systematic thinker can omit Ethics without being blatantly incomplete.

465. Ethics concerns itself with a wide range of issues. Firstly, it seeks to define the desired and undesired objectives and aspirations[200] of an individual and a society from living. Second, it provides the basis for driving and judging human action accordingly. Third, Ethics concerns itself with finding a satisfactory basis for these stated objectives and aspirations, be it in rational reasoning, utilitarian considerations, or individual drive; Ethics looks into the origins of such objectives and aspirations. Fourth, beyond Action itself, Ethics looks into the motives of Action, or in other words the *will* behind the Action. Ethics concerns itself with the Action and the will behind, and it attempts to find which is the right basis for judgment. Five, Ethics looks into including all such objectives and aspirations into one intellectual system in a coherent manner.

---

198 We do not mean that we agree with Kant entirely on the subject of Ethics. In particular, we refuse the *a priori* nature of Ethics as Kant envisaged it. Where we stand with Kant is on the importance and supremacy of Ethics for us humans, our thoughts, and our actions.

199 Latin for 'wise'.

200 Which are often referred to as 'moral values'.

On Ethics

466. Ethics is the discipline, and Morality is the outcome system of this discipline. From Ethics are derived the mechanisms of Law and Politics; Morality is their inspiration and their guiding force (or at least should be).

467. Ethics is a wide, intricate, and important subject that raises many questions among which:

   a. What are the origins of Ethics?

   b. Is there one Morality? One ethical system? Is Ethics the *discovery* of this system, or is it the discipline of *defining* Morality?

   c. What should we base ourselves on in the search for Morality? Pure Rationality, Economics, Emotions, Subjectivity, Instinct, or Biology?

   d. What are the key characteristics of Morality? Do such characteristics follow a certain hierarchy?

   e. What is more important in Ethics, Action or the will behind it?

   f. Does Morality change with time, or is it one across times and ages?

   g. Should all humanity share one Morality, or is it possible to have different moralities of equal stature? How do we then reconcile these moralities when they face or oppose each other?

   h. How do we deal with situations of uncertainty and rational breakdown when it comes to Ethics?

468. For us, Ethics is not about Truth. Truth is of the domain of Knowledge and Epistemology which we have already elaborated on. Naturally, there is a close interaction between Ethics and Knowledge, but the two are not the same and should not be inferred to be the same. Many historical mistakes have been committed because of this forced amalgamation, undermining in the process both Ethics and Truth. Many things were considered true because they corroborate with pre-defined ethical systems and turned out

to be wrong later. Examples of such are the health dangers of eating pork meat or the rotation of the Sun around the Earth.

469. Ethics is not Religion. Indeed, historically the two have been brought together very closely, particularly in the Western/Mediterranean/Middle Eastern civilisations. It is likely that Ethics, even if in rudimentary forms, has preceded Religion. We can imagine that early humans have had a form of basic culture in which Ethics cannot but take place before even devising sophisticated rituals for burying their dead[201] or looking to the stars for answers to deep questions.

   a. The main historical reason for the co-mingling of Ethics and Religion is that the latter helps provide a basis for establishing a certain Morality that is more difficult to refute. In other words, Religion helps dogmatise Ethics, which makes the question of the origins of Ethics unquestionable, but also helps provide the needed 'supra-natural' authority for the key custodians of the ethical, and behind political, systems.

   b. It is possible for a community of humans to have a deep rich culture and an advanced ethical code without a developed metaphysico-religious system behind. Morality is part of the human culture and tradition, more so than religions themselves. Therefore, we find for example the Chinese culture to have an elaborate ethical system without the kind of religious stories and dogmas that we are used to in Abrahamic religions.

   c. Do Polynesian tribes or hunter-gatherer societies lack ethical systems because they may lack a well-developed religious system? Of course not.

470. We shall state that **there is no categorical proof that Morality has to be absolute or one.** From a rational and historical point of view, the necessity of uniqueness and eternal immutability

---

[201] Rituals and treatment of the dead are commonly considered as one of the first signs of birth of religions from an anthropological point of view.

of Morality is far from being demonstrated. The evolution of Morality across our human history is the anti-thesis of an *a priori* Morality, a Morality pre-defined, anterior to humans.

471. Different human societies, cultures, and religions have had different ethical systems, with some of their aspects opposing each other. Moreover, within the same culture and religion, Morality did evolve to something different with time. We find Morality to adapt to the 'spirit of the time' in many ways. We have given several examples of such already, but we shall mention a few more: the ethical approach to usury, to homosexuality, to human or animal sacrifice, to equality of men and women, and to torture, have all changed dramatically within the context of many cultures. If our ethical approach changes with time, how can we then not admit that Morality itself is changing? This naturally does *not* signify that everything within a certain Morality changes constantly; there are many things that we may hold unchangeable, such as family values or respect for individual property. But to admit the other extreme is also foolish.

472. Ethics is central, but there is no one ethical system; Ethics is supreme, but there is no one metaphysical or *a priori* system of Ethics that we could all seek and follow. The importance of Ethics is not in its dogmatisation; the importance of Ethics is in its possibilities, and it is in these possibilities that our liberty takes its full measure.

473. There is a degree of perspectivism (Nietzsche) in Morality that cannot be easily denied. It is a perspectivism from the point of view of timing, civilisation progress, and Culture more generally.

    a. The value of Life, human or other, is as much as we attribute to it in practice and not in theory. There is no denying that the morality concerning the sanctity of Life has been slightly altered with time, and it is still not at perfect par across cultures around the world today. The value of Life is practically reflected according to the varying ways we deal with birth (giving life), education and nurturing (promoting, enhancing, and defending life), and death (terminating life). The sanctity of Life is not only reflected through the generally stated guideline, through pretensions and theories, but also through the everyday practice and treatment of Life by society.

- b. As we have seen, Nature itself is neither intrinsically good nor bad; it does not point in any one particular ethical direction. The process of living forms does not have a deterministic purpose or finality, even if we are followers of the most crude of the mechanistic views of existence[202]. Different living forms show different perspectives on a wide range of topics, from family structures, to interaction with members of the same species, to social hierarchy.

- c. Moreover, the notions of Good and Bad are themselves continuously evolving ones. They are as much the product of time and human culture.

474. It is very difficult to judge an act, whether it is good or bad, without its historical context. It is also more difficult to judge whether a man is good or bad independently from context. Many key historical figures, which we generally consider to have been great, committed acts very few today can agree with. Consider the approach to slavery for example; most great leaders and thinkers in distant history had slaves. Some even had kids with these slaves (e.g. Thomas Jefferson) and did not recognise the legitimate rights of these descendants[203]. We always like to think of historical figures in the light of our current morality, and we idealise them. But when we are faced with historical realities, some form of disillusionment takes place.

- a. Kings in the Middle Ages were considered by their followers not to commit any wrong; terrible abuses have ensued even from the most righteous of kings.

- b. We express shock at the level of racism in Germany in 1930s. The reality is that most of the remainder of

---

202 We remind the reader that uncertainty and chaos can ensue from the most deterministic models.

203 From our current view of what should be a right for every child.

Europe was not that different at the popular level. Yes fascism, nationalism, and xenophobia did not come to take control of power in the same way outside Germany, Italy, or Spain; however, to consider from there that such feelings were not present at a common level in other European populations, that the French or the English were utterly immune, is a historical hypocrisy, a typical rewriting of history by the winners of wars. Eugenics was an unfortunate 'fashion' in many Western countries at that time.

    c. Some of the statements from Churchill[204], considered to be one of the greatest politicians in English history, would constitute a real shock if uttered today by any politician. Here is an example from 1919 destined against the Arabs (they happened to be not too conciliatory with him): "I do not understand the squeamishness about the use of gas, I am strongly in favour of using poison gas against uncivilised tribes." It seems that Churchill of 1919 was not that different in his approach to containing rebellions from Saddam Hussein of 1988 with the Kurds…

475. A less moral person today can be more moral than a moral person in History by the reference point of current morality.

476. Hence, the quest for Morality is not a search for a single hidden moral treasure; it is rather a continuous process of collective intellectual and emotional building that is unlikely to lead to something final as long as human cultures endure.

477. All ethical approaches that have assumed a supra-human origin of Morality have faced unsolvable difficulties. Indeed, the most natural way of assuming Morality to be absolute and unchangeable is by attributing its origin to something absolute and unchangeable.

    a. However, Morality does change and raises then the question of the changeability of its creator.

---

[204] For the sake of example and not to focalise on any one particular politician.

b. And what about the ethical nature of this creator? Historically, those who attach Morality to God have had, and continue to have, difficulty escaping this problem. God has to be absolute and Good. In this case, where does the Bad come from? Morality cannot exist without defining the Bad, without defining that which the society recognises to exist but does not aspire to. If God has only the Good in him, then the existence of the Bad requires the existence of something from outside God, which amounts to saying that God is the only absolute, but Morality is not fully in God. Or in other words, God is not the creator of everything, which is against monotheistic theories.

478. Ethics are of the domain of Anthropology. From the day human beings have attempted to define their relationships to each other and to the wider environment, Ethics were born. We have Rationality and Emotions; we live and interact with our environment; and we are a particularly social kind of animals. All of these attributes are covered by Ethics. Even animals have ethical codes; there may not be a rational basis for their rules of behaviour comparatively to Humans (or a lower degree of rationality), but animals do nevertheless also have some form of instinctual ethical code when interacting.

479. As to the objectives and aspirations, Morality has been generally approached historically from two different starting points:

a. Morality should have goals that are clearly defined, and it is these goals that matter more so than the means. It is the method of defining the immutable Good and targeting the best ways of achieving it. It is 'The end defines the means' approach to Ethics. This is what is commonly called in the discipline Consequentialism. The consequences are the basis of the ethical approach, and actions are judged accordingly. Consequentialism can be divided into many different sub-categories depending on what is that which we are seeking in the consequences: Individual happiness? Material benefit for society on overall basis? Predominance of a certain culture?

The difficulty of an approach based on consequences is that, in an infinitely inter-related world, we need to ask the question of which consequences we are really looking for? Short-term or long-term consequences? Immediate consequences or a longer chain of consequences? And what if the consequences are altered by unexpected randomness? Would they remain a valid basis of the ethical judgment? And how are we to judge the consequences in situations of great uncertainty or where the outcome is purely probabilistic?

b. Virtue is what counts; the will behind the action in a particular situation, regardless of the results, is what matters. This obviously necessitates defining all virtues in all different types of situations, which is cumbersome and rather impossible, but it still constitutes the most traditional approach of almost all religions. Some simplify this approach by saying that intentions are what count.

Unfortunately, human psychology is greatly more complicated than that. One can easily have good intentions at one level and selfish intentions at another[205]. And should we judge the intentions in a vacuum or in the context of the influence of the environment on the individual? Aren't intentions greatly altered by cultural norms and long-term conditioning?

480. Given the inter-related nature of all things and uncertainties resulting from dynamic environments, this separation is rather fallacious. Certain behaviours even if undertaken with good intentions can easily lead to moral complacency, ultimately corruption, and therefore can end up turning destructive in the long run. On the other hand, consequences alone are not a

---

205 Think about someone who does a virtue in order to gain a place in Heaven. Does she have good intentions or selfish ones?

sufficient judgment criterion given the innate uncertain nature of things. The environment can also impact and condition intentions, and therefore consequences do influence the will over the long run.

481. Will and Consequences are in an endless circular relationship not that different from the one between Nature and Nurture. It is for these reasons that the distinction between the two methods is a weak one. Will is very difficult to judge, and its drivers are many and uncertain. The human psychology is not without its deep complications, which have immediate impact on the way we deal with concepts such as internal will or virtue.

482. We should mention a third approach to ethical objectives and aspirations, which is more passive and less defining. It is the approach of observing the general behaviour of a society and deriving from it the required objectives and aspirations based on the opinion and behaviour of the majority. It is in this sense that we mean this approach to be more passive than defining. It is a 'morality by voting' that we reject. Morality has to be capable of opposing the opinion of the majority, should that opinion deviate from what is acceptable. Otherwise, we are prone to pure populism in Ethics. Morality does change with cultures, communities of people, and time; however, it should not be driven by the whims of the majority, which can be fast-changing, and lose all respect in the process. Morality should not be the victim of shallow political dealings, propaganda, or marketing. This reminds us of a phrase from Edmund Burke in the context of legislation, which can as well apply to Ethics more broadly: "When the leaders choose to make themselves bidders at an auction of popularity, their talents, in the construction of the state, will be of no service. They will become flatterers instead of legislators; the instruments, not the guides, of the people."

Necessary Elements in a Morality

Failing to provide an all-encompassing treatment of the discipline of

Ethics, we shall dedicate ourselves in this part to what we consider to be the necessary characteristics of Ethics and ethical systems. We hope in the process to better frame the thinking about Ethics.

483. Ethics naturally involve a great degree of Rationality. Rationality plays an important part in human cultures and is therefore a key builder of Ethics. However, Ethics is not to be confused with Rationality or some sub-set of Rationality. Rationality is of the domain of Truth and Knowledge, whereas Ethics is of the domain of Action and Living. Naturally, both greatly influence each other but without entirely being the same.

484. All ethical systems that have so far based themselves solely on pure Rationality, from Spinoza to Kant, have been wrong, incomplete, or are obsolete and impractical. Much has been tried to position Ethics irremediably in pure Logic and Rationality without the recourse to other aspects of the human culture to no avail. From the Categorical Imperative to pure utilitarianism, many attempts have been done to try to argue Ethics in pure Rationality and give it a fully rational unquestionable ground. These attempts have helped the discipline of Ethics tremendously, without really giving it a final framework to work in. They usually hide behind a deterministic bias and a love for rigorous science and logic.

485. Ethics have to involve Emotions not only Rationality. We have instinctive and innate emotions that should find their right place in our ethical systems.

    a. Any Morality that does not take account of emotionality is bound to become obsolete or dangerous. Emotionality is an important component of human behaviour that should not be ignored. Emotions are more difficult to treat than Rationality, as their rules are different. However, omit Emotions from the ethical equation, and they shall come back running in one way or another. Force a purely rational system for a long-time, and you will see emotional radicals ultimately gaining influence over Ethics. This has happened historically with the Romantics.

    b. Historically, emotionality played little explicit role in grounding Morality, but it occupied a very important place implicitly. Many philosophers and religious thinkers adjusted moral values to be consistent with some of their deep intuitions and human cultural traditions. They have also done so to avoid alienating natural feelings of their populations and to obtain approval for their ethical systems. However, thinkers in Ethics have typically used Rationality to justify these values and not emotionality itself; they have post-rationalised some of the emotionality related to Ethics.

   c. Emotionality alone can lead to excesses but can also serve as a great safeguard against rational excesses. From some of our most intuitive and instinctive emotions, we derive some of our best ethical objectives and aspirations. Once a person accepts Compassion, it is very difficult emotionally to argue against equality of chances, equal liberty to all, and equality of treatment and solidarity in society; this is typically an emotional decision more so than an intellectual one at first for most people. One does not usually start with utilitarian calculations to justify equality; it is an emotional judgement that is subsequently rationalised. There is something in our emotions and intuition that feels right about the idea of everyone deserving equal chances in life. Once a person accepts reproductive instincts, it is very difficult emotionally to argue against family values or sexual ethics.

486. There is an important interplay between pure Rationality and Emotions when it comes to Ethics. Each alone can result in much excess, but none can be omitted in the ethical exercise.

   a. The incorporation of an element of emotionality in Morality should not render it irrational. Without Rationality, the entire edifice of Ethics from an applicability and sustainability point of view would become impossible.

487. Rationality in Ethics is not only about pure abstract logic. Ethics relate to Action and Living, and objectives and aspirations have

therefore to be of practical nature. The collective material world, or what is also known as the Commonwealth, is fundamental for the survival and progress of the species. A sustainable ethical system necessitates a utilitarian element. Emotionality alone does not provide a valid way of judging between two different ethical systems; applied rationality or a certain measurement of the overall utility however can. By attempting to measure the consequences, we obtain greater objectivity and a better reference to experience. This in turn helps provide ethical systems more credibility but also a necessary feedback from experience.

488. Now that we have anchored Morality in Rationality, Emotions, and Social Utility, we can proceed to mention some of the key characteristics of an ethical system. Morality has to:

    a. **Be consistent**. As with any systems that rely on Rationality, Morality needs to be intellectually consistent. The objectives of a Morality need not to contradict each other, but should they do, there needs to be a hierarchy of objectives in order to address these difficulties in a coherent manner. The applications and judgment criteria of Morality need also to be consistent, without which Morality loses any intellectual credibility. While complete consistency and comprehensiveness may not be possible, a high level of consistency remains a key requirement. Kant's Categorical Imperative can be considered as part of the consistency condition of an ethical system; it is a necessary condition without which the generalisation of any conduct leads to blatant absurdities.

    b. **Be practical**. Morality needs to minimise confusion in the daily application of its precepts. In an uncertain and ever-changing reality, eliminating uncertainty entirely is not possible; however, frequent confusion opens the door to disrespect of Morality and varying interpretations of it. Moreover, Morality concerns itself with deeds and living, and it should therefore be as simple and as easy to apply as the situation makes it possible. Simplicity helps facilitate applicability as well as acceptability. Action does sometimes require fast and clear ethical interpretations, which only a practically oriented Morality can provide.

c. **Be coherent with basic human instincts**. It is in this way that emotionality can take its rightful place in the ethical system. Key examples include: self-preservation, reproduction, maternal/paternal instincts, social bonds including empathy & sympathy, a perimeter of liberty, some form of right to individual property, some form of self-expression, and some form of equality of rights and obligations.

d. **Possess common sustainable utilitarian objectives**. Similarly to emotionality, it is in this way that applicability and objectivity are reinforced. It is also in this way that Morality can be confirmed through its utilitarian consequences. Key examples include: preservation of the species, control over and protection from the environment in a sustainable manner, and minimisation of the number of people under the misery line.

e. **Be capable of evolving** with the change of our knowledge and material and immaterial conditions. Of all characteristics, Capacity to Evolve is the one most overlooked. It is also the key reason for why many moralities have historically been compromised in the views of societies. We cannot pretend to have a complete understanding of the Universe and our existence. As such, our Morality needs to reflect our evolving understanding and technology, as well as our continuous altering of our environment. Extremely rigid moralities and dogmas that are never allowed to be discussed are bound to be washed away with time. Practicality and Capacity to Evolve are attributes of nimbleness, and there is no more important requirement for sustainability than nimbleness; Morality has to be somehow nimble without going into the extreme of easily changing and lose in the process respect and stature. Naturally, rigidity of values needs to be commensurate with the place in the hierarchy of Ethics these values occupy, which brings us to the next characteristic.

f. **Be hierarchical.** A hierarchy of moral values is a necessity for the consistency of the system of thought, to address possible difficulties and confusions, and for the sustainability of the system. More so, in a state or community structure, Morality can never be fully individual. By definition, when human beings join together in a community, society, or state, they give up part of their individual freedom for the communal good. Hence, Morality becomes as much a communal subject as an individual one with direct consequences in terms of Politics and Law. There is still space for personal morality and individuality in Ethics, but there are limits defined by the communal structure. For example, individuals can be morally free to choose whether to marry or not when it comes to relationships, but they cannot be free to choose their moral values with regard to murder or stealing. This requires a clear hierarchy between individual values and collective values, as well as a serious consideration for the space in which individuality can express itself in Morality.

g. **Minimise collective psychological disturbances.** *All else being equal,* Morality has to seek not to oppose that which is of cultural importance including the most important of customs and traditions. It is in this way that Morality can take into account the continuity of the history of the society it applies to. Once Morality has fulfilled all other characteristics, it should seek to walk the path of least resistance from a cultural point of view.

489. A note of caution: Utilitarianism is an important concept of Morality. However, as we discussed with Consequentialism

previously, it is a very difficult one to nail down satisfactorily. No matter how pragmatic one is, it is, as a rule, extremely difficult to demonstrate satisfactorily a permanence of utility from any one particular moral code under all possible circumstances. And even if we relax the condition of universality under all circumstances, and narrow the condition to most circumstances, we will find ourselves in difficulty with the definition of this 'most'. Second, the definition of the notion of 'utility' is far from being clear or universally agreed upon. Is it happiness? And how do we define happiness universally for all characters and personalities? Some people can be happy with more wealth or material possessions, some with less; wealth and happiness highly depend on cultural influences. Then happiness over which timeframe? Long-term or short-term?

490. The last three characteristics, Capacity to Evolve, Hierarchy, and Cultural Consistency, allow for a change in Morality without dramatic moral experimentations and dangerous moral revolutions that open the door to great uncertainty. Careful evolution of Morality allows it to remain respected and revered, while frequent Revolution in Morality is dangerous and ultimately results in wrong collective despise for the concept of Morality itself.

Difficulties of Application

491. Defining and living by a Morality is far from being easy. One lives long enough to be faced with multiple challenges and possibilities of re-questioning on that front. Living by a code of conduct always raises the question of the validity of the exceptions to the rules in many circumstances. Even once defined, applying Morality in real life over long periods of time typically exposes us to many grey areas. We all have an experience of this; we talk about 'white lies' or we say, "Doing a little bad for a greater good"... This is naturally related to what we put more emphasis on, consequences or inner drivers, but the challenge of the exceptions to the rules is present in both approaches.

492. Of all the difficulties in applying Morality, we find the most challenging one to be what we choose to call the Problem of Continuum. At the scale that concerns us most in terms of Morality, Life around us is a continuum. There are no intrinsic limits; everything is connected to everything and impacts everything. It is a greatly complicated and unending chain of interactions and developments. Whatever we choose to define as boundaries and categories is mostly nothing more than a human interpretation. The lines and boundaries we draw are mostly for our own easier understanding and control of reality. The Universe itself cares little about such definitions and separations[206].

493. The difficulty with continuums is the following: if what we define as limits, categories, and boundaries for the application of Morality[207] is actually artificial, then this by itself poses the moral question of what attitude we should take or interpretation we should hold at the cusp of such an artificial line. If red is good and pink is bad, as we move from red to pink when do we stop calling things Good and start calling them Bad? There is no objective line that we can argue for comfortably in such situations. And we cannot say, as may be the case with common measurement units like the meter, a bit less or a bit more to define a meter will not create much of a difference. In Morality and more so in Law, a bit more or a bit less of something might be the difference between going to jail or not going to jail, committing a felony or a sin or not committing a felony or a sin… Is there really a major difference between someone who is

---

[206] If one chooses to use phenomenological terms or admits something of the kind, all universals are somehow inter-related in some sort of a continuum. For example, we can move in grades from the essence of the colour red to the essence of the colour pink. When do we stop calling it red and start calling it pink? The answer is: probably at some arbitrary level. In Physics, there are well-defined minimal units and minimal measurements (quantums), but, for all practical purposes, most of what is available to our consciousness, tangible and intangible, particulars and universals, is somehow inter-related and forms continuums.

[207] And such definitions are fine and necessary when it comes to Morality or any human reasoning.

18 years old plus one day and one who is 18 years old minus one day? Can we really say that there is no moral problem when we consider such two individuals as having different moral status disregarding everything else?

494. No matter what other reasoning we try to apply to mitigate the Problem of Continuum, such as taking other factors into account, relying on some other adjacent method of separation, or applying common sense, it is indeed very difficult to eradicate the problem entirely. We can even adventure to say that the Problem of Continuum exists as soon as Morality and its practical rules are defined, the same way circular references exist as soon as Causality is used... We find ourselves led back to the same old problem of the Absurd.

495. One of the difficulties the writer continues to struggle with in the context of the Problem of Continuum is with regard to the moral approach to abortion. It is not the usual opposition between pro-life advocates and pro-choice advocates that bothers me. It is a more fundamental but obviously closely related question. It is that of the definition of a human being: at what biological stage can we consider the foetus to have become a human being?

From this perspective, pro-life proponents have a more convincing, consistent view although not without its question marks. They claim that a human being is whenever an egg is fertilised, i.e. once the full human DNA is put together. We can consider the result, regardless of its morphology, a human being, even if it is just a collection of few cells. Obviously a cell is a cell, and it is rather difficult to conceive it as a human being. We create cells and we lose them every day while we live. Nevertheless, the definition remains more neat than in the case of the pro-choice standing, and here is why: pro-choice advocates generally consider that a foetus should not be looked at as a human being until it has reached a certain level of biological development. Some even say that as long as the foetus is attached to the body of the mother, it cannot be considered as a human being as it is entirely dependent on the mother's body. Both arguments raise questions of the type of the Problem of Continuum. Let us illustrate how.

> a. If we choose the threshold to consider the foetus as a human being as X months of gestation[208], are we really saying that at X months minus one day the foetus is not a human being, and at X months plus one day it is? One must admit that this is quite arbitrary.
>
> b. Now let us consider the other approach that says a foetus is a parasite organism till it is born, and the X-month threshold is just there for health reasons—it is dangerous for pregnant women to abort when the foetus is too developed. Let us then consider two pregnant women at nine months. At nine months and two days, one of them delivers the baby, and it is considered a human being. The other woman does not deliver till nine months and seventeen days. Can we really say that for these fifteen days the first baby is a human being and the second is not? We know well that delivering a baby can get delayed or accelerated for various reasons and in various ways that are *not* purely related to the exact development of the foetus. In other words, gestation cannot be thought of as a checklist that, as soon as it is completed, the baby decides to come out. Case in point: premature babies born at seven months of gestation.

496. It is these kinds of serious questions the Problem of Continuum can raise in Ethics. And we can continue with such logical and moral questions endlessly... We are not advocating a pro-life or pro-choice stand here; we are only illustrating some of the difficulties of moral application. If I become pro-life one day, it will definitely not be for the traditional religious reasons; however, whatever my position is, it will seek to minimise the Problem of Continuum while acknowledging that it cannot be fully evaded. I have yet to find a pro-choice justification that minimises the Problem of Continuum as much as the pro-life one.

---

208 Take 3 for X for example.

497. For many of the moral difficulties, the Mass or the Average can serve as an effective regulator. We all experience moments of weakness, we all fall at some point or another into temptation or into bad behaviour, and we all are eventually pulled back into normalcy by the Average, the Mass. Taking a scientific view, it resembles random movements away from the mean where such movements nullify each other, and the Average remains determinant over the long-run. It is what Herman Hesse referred to as the sphere of the bourgeoisie that the genius escapes from; the same analogy could be used here. Saints and demons escape this sphere in different directions. The Average is moral but not to the extent of the Saint; it can be wicked but not to the extent of being devilish. The Average follows Morality generally but never entirely to the letter. Such an analogy does not mean that the Average is static or constant; the middle class or the bourgeoisie does evolve. There is however a pull of the individual towards the Average more often than not.

    a. Here again there are exceptions to the rule. The Mass can lose its head; a majority is capable of crushing or eliminating a minority. Thus, the importance of an independent moral body that can exercise moral leadership and can serve as a safeguard against the excesses of the Mass. We are not advocates of Descriptive Ethics that makes the behaviour of the Average the defining force in Ethics.

    b. Most of the time, the Mass plays its role of the pacifier or the averaging force, in an efficient way. However, in large sigma situations[209], we require something independent from the Mass that regulates Morality to preserve its overall integrity. The Mass can become self-destructive, and an independent body has to be able to protect against that.

498. Another key difficulty in applicability is around the common denominators of Morality across its different variations, across different cultures, or between moral centres that possess equal

---

[209] I.e. very low probability but extreme situations.

On Ethics

power. Are there any values, objectives, and aspirations that can serve as common ground to all humans, of all cultures and backgrounds, upon which we can build the centre of all moralities?

499. This question can be of some apparent simplicity at first thought. Who would not be against lying or cheating from a moral point of view at first instance? However, the question of key denominators becomes enormously more complicated when looked at in details. Even with cultures of similar origins, difficulties abound.

   a. An example of such difficulties is defining under which conditions (if any) we have the right to kill another human being. There can be a general agreement on the right for self-defence, and, with the exception of some hard-line pacifists, the right to kill in case of legitimate military confrontation between professionals (i.e. soldiers), except when surrender occurs. But how about the right to apply a death sentence? Even Europeans and Americans, who share the same philosophical and cultural backgrounds to a large extent and can be considered to be at very similar levels of economic development, are today in disagreement on the subject of death penalty. It is these kinds of details that make the definition of universal common grounds for Morality very arduous.

500. It is worth stressing at this stage that these difficulties should not serve as an excuse to question the necessity of Morality.

   a. Morality is non-static and subject to evolution. So difficulties of drawing commonalities or disagreements are no justification for rejecting the concept of Morality itself.

   b. No matter whether one subscribes from a philosophical point of view to utilitarianism or not, from a very concrete perspective, human civilisation would not have progressed without having defined key social values. Some like to link Morality to direct utilitarianism; others prefer to talk

Reflections on Fundamental Matters

about indirect utilitarianism[210]. Regardless of the point of view, rules of the game are indeed required to generate long-lasting human utility.

c. More importantly, the concepts of Freedom and Free Will are nothing without Morality. When Morality is separated from Religion, as it should be, most people struggle in justifying the basis upon which Morality should exist. After all, if God does not exist and did not order certain rules of social conduct, then what is the basis of Morality really? **It is in fact the rejection of a Morality prescribed by God, a Legend, or a Myth while adopting a Morality nevertheless as part of an individual life what constitutes the basis of Freedom and Free Will.** Morality is and should be a free choice: I, as a person, choose freely not to kill, not because a God will punish me if I do so; not because another man is an image of God; but because I choose freely the value of respecting the life of any other member of Humanity. We repeat, Morality is in our view the most important reflection of Freedom.

501. Yes there are differences across cultures and religions; yes there are debates about whether Morality should be individual or common; yes some people (e.g. Albert Camus) talk about Integrity instead of Morality; but the notion of necessity of a Morality (or equivalent) is essentially universal across human cultures. An easy though imperfect way of understanding Morality is to think about it as a synthesis of human active wisdom, within a certain cultural and political context, transmitted and refined from generation to generation.

502. An approach to joining different moralities together is possible, even if difficult. As almost anything related to the subject of

---

[210] The difference is that one considers that every case of conduct according to Morality leads to a direct increase in utility, while the other considers that, on average, the more people behave ethically, the more utility emerges indirectly in society over History.

Morality, this requires at first a free conscious choice to do so at the collective level. Without this free choice, little in Morality would be possible, and even if possible, sustainable. There is also a need for a hierarchy of Ethics with the highest rank occupied by the key denominators common to all human societies. And these denominators need to be (sooner or later) explicitly defined if we are to avoid political confusions and misunderstandings. Some may consider the Universal Declaration of Human Rights to be this denominator. However, this declaration does draw some criticism, particularly of political nature.

503. *Moral and Legal are today differing concepts.* The distinction between Moral and Legal is a growing concern from a historical point of view. At the inception of Law[211], Law and Morality were not that different; they were what is desired under a certain culture and defined by the leader of the community. The easiest historical definition of Law is to say that it is the part of Ethics that is explicitly covered by the scope of the government an individual is under. Law includes a dimension of power and enforcement. However, with social, cultural, and geo-political evolution, we find ourselves today with more difficulties emanating from the varying number of moralities we have, as well as the differing, and sometimes opposing, legal codes.

504. The identification between Moral and Legal is not valid any longer. Furthermore, some of what is legal is not necessarily moral. This can create serious conflicts in daily conduct. For example, prostitution can be legal under the civil code and still perceived as immoral for the majority of a population. A police officer may be required by Law to execute someone, while her inner morality is against this kind of human killing. Euthanasia is illegal in most countries, while it could be considered moral and merciful by the larger faction of the population. Law can be the victim of politicking, while Morality is of higher individual and collective expression.

    a. Hence, the difficulty of application is double: it is between differing moralities and differing legal codes that need

---

211 Morality does indeed precede it.

to be reconciled, but also between a particular morality and a particular legal code that co-exist and have to be reconciled. Various legal and moral codes can oppose each other on several aspects, while any community is required in our current times to have a Morality and a Law that are simultaneous but can be distinct.

Key Values

505. We find the issue of defining and applying Morality easier to approach not from the purely holistic angle of defining a complete and coherent system that stands the test of time, but alternatively from the point of view of listing a set of Key Values, which, for all practical purposes, serve as very acceptable notions across cultures and ages. Morality can then find its shape starting with these Key Values by applying Rationality, consistency[212], and a degree of validation through Utilitarianism. These Key Values by themselves contain a central element of emotionality.

506. Adopting these Key Values goes a very long way into achieving what is sought by Morality. These Values would not make a person necessarily a saint[213], but by striving to remain faithful to them as much as possible, we believe societies and individuals, through their actions, can create an environment of important psychological positivity and utilitarian synergy which will come to further shape Action, Thought, and Will in the direction of these Values, and in turn benefit Life and living forms. I admittedly have not been able to remain faithful to these Values at every moment of every day; however, they remain my guiding stars. I like to believe that as long as I continuously do a genuine honest effort to get closer to them, I become in the process 'better' and more satisfied with my identity, which I am continuously forging.

507. Moreover, these Key Values could be, almost by definition, the

---

212 Intellectually and with the culture and history at hand.

213 Turning everybody into a saint is in any case utopic.

key denominators across different moralities and cultures we are seeking.

Of these values come first:

508. **Compassion**, towards other humans, living forms, and the Universe. *Compassion is the most noble of Values.* It should be the cement of social structures and the source of social cohesion[214].

   a. Compassion is the ability to relate to everything around us, to the humans, and to other living forms around us. To have empathy regardless of the history of the relation we have to each other, even in case of great animosity; to put oneself in somebody else's shoes; to have sympathy for the difficulties of others as they can very well be our own, and for the bad circumstances or the environment these living forms have been dealt, out of their own full control and choice.

   b. We will always hit the Absurd, we will all ultimately die, and we are not that special *a priori*, neither collectively nor individually. Therefore, the more we wake up to the irrelevance of all knowledge and purpose around us in the standard of the Universe, the more we are likely to appreciate ourselves and our kind. And the more we are likely to appreciate Life, the more we find ourselves to be compassionate towards other humans and the environment generally.

   c. Some religions advocate Universal Love. We find such advocacy exceptionally beautiful and noble; however, we have yet to meet someone who really loves *equally* everything around her, constantly. I am not capable of such a universal feeling maybe out of my own deficiencies. And if this advocated Love starts being asymmetric, then we fall back into the debate of what is Love and what is not Love, and what is this lowest common denominator

---

[214] Yes, it is Compassion that should be the cement of society, not the Leviathan nor Fear.

of this loving feeling... However, Compassion can be more easily applied to all and can constitute this lowest common denominator of the loving feeling. It is therefore no surprise that Compassion is present in almost all religions and philosophies of positive living.

d. Genuine Compassion has several positive side effects to the environment we create.

   i. If I enjoy freedom or material comfort, and I meet a person who does not enjoy these, my feeling of empathy should make me want to wish and seek that this person would enjoy these one day with the right amount of effort and good action. At the very least, I would understand and be supportive when an individual is trying to work his/her away ethically and with hard work towards these benefits that I possess. *Freedom and equality of conditions and chances are better served with Compassion.*

   We have always found artificial the concept of forced equality, of totalitarian equality in everything, which is both inapplicable and hypocritical in many ways. Economically, forced totalitarian equality has frequently proven to result in all sorts of complacencies and inefficiencies.

   ii. If I am asked to judge someone, Compassion makes me do so with an eye to the conditions and history that led the person to commit a specific act. *Blind sense of vengeance and self-righteousness are muted by Compassion. Rash judgement of the Good or the Bad, Success or Failure, is always moderated by Compassion.* Recall how you find yourself approaching things differently whenever you think that what bad circumstances happened to another person can equally happen to you? *Forgiveness is more possible with Compassion. More balanced and effective justice is possible with Compassion. Abuse, physical and mental, is more muted with Compassion.*

iii. *Compassion results in a feeling of universality between human beings of different cultures and backgrounds.* If I meet someone from a different social background, language, skin colour, or religion, I am less likely to be carried away by feelings of discrimination or prejudice if I am willing to put myself in the other person's shoes. *A feeling of fraternity in Humanity results from Compassion,* and it is not a shallow simplistic fraternity. I may not necessarily want to embrace any person I see in the street, but through Compassion, I would nevertheless have a deep-down realisation of the equality of our Human Condition.

iv. Compassion should not be limited to other humans. Compassion should include everything around us, including living beings and matter. If Compassion for matter is a difficult concept to imagine, then the reader can substitute it with respect for matter. We do not mean to go and hug every tree in the forest or every bear in the mountains; we mean a certain level of sympathy and empathy for all that is around us. *As we realise that we are not fundamentally all that different from what is around us, that we all influence and interact with each other constantly, the feeling of compassion and of association grows.* It is rather difficult to imagine someone caring for everyone around him on the one hand, and abusing animals and Nature savagely on the other. Typically one attitude reflects the other. Usually people with great love exhibit great love for everything around them including animals, flora, and things. Saint Francis, the saint of great love and sacrifice for fellow humans, was notorious for his love of animals; he is in fact the patron saint of animals. Several psychological examinations correlate compassion towards animals with compassion towards human beings. And as such, if the principle of Compassion to the world around us is applied, many environmental problems can become easier to approach. If we are compassionate about Nature, we will not destroy it in an irrecoverable manner. We would still use it to our advantage, but we would additionally provide it the respect and conditions of existence it requires. With Compassion, we would not dump or leave our waste in outer space as if it is the ultimate trash bin. We will show respect to animals and living forms even when we kill them to eat them[215].

    v. *Compassion is the ultimate safeguard against violent emotions.* "Do to others what you would have them do to you."[216]

509. **Moderation**, intellectual and in deeds.

    a. Lack of Moderation is the root cause of almost all atrocities and evils. At the core of every terrible deed is excess, material, political, or psychological.

    b. Understanding the ultimate limit of our knowledge, the large number of exceptions to the rules, the fundamental existence of absurdity as part of the web of this Universe, and the unpredictability of many phenomena, results in moderation and modesty[217], both intellectually and in action. It is enough to read a bit of history to notice how many good ideas, intentions, philosophies, ideals, and political systems became perverted through excess;

---

215 There are different ways of killing animals for food, ranging from the wasteful and savage to the more merciful, quick, and minimising in pain.

216 Luke 6:31.

217 Which will also be cited as Key Value.

how many insightful views looked foolish after fact; and how the 'greatness' of Man can come crushing down so quickly in front of Nature and the Universe. Civilisations crumbled; economic systems crumbled; dominant species disappeared... The world is a complicated and intricate place whether we like it or not.

c. Addiction of any sort (e.g. money, drugs, fame, love of self, ideology) is an antagonist of Moderation.

d. *Even good intentions and good principles can turn evil through lack of Moderation*; historical examples abound.

　　i. Lack of Moderation in religious zeal during the Middle Ages made the clergy assume that the worst threat against a blasphemer is him/herself. The resulting Inquisition led to monstrosities for hundreds of years, some at the hand of people who are still considered today to be saints. There is no religion that made of Love a central theory more than Christianity, and yet lack of Moderation led some of its disciples, even at the top of the hierarchy, shockingly astray, and conducting themselves in plain contradiction of their central doctrine.

　　ii. We could cite *La Terreur* following the French Revolution again, and how many of the noble ideas of the Enlightenment found themselves usurped through lack of political moderation and an excessive drive to impose a new political order at any cost.

e. Depending on historical circumstances, predispositions, and other environmental factors, many people approach life with an innate positivism; these are the builders of systems of all kinds, the optimists, and the motivators. Others, on the contrary, approach the living with an innate negativism or scepticism; these are the critical minds, the sceptics without whom we never realise the flaws in our action and thinking, and the destroyers of naivety. *With Moderation, both types are equally beneficial, and without it, they are equally dangerous.*

  i. Without Moderation, positivism leads to blind dogmatism and terrible totalitarianism that leaves no room for a different opinion. Belief becomes fanaticism; everything must be made to fit the mould or rejected and eliminated.

  ii. Without Moderation, negativism leads to complete inaction. Failing to moderate negativism renders everything endlessly questionable and flawed. Nothing can be built on such an attitude; no good can result; nothing is possible.

f. Moderation in the use of the resources around results in efficiencies, good economics, less boom & bust cycles, and less environmental destruction.

g. *In Moderation lies equanimity.* Equanimity is a key attribute of leadership and decision-making under extreme circumstances and uncertainty. The historical figure of this style of leadership, or what transpires from him, is Marcus Aurelius. Abraham Lincoln was also known for his equanimity.

h. The prevailing criticism against Moderation is that it makes one stand in the middle on any topic, it makes everything dangerously relative, and no clear action on anything is possible. We reject this criticism. *You can be moderate and still define for yourself a strong morality or a strong identity.*

  i. Let us take the example of identity. There is no shame in having a strong identity; to choose one's own values and stand for them; to affirm one's convictions. The danger is when this sense of identity starts spilling over on others against their will in a forceful manner. The attitude of

On Ethics

"either you agree with me or I wipe you out" is where trouble starts. Not knowing or refusing to accept the limits of one's identity, either consciously or unconsciously, is an open door to excess. It is such an attitude that perverted many philosophies of the self in Europe and resulted in monstrous political ideologies (e.g. Fichte). The aim of torture, whether mental or physical, is to dominate the consciousness of the other, to overtake one's identity and control it.

    i. Moderation is not an 'everything-is-relative' approach. By definition, Moderation has to reject the mould of total relativism. Moderation should not be taken as a call for inaction; it should rather be taken for what it is: Moderation when in action, a truthful knowledge of the limits of each and every one of us. Moderation does not mean that one cannot defend him/herself when attacked. Even in war, there can be Moderation.

    j. Moderation, much the same as Compassion, and more by direct definition is also naturally a safeguard against violent emotions.

510. **Honesty**, especially intellectual and psychological honesty. The more accurate term reflecting what we have in mind is Anti-Hypocrisy. However, it is never nice to define a Key Value as a negation, so Honesty as moral objective and aspiration can well do.

    a. What we mean by Honesty is not the shallow one of telling the truth or not telling lies. It is the internal moral, psychological, and intellectual honesty, consistency between words and deeds, thoughts and actions. It is the attitude of "putting our money where our mouth is."

    b. If you follow your thought freely, you should accept wherever it leads you and not evade it out of cowardice or laziness. With the following caveat: attach Moderation to your thought commensurate with the level of certainty of your knowledge. When one follows his/her thoughts rightly and in an enlightened manner, many prejudices and ancient beliefs are bound to become flawed.

c. *Honesty, true honesty, forces consistency, internally, in our thinking and feeling, and externally, in our attitude towards the world.* How many times have we seen this in our experience? Whether in what concerns us personally or the people around us: we say something, we preach something, and we find ourselves doing the opposite. The worst of us are those who use such preaching as social or political tools while behaving differently under cover

d. Honesty is not easy; Honesty can come at a cost. It is capable of disturbing an internal balance built on false premises. It can risk marginalising those who hold it if the conclusions it reaches are not to the general liking of the society we live in. Societies can be hypocritical; Honesty can provoke much resistance, and its consequences can be terrible on those who define themselves based on the general social approval they receive.

e. While a certain level of contradiction and hypocrisy is impossible to eradicate in our nature, a great measure of Honesty is possible. The range of human behaviour when it comes to hypocrisy spans from those who look to benefit personally from it (they tend to abound in politics and social affairs); to those who are not conscious that they are actually practising it; to those who are aware of it but are too consumed by other priorities to fight it properly.

f. Lack of Honesty has a long-term eroding effect on the image of an individual or an institution. No matter how good is the eloquence, it will ultimately fail in covering satisfactorily all the lack of Honesty in action. *With Honesty, respect is cemented; without it, disillusion and suspicion ultimately set in.*

   i. Rome and the Church had tremendous historical

aura. It was however the lack of Honesty between words and behaviour that ultimately constituted the soft belly exposed to those who wanted to diminish the power of Rome. The Franciscan movement was the last shield of the Church pre-Reformation. Alas, the followers of Saint Francis were as dishonest as their peers… It is equally the strong level of honesty and attachment to doctrine that the Jesuits forced post-Reformation that allowed the Church to gain back some of its lost aura. The cover-ups of the child abuses is a more modern example of the terrible eroding effect a lack of Honesty, when discovered, can result in.

    ii. We are not singling here the Catholic Church with our examples on purpose; it does happen that these are some of the better-documented examples. What applies to it, applies to many other orders, movements, and religions. Issuing *fatwas* that protect immoral and unethical behaviour for the sake of a particular political line or objective is another example of the blatant lack of Honesty religious leaders can practice.

g. We like to think that lack of Honesty has an equally long-term eroding effect on the inner psychology of most individuals. In the same way an institution ultimately loses people's respect, one can lose self-respect from lack of inner honesty. It is more difficult to be comfortable with what one sees in the mirror when covering a great deal of hypocrisy and lies.

511. **Modesty**, again especially intellectual, and especially towards the Universe.

"Pride goes before destruction, a haughty spirit before a fall."[218]

---

218 Proverbs 16:18.

a. The Modesty we refer to here is the one that consists of *realising one's own limits, not only within human societies, but also, more importantly, in the broader universe of things.*

b. Modesty is not necessarily vis-à-vis a creator or some supra-natural powers and beings; it is not a form of forced self-mutilation either. It is not an artificial modesty that proceeds with little inner conviction or more out of fear or calculation. True Modesty is about the conscious realisation of one's own limits in every field of Thought and Action, and living this realisation to the maximum possible.

c. As we said before, the realisation of the Absurd; the power of the environment; the historical disillusionments in Thought and in Action; the role luck and circumstances play in individual and collective affairs; and the intricacies of Life and the Universe, cannot but instil in us a feeling of deep and true Modesty.

d. We all think we are special, and many of us think that they are destined to some form of greatness. We like to think at first that we are capable of controlling everything around us through our technologies and capacity to invent, when in reality we control much less than we think. Luck, timing, and/or social conditions at a particular point in time, all play a great role in historical development, while we often like to attribute the result solely to ourselves.

   i. An economy goes well, and we think that it is due to the great insight of a particular minister or government. We win a war, and we think that it is only due to one particular tactic, leader or speech. We manage to resolve one major problem, and we think we understand it all.

   ii. Human advances or individual successes give often room for delusion and feeling of personal grandeur.

Modesty helps limit some of these attitudes.

e. No one is really great enough or fantastic enough to have created something out of nothing; *there is always a credit in any thought or work to something or someone before*. In reality, those who claim otherwise either do so out of some form of megalomania and self-love, or to usurp some kind of unjustified power.

   i. Knowledge, Wisdom, Material Progress, and Civilisation are all gradual accumulative phenomena for which no single individual can take credit. Each step along the march of these phenomena has depended on the step before and would not have been possible without it.

f. The smartest of the smart, the strongest of the strong, and the most cunning of the cunning, are in the crushing majority of times weaker than a collectivity of humans.

   i. What we manage to create in common almost always outweighs the individual.

   ii. *Wikipedia* is better than the best of the Diderots or the D'Alemberts.

g. And this collectivity of humans is certainly always weaker than the environment around.

h. We sometimes have it going for us, as an individual or as a group, but extremely rarely things last for long periods of time. Any long-enough reading of History, Evolutionary Biology, Geology, or any other discipline that ponders over long periods of time makes this abundantly evident. It is this realisation that leads to true Modesty, gratefulness when things go well, and a form of stoicism and acceptance when things go wrong.

i. Modesty and Moderation are related values: there is definitely some form of Moderation in Modesty and vice versa.

512. In a world where History has provided ample examples, and in many fields, that almost no political, social, or economic system works all the time and under all circumstances, these Key Values can serve as guiding principles in the stream of continuous changes we can find ourselves.

513. These four Key Values are a mixture of utilitarianism and emotional preferences; they are a minimum that does not exclude other values.

514. These Key Values constitute strong pillars of sustainable and productive social structures. They do not promise eternal happiness in this life or some next, but they can drive healthier social dynamics. They create a virtuous and productive social cycle that becomes increasingly difficult to break.

515. Those familiar with oriental philosophies might find a lot of similarities in these values with what they already know. Of course, they also constitute key components of most Western religions. Aristotle talked about the Golden Mean, which loosely relates to Moderation. None of this is a surprise, and no one can really claim monopoly over such values.

516. The point here is simple: as long as these values are truly lived and practiced, it matters little how they come to be in the person living them.

517. Even with this small number of Key Values, there is a necessity for a hierarchy of values. Therefore, these values have been stated in their order of importance in the eyes of the writer.

518. The happiest men tend to be the most moral. The more accurate statement is actually its negation: the less a man is happy, the more subject to moral breakdowns he or she becomes.

ON RELIGIONS

"God has no religion." Henry Whitney Bellows

"A religion is a system of symbols which acts to establish powerful, pervasive, and long-lasting moods in men by formulating conceptions of a general order of existence and clothing those conceptions with such an aura of factuality that the moods and motivations seem uniquely realistic." Clifford Geertz

"Une société sans religion est comme un vaisseau sans boussole [...]"[219] Napoléon Bonaparte

"[...] la religion [...] rattache au ciel une idée d'égalité qui empêche le riche d'être massacré par le pauvre."[220] Napoléon Bonaparte

Tarek lived in a small village in a remote region of what is known today as Syria under Byzantine or Eastern Roman rule. Tarek was a Christian, living conservatively in the tradition of his forefathers and everyone around. Living in that part of the world in the 8th century AD, Tarek

---

219 A society without religion is like a ship without a compass. (John H.T. Francis translation)

220 Religion attaches to Heaven an idea of equality, which saves the rich from being massacred by the poor. (John H.T. Francis translation)

had witnessed incessant infighting among different Christian factions, particularly Nestorians and Orthodox Christians. Each side claimed to know the Truth about Jesus, to have solved the Mystery of Jesus, each argued well, and each refused to concede to the other. Tarek did not care much or understand much about all this infighting. He was a simple man, he knew that he believed in Christ and God, and only wanted to live life peacefully in the tradition of his village and his family. Tarek had a wife and two young children to care for; he loved them very much and constantly worried about their safety with all the religious wars going on. All that Tarek knew from these wars is that they have taken many people, some of whom he knew closely, and he was greatly saddened for losing them. Tarek's wife covered her head whenever she went in public, as was the tradition back in the days for women of all religions. His mother did it, his sisters did it, and his wife did it; it was part of the general customs of the age. Tarek loved Jesus and Mary, heard stories of the Bible regularly, and was always moved by Jesus' humanity and compassion. One day, a sudden unexpected development took place in Tarek's life. An army from the Arabian Desert invaded the land and conquered most of the villages around. Most villages ceded without much fighting, and the Christian armies of Byzantium fled without much resistance; they were already greatly diminished by the incessant Christian infighting. Tarek did not know much about his new conquerors. In practice, they appeared respectful of people, took no hostages, sacked no homes, were very respectful of women and families, feared God, prayed regularly, and kept most things as they are—roads, institutions, and buildings. Tarek heard that the new conquerors also believed in one God. They respected Jesus greatly, called him a Messenger of God, and considered Mary the most respected and purest of all women. The conquerors also fasted, talked about Abraham and Moses, and believed that Jesus will come back at the end of times to judge us all. The only new belief the conquerors held that Tarek had not heard of before was that of a prophet by the name of Muhammad, who came after Jesus, died only recently, and on behalf of whom the conquerors were spreading the words of God. Muhammad was considered the last of the prophets of God. The conquerors held a different book than the Bible, which they called the Koran; but then again Tarek was never really allowed by the Church to keep a Bible and did not know much about the difference. Most of all, Tarek was delighted that the religious wars around were ended, and that a new age of peace and prosperity had come. Tarek welcomed the new conquerors and adopted their religion—he continued to love Jesus and Mary and pray for them. Tarek grew to know the stories of Muhammad. His descendants always believed that Tarek became a Muslim out of some deeper religious considerations.

Jacob lived in a middle-class community in a normal quiet suburb. Most of the neighbours in the community shared in the same religious practices. Some were more deeply religious than others, but overall Jacob could not say of the community he lived in to be overly religious. They had their Shabbat, their Passover, and their Hanukkah. Jacob himself did not care much about religion or religious duties and ceremonials. He never engaged in religious discussions, and when he was taught religion at school, he mostly day-dreamed through it. Jacob loved having fun; he was a cordial and joyful young man with no prejudices. He never cared to know who followed which religion and who believed what. For him, life was too short to worry about those things. One day, Jacob woke up to discover his community the victim of vicious attacks because of its religion. Some of the key religious symbols in the community were desecrated, and a couple of young men were tortured and killed. Jacob did not know the victims personally. A mood of great shock, anger, and fear swept his community. Jacob could not but feel provoked and threatened. He came to discover that his religion is part of his identity independently from how he felt about its content. Jacob associated himself more strongly with his religion from then on while still not bothering about the details.

Jessica had a troubled childhood and a difficult life growing up. Her parents abandoned her at a young age for unknown reasons. She spent her childhood going from one foster home to the other. She was rarely looked after, suffered too early in life, and in the process lost all capacity to trust anyone. Jessica was eager to come of age and be able to escape from the vicious environment she grew up in. Only Jessica did not know what to do with her freedom once she became eighteen. She went from one relationship to the other, and from one odd job to the other. She never managed to trust anyone, and she constantly felt deeply lonely and isolated. She was incapable of building long-term relationships or committing to one job for a long time. Jessica took to drugs and became highly addicted which worsened her condition. She spent all the little money she made; her addiction drove away everybody she knew, and she was about to die alone, on the street, suffering from sharp withdrawal. On one of her daily walks, a wonderful nun discovered Jessica and took great pity on her. The nun took the young woman under her care and brought her into her monastery. She helped Jessica break her addiction and was always patient and caring with her. Jessica did not always react well–it was a natural defence reflex she had acquired since childhood. But the nun was patient and caring, and Jessica could see the love and care in her eyes. Jessica never experienced this level of care and attention before. The nun talked about God and his Son, their great love, which all of us need to replicate, and how Jessica needs never to feel lonely anymore; Jesus is always there and she can always trust him. Jessica, in her character, was not naturally inclined towards religions. However, through the nun and her religion, through the crises and the subsequent life-changing experience, a large part of the void in Jessica's psyche was filled with love and care. Jessica started to believe again that there are people she can trust. Moreover, she started to find some meaning and purpose in her life, and she came since to associate herself with the religion of the nun. Religion filled the great need for love and compassion Jessica had constantly lacked; the nuns became Jessica's family.

Constantine cared very much about his social status; he had great political ambitions. Constantine lived in a deeply religious community where religious ceremonials took a great part of daily life. Constantine understood the importance of religion since a young age and attempted to constantly use it to advance his career. He never expressed any genuine personal view on religion; always appeared in line with the general religious doctrine; made sure to constantly position himself as a great defender of religious belief; and took part in all socio-religious events. No one really knew what Constantine thought in private as Constantine grew up continuously devising better ways of hiding it. All

On Religions

that Constantine cared about is gaining political office, and he knew that appearing religious was essential in politics.

Pascale was born curious. As a little child, she constantly asked too many questions. Pascale grew up to be an educated independent woman. She was a highly rational person and found as she grew up many inconsistencies in religions. Pascale therefore devoted her career and life to Science and Knowledge. However, despite everything, many of Pascale's childhood questions remained unanswered. "Where do we come from? What is the purpose of our Life? Why is there so much bad and suffering in this world? What will happen to me after death?" These were the kind of questions that weighed on Pascale's mind... Most importantly, Pascale always feared death and what might become of her when she dies. She did not have any convincing answers and was not able to find any in Science that satisfied her emotional side. No matter how much Pascale tried to rationalise her death, she could not shake off this fear. Pascale became increasingly dominated by her emotions. One day, Pascale could not do with the questioning any longer; she decided to embrace Religion even if she was not convinced by many of its precepts. Her close circle of friends was surprised. Pascale was known not to engage in anything without thorough rational examination. When they asked her, Pascale answered, "Well I have spent my life trying to answer these questions that torment me to no avail. I am quite advanced in age now, and I cannot shake off the fear of death. I have decided to accept Religion even if I am not entirely convinced rationally. After all, what do I have to lose? If I turn out to be wrong, I will die anyway. But in the likelihood that I turn out to be right, I can at least guarantee myself salvation after death and in the meanwhile enjoy having some answers to my questions..." And so it goes with the classical religious calculation many undertake[221].

519. From what has been said so far, one can draw a conclusion against religions. The reality is (again) more complicated than at face value.

---

221 Inspired by the actual life of Blaise Pascal.

Reflections on Fundamental Matters

520. But before we talk about Religion, we need to ask ourselves what is *really* Religion? How is Religion different from Culture, Social Customs, Ethics, or Philosophy? Is it a certain combination of all of them or is Religion something of its own?

521. From the First Premise we have stated in the beginning of this essay, we cannot define Religion in relation to a special independent substance or nature (the 'supra-natural'); this would simply correspond to moving the problem from one field to the other. Moreover, many religions themselves (e.g. pantheistic religions) reject the separation into different substances. We cannot therefore in practice apply a definition to a set of beliefs that may actually reject the basis itself of the definition. Moreover, the definition of Religion in reference to a god-like aspect or belief does not work well either without diluting the definition of 'godness' to such a degree that we could do without it.

522. We shall therefore define Religion as a certain combination, a phenomenon that cuts across Culture, Ceremonials and Customs, Cultural Symbols, Metaphysics[222], Individual and Social Beliefs, and Morality. It is the collection of all of those components put under one roof, under one name.

    a. Not all components of Religion are as developed in every particular religion, but all of them are present to a minimal extent.

523. But is Religion any combination of the above? Or is there any particular pattern across different religions?

It is difficult to historically point to any one particular component as being the primary driver or the origin of all religions. Metaphysics definitely plays a very important role in Abrahamic religions (particularly Christianity), in Buddhism, and in Hinduism, but other religions could be more cultural, moral, or social in nature than metaphysical. Among those are many indigenous African religions, folk religions in general, and

---

[222] Including the nature and origin of Being, of the Universe and of us Humans.

On Religions

Confucianism[223] which concerns itself more with social conduct than Metaphysics. Many old religions have developed first from Ceremonials (such as the burying of the dead or the ceremonials around harvest time), Customs, norms, and social traditions, following which more metaphysical or elaborate intellectual systems were added in order to tie the different components of the religion together.

524. If Religion cannot be defined by a particular primary component or a particular pattern of origin, then how do we manage to name something Religion? How do we differentiate Religion from any random combination of the components we have stated?

In addition to the combination of the different components mentioned above in one system of thought and belief, what ultimately defines Religion is *social acceptance and perpetuation over time*. A Religion is a certain combination of Culture, Ceremonials and Customs, Symbols, Metaphysics, Beliefs, and Morality that gained a particular social critical mass for a long-enough period of time. Social acceptance and perpetuation over time are what makes Religion different from a cult. What are religions other than particular cults that gained social acceptability and perpetuated over a substantial periods of time? Religion is therefore not only defined by its characteristics, and definitely not by its origins; it is also defined by the *result* in terms of the perpetuated social impact it creates.

525. We realise that this definition of Religion is unlike many of the traditional ones. Traditional definitions of Religion relate it to particular socio-cultural and ethical characteristics or to having the metaphysical and the supra-natural as subject-matter without giving due emphasis to the results Religion effects in society. With all due modesty, we find ours to be more encompassing of what we

---

223 Some may not consider Confucianism as a religion given its social and ethical focus rather than its focus on metaphysics; it represents a bias towards liking a primacy of the supra-natural or metaphysical in Religion. Metaphysics do have a place in Confucianism, such as a religious respect for ancestors, taken from prior Chinese folk religions.

have an intuition of today as being Religion while avoiding some of the intellectual difficulties we have previously discussed.

526. The components of Religion may exist (or have existed) under one system without them gaining substantial social critical mass that endures because of historical circumstances or purely for random reasons[224]. In this case, we rarely call these phenomena religions. Circumstances and general social dynamics play a key component in the creation of a particular religion and are an integral part of the definition of Religion itself.

527. Religion is a social phenomenon that drives or forces commonality among different individuals across the dimensions we discussed. The concept of 'individual religion' is a weak and unnecessary one and can be easily confused with individual philosophy, 'approach to life', or other. Individual religion does not have the same weight as Religion in the social sphere.

528. To Religion is often associated a religious institution, which can be of varying levels of complexity.

529. Religion is often perpetuated through both oral and written traditions.

530. To Religion is always associated a religious community, and the distinction between different religions is often based on the distinction different religious communities make, which is then reflected through differing religious institutions.

   a. Person A and person B belong to different religions if they associate themselves with religious communities Ca and Cb, while Ca and Cb consider themselves not to belong to the same religion, regardless of the extent of the underlying religious or intellectual similarities and differences. *Hence, religious differentiation is mainly political.*

---

[224] We can give several examples of pseudo-religious movements that did not succeed in becoming proper religions such as the movements created by Pelagius or Peter Waldo, or that of Hellenized Jews outside of what is today Israel/Palestine. On the other hand, Luther and Calvin's movements did succeed and came to define a particular religion, Protestantism.

531. From the definition we have given to Religion, it is difficult to draw a simple judgment on it. While remaining critical, we therefore refuse to draw a general conclusion on Religion. Culture, Customs, Ceremonials, Symbols, Beliefs, not to mention Ethics and Philosophy, are all important aspects of Humanity, and they are all in Religion. Throwing Religion away is synonymous with throwing pillars of Humanity away or calling for their disappearance. Every time something likes this was attempted in History, a form of Religion was in reality replaced by another. It is indeed difficult for Humanity to try to eliminate what makes it human.

532. What we can however reject is particular religious practices and/or beliefs. What we can also criticise is the act of drawing all such aspects of Humanity unnecessarily under one all-encompassing system. Some systems are typically found to be weak in consistency, blatantly false in some aspects, and/or of poor utilitarian value. **It is not necessary to have Religion, but it is necessary to have all the underlying components of Religion,** as they are in reality underlying components of Humanity.

533. So why is it then that these components come from time to time under the banner of one religion? And why do religions perpetuate for so long?

The reason is *political effectiveness*; it is the marriage of Religion and Politics, under which material, socio-cultural, political, and symbolic anthropology can all find their respective places. There is, particularly with a lower level of social development, more effectiveness in *pushing* commonality of Culture, Beliefs, Customs, Ceremonials, Symbols, Metaphysics, and Morality under the banner of one religion rather than each developing separately. Religion provides an apparent sense of coherence[225], as well as better means for perpetuation, through well-crafted stories and legends, and through political and institutional inertia.

---

225 Though not of a full intellectual consistency.

534. Religion is more reflective of Humanity than God. Religion is a reflection of a community of humans in all of its aspects, intellectual, physical, moral, and artistic. Religion is a reflection of past and present experiences of a particular community of humans, and how it perceives itself and its identity. God, creator of all, would be limited if He is contained within one particular religion. *Through Religion, we often attribute what we like to see in us, our ideals and our aspirations, and the ideas of our most sublime and purest, to something outside us, something eternal and immutable.* We look far in order to better reflect what is inside us. In Religion, we find some of our greatest heroes and martyrs, our best conduct in the face of hardship and malice, and an ultimate victory and happiness we greatly long for.

535. Religion deals with our social identity, with our deep emotions, and with existential questions; it provides us a sense of belonging and a meaning in an existence where no meaning is readily present. Religion contains a code of conduct and likes to position itself as an ultimate refuge in terms of uncertainty.

536. Most importantly, Religion does all of that in a rather simple manner accessible to a society with a lower level of development.

   a. Religion relies on well-crafted stories and legends, and the impact of storytelling is great on humans. Storytelling is indeed central for propagating religions, and most holy books are concerned with stories rather than dry edification.

   b. Religion uses art, visual and musical, to more easily reach into our emotions.

   c. Religion knows how to use the approval of the Mass to further strengthen its position. Religion builds great institutions and monuments, which it represents as testimony to its greatness[226]. Religion affirms itself with

---

[226] In reality this attests to the greatness in our Humanity rather than Religion itself. The Vatican attests to the greatness of the Roman and European heritage rather than that of Jesus Christ. Angkor Wat attests to the greatness of the Khmer Empire rather than that of a particular form of Hinduism.

confidence, and he who shows greater confidence typically draws more people towards his convictions.

537. Humans create their own web of meanings through their mental processes[227] and Cultural Evolution; Religion has served historically as the spearhead in this search for meaning. For all these reasons, Religion lasted and continues to do so despite many of its rational deficiencies and mistakes. This is what makes the political effectiveness of Religion.

538. When we have great things to lose, we turn towards Religion; when we have lost someone important to us, and all that we need is consolation and an ease of the suffering, we turn towards Religion; when we feel utterly helpless in front of adversity, we turn towards Religion; when we feel alone and afraid, we turn towards Religion; when we are humiliated by Life and our ambition and arrogance are destroyed by circumstances, we turn towards Religion.

   a. In all such situations, the control of our rationality is weak, and our survival instinct is at is strongest; our emotions take control. Religion greatly benefits from such situations for its survival. Indeed, Religion draws more of its power from adversity than earthly happiness.

539. Power holders have since long found an opportunity in attaching themselves to particular religions as a way of strengthening their legitimacy and grip on power.

540. As Religion drew closer to government and politics, two things happened:

   a. Particular religions became state religions and each god, or set of gods, became specific to a particular society, culture, kingdom, or city. Gods were invoked in order to favour certain populations in battle. Through this, religions became synonymous with political identity. This did not necessarily have to be the case, but it happened.

---

227 As per the Second Premise.

i. In ancient Antiquity, different cultures used to 'borrow' from each other deities without scruples. Fertility goddesses had different names in different cultures but shared striking resemblances. When Alexander the Great invaded Asia, he did not mind calling himself son of the patron god of any nation he conquered, and the populations he invaded accepted it mostly without resistance[228]. Alexander became son of Zeus and Baal. Phoenicians, Romans, and Greeks exchanged deities and legends.

However, a tendency towards religious identity grew with time. Yahweh became the God of the Jews and only them. Christianity became the religion of Europe and the Roman Empire. Later on, Catholicism and Protestantism became the religion of Western and Central Europe, and Orthodoxy became the religion of Eastern Europe and North West Asia. Islam became the religion of the Middle East, North Africa, and Central Asia. Few places escaped from the identification between religions and politics.

b. Law drew closer to Religion, and in the process Morality attached itself to Religion. Moral values became indoctrinated which provided them a dogma-like status. Through this amalgamation, monarchs derived not only political but also moral power; their sources of power became unquestionable. Historically, there was very little difference between religious morality and state law in most cases; all governments included a form of implicit or explicit theocracy (at least in Europe, East Asia, and North Africa).

i. Popes and Khalifas had explicit theocratic authority; they sometimes managed to govern politically and retained religious monopoly.

---

228 Tyre was an exception, and he wiped it out.

ii. Kings and Sultans did not enjoy religious monopoly[229], but they were assumed to be given power to rule by God (through the Pope or the Khalifa), and hence enjoyed implicit theocratic power and religious immunity against sin.

541. The distinction between Religion and the State (both politically and legally) resurfaced only at the end of the Middle Ages and was magnified at the time of the French Revolution.

We shall briefly elaborate now on the different components of Religion in this order: Culture (incl. ceremonials and customs), Symbols, Metaphysics, Beliefs, and Morality.

Culture

542. Human Culture is the ultimate human expression. It is the distinct living behaviour of the Human as an individual and as a society. Culture is the general style of living of a particular group of humans transmitted from generation to generation; it includes language, customs, ceremonials, style of habitat, style of economy, type of education, social hierarchy and structures, family structures, Ethics, art, and naturally Religion. We have described the concept of Cultural Evolution and Civilisation as percentage of the environment influenced by humans before.

    a. Religion has historically played a central role in defining the style of human expression and hence naturally finds its presence in Culture. However, Religion is not a necessary defining component of Culture, but rather a more general and more vague phenomenon that gathers under its roof many cultural elements.

543. Religion can come to play a central role in social identity through its influence on Culture. Indeed, many communities and individuals can come to define themselves (at least partially) through their religion. Religion is part of the identity of many, and in the

---

229 Except in some minor cases such as the English Crown after Henry VIII.

opposition between different identities, Religion can be a central component. Samuel Huntington called it the clash of civilisations as a proxy to the clash of religions, and Amin Maalouf referred to it as the 'lethal identities'[230].

> a. As with the story of Jacob in the beginning of this chapter, we can be judged culturally according to the religion of our birth regardless of our particular attitude towards it. And we all carry the religion of our birth, if we were given one by our family or the culture we were born into, to behave by it, oppose it, or alter it. In other words, *Religion does serve as a cultural anchoring point whenever and wherever it exists.*

544. The power of influence of Religion is greatly enhanced through ceremonials and social creativity. There are ceremonials for birth, for marriage, and for death; there are ceremonials for the days of rest (weekends), for major holidays, and for changes in seasons. We humans have a natural interest in events such as reproduction and birth, the joining in romantic partnership, death, days of rest from hard labour, seasonal changes, and key anchoring points in time (e.g. New Year celebration); all such events have invariably played a defining role in various cultures. With Religion, where it exists, almost all such events are wrapped up tightly in religious cloak. The natural and cultural way of dealing with such events becomes, at least partially, a religious one.

545. We can find an atheist born initially in a Muslim community being moved by, or identifying with, the famous call to prayer; we can find an atheist born in a Christian community being moved when hearing church bells as an expression of joy. The panoply of rich colours and senses in Hinduism are greatly cultural. The dressing codes in many parts of Asia are largely influenced by Religion[231].

546. Religious music, paintings, dressing, as well as elaborate ceremonials have served (and continue to serve) as an artistic inspiration to many, independent from religious belief. European

---

230 In French *Les Identités Meurtrières*.

231 E.g. Buddhist dressing or Shinto dressing.

classical music, particularly German, is intricately related to Religion –whether in Mozart's *Requiem* or in Bach's *Missa in B Minor*, we cannot ignore the influence of Religion on the musical culture. It is unlikely that Michelangelo was an ardent catholic, and yet most of his creations were of a historico-religious nature. Are we to reject these forms of art because we do not associate ourselves with the religious dogmas?

547. Fully eradicating the influence of Religion from Culture and social identity once it sets in is indeed a very difficult task. Often, those who have attempted to do so either failed or ended up just replacing one form of Religion with another.

   a. Early Christianity could not eradicate all pagan and other religious cultural influences from the populations it ruled over; it ended up adopting and slightly replacing many traits. The deity of fertility was replaced by Mary; the pagan and Jewish Easters were replaced by the Christian one; and the ceremonials of blood and sacrifice were substituted by the blood and flesh of Jesus Christ.

   b. Persian culture had great influence on Islamic religions. Persia was a developed society culturally and religiously, and Islam adopted, sometimes with some change, many of its cultural aspects. It is no wonder that Shia Islam, which has long been present in Persia, is the more ceremonial kind of Islam. The celebrations of *Ashura* remind us, as much as the ceremonials of crucifixion in Christianity, of the pagan rituals of blood and martyrdom, of the rituals of the slain god or hero (e.g. Adonis or Dionysus). The historical delineation between Good Gods and Bad Gods is primarily Persian and Mesopotamian; it is likely to have spread from there or was adopted by the Jews (mainly during their deportation to Babylon), by the Greeks through Alexander's conquests, and later on by Christianity and Islam.

   c. The aftermath of the French Revolution provides an interesting look at the difficulty of completely eradicating religious influences from Culture once they set in. French revolutionaries were aware of the religious influence on the way of living and sought to eliminate all such influences as quickly as possible. They brought back symbols from the Roman era to replace more Christian or royal symbols (such as the fasces), replaced the Gregorian calendar with the French Republican calendar, and created new ceremonials. What they have in reality attempted is not to eradicate Religion but rather replace it with a different 'revolutionary religion', more pagan and historical in nature. The reason we call it a religion is due to the fact that all such cultural changes took place under the one umbrella of revolutionary belief, which is nothing more than a pseudo-religious umbrella. Year 0 in the French Republican calendar corresponded to the day where the First French Republic was proclaimed instead of the (supposedly, but wrong) birth year of Jesus Christ. Different cultural aspects were not given their proper time to develop distinctly but were rather forced through the mould of the Revolution, the same way they had been forced before through the mould of Christianity. A similar dynamic took place in the Soviet world with the coming of Communism. Such attempts have had a very mitigated effect, and as soon as the new mould was gone, the old Christian one was brought back.

548. Of all the ways of transmitting Religion, we consider cultural transmission to be the most influential psychologically, more so than preaching or holy books. The power of cultural influence is great and subtle; it infiltrates many aspects of the environment we live in and becomes the *de facto* standard of living. When Religion attaches itself to Culture over long periods of time, the power of Religion becomes very difficult to shake off easily.

Symbols

549. Symbols could be considered as an integral part of Culture. However, we have chosen to separate them here for two reasons:

On Religions

(1) The general realisation of their growing importance as a distinct anthropological tool; and (2) Their prominence in Religion.

550. Symbols are a widely used tool by Religion. Without hearing any talk, without reading any words, and without seeing any actions, we can infer from few static images much about a group of humans, their culture, and their Religion (if they had any).

551. In Symbols lies an immediate summary of our cultural identity and if religious, of our religious identity too. We give ourselves great meaning and identification through symbols. When we have travelled far, we know that we have returned home when we first see certain symbols.

552. Symbols are not only in the signs we hold on our religious institutions; symbols are everywhere. They are in the way we dress; on the jewellery and ornaments we wear; in our flags and on our passports; in our public decorations; in the style and architecture of our buildings; in the colours we more often display; and in the make-up and hairstyle we choose.

553. Religion as much as Politics understands the importance of Symbols: Religion is as much symbolic as anything else. Religion greatly perpetuates through such symbols in some of the subtlest manners.

554. The Cross, the Crescent, the Star of David, and the Swastika[232] are on our religious buildings; on our clothes; in our ornaments and on our jewellery; in our country flags and the flags of many of our institutions and organisations[233]; and in the logos of our official documents. We find in them allegiance of a particular kind and a great deal about the history of our society, regardless of our individual religious convictions.

   a. We recognise a Muslim or Hindu community from the way women dress or what they decorate their hands or forehead with.

---

232 As the original ancient Indian one, not the one later usurped by Adolf Hitler.

233 In the symbols of Royalty, of Military, and even of humanitarian institutions such as the Red Cross or the Red Crescent.

b. There are different forms of the Cross depending on which Christian religion, order, organisation, or institution we are looking at: a symmetric or an asymmetric cross; a thin cross or a fat cross; a cross of a particular colour; a diagonal cross as opposed to the vertical one; or a cross with three crossbeams instead of one. We also look at the style at the ends of the Cross or the letters written on it.

c. We recognise a Shia Muslim community from a Sunni Muslim community by the predominance of the black colour, and a Moroccan Muslim from an Indonesian Muslim by the architecture of the mosque we are looking at.

d. We can come to know a male Jew or a male Sikh from his hairstyle.

555. Pagan religious symbols still exist in our days, but their meaning was often greatly altered by subsequent religions that attempted to eradicate or create animosity towards pagan practices and their symbols.

a. The pentacle was a great symbol of the old, which became synonymous today with witchery and evil. The pentacle was greatly revered by Pythagoreans; it was considered a symbol of perfection and health, and a symbol of protection or wisdom by many old pagan orders.

b. Bullhorns and horned deities were predominant in pagan times and were associated with power and fertility. Christianity turned the horns into the symbol of the devil to fight pagan practices.

556. Not all symbols of the old were however rejected or turned into something devilish. We can still find symbols that maintained an almost universal coherence in interpretation.

a. The crescent was a symbol of old religions before Islam. It was the symbol of Baal-Hadad in Mesopotamia; solar deities are also often shown as a disk or a face in a crescent. The crescent is also sometimes formed with two olive branches as in the case of the United Nations flag or the Menorah. Mary stands with open palms crushing the snake on top of the globe and the crescent.

    b. The symbol of the hand is present in Jainism and in *Hamsa,* which is used by many Middle Eastern cultures[234] to protect against the evil eye. The symbol is sometimes called the hand of Mary or the hand of Fatima. The Buddha is also shown frequently with the famous open palm.

557. Religion where it exists shapes our cultural symbols and our colour choices, which in turn contributes to our individual and collective identity, and a sense of meaning and belonging. We all have images, forms, and colours in our minds that are shaped, consciously and unconsciously, by symbols and hence by religious symbols. We live in a certain environment with a particular interpretation and attitude to such symbols. Our reaction to the visual is partly a reaction to the symbols we see. We interpret Symbols as a sign of friendship or a sign of threat, as a sign of belonging or a sign of animosity.

Metaphysics

558. Historically, religions helped provide speculative answers to difficult existential questions over which humans needed urgent comforting. Humans hate uncertainty, particularly in difficult times, and the metaphysical part of Religion is often there to console them.

559. Religion was mixed with Metaphysics in many ancient civilisations but not always: Greek philosophers were not religious men, and the Roman Empire until Constantine and Justinian continued to have its thinkers in Metaphysics separate from the religious institutions. However, it is only after the Renaissance that the full separation of Religion and Metaphysics was effected. Naturally, Metaphysics is still an important component of Religion, but

---

234 Christian, Jewish, and Muslim alike.

Religion does not enjoy a monopoly over Metaphysics or Ontology in the majority of societies today.

560. Religion has often positioned itself as the one capable of solving the 'mysteries' of existence we are faced with. This positioning was useful to Religion, up to a certain point in History, and religious metaphysics became the driving force behind the unity of all the components of many religions. Customs, Symbols, Morality, and Beliefs were all unified by the Metaphysics of Religion in Abrahamic and Mesopotamian religions. It is through Metaphysics that Religion attempted to rationalise all of its aspects in a coherent body.

561. Dogmas are a necessary component of Religion and constitute the underpinning of religious metaphysical theories. These dogmas are used to make the morality promoted unquestionable but also often go beyond as a way of providing answers to long-dated questions of the Human Condition such as "Why are we here? Where are we going? Or where does the World come from?"

562. Not all metaphysical theories in Religion were however there to address these existential questions. Some metaphysical considerations were of a more practical nature.

    a. Agricultural cultures cared much about understanding the weather and its cycles. Hence, they did everything they thought possible to improve the odds of them having more fertile crops. Religious metaphysics reflected such preferences in great part.

    b. Sailing or commercial civilisations cared much about safe sailing and not drawing the wrath of the seas. They had often thought the moods of the seas to be controlled by a god, and they developed elaborate metaphysical theories accordingly.

    c. Most warring civilisations had their war deities, to which they prayed for victory.

563. The primacy of Metaphysics in many religions contributed greatly

to the development of Philosophy, Science, and Knowledge in society. But the combination of rationalisation and irrefutable dogmas came later to represent the Achilles' heal by which Religion lost its aura. In other words, Metaphysics helped give Religion a higher status, a way into the rational mind, and some consistency across of all its aspects, but it is also the current root cause of religious disillusionment.

564. Metaphysics are the most dangerous part of Religion. They allow for Religion to be more rationalised, but often in the wrong rather than in the scientifically right, and also make Religion in the process easier to manipulate rationally through varying metaphysical interpretations. With scientific discoveries, History made a mockery of almost all of religious metaphysical theories over time. Many religious metaphysical theories have been used as justifications to wage wars, plunder rights, or impose divine dictatorships.

565. Some will argue that this is only Religion being misinterpreted; we beg to differ. Morality can come to represent what is most noble in Religion, and Metaphysics what is most dangerous. Elaborate speculative dogmas of the kind found in religious metaphysics can lead to excessive behaviour and political deadlock. When two people have opposing dogmas they each consider irrefutable, there is no room for reconciliation without the defeat of one by the other. Willingness to accept the other goes against the metaphysical dogmas as originally envisaged; it is a historical compromise we forced out of the realisation of the terrible nature of religious wars and radicalisation. When wars and massacres constitute integral parts of religious books and are made sacred as such, how can one really be surprised to find warmongers in the name of religions?

Beliefs

566. In Religion, there are inalienable beliefs. Beliefs are different from Metaphysics, and the two need not to be confused. Beliefs are not only concerned with supra-natural events, miracles, and

deities. Metaphysical dogmas are beliefs, but not all beliefs are metaphysical.

567. *Beliefs are an important and necessary component of Humanity.* They are what we hold as starting points of most human disciplines, intellectual, artistic, or moral. There are metaphysical and ontological beliefs (such as "I think therefore I am"), epistemological beliefs (such as mathematical axioms or the law of identity), aesthetic beliefs (such as the existence of the Sublime or Perfection, the beauty of symmetry), and ethical beliefs (such as holding that all humans should be equal in rights and duties). We cannot do without Beliefs, as nothing is possible without them.

568. Religion cuts across Beliefs, the same way it does across Metaphysics, Customs, or Morality. Religion attempts to organise such beliefs under its one umbrella. Most religious beliefs start by being metaphysical and moral in nature, but they proceed with the advance of Religion to the domain of aesthetic and epistemology. It is in the latter that they typically find their doom.

569. What could be at fault in Religion is not the fact that there are beliefs but rather the scope of the religious beliefs. Beliefs are important, but what is even more important is *to know what should be of the domain of Beliefs and what is not*. In other words, knowing what is a necessary and insurmountable starting point, and what is too elaborate and speculative to serve as a proper belief.

    a. If I choose to believe that there are flying cows, it is not Beliefs themselves that are wrong and dangerous but, rather, my choice of application of the realm of Beliefs.

570. There are generally two types of Beliefs:

    a. Those beliefs that can be falsified (i.e. capable of being proven wrong) by experience, either in our current time or in the future.

    b. Those beliefs that we have very solid reasons to think them not falsifiable and hence, by definition, can serve collectively as a starting point for human intellectual, artistic, physical, and social activity. For beliefs of this category to be respected and accepted, they need to be as simple as possible and necessary for a particular human activity. They are also necessary for the process of validation itself. Without initial beliefs, which some prefer to call intuitive beliefs, we cannot talk or falsify anything, we cannot experience anything or put anything to the test, and we cannot talk about Logic or Mathematics. These types of beliefs are rarely considered each distinct belief by itself, separately from the others, but, rather, as a *combination* of different beliefs that yield systems of Thought and Action.

571. Different religions have taken ownership of both kinds of beliefs:

   a. In what concerns the first kind (e.g. belief that we came directly from God and are not related to the other animals; Armageddon; belief that pork meat is more harming to health than cow meat or poultry; or Noah's flood), Religion has been proven wrong on a great number of them by Science. What has not been proven wrong yet is very little and appears in the context of our current knowledge too selective and biased in the belief. There are some such beliefs that have been proven right by experience, but it is no greater percentage of success than that of popular beliefs that have been proven to be true. The trouble is that out of religious dogmatism, most people still refuse to face the results of experience in the name of Religion. It is not so different, but greatly more sensitive, than refusing to admit that babies do not grow in cabbage patches.

   b. In what concerns the second kind of belief (e.g. the seven Great Mysteries in Christianity[235]; God as a way to deal with the Absurd in Kierkegaard; there is only one God; Jews are the Chosen People; or pantheistic beliefs in Buddhism), there are merits and necessity of

---

[235] Baptism, Chrismation, Eucharist, Holy Orders, Holy Unction, Marriage, and Penance.

Reflections on Fundamental Matters

some despite our probable disagreement with them. They are no different from atheistic beliefs or many of the philosophical beliefs. *What is clear is that beliefs of this kind are most of the time opposing and irreconcilable across different religions.* A choice is therefore often necessary among them.

572. The trouble with Religion is that by tying the first kind of beliefs to the second, and to everything else in Religion, and by being proven wrong on many of the first beliefs, it has compromised itself irremediably.

573. There is a place for Belief as a cognitive capacity next to Rationality and Intuition. However, its proper form is far from what is generally conceived in Religion.

   a. Can we really believe that Saint George did in fact kill a chimera or a dragon[236]?

574. The history of religious belief is full of wrong assumptions that later on, once defending such assumptions becomes plainly impossible, are mitigated by claiming one of the following:

   a. These assumptions were actually more symbolic or allegoric than anything else.

   b. It is the fault of some people within the religious institution who gave the wrong interpretations and not the fault of the religious beliefs themselves.

   c. To deny that the wrongly proven beliefs ever existed, or that they were instrumental.

575. Four important examples were given in the chapter on Knowledge. The Bible evolved from being a book to be analysed letter-by-letter to more of a symbolic book, particularly some parts of the Old Testament and the Apocalypse.

576. Today, if one is to be converted to a particular religion and is told that some of the old stories in its holy books should be taken for actual historical facts (e.g. there was literally a war that historically took place in Sri Lanka, led by Rama and Hanuman, to locate

---

[236] An obvious copy of the mythical story of the Chimera and the Bellerophon.

Sita), one could rarely imagine an enlightened, educated, and well-experienced person to easily hold such stories as true.

577. Reformations (and counter-reformations) have taken place in Christianity, but they remain far from being enough in terms of rectifying the scope of religious belief. There are two key figures in the reformation of proper religious beliefs whose wisdom has not yet crossed to the mass of Christian believers: Kierkegaard and Dostoevsky. Both remained religious despite their existentialism and agnosticism.

578. Belief is not about taking for true what is rationally wrong or proven by experience to be wrong, and Belief is not about elaborate speculative stories. Proper Belief is about overcoming the limits of Rationality, the areas where Rationality breaks down, and overcoming the Absurd, with a certain religious inclination. Some choose to do so when reaching the Absurd; others refrain. The first are called agnostic theists, and the second are called agnostic atheists. In reality, all said and done, they do not differ as much when it comes to practical daily life and usually exhibit great mutual respect; they use and build on many notions and concepts from each other.

Morality

579. Morality is naturally a key component of Religion. Religion, where it exists, typically makes of Morality one of its central pieces.

580. Historically, Religion has been instrumental in the spread of Morality in many cultures around the world. Morality was more convincing to early civilisations thanks to Religion. Arguing Morality through Rationality, Game Theory, or Utilitarianism was not as easy thousands of years ago; such tools require a minimal intellectual and cultural development for them to be effective. The religious function of promoting Morality is therefore in large part beneficial. Who can really argue against the religious forbidding of murder? Lying? Stealing? Or who can oppose a religion advocating Compassion?

581. It is through Morality that different religions can find common

ground for co-existence and through Metaphysics most of what causes them to conflict and fight.

582. Deeds are more important than Words. We therefore hold great respect for many of the religious figures and saints. We have great respect and appreciation for them from the basis of our common humanity and the deeds they have done.

On Political and Economic Systems

"[...] the greatest of penalties is being ruled by a worse man if one is not willing to rule oneself." Plato

"[...] the ideas of economists and political philosophers, both when they are right and when they are wrong are more powerful than is commonly understood. Indeed, the world is ruled by little else. Practical men, who believe themselves to be quite exempt from any intellectual influences, are usually slaves of some defunct economist." John Maynard Keynes

"The political problem of mankind is to combine three things: economic efficiency, social justice and individual liberty." John Maynard Keynes

Once upon a time, there was a group of sophisticated talkative sheep. They grazed in the fields, migrated from one place to the other depending on the seasons and availability of food, gathered together in the night for comfort, warmth, and protection from predatory wolves, and otherwise spent their time in peace and tranquillity. The sheep were distinctly aware that they could never get all that they had wished for, but life was simple and understandable. For one, the wolves will never go away, and these ferocious predators will capture some of the weaker sheep from time to time; it is the price for the rest to escape. Also good food has to be looked for and does not always grow in the same places. And finally, winters can be cold and brutal, but they have each other to make it less so.

One day, a smart and ambitious blond sheep had enough with the general quality of food. It started to voice its opinions more loudly than the others. It argued that the food they are all eating is monotone and boring, and whenever one of the sheep finds a good pasture to enjoy, all the others from the herd come along to share in the discovery. The blond sheep had an idea: that every sheep should have its own defined piece of pasture, to take care of and to grow, so that every sheep can enjoy its own food without competition from the others. All sheep loved the idea! They separated in the wide fields; each looking for what it thinks is the best spot on which to mark its territory. The sheep lived in independence for some time. However, the sheep started soon realising that their number was dwindling faster than expected. It seemed that, by each being alone, they were more vulnerable to predatory attacks, even from creatures that barely constituted a threat before, while the cold winter claimed more of the older ones who were left alone to fight the frosty nights.

A black sheep came out of the group to voice an opinion in radical opposition to the blond sheep. The black sheep claimed that there is great strength in sheep unity, and that to the contrary of what the blond sheep was advocating, all sheep need to come back more together and get more organised in the face of the dangers to their existence. All sheep loved the idea! They came back together and appointed the black sheep as leader to organise them. The black sheep had so many fine ideas. It gave speeches every week about how this or that particular aspect of their life should be better organised. By the end of one year, there were so many speeches and so many rules that the sheep started getting bored; they started seeing the black sheep as a symbol of long speeches and complicated rules, which very few had real interest in. The sheep started wandering and listening only half intently.

A white sheep emerged from the herd with a new idea: that of each sheep building its own house. This way, the white sheep argues, every sheep could enjoy the protection of its house while getting rid of many of the protective rules the black sheep put in place. The white sheep looked like a reformer, and it sounded smart. It possessed a new technology for building sheep houses the herd had never heard of before. The concept of a house was entirely new to the sheep community, and it looked neat indeed: an individual space for each, a door they can close when they feel a wolf attack was coming, and the pasture outside to enjoy whenever they needed to. All sheep loved the idea! They commissioned the white sheep to build each one of them a house, and they dismissed the black sheep and its speeches. The sheep urban community grew bigger and bigger every day. The white sheep had its best times; everyone praised it for its invention, everyone coveted it, and everyone went to it for questions of any sort; it was the genius of the community. But then a bizarre thing happened; winter came along, and storm after storm destroyed the houses one after the other. Grass around the houses became scarce, and the wolves, hungry and frustrated by the sheep hiding out for so long, turned even more savage and aggressive than usual. The sheep found themselves with destroyed homes, good grass miles and miles away, and threatened by a pack of even more ferocious wolves.

A generation of new blond sheep gained more influence within the community; they went to claim that the blond way was the right way. If every sheep were left alone to do as it pleases, then none of this would have happened. The blond influence came back, and the cycle was about to repeat itself.

The story of political and economic policies of our times is not very different from that of these sheep.

> 583. Politics exist for a large part because human desires conflict. The primary cause of conflict is egoism, not only of the individual as an entity, but also of particular traits within each individual, leading to some of the contradictions we discussed. Politics aims at working out these conflicts and contradictions in light of the Morality in place. Politics and Law provide a way of resolving conflicting human desires by means other than continued brute force.

584. Economics interests itself with particular mechanics which output is of value to the ethical system. This particular output is often named utility or material benefit. However, not all moral values are outputs of the mechanics of Economics, and the concept of utility or material benefit has been varying and proves difficult to define well.

585. Hence, both Economics and Politics are indispensable for human affairs regardless of our subjective personal tastes. And both Economics and Politics should be subjected to Ethics.

586. Economics and Law are in effect branches of Politics.

We shall not talk here about all aspects of Politics and Economics, which would require volumes by themselves. We shall rather focus on political and economic *systems* in order to characterise them and be able to express some of our views on the subject. Indeed, policy-making affects the human and non-human environment, be it in the fields of Politics or that of Economics. It is for this reason that we shall focus on it here. We will provide a brief historical approach on the subject of political and economic systems; we will state our views on these systems and their characteristics similarly to what we have done with regard to the ethical system; and finally, we will point to some of the important consequences of policy-making even to those who believe not to be concerned by it.

The Search for Perfection (again)

587. In a world of increased intellectualisation and rationalisation, political and economic systems have become a subject of great academic and social interest alongside scientific and philosophical systems. The search for the perfect political or economic system has interested most social thinkers in modern times. The same way theories of matter have been developed and proved effective and beneficial in their results, it has been the wish of social thinkers to develop similar theories in the realm of societies.

588. We talked about the human fascination with systems of Thought

On Political and Economic Systems

in general in the chapter on Knowledge. It is also natural that when an ethical or philosophical system is developed, we often desire to extrapolate it into the realm of Politics, Law, and Economics.

589. Many systems have been developed and continue to be developed in Politics and Economics, and most such systems have been implemented in a way or another. Some systems attempt to integrate a great deal of Science and Mathematics[237], while others are more qualitative; some systems were developed mostly in abstraction and then implemented, while others came to be as synthesis of notions and mechanics that were already in use.

590. Examples of systems in Politics include: Dictatorship, Monarchy, Oligopoly, Plutocracy, Aristocracy, Military, and Republic. There are several variations on these such as Constitutional Monarchy, Absolute Monarchy, Tribal Oligopoly, Economic Oligopoly, Ethnic Oligopoly, Parliamentary Republic, Nationalistic Republic, Communist Republic, Anarchist Republic, Nationalistic Militaristic Rule, Troikas, One Man Dictatorships, Federation, or Confederation.

591. Examples of systems in Economics include:

   a. When it comes to ownership of productive assets: Capitalism, Communism, or Aristocracy;

   b. When it comes to market exchange: free markets, free markets but with barriers across major markets, or controlled markets;

   c. When it comes to the role of government: Keynesian, Socialist/Dirigisme, or Libertarian; and

   d. When it comes to money regulation: no regulation, monetarist approach, interest rate vs. money printing as monetary tool, focus on inflation, or focus on economic growth.

592. There are proponents of all such systems at different points in

---

[237] With the hope of providing more solid footing to the system but without really succeeding most of the time.

Reflections on Fundamental Matters

History. Preferences for one system over the other can have one of many causes: ethical considerations, personal experiences, social position, emotional prejudices and biases, egoism, or altruism.

593. We find substantial intellectual work on almost all abovementioned political and economic systems. The attitude of the proponents of each system is typically to claim that they are in the right, while the opposing camp is in the wrong. Their system explains it all and explains it well, while any other systems should be disregarded.

    a. Proponents of a particular system always focus on the negatives of the system(s) they do not like and use any examples of underperformance, especially recent ones, as 'proof' that other systems are flawed. They therefore conclude that the system they are advocating is the right one.

    b. Proponents of a particular system constantly seek to find any possible mitigation for periods of underperformance in their own preferred system.

    c. Proponents of a particular system almost never admit the reality that nothing works all the time. They like to constantly appear as knowing all things and capable of explaining all things through the lens of their system.

594. The result: we collectively zigzag from one system (or political party) to the other with promises that the newfound system will solve all of our problems, that is until we succumb to the next political and/or economic disillusionment.

595. People tend to think politicians are smart and know it all, and politicians of course think themselves even more intelligent than people think; the reality is far from it.

    a. If there are any given attributes to be given to politicians, they are rather their capacity to mobilise people (through charm, eloquence, control of information, material wealth, professional reputation/career, and less often than people at first hand think, ideas) as well as their ability to conceal a lot of their true feelings and ignorance in order to appeal to the widest audience possible.

b. Intelligence is not a key trait of daily politics; it is however a necessary attribute of great long-term political thinking and governing.

596. Most governing systems are a product of circumstances, and some have proven to be beneficial, albeit within a certain timeframe. Governing systems equally impact future circumstances, and the interplay between governing and circumstances is a natural manifestation of the general interaction of things.

597. What is however more evident is that no political or economic system has proven so far to be applicable to all types of societies, at all times, and under all conditions. No one single path seems to exist for reaching the desired social outcomes whatever they may be. All systems seem to underperform either in particular circumstances or generally after a certain period of time.

598. When it comes to political and economic systems, the idea of some prescribed eternal state of equilibrium is not only false but also greatly dangerous for policy-making. Apart from defective system engineering, the root causes for opposing this utopic view are the interactive nature of things, Reflexivity, and the inherent existence of chaos in our world affairs. He who says differently is usually doing so with the purpose of marketing a certain particular system of his/her preference.

599. The common reasons behind potential breakdowns of a political or economic systems can be many:

　　a. The system itself can be inefficiently conceived and can therefore produce sub-optimal results even if everything works out as intended. In other words, the mechanics of the system might be ill conceived.

　　b. The incentives put in place can be beneficial at the start but turn out to be self-destructive in the long run. For example, a system promoting competition can be beneficial for economic dynamism, but we know all too well that competition can turn ruthless and unethical if not regulated properly, or that it can in the process result in oligopolies and monopolies of power that in turn come to undermine the incentive to compete.

   i. Many large institutions, abusive of the right to compete, have been created from what some macroeconomists call 'free competition'.

   ii. The dynamics of boom & bust also fall under this category; the bust can sometimes be of destructive magnitudes.

c. The system might be omitting important social considerations that will come to undermine the entire system and the way its functioning was envisioned. Examples can include a culture of corruption, which will make governance as intended impossible, or a culture of tribes or acute ethnic opposition, which will make equality difficult to apply strictly. Equally, it might be valid at first to ignore certain considerations for the sake of simplicity, but for unforeseen reasons, these considerations can become greatly influential in particular critical situations[238] at a later stage. No system can factor in all possible considerations without becoming monstrously complicated and in the process inapplicable.

d. Paradigm shifts and dramatic externalities do take place and can undermine the good functioning of a system.

   i. Rapid industrialisation can render a system based mostly on a culture of agriculture obsolete and ineffective very quickly.

   ii. A similar dynamic is taking place in our age of the Internet.

600. We are not inferring that all systems are alike. There are some systems that are very poor in most circumstances, and there are definitely many poor systems in light of the prevailing

---

[238] We described the increased sensitivity to noise or initial conditions of many dynamic systems close to a critical state in the section on Interaction and Reflexivity.

On Political and Economic Systems

circumstances. However, there are also situations where several systems can work with each having its proper limitations. The choice in such cases becomes a matter of resolving contradicting desires in society more so than trying to engineer a better system.

601. We can draw valid lessons from opposing systems without becoming irrelevant politically or economically:

    a. Market efficiency and protection of private property are right wing ideas at the core, while a minimum social net and market regulation are left wing ideas; very few economic systems in the developed world today do not include these four elements.

    b. What one can take from Conservatism is that rash revolutionary experiments often result in disorder and unintended consequences as proven by the French and Bolshevik revolutions. What one can take from Reactionaries is that for a political system to survive over long periods of time, it has to evolve and incorporate new conditions.

602. We ask the reader to beware of ideological propaganda that can in reality be very different from the actual political or economic system in place. Some claim themselves to be more liberal or greater proponents of freedom than they actually are, while others can be labelled more socialist or communist that their current system in its working is. Some can claim that they are proponents of cultural or religious diversity and integration while having system rules that attest to the contrary. All of us ought to pay more attention to the systems and their actual working rather than take words at face value.

    a. In many ways, China today is more capitalist than many countries in Europe or the Americas.

    b. Some red states[239] in the United States are top beneficiaries of social welfare measures, such as food stamps or healthcare benefits.

---

239 I.e. of Republican or right wing inclination.

c. Many countries where freedom of speech is sacred have their media outlets mostly controlled by particular factions of society.

d. The Middle East is full of countries claiming religious diversity and integration while each having a sectarian political system in writing or in practice.

These subtleties bring us to the topic of Democracy, great and simple to understand at face value but full of nuances and diversity in doctrine and application, as we shall see. There are many democratic systems, and they can be very different in practice than what their proponents generally think.

Quick Synopsis of Democracy

603. Democracy is the vote of the many. Democracy is often positioned as one system or one ideal; in reality, it has different degrees and can take different forms.

604. The idea of Democracy is indeed very old, but its applications show a great deal of nuance. The circumstances under which democratic systems have operated in History point to very different possibilities of outcome.

605. In ancient Greece, Democracy concerned only Greek males of age; it excluded females and slaves. Slaves in the nascent American nation had no say either, and Democracy did not prove in any way capable of overcoming ethnic segregation—only an outright and bloody civil war did. The largest democratic country in the world today, India, suffers from endemic corruption. Indonesia suffers from challenges similar to that of India. Ethnic diversities can turn elections into ethnic competitions, where defining voting circumscriptions becomes more important than the voting itself in determining the result of an election; the race towards demographic multiplication becomes in such situations the only meaningful political game[240].

---

[240] Iraq, Lebanon, Nigeria, and Ukraine are examples of such.

606. The first important question in the vote of the many is to define what is subject to vote and what is not. We can subject taking public office to the vote of the many, but we can also organise a daily vote on what a president or a queen should wear. The first is important, while the second is utterly futile and counterproductive. A great deal of difference in democratic functioning comes from the frequency of vote, the subjects to be voted on, how the vote is framed in the first place, as well as the conditions under which the vote is taking place.

   a. For example, direct and indirect voting systems can lead to completely different results and behaviours in otherwise similarly democratic systems. The 2000 US presidential election would have yielded a different outcome (and maybe behind also a different outcome in terms of geopolitical wars and acceleration of the US federal deficit) if the popular vote were to be the norm in the United States. Similarly, election by the majority vs. proportional representation can also yield very different parliaments with distinctly different behaviour of the constituting groups in terms of attitudes towards radicalisation or compromise.

607. Powers given to various institutions in a Democracy can result in dramatically different governance systems. We find Republican Democracy, Constitutional Monarchy, Communist Democracy, Anarchist Democracy, and Militaristic Democracy. Democracy can apply to the legislative branch, part of the legislative branch, the executive branch, or a combination of the two. Democracy can also apply to regional governance, such as municipal elections, state elections, or any similar.

608. Moreover, the exact same democratic system will also look very different in application and effectiveness depending on the conditions imposed on it by the outside environment. It would look different in situations of prolonged war or peace; in situations of acute economic crises or prosperity; in situations of foreign

invasion and control vs. complete independence and freedom; or finally in situations of global xenophobia or cosmopolitanism.

609. No democracy is a democracy all the time and under all circumstances. Concretely, any democratic system includes explicit and implicit restraints that are put in action in case of existential threats to the system. The general view is that a government should be able to defend its own existence against threats from the inside and the outside[241].

   a. We call some of the explicit restraints Marshall Laws or Emergency Laws. Power in these circumstances becomes centralised in one individual or a small committee, sometimes for long periods of time.

   b. There are also implicit restraints. For example, the media can auto-censure itself; everybody can beat the same drum in situations of war regardless of personal conviction, out of fear for one's existence, out of gregarious attitude, but also simply because it is not easy to go against the general current.

610. We are not arguing that contingency plans and restraints are necessarily bad under all circumstances. We are only drawing attention to the difference between a general utopic idea of Democracy and the realities of democratic functioning. After all, in any governance system, there is a balance to strike between speed and efficiency on one side, and democratisation on the other. In extreme scenarios, speed and efficiency count more.

611. Thinking about Democracy as a cure to all the world's challenges or an end state by itself is wrong simplistic idealism. Stating this is not intended to justify dictatorships of any sort. In reality, tyrannies lead more often to worse results on the long-term if they do not transition eventually to some form of electorship. The aim of what we are saying is to render Democracy a stronger and more enlightened concept, less easy to usurp or become disillusioned

---

241 Defends itself from what exactly is an important consideration, as in there lies a fine line between legitimate self-defence and disguised dictatorship.

by. The vote of the many has distinct advantages but also pitfalls that cannot be ignored.

612. Among the definite positives of the vote of the many we can find:

    a. Accountability of governance.

    b. A process of regular checks through election capable of counterbalancing corruption and complacency[242], which tend to take place in institutions with no change or accountability in them.

    c. A form of equality, albeit limited. Theoretically, anyone can access some form of public power in most democratic systems; the reality is however more subtle than that as access to public office depends on many other ingredients than just the popular vote. Nevertheless, wealth and aristocratic segregation can be better fought with Democracy.

    d. Greater resilience to the governing system. Through regular elections, a political system can allow itself to change direction regularly as times and circumstances vary; new externalities and conditions of the general environment are continuously incorporated into the next vote in democratic systems.

    e. Greater satisfaction to human self-esteem through a sense of participation. Democratic systems are not perfect, but through the process of participation in public life, individual voters gain a sense of ownership in public affairs. People feel the government to be their own more so in a democracy than through any other governing system, particularly when the vote of the many is regular and is perceived as capable of bringing major change in public life from time to time.

613. There are also some clear difficulties and drawbacks of the vote of the many we need to be aware of:

---

[242] Not in all instances though.

a. The concept of one-person one-vote can give sub-optimal results such as dangerous populism in the form of a Hitler or a Robespierre, or religious radicalism that leaves no room for another opinion or belief.

b. Democracy applied to the wrong field can equally be detrimental and dangerous. In ancient Athens, Democracy spread to everything including court processes. An accused was judged by a jury from the general public (who held office for short periods of time) similarly to what we have today in the US in many proceedings. However, the key major difference with the US was the absence in the Athenian Antiquity of a qualified judge whose crucial role is to uphold equality of treatment and procedure. The result was a pure sheer manipulation of the jurymen by both plaintiff and defendant; legal victory was more determined by who was more capable of manipulating the jury during the trials.

c. We mentioned what democracies can result in when applied crudely to countries with a history of acute ethnic tensions. Of course, there are ways of containing these dangers such as the establishment of a proper senate that protects minorities. Constitutional courts or similar organisms serve an equally beneficial counter-balance. Unfortunately, these structures rarely exist in countries with ethnic tensions, and even where they exist, they rarely operate as they theoretically should.

d. A subtle consequence of the race to short-term popularity in Democracy is focusing society's priorities on the wrong subjects. One particular issue can sometimes dominate the results of an election over all others, regardless of the importance of this issue in the grand scheme of things. A particular affair, a certain tax, or a certain security fear, can overshadow other greatly important issues because of the influence of the present moment. Some of these situations are manufactured on purpose in order to evade more difficult topics. Democracy can seem like a game of charm more so than a serious approach to governing because of the importance of short-term popularity, particularly in tight elections.

e. Grave inconsistencies and political oscillations can emanate from popular vote. Consider the political willingness for further integration in the European Union. In times of prosperity, the general public will was for further integration, while today, in more difficult economic times, the will is for further independence, as well as a reduced funding of the European institutions[243]. A project such as the European Union one is a long-term project that spans several generations. Economic conditions are likely to oscillate between the good years and the lean years all along. Europeans should ask themselves, "Are we to stay the course in the European integration or change our views on it with the changes in shorter term economic conditions?" The same can be said about funding for Science, space programs, environmental protection, or the fight against famine. Public opinion on these subjects does vary with the change in economic conditions in sometimes absurd manners.

f. When the vote of the many counts, the ability to address the largest number counts as much. Hence, the role of the media is very important in Democracy. The media industry in an environment of no self-control, or where media outlets work for or are funded by special interests, can be very effective in manipulating opinions. The role of the media is even more determining on subjects where the general public lacks education. Stories and opinions widely perpetuated by the media exert an anchoring and availability bias in the mind of voters, which can result

---

243 Which remains very low as percentage of GDP in comparison with major federations and countries, once again unlike what the general media often portrays.

Reflections on Fundamental Matters

in a dramatically different behaviour of a democratic system.

614. Democracy is simply a process of decision-making through mass election more so than a well-defined political system. A process and a political system cannot be confused, even if the political system does use the democratic process as key basis. Politicians in many influential countries like to give eloquent speeches about spreading Democracy in the world; such grand callings mean very little without the necessary definition of the governance systems to put in place.

615. Systems with sound democratic elections and free of manipulations yield, on the balance, more optimal long-term results and prove to be more resilient. However, this is not necessarily always the case. For such systems to be successful, other considerations have also to be taken into account. Some are particular to the society we are looking at[244], while others are of a more general nature. Naturally, we can only talk about the general ones here and can consider them as necessary conditions for the success of a system relying on Democracy:

   a. An effective counter-balance to the popular vote. This counter-balance usually takes the form of an auto-governed legal system (including constitutional courts), but this is not the only possibility. Sometimes upper and lower legislative structures are also necessary counter-balances.

   b. An effective and efficient functioning of all institutions involved, including lack of corruption. History is full of examples where disorder and anarchy have helped military tyrannies take advantage of popular frustrations. Moreover, the results of a democratic election become worthless if the candidates elected to undertake certain tasks find themselves at the command of institutions incapable of doing much, or where the public vote is

---

[244] E.g. ethnic diversity, demographic distribution, or political history.

On Political and Economic Systems

usurped by corruption and backdoor calculations and lobbying.

c. An effective and uncorrupted monopoly of physical power (military and police). Without a disciplined and enlightened monopoly of physical power, democratic systems can quickly turn into a ruthless ruling of a majority at the expense of a minority. *An effective legal system with a strong enough military is sometimes the only practical safeguard for the loser in an election.* Moreover, monopoly of physical power guarantees greater public safety, which takes us away from the politics of fear into a more constructive political debate.

d. Some level of specialisation and elitism is necessary, no matter how much this condition opposes our longing for universal equality. A judge cannot be given responsibilities and be expected to perform her duties without proper legal qualifications; neither is a general, a doctor, or a president. Although in theory, democratic systems allow for anyone to make it to any position open for election, in reality, the way most democratic systems work includes some implicit form of filtering based on qualifications. In France, it usually takes the form of educational credentials; in China, a certain curriculum within the Communist Party is required; and in the US, there are Democrat and Republican Party, sometimes gruelling, elections.

e. An auto-regulated independent media[245]. The importance of this condition could not be stressed enough, especially in an age where the media still commands large influence despite the rise of the Internet and alternative journalism. If media airtime can be purchased freely by anyone, those who are able to gather the most capital would dominate both media presence and elections. A candidate needs to be known before getting elected, and we live in a world where it is still not easy to be known without media support.

---

245 Economic independence in particular.

616. A democratic system that is not capable of counter-balancing some of its unintended consequences is doomed sooner or later to fail.

    a. Tyrannies can take advantage of the frustration from disorder or grave security fears to seize power.

    b. Similarly, populist tyrannies can take hold of a society with endemic and increasing material inequalities if they are not addressed from within the system in time. Democratic systems, despite allowing in theory anyone to make it, can still result over time with social and material inequalities. The rule of the many can become from all practical points of view, a concealed rule of the few at the top working for the special interests of these same few. Democracies can lead in these situations to plutocracies or oligarchies, and in the past aristocracies. Rome was taken over by its military when its democracy led to increased inequalities and became effectively an aristocracy. This is one of the distinct cases where Democracy slips back into Dictatorship.

617. **From a historical standpoint, it seems that security disorder, blind populism, and social inequalities are the three key threats to the longevity of democratic systems.** They are largely internal threats.

Approach to Political and Economic Systems

618. We ought to care about which approach our society is taking to political and economic governing. And we equally ought to not be naive when it comes to the dynamics of Politics and Economics, the conflicting desires of humans, and chaos in our existence. As with much else, there is no simple everlasting solution to the problems of Politics and Economics.

619. This does not necessarily mean an advocacy towards Anarchism[246],

---

246 Although philosophical anarchism is not as pejorative as commonly or politically portrayed generally—Anarchists, apologies...

On Political and Economic Systems

and more importantly this should not instil in anyone a defeatist attitude of the sort that says that nothing will ultimately work all the time so we should not even bother.

- a. We would not be where we are today if some of our ancestors did not bother. History is far from being pretty, but though all of the human experiences, good and bad, the general utility has increased to the benefit of the majority because some have cared about political and economic systems. Those who believed in a better tomorrow have made great sacrifices, and *it is in reality through this belief itself that they managed to shape a better tomorrow.* We are capable of exercising an effect on our environment, even if sometimes limited and even if imperfect, and it is what makes the power of ideas great.

- b. There is also strength in collectivity. Arguably at our current level of advancement in many fields, it is almost impossible to progress any longer without a collective effort. And he who talks about collectivity needs to define mechanisms through which this collectivity of humans can operate; this is precisely the key purpose of political and economic systems.

620. There is strength in collectivity, but there is especially more strength when each member of society is enlightened and adds to the group, not when he or she is used as another pawn in validating a single doctrine till it is too late and the ship has fully sunk. In any collectivity, individuality, both physical and intellectual, remains very important.

621. **When it comes to political and economic systems, it is better to be nimble and practical** rather than too ideological and wanting to be precise, as conditions change, the world of human affairs is inherently uncertain, and our knowledge of it remains limited.

622. Inertia and human reluctance to change, including vested interest of various sections of society, are the enemies of nimbleness and practicality.

623. Systematic thinking needs therefore to be applied with moderation: not an attitude of believing that a particular system will always work; that your political party or leader has the magic solution to everything; that your country is always the greatest and can do no wrong; nor an attitude that says that any serious effort is useless since there is no stable solution to our problems and aspirations.

624. Whatever is the chosen system,

   a. It should reflect the common Morality and the moral objectives of the society it applies to.

   Moral objectives define what is desired and not desired by a certain society, which a political system has to respect in order to maintain a long-term sustainability and adherence by the largest proportion of the population. It is also what the political and economic systems should point towards. Individual Rights, Human Rights, Civil Rights, and Protection of Individual Property, all emanate from Morality, without which a political system loses its fundamental compass.

      i. Let us illustrate with an example from commerce. Free markets operate rather well under the large majority of conditions. However, free markets by themselves are amoral; they have no notion of what is good and what is bad, what is desired morally and what is not. All that market participants seek to achieve is maximising individual utility. It is the role of regulation to balance market functioning with Morality, including protection of the weak and the poor, basic equality of opportunities, environmental preservation, and insurance against dramatic events for which markets are known to be poor to account.

   b. It should be capable of evolving and adapting in order not to lose all effectiveness under changing conditions.

   A system would need to include in itself proper

mechanisms for changing, evolving, rectifying mistakes, and internalising new unforeseen conditions. *A good system is not a system that always functions well; it is a system that is capable of recognising when it steers in the wrong direction, rectifies itself (hopefully as quickly as possible), and synthesises such experiences for later use.* Democratic systems, when operating properly, can allow for punishing abuses of power or mistakes at subsequent election-rounds, at least as they become flagrant at the overall level.

c. It should allow for the broadest individual liberty possible while respecting the above two conditions.

Complete and absolute individual liberty is not possible in a society of several individuals; more so, it is inefficient. My individual liberty overlaps with that of others. Some of what I desire can risk coming at the expense of other individuals. One of the roles of a political system is to balance out all individual liberties and aspirations into something workable while allowing each the maximum individual liberty possible. This is one of the essences of Liberalism.

The greater the *possible*[247] liberty of individuals is, the greater the sense of fulfilled self-esteem is, even if this liberty is not fully exercised. We are creatures who constantly look for individual affirmation; a perimeter of liberty that is too narrow works against our self-esteem and, more often than not, results in erratic behaviour against the system that is limiting this liberty. Greater liberty allows for greater diversity and helps limit dogmatism and conformism. The latter constitutes a major threat to the system's capacity to evolve in the face of changing conditions. Diversity is a key aspect of the functioning of a free market. Without it, most of the innovation and personal entrepreneurial expression would be stifled. Diversity helps protect against totalitarian and mono-colour political systems of any sort.

---

247 As opposed to the actually utilised one.

d. It should contain a system for efficiently dealing and effectively answering human contradicting aspirations.

We saw from the chapter on Human Contradictions how inherently contradictory we can be, even when paying the most attention to our inner contradictions. As with the case of individual liberty, a political system should incorporate ways of satisfactorily dealing with contradicting human aspirations, both at the individual as well as the collective level. Voting is one of the ways of resolving human conflicts and collective contradictions without having to use force.

625. These are for us the four pillars of a good political and economic system, beyond the generic labels we find in everyday politics between left wing, right wing, or centre. All political lines and parties have evolved with time, and the definitions and lines of separation on ideological bases have become blurry and confusing. The distinction today is more of a 'branding' exercise than that of ideas and practice. What is far right in one country can be centre in another, and those who remain stuck in an older age of Cold War seem to us rather mentally stuck in a past that helps evade facing the current reality of global politics and economics.

626. Here again, whatever changes need to be implemented to an existing system, it is better to do it in moderation, and through smaller steps, over abrupt changes that sometimes lead to worse situations and unforeseen consequences.

a. If we compare the consequences of the French Revolution to that of the Glorious Revolution thirty or forty years later, the difference is notable both in terms of prosperity as well as system stability.

b. The abrupt dismantling of the Soviet Union resulted in plain theft of public equity by oligarchs, whereas China is working itself slowly towards prosperity, one step at a time, away from ideological Communism.

On Political and Economic Systems

    c. Almost everybody agrees that the US decision to dismantle all key institutions in Iraq[248] following their military victory has only accelerated the path that the country took towards chaos and allowed many dormant sectarian problems to resurface. It cost thousands of lives and billions of dollars to restore some order following this rash dismantling.

627. Finally, the effectiveness of a system needs to be judged in the light of some of the characteristics of the society it applies to: level of evolution (including education and political sophistication) of the society in question; composition of the society (e.g. mono vs. multi ethnic); history of political systems (we cannot pretend that a society is a clean slate–social memory does count); and the key paradigms of the time (e.g. a period of baby boom, technology boom, wars, or economic depression).

628. One of the current social realities we struggle with is the poor level of value allocation in comparison with human utility, societies, particularly developed ones, bestow on various human activities. There seems to be a grave disconnect between what we consider to be the most important problems of our times, and what types of human activities our societies reward the most. The proportion of rewards between different human activities is gravely skewed in many instances.

    a. As an example, there is no justification for a pop singer to earn 20 or 100 times more than an astronaut; is a successful singer really providing humanity 20 to 100 times more utility than a successful astronaut?

629. Structural considerations[249] go a long way in explaining these disconnects of rewards. Scale effect and concentration can distort value greatly.

---

248 Particularly security ones.

249 Such as monopolistic vs. more competitive industries, or large-scale and/or oversupplied structures in some sectors, which can make a mobile phone cost less than a massage.

630. Regardless of the reasons, a comparison of monetary value and social utility in our current societies often shows mismatches with which very few people would objectively feel comfortable. And if Morality is the guide of Politics and Economics, we ought to care about such mismatches, and not just shrug and say this is the way things are. Regulation does not have to be cumbersome; it can be smart without being cumbersome.

631. Disconnects of value are not necessarily a pure product of a more liberal or socialist economy. France, which is known for its more socialist stance than the United States, shows similar disconnects and inequity of proportions. Is it right that, concerning the proposed 75% taxation on income above a million euros in France, those who are most affected turn out to be footballers and singers? What does that tell us about society's priorities? It does not seem right from a moral and social point of view, and yet it is the reality in many economies.

632. It seems that we live in times where immediate and easy material pursuit and entertainment are the two key priorities of almost all factions of societies over other considerations. It seems to us that there were prior times where intellectual or artistic pursuit for the sake of Knowledge, Political/Social Ideology, or Art were more important priorities, at least in certain social circles. Humans, at all times, have aspired to greater material well-being. However, the difference is in what becomes of one's priorities once a sufficient well-being is secured; some continue to focus on amassing greater material wealth, while others change priorities to something more abstract and important to Humanity as a whole. In our days, we cannot fail to notice a normalisation of social desires towards the easy and the immediate, over those activities that require more hard work and sacrifice. Financial speculation, exorbitant spending on sports entertainment, fascination with becoming the next pop or Hollywood star over a theatre actor or a music composer, and more lucrative remuneration from plastic surgery technologies over many other scientific experimentations, are all reflections of this bias towards the easy and the immediate.

633. Simplistically human activity can be put into three categories:

   a. Value-transfer activities; financial speculation and gambling are the easiest examples to give. But more generally, it can be defined as activities where the amount of value transfer is equal or higher than any value potentially created by that activity.

   b. Value-creating activities; scientific research, technology, teaching, developmental NGOs[250], *Wikipedia*, policymaking, transportation, i.e. activities where the resulting long-term value creation outweighs the immediate value of the activity itself. In other words, value propagates and multiplies in society as a result of such activities.

   c. Value-preserving activities; law, police, fireguard, army, insurance companies, security companies, i.e. activities that seek to protect created value. The act of preservation could be against externalities, environmental or human, as well as internal activities not in line with Morality. The utility of value preservers is often forgotten until bad things happen, and we suddenly are reminded of their importance.

634. Some may wonder, how about value-destroying activities? Military has value-preserving roles but also value-destroying roles. We have omitted this category on purpose. Value-creation and value-destruction bring us back to Morality and what is considered to be a positive value. What can be a destruction of value under one morality is not necessarily so under another. Was NATO[251]'s intervention in ex-Yugoslavia value-creating or value-destroying? Most would agree that it was rather value-creating despite the short-term destruction and loss of life. It is for this reason that we will not elaborate on the opposition between value-creation and value-destruction here, as it would take on many unnecessary digressions.

---

250 Non-Governmental Organisations.

251 North Atlantic Treaty Organization.

635. **The long-term sustainability of economic and political systems is greatly enhanced by the proper reward allocation to value-creating and value-preserving activities over value-transfer activities.** Such an attitude protects long-term investments and effort over immediate volatile gain; it protects the hard-working taxpayer or the investor who risks substantial amount of hard-earned wealth from the gambler or the individual who tries to maximise welfare benefits instead of creating value in society. It rewards the right behaviour over the wrong one. *It is not the job of market participants to define their political and economic morality while operating in the market in order to balance out the deficiencies in the overall system*; the system itself has to incorporate such moral factors to ensure long-term sustainability.

    a. A lot has been said about the banking industry and its 'evils'. Even before 2007, we could often read opinions about how the American economy is sooner or later doomed; how young Americans do not study Science and Engineering anymore, or even if they do, they never work in these fields; how the brightest go into Finance or maybe Law[252]. These young Americans are not really to blame; and we are not so sure that economies are destined to doom because of that either. Most are hard-working smart individuals many would love to have in their organisations. Their job is to maximise their individual utility; we, voters, on the other hand, are to blame for sanctifying politics that protect such a biased reward structure; we, policymakers, who are supposed to come up with the rules of the game; and we, academics and journalists, who are supposed to voice up our ideas about such deficiencies *before* the damage is done. It is rather hypocritical to put all the blame on only one faction of society who works in Finance when the blame is to be shared. The reality is that many of these individuals would still have chosen to do the same job for

---

252 Similar points have been made about Europe's brightest taking a one-way ticket to the City of London.

less. Given the level of stress and anxiety in Finance, very few individuals are likely to last a long time if they did not actually enjoy it.

Let us look at how we compensate our scientists and inventors on the other hand. Have you heard of anyone becoming a multi-millionaire because he discovered a great new theory in Physics or a great new theorem in Mathematics? Have you heard of anyone who has dedicated her life to expanding the boundaries of Humanity into outer space become very rich out of it? Did Donald Davies make billions from his indispensable contribution to computer science, and what later became the Internet?

636. Civilisations grow from the increased focus on value-creating activities, sustain from the increased focus on value-preserving activities alongside the value-creating ones, and auto-decay from a primary focus on value-transfer activities over the rest in comparison with other civilisations.

637. Measuring value accurately is not easy, and predicting which activities will have a greater multiplying effect in society is not always obvious and can be subject to circumstances. But societies need to pay attention to the change in focus from value-creating and -preserving activities to value-transfer activities, and this is possible at a general level. The attitude of paying attention to this change of focus is itself greatly beneficial, more so than the accuracy of value measurement, as in it lies the greatest defence against general complacency.

638. Why are all these considerations about political and economic systems important? The answer takes us back to the important influence of environment. Politics and Economics are great drivers of the human environment and are responsible for setting long-term conditions for human life. Their impact can therefore be found in anything. From what we study, to what and how we eat; from what we earn for our work, to how we interact with

strangers or neighbours; from what we fear, to how we behave; Politics and Economics impact all of it either directly or in more subtle manners. In particular, we will highlight three important reasons for good politics and economics:

    a. A sufficient material well-being for the highest number of humans.

>   Eradicating poverty and providing a sense of equity among all individuals in a sustainable manner[253] result in better conditions for progress, whether in thought or in action, and be it technological, social, political, or other. Whether human conflicts are primarily driven by material considerations or by ideological reasons, there is almost always a material element involved in wars and acts of violence. *A starved person cannot be an innovator, a researcher, a scientific, an economist, or simply a good citizen. The worst in human nature usually awakens in situations of deprivation.* Need can drive the destructive impulses of anyone towards the human and/or natural environment. It is no surprise that we find today the greater risks of animal extinction and destruction of natural habitats to be in some of the poorest regions of the world. It is no surprise either that innovation almost always goes hand-in-hand with material progress.

    b. Psychological well-being for the highest number of humans.

>   Humans are not only material beings; they seek freedom, will for political expression, cultural expression, creation of beauty through artistic means, and other intangibles. All of these goals are not properly catered for without the right political and economic systems in place. Even in situations of material sufficiency, sooner or later, pressures for psychological and political well-being will make their way to the surface in societies.

---

[253] We mean by that equity of chances, not necessarily a forced artificial equity of wealth.

c. A decaying political and economic system in a developed society will eventually sap the foundations themselves of this society.

Through bad politics and economics, the good risks being destroyed with the bad, and much of what was achieved risks being compromised. Bad economies or complacent military brought to the ground great civilisations throughout History. Asian armies invaded Byzantium; Mongols took over China; barbarians invaded Rome; and rural Spartans vanquished educated and sophisticated Athenians. In all of these examples, the latter had a notably greater level of civilisation, but it was not enough to preserve it. And in all of those examples, it took Humanity a long time to recapture some of what it had lost. This could happen again. We invite the reader to imagine what will happen to Human Rights, Women Rights, or Civil Rights if the societies that uphold them the most today collapse economically or politically. Extremist views flourish in such situations of collapse, and external threats become more effective; we worry about that, particularly in what concerns the European Union today. Through a process of auto-decay, great human achievements can be buried along with all that is complacent and inefficient.

Power: A Key Paradigm of Living Beings

"[...] the fundamental concept in social science is Power, in the same sense in which Energy is the fundamental concept in physics. Like energy, power has many forms, such as wealth, armaments, civil authority, influence on opinion." Bertrand Russell, *Power*.

There was once a little boy who wanted to change the world. He was born into a family of modest means, but he was very smart and ambitious. More importantly, he was genuinely concerned with the plight of humans and wanted to make a difference for the better in the world–he was a Don Quixote in the making. The little boy took upon himself to talk openly when he saw humans behaving ridiculously or in a manner that would come to hurt them in the long-run. He never understood why people in his neighbourhood could be so contradictory; that they can express dissatisfaction with their everyday life but do nothing about it; or that they focus on the small picture rather than what matters the most and complain about it afterwards. The little boy decided to openly point out these contradictions and this absurd behaviour in the hope that people would listen to him, pay attention to what they are doing, and change their life for the better. The little boy went on for years doing so to no avail; although some of the neighbours recognised that the little boy was smart, and that he was probably right in what he was saying, they, most of the time, smiled when listening to him or simply ignored him and went on doing what they used to do without changing much. "How can people simply acknowledge something and not change?" the little boy wondered. He grew more frustrated with time but kept on pointing out the flaws in people more vehemently. The neighbours, who the little boy mostly addressed, got equally frustrated listening to him and started perceiving him as a nuisance. Eventually, they stopped paying attention to him. The little boy grew desperate; he realised that whatever he said, he could not make a difference. People even came to ignore him completely, which made his situation worse. One day, the little boy sitting in his room, all grumpy and angry, his grandfather passed by. The little boy's grandfather was definitely not as smart and observing as the little one, at least that is what the little boy thought. The little boy always thought that he knew it all, while his grandfather always led a simple, relaxed life. The old man asked the little one why he has been in such a miserable mood lately. The little boy told his grandfather his story, and his eyes watered while he was talking. The old man listened intently and seemed to genuinely feel for his grandson and his frustration. When the little boy finished, the grandfather took a deep breath, held silence for a moment, and then said, "Listen my dear boy, I have come a long way in life, and I may still not know a lot about it. But I know this: people will not listen to you and will not give you attention without Power. Even if what you are saying is right and is for their own good, they will not take it seriously enough without some form of Power. This is what you have been missing all along. People will walk by you in the street and not even notice you if you do not have Power. And even if they listen, even if they recognise that what you are saying might actually be true, they still would not take it as seriously as when you have Power of some sort." The little boy was startled and immediately realised how naive he was all along about human affairs.

639. If Morality should be the long-term compass of Politics and Economics, Power is in reality their everyday closest driver.

640. Power is the extent of the influence a living being (or a group of living beings) *can* have on the behaviour of other existing

Power: A Key Paradigm of Living Beings

beings through interaction, and the capacity to resist this same influence when subjected to it. Indeed, Power includes the ability to influence Morality itself.

641. If interaction is the key paradigm of existence, then Power is a particular facet of this interaction that mostly relates to living beings[254], either at the initiating or receiving end.

642. The subject of a living being's power is both the inert and the living world. In the case of interaction with the inert world, Power is mostly measured in absolute terms and is essentially about Physical Power. In the case of interaction with the living world, Power is mostly measured in relative terms to other living beings and can take many forms, including the traditional physical one.

643. In our days, Physical Power is more prevalent in the world of living beings excluding humans than in the world of humans itself. The world of humans seems to exhibit today a larger and more sophisticated array of Power forms, which do exist, but in a more limited manner, in the animal world. As a rule, the greater the level of cognition of living beings is, the subtler the forms Power can take.

644. Power over non-cognitive nature[255] is about Physical Power; it is about the power to manipulate or take advantage of Nature for particular interests, while being able to protect oneself from harmful threats. Physical Power is unhidden power. It is not subtle, and it does not appeal to the mind. It threatens the body. It acts through harm or fear of harm, through action or fear of action. It is the power of the alpha lion or the alpha wolf in its pack.

645. But it is Power among and between Humans that is often the subject of most interest to us. Like all animals, we care much about how powerful we can be vis-à-vis others, without realising

---

254 We will focus on Power in the social sphere in this chapter and not necessarily as it is more purely defined in Physics (as Energy divided by Time).

255 We mean by non-cognitive: inert nature, flora, and other living forms with very basic or non-existent cognitive capabilities such as microorganisms.

that in the grand scheme of things, all our collective power comes to nothing at the level of the Universe.

    a. When we acquire Power, we are no different than a peacock proud of having won a duel. The same way we would look and smile at such a naive attitude of the peacock not realising the greater power dynamics around it, the greater Universe could laugh at our world of human affairs and our narrow perceptions of Power.

646. Power is indisputably one of the key defining attributes of human affairs, politics, and economics. It is not the only attribute[256] of our world, but, without understanding Power, much about human affairs remains in the dark.

On The Forms and Drivers of Power

647. Intra-human power includes Physical Power, but also many other subtle forms of Power. In order to talk more effectively about Power in the human world, we shall separate this world first into two categories:

    a. The realm of nations, military, and institutions that control organised groups whose profession is to exercise Physical Power/violence and protect from such.

    b. The realm of the 'civil' world, be it at an individual level or at a group level[257]. A police force falls under this category, as ultimately the role of the police (at least on paper) is to protect and execute the commands of civil law.

648. Power balance in the realm of nations and military is ultimately a count of the *potentiality* of Physical Power, even if not exercised on a regular basis.

649. Diplomacy and bilateral agreements exist between nations, and

---

256 Compassion can be one as we have previously stated.

257 E.g. a civil organisation, a company, a religious institution, a professional order, or a civil party.

Power: A Key Paradigm of Living Beings

there are international bodies such as the United Nations, but they all ultimately have their basis in the potentiality of Physical Power of the nations in question. There is no international independent body today capable of policing the large nations on Earth[258]. Ultimately, their dynamic is a dynamic of pure Power comparison.

650. Atomic weapons have greatly balanced the potentiality of Physical Power around the globe, regardless of nations' other Physical Power attributes[259]. At least nine states[260] today possess an arsenal of nuclear bombs; it is for this reason that global world wars between these nations are today a more remote possibility than a century ago even in situations of direct animosity. The United States is indeed the most capable country militarily, with a strong deployable force around the world; however, for all of this deployable force, the US would not be capable today of using the threat of Physical Power in a deliberate and open manner against China or France for example because of the potentiality of atomic weapons they possess. Nuclear nations operate today on the basis of a small tit for a small tat or threaten each other indirectly[261] and in a limited manner.

651. A new form of Physical Power is growing. Our age is no longer the age of atomic bombs and carrying missiles only; it is a world of information and greater electronic control of Physical Power. Hence, power over information, electronic control and hacking, and electronic spying can have a disrupting role over other forms of Physical Power. In greatly digitising Physical Power, more influence is potentially given to what we can call Electronic Physical Power. Nuclear capabilities of which a nation loses electronic control amount to no nuclear power.

---

258 As is the case in the civil world with the legal system and the police.

259 Air force or naval capabilities for example.

260 The United States, Russia, France, the United Kingdom, China, India, Pakistan, Israel, and North Korea.

261 By assisting each other's smaller foes.

652. Cyber War seems to be the new Cold War. It is the new small tit for small tat nations are giving themselves into. The world is less today that of spy agents infiltrated behind enemy lines, and more that of capacity to access and hack major Physical Power intelligence and command centres. The aim of this Cyber War is to disrupt, create a lack of confidence, and steal important proprietary information. Unlike Cold War, Cyber War has lower barriers-to-entry. Many organisations, including criminal ones, can also join in the game. In our world, Physical Power is not only about the end brute force, but also about the technology that controls it which is highly digitised.

653. Economic Power counts between nations, but it is simplistic to think that Economic Power can stand any chance in the face of physical military power in extreme situations.

654. Economic Power and Commerce count in regular daily world affairs; however, when it comes to extremes and large-scale confrontations, only the potential for Physical Power counts.

   a. China, Japan, and Germany are economic powerhouses and also key lenders to the US. Although it is an extremely unlikely scenario, should the US decide one day not to honour its debt towards some of these lenders, these nations have no chance of forcing the US to pay. They may decide to stop lending to the US, which will be equally disastrous to them as the US is one of the key markets for these lenders, but they are currently in no position to force the US to pay.

655. *It is only the institutions that control the monopoly of Physical Power that are ultimately the guarantors of the preservation of Economic Power.* The economically powerful needs the militarily powerful as a friend in order to preserve his/her property. If I own large pieces of land but cannot defend them from being confiscated forcibly, nor count on a legal system for such a protection, noting that a legal system ultimately relies on Physical Power for enforceability, then all my wealth is but a mere illusion.

656. Moreover, Physical Power can breed Economic Power, and all

Economic Power has its origins in violence. Civilisations have controlled resources and defended them through Physical Power. Kings have taken possession of large pieces of land through Physical Power. Borders continue to change through Physical Power; control of oil, water access, air access, and outer space all depend on Physical Power. Nietzsche's views are notorious for being extreme, but they are not far from the reality of human affairs in this particular context: "[...] almost everything that we call "higher culture" is based on the spiritualization and deepening of *cruelty*."

657. Naturally, Physical Power can be enhanced through Economic Power. A strong economy can provide better resources for a larger and more effective Physical Power. The two go hand-in-hand in many cases, but Economic Power is not a guarantee of Physical Power. If a nation relies on a militia or mercenaries for Physical Power, then this nation is much weaker physically than it really thinks.

658. In extreme situations, what is more important than absolute Economic Power for the general sustainability of a nation's or military's power is a certain level of economic self-sufficiency for a long-enough period of time. Foreign dependence on indispensable resources can greatly jeopardise the sustainability of Physical Power.

    a. For example, the US economy is more sustainable than the Chinese one in extreme situations, not because the US GDP is greater than the Chinese one (a fact that will change soon), but, rather, because the US is on a shorter path towards resource self-sufficiency. China does not have today enough internal energy sources for long-term sustainability, which the US is on the path of realising. And without energy sources, Physical Power is greatly compromised.

659. Outside the dynamic of nations, in the realm of the civil world, intra-human power is mostly about the capacity of influencing

and/or controlling the thinking, emotions, subconscious, and actions of other humans.

660. Power in the civil world takes different interesting forms among which economic (corporations, wealthy investors, institutions that control money supply, consumers); political (elected or inherited); physical (bar bouncer, security staff, army, police); sexual (good looking people can be more convincing sales people); emotional/psychological (priest, sage, guru); technical (doctor when you are sick, mechanic when your car is broken); through control of information; through fame or access to a large network of people; or through reputation (a form close to psychological power). The harm or fear of harm we discussed with regard to Physical Power is present in various degrees in the above, but many subtle ways are used to mask this threat of harm, make it indirect, elude to it without exercising it, or control it through influence.

661. Which type of Power is more effective in the realm of the civil world largely depends on the social structures in place as well as circumstances. In times of war, the army protecting you has more power over you than in times of peace. If your Air Conditioning ("AC") system is broken, and you are agonising from heat, your AC mechanic would have a higher status than Alexander the Great till the AC is fixed.

662. What is important to note is that, at first instance, we tend to confuse Physical Power and Power in general. In reality, and particularly in the context of what we call civilised human societies, Physical Power is far from being the only dominant form of Power and can sometimes be easily overwhelmed at the aggregate level. It is true that between nations and different monopolies of violence the relation is ultimately that of Physical Power, expressed or not; however, all such nations and monopolies of Physical Power derive their long-term legitimacy from civil approval, or at least obedience, making for some limitation of Physical Power in the human world.

   a. In the Middle Ages, the surviving and thriving of a more intellectual institution like the Church in the sea of warring barbarians in Europe attest to some of the limitations of Physical Power in the realm of human affairs, even in more barbaric ages. The individuals making the Church might have been easily disposed of or bullied, but the aura of the institution remained, mostly for psychological reasons emanating from the status and level of influence it had on common people. Even barbarian kings were superstitious and feared the reaction of their followers if they went too far in desecrating the institution believed to represent God on Earth. As with any form of Power, organisation and a sense of discipline in the face of anarchy help tremendously. The Church had an effect on people, and people are the ultimate source of long-term legitimacy of organised Physical Power.

663. One form of Power can naturally help acquire another form of Power. Economic wealth can facilitate political power, and so does a high position on the information or reputation chain. If we have money, we can buy Physical Power (e.g. a bodyguard). If we have technology, we can invent new ways of making old fashioned Physical Power irrelevant.

664. We can therefore divide Power forms into two major families:

    a. Physical Power and physical endurance, including all the technologies allowing for such.

    b. Abstract Power and psychological endurance; this family of Power forms is based on the many different ways of influencing the mind and body.

665. Ultimately, the two families have strong interconnections, and the second is mostly used as a 'civilised' and indirect way of the first; in our days, we try to convince someone of a particular course of action rather than beat him/her into it. However, the two families have distinct characteristics, and the second is the more interesting and less explored.

666. The higher the degree of civilisation, the more subtle Abstract

Power becomes; the greater the human footprint on the environment, and the wider and more intricate human affairs, the greater the necessity of Abstract Power over Physical Power is.

667. Fear is a great ally of Power. Fear influences the behaviour of individuals like nothing else and plays on that which is the most basic of our instincts: survival. Holders of Power often use Fear as a tool to consolidate Power. Fear from the unknown can increase the power of Religion and Speculation.

668. Desire is the second greatest ally of Power. When humans desire something, anything, the agent capable of providing or suppressing that which humans desire is capable of influencing their behaviour. And naturally, the greater the desire, the greater Power is. Creating scarcity, sometimes artificially, is one of the common ways of realising Economic Power and fame.

669. Fear and Desire have to be communicated. Desire is not fixed and can be created, accentuated, or reduced; Fear can be real or fake. Communication is therefore not only an objective medium but also an intrinsic driver of power dynamics. We require information to fear or to desire, and those who control information will influence us.

   a. We cannot suppress communication of information, nor should we. We should fight a monopoly of communication, but the writer is equally weary of a world where anyone can communicate anything to everybody irresponsibly or without a duty of basic recourse to facts or Truth.

670. Fear, Desire, and their communication, are all present in the various forms of Abstract Power.

671. Perceptions and psychology play a central role in abstract forms of Power. There is a difference between where Power resides and where society perceives it to reside. Power myths can be effective and are often prevalent. In the subtle world of humans, it is enough for powerful people to be convinced that a certain individual possesses more power for the latter to exert greater influence in

society. Power is about influence; influence and psychology are closely related.

672. Power can reside for a long time in the wrong place out of false common perceptions.

    a. An institution or a government perceived to be able to constantly pay what it owes could continue to borrow beyond what it really is capable of paying for on the long run. Excessive financial leverage is only called excessive when the borrower has lost the perception (as opposed to reality) of being able to honour its debt in full.

    b. During the colonisation times, European minorities were able to control larger populations and lands in many colonies out of a wrong perception of their invincibility and greater sophistication.

    c. Pharaohs managed to rule large populations out of the psychological belief that they were deities.

    d. Even in our days, many dictators continue to command large populations where the balance of Power is clearly in the hand of the people. The Arab Spring attests to how vulnerable Power actually is when perceptions change: it was enough for one country, Tunisia, to show the rest of the Arab World that dictatorship power can be broken by the people for the revolt movements to spread to several other countries including Egypt, Libya, Yemen, and Syria.

673. The stress of times will ultimately make the difference between what is wrongly perceived as powerful and where Power truly resides. Nevertheless, such revisions of beliefs can take a very long time to materialise.

674. The psychology of Power is an important art that many rulers understand and try to master. Power in the civil world goes hand-in-hand with the general psychology in place. Hence, we find links between Power and Religion; Power and mystification; Power and grand monuments; and Power and good health. We also find the use of Fear in order to display 'outstanding' courage; a great level

of artificiality or selection of public appearance; and a certain distancing from what is really the 'normal human'.

   a. The healthy, powerful, and charismatic image of a head-of-state or a leader is often perpetuated across most cultures. Franklin D. Roosevelt and John F. Kennedy were portrayed as such even when they had recurring health problems, so was Hugo Chavez and Kim Yong-il.

675. The perceptions of Power and psychological power games are not only a characteristic of Humans. Animals also go through great rituals to make enemies believe that they are more powerful than they really are. In many situations, animals do not actually fight; adversaries stand facing each other and try to look as scary as they can. In the world of humans, this amounts to the gesticulation, the frowning, and the shouting to intimidate others.

676. It is through the perception of Power that many forms of Abstract Power manage to command Physical Power. **What counts is where the Physical Power perceives ultimate Power to reside**, in a single person, in an institution, in a college of men, or with the people. It is the legitimacy and perception of Power that counts the most.

We Care More About Power Than Truth

677. The definition of Power encompasses many others in Sociology. For the believers in materialism, materiality falls under the umbrella of Economic Power. For the religious believers, a large aspect of religions (but not all) is about psychological and emotional influence, which falls again under the notion of Power.

   a. As we have seen before, many drivers of human behaviour have been put forward in History from Religion, to the search for Truth, to materiality, to nationalism, and to the sexual subconscious; there is none in our view that covers a wider scope of application than Power.

678. We are *not* trying to imply here that all human behaviour can be explained by a magic formula that corresponds to the dynamics

of Power. The reader at this point has hopefully realised that we are not fans of this kind of totalitarianism of ideas and total systemisation. However, in the most frequent cases, humans behave according to their material, physical, and emotional interests, and out of fear of harm; both are ultimately driven by the dynamics of Power to a large degree.

679. Power played, and continues to play, a very important role in shaping History both at the humanistic level but also at the biological/DNA level.

680. It is through Power that geographic boundaries have been defined, religions and political systems have been spread and maintained, and all natural resources are being exploited today; it is through Power that certain languages are more spoken than others in the world; it is through Power that moral values have been instituted at first; and it is through Power that Law has always been enforced.

681. History is written first by the powerful and then ultimately rewritten by the real historian searching for the Truth. Even if the powerful does not fully define History, at least he/she anchors it where it suits him/her best. In other words, the powerful sets a certain standard in History against which the real historian has to work.

682. Science matters less than Technique in human affairs: this is a simple reflection of the dynamics of Power in the human world. Science is today regarded as a highly desirable activity in a civilised society. In reality, from a historical perspective, Science only started to be important and taken seriously by the majority when nations and rulers realised the potential for Power they could acquire through this activity that is labelled Science. If Science only resulted in the Big Bang Theory and the Standard Model, and not in powerful ships, canons, planes, and bombs, it would have likely been less popular, maybe as popular as Philosophy is today. The hard reality is that a large majority of people will only make the effort towards something that will make them acquire Power, realise their interests, and put them away from harm. Intellectual

curiosity and the search for Truth are unfortunately a priority for the few only[262].

683. When it comes to influencing other humans, being powerful is more important than being right, at least on the short-term.

    a. The religious man derives his power from human emotional insecurity and wondering in the face of Existence. In situations of misery or great sadness, men of religion command great power, as in such situations humans are in most need of hope; Religion provides that hope. Being right becomes less important than providing hope in situations of emotional distress.

    b. The rich derive Power from their greater economic capacity, but also from the human craving for greater materiality. The thinking goes something like this, "He/she amassed so much money so he/she must know what they are talking about. We ought to listen to them intently because they must have a magic formula the others do not have." This is a prevailing kind of reasoning, even if the money came from pure sheer stealing!

    c. Some thinkers can command intellectual power beyond what is fair. Because society gives the thinker a recognition of higher rational capacities in the form of a PhD or a distinction, he/she can become eligible to provide judgement without fault in the eyes of many, even if it is on subjects where uncertainty is core. How many times have we listened to great imminent economists making false predictions, and how many times have we heard politicians invoking the opinion of some economists as if they were sacrosanct?

684. We are wired to listen more to the 'wisdom' of the powerful than the wisdom of the weak, regardless of the individual merit of each. We tend to obey more the powerful than the weak and provide subsequent rational reasons for why we are doing the will of the

---

262 We are hoping to help change some of that through this book.

powerful and not that of the weak. We are taken more seriously when we have Power, independently from the way through which Power was acquired.

685. Humans are not only attracted to the powerful for their apparent wisdom, out fear of their spite, or as a role model; we are also attracted towards the powerful subconsciously and for evolutionary reasons:

   a. Various studies show that women, even unconsciously, are more attracted to powerful men. From an evolutionary perspective, the powerful is more capable of taking care and protecting the children than the less powerful and therefore represents a better candidate for gene transmission. Many animal species go through very specific power rituals during mating season for this same exact reason.

   b. We subconsciously associate beauty with physical health and body symmetry. Several studies also show that our intuition (or our unconscious) is capable of picking up the symmetry in the face and body of someone we are looking at much more quickly than our consciousness. And consciously and unconsciously, we associate symmetry with good health; and good health means good genes from an evolutionary perspective.

686. The living nature itself is more drawn towards the powerful as part of its race towards better self-perpetuation.

687. In our present age, individual power counts more than in past ages. The trend particularly accelerated with the growth of relativism of opinion following the Renaissance. Changes in the structure of societies, loss of intellectual monopoly by some institutions like the Church, the Reformation, the various humanistic movements, Liberalism, the Romantic Movement, the Civil Rights movements, and the emancipation of women, are some of the key causes behind the growth of individual power. The Internet and Globalisation are also two great modern contributors.

- a. Religious institutions do not command[263] any longer the same level of influence than centuries before. Nuclear proliferation has rendered world wars less probable, and in a time of greater peace, the role of armies in influencing populations has relatively diminished. Even the role of government has been reduced with globalisation and the easier movement of people. It is not inconceivable that the recent sovereign financial crises will contribute to weakening further the power of the State vis-à-vis the individual. Political parties and syndicates command less influence than in the ideological ages of the Cold War. People increasingly realise that the state of nature and natural divine rights of the past[264] are no more. This opens the door wider to new values being created in societies through individual influence and Power.
- b. Likely, the Corporation is the last institution standing intact in the face of individual power.

688. People's natural appetite for Power varies; some like to command while others like to follow or not be in the responsibility seat. This partially makes for why Power alone cannot be used as the driver of all human behaviour.

689. What stands in the face of Power and human appetite for it? We can think of three limiting factors:

- a. Power itself.

    Power can be limited by Power, of the same kind or of a different kind. Many powerful do not respect anything else than Power and cannot therefore be stopped but through Power.

    - i. We note here that Power cannot be limited or faced by what is right and true directly. It is only when Truth gains enough critical mass in society that it can stand in the face of Power. In

---

263 On the whole, there might be exceptions in some geographies.

264 Legacy of Hugo Grotius.

other words, Truth needs to become popular and famous, and it needs to acquire some form of Power in the process, in order to stand a chance of facing another form of Power.

b. The environment.

Power naturally operates against a certain environment. Power can breed more Power, but no Power is infinite and there is always a certain environment that limits any form of Power. The environment is ultimately the humbling force to all forms of Power. Moreover, Power exerts an influence on the environment, which can come to create an eroding effect on Power itself.

   i. Let us take the example of fame. Fame can be a great source of Power when things are going in one's favour, but it can also become the cause of a great and quick demise when things are going against one's favour.

c. Personal ethics.

Personal ethics is the most important limiting force that comes from inside the Human. Power can be checked by Ethics; we have a rational conscious side, and we are capable of controlling our power rather than act as automatons looking to maximise Power at all cost.

   i. Individuals with the greatest appetite for Power and with no personal ethics are those most hungry for pure Physical Power; the environment and other opposing forms of Power become their only limiting force. Nothing would stop them otherwise.

690. Power is always there as long as there are living beings. It can move from one being to the other, and from one organisation to the other. It has its own proper dynamics and can manifest itself in many different ways. Power can get created with the creation of new desires and fears, it can transfer from one agent to another

with the change of circumstances, and it can disappear with paradigm shifts. Power can be created, acquired, or can come as a product of circumstances. No agent has been able to maintain Power indefinitely, and no one form of Power has proven constantly superior to others under all ages and circumstances. Time effects changes to Power, and there is very little possible to stop it. Actions of holders of Power can help lengthen their grip over it, but eternal Power is an illusion. Change is in Power as Change is in living beings, and Power cannot do anything to escape it.

Some final words.

691. Changing behaviours in a society requires, almost by definition, Power more so than anything else. This Power needs not to be brute; it can be subtle, and it can be through transmission of information. However, for the behavioural change to 'stick' and not vary simply with the change of power holders, it has to enjoy a long-term moral value.

692. **Power itself is neither good nor bad.** Power is an attribute, a fact like Mass in Physics. Either one has it in a certain form or he/she does not. Having Power does not say much about the person or the institution who has it; it is only Action and the use of Power in the context of living that reflects the moral status of the person with Power. Some of the greatest and worst humans had almost equal Power.

693. Influence through Power is not necessarily a negative. When we think about Power, we tend to associate it with bullying or unwarranted violence exercised. In reality, Power is greatly more present in our daily life, and some of its long-term positive faces are taken for granted. Power can be as much disciplinarian and educative. It is through the power of the parents that children are raised, and through the power of society that younger members are educated in a certain way. A newborn left on his/her own would result in a much different person without such power dynamics. Importantly, democratic and civil traditions are, from all practical perspectives, transmitted through the dynamics of

Power: A Key Paradigm of Living Beings

Power rather than through complete individual conviction of each and every member of a society.

    a. When the Founding Fathers of the United States envisaged a certain concept of a nation (without many of the ills that were plaguing Europe), these values were transmitted from generation to generation less so by the force of conviction, and more so by the influence of society, which is a form of Power.

    b. We learn at first, when we are young, not to cheat or not to steal out of fear of repercussions rather than out of full analytical conviction that this behaviour results in better overall results in human societies than everybody cheating or stealing from everybody...

694. If every new generation had to re-question *every* value of the older generation, no time would be left to do anything else. It is Power that allows this not to happen. Power can provide a necessary continuity and resilience to a political, social, and/or moral system.

695. Given the capacity to influence through Power, the more Power one has, the more important the moral standing of this person with Power is. With Power comes greater ethical responsibility. The worst combination is to be unethical and very powerful; the negative impact of one's actions in this case is great. As Aristotle said, the corruption of the best (i.e. the most powerful) is the worst, and the education of the most powerful is the most important.

696. Power is present everywhere in Nature; we all need Power. We all need also to understand where Power truly lies and according to which morality this Power is operating. We equally need to realise that Power can come in different forms, and some forms can be better suited than others depending on the situation. And finally, we would be naive to think that any acquired power is endless, unmatchable, or never changing. We would also be naive to think Physical Power supreme. Power can temporarily blind us to the Truth, and when we acquire it, it can actually blind us to what we really are, and the way through which we acquired Power in the first place.

The Ingredients of Success

"Ce qui vient au monde pour ne rien troubler ne mérite ni égards ni patience"[265] René Char

"Knowledge may give weight, but accomplishments give lustre; and many more people see than weigh." 4th Earl of Chesterfield

Once upon a time in far-away land, there were three brothers: the shrewd and intelligent one, the energetic and moderately smart one, and the light-hearted but not so smart one. The three brothers were born in a humble village where most people worked their land and lived together within the broader family, from lack of resources to build their separate domiciles or cultivate their own separate estate. There was only one school in the province, and many small villages scattered throughout the land shared it. The three brothers were taken care of by their uncle as their parents passed away when they were young. The uncle was unmarried and possessed a large house, a piece of land, and some cattle—enough to cater for the needs of the four of them.

The intelligent brother went to school every day and was always occupied with how to make money. He was slightly arrogant (some people would

---

265 What comes into the world to disturb nothing deserves neither respect nor patience. (John H.T. Francis translation)

just say proud) and very confident in his ability and intelligence. He had good grades and worked during his free time from school on devising ways of making money, including selling gadgets to kids or assisting neighbours with small works. When he finished his studies, the intelligent brother managed to land himself a well-reputed professorship job. Becoming a professor at his time was very prestigious indeed; it secured him a life-long occupation in the public sector, a good salary, several benefits for him and his future family, not to mention the three months of vacation a year.

The two other brothers did not have the same capabilities when it came to education.

The energetic brother left his village looking for a job in the city. After trying several odd jobs, he landed himself on an interesting business idea. Many international companies required customisation services; they needed advice on how to customise the products and services they are trying to sell to the local culture and country they are targeting. There were few reliable and dynamic people international companies could use for these services. The energetic brother quickly understood that by making these international majors trust him, and by building a reputation for professional integrity, he could enjoy long-term relationships with them and benefit from their recurring business. And that is exactly what the energetic brother set on doing. He borrowed money, set-up his own small company, and worked hard, day and night. Things turned out according to plan; the business grew, and he started to recruit more people to help him. The young company witnessed remarkable success. The energetic brother made good money and quickly became the richest and most successful of the three brothers, and one of the richest individuals of his original village. He married a beautiful woman and spent his time between long work hours and home. He was generous with his wife, kids, as well as the broader family. His business was in excellent shape, his reputation was golden, and profitability was great. He bought a beautiful house, a nice car, and always the best of clothes, toys, and jewellery to his family.

The third brother also left for the city; he equally started living from small odd jobs (washing dishes here, transporting things there). After some years, he was however lost and afraid; none of what he tried led to anything serious. And seeing the success of his brothers, his sense of failure worsened. Eventually, the third brother came to meet and befriend an old gentleman. This gentleman lived abroad and used to come back home every now and then. He used to always complain about the difficulties of growing old in a foreign place and his longing to spend the last of days in his homeland. The third brother saw in this gentleman a father figure–the early death of his parents had something to do with it. One day, the third brother sought refuge from his doubts by going to the old gentleman and confiding his failures and his utter confusion about his future to him. The old gentleman's eyes shined instantly and said to him, "Why don't you come and join me abroad? My business is not a glamorous or prestigious one, I sell meat, but in such an under-developed country, no one else bothers to try to compete with me. It is decent money. You won't do great, but you will make a decent living." The third brother accepted reluctantly; the lack of options drove him to it. The old gentleman had only one condition: that the brother marries his one and only daughter. The daughter was a strong-headed, far from charming, small sized, older woman. The third brother acquiesced nevertheless, without really thinking things through at that particular moment. He later regretted his rash decision, but it was too late; he was already on a ship sailing to his new land of opportunity. Being light-hearted, he enjoyed the luxury of forgetting and taking things lightly anyway. And so, the third brother travelled abroad and spent his time learning his new occupation and taking over from the old gentleman who was delighted with the extra time he enjoyed; the old gentleman could now travel back and spend more days in his native land. The third brother and his wife lived their days in this foreign boring land, focusing on selling meat, doing their repetitive tasks, and saving little by little, mostly due to the lack of any options of spending the money or means of enjoying life.

The intelligent brother had plenty of time to spare thanks to his easy, good-paying job. He had time to think about additional ways of making money. His top objective was simple and long been there: his uncle's estate. His uncle was getting old, and he was losing his senses. His two brothers were always away; the entrepreneur was completely taken by his exciting business, and the third brother was abroad. Through a mix of emotional manipulation and simple continuous presence in front of his uncle, the shrewd brother managed to have his uncle assign his complete estate to him after his death. And so it happened that, to the surprise of the two other brothers, the shrewd one snatched the entire estate of the uncle, which should have normally been divided equally among the three brothers. The entrepreneur, generous by nature and not needing the money, preferred keeping quiet on this injustice. The other brother was more spiteful, despite his usual light-heartedness, but there was little he could really do. And so the intelligent and shrewd brother added a large estate to his secure job and various other public benefits.

Years passed and all three brothers had children and lived well in their own respective families. The brother abroad had three kids who by now started to become teenagers. Worrying about their upbringing and the nature of their education in such an underdeveloped land, having amassed a decent saving account from all those years of work, and pressured by his wife to take her back home to their native land, the third brother decided to sell the business and return home[266]. He was unclear on what to do upon his return. His savings, plus the proceeds from selling the business were quite decent, but they risked being quickly eroded if not put to good use, especially that after a long period of lack of entertainment abroad, temptations to enjoy life and catch-up were great now. People came up to welcome the third brother, and so did his brothers. The returning brother enjoyed his first months meeting back old acquaintances and family, visiting the village, telling of his stories and 'adventures' abroad, and receiving all sorts of advice on how to best utilise his hard-earned money. The returning brother then settled on buying a small building in one of the cheap suburbs of the city, at a bargain price. He planned to take up residence there and rent the rest (seven other flats) to families working in the city but unable to afford living in it. By opening a small grocery shop at the entrance of the building and benefiting from the rental income from the apartments, the third brother calculated that his money will not risk being spent unwisely, and the returns will be decent enough to provide for his family.

---

266 The old gentleman passed away years ago.

The Ingredients of Success

The three brothers are now in their sixties. The professor is approaching his retirement age; with his pension and the estate inherited from his uncle (plus his savings of course), he was counting on a good, fat, long retirement period, enjoying life in the village, cultivating, taking care of farm animals, and the rest. In the meantime, the successful entrepreneur went through the unexpected. After flying so high with success, his business started drying out slowly. Customisation services were easier to do online now, and many free lancers jumped on the opportunity. There was no need anymore for a centralised, trustworthy point of contact, and as a drying river, the inflow of money from his business started depleting month after month. The entrepreneur did not see this structural change coming and had little experience and knowledge of this thing we call the Internet. After a period of denial, hoping that things would return back to normal, he started ploughing more money into his business to save it: traveling all over the world to promote his company; launching several marketing campaigns; and doing work for free in order to demonstrate the quality of his offering. Through the combination of his generous lifestyle[267] and the new investment requirements in his business, the entrepreneur found himself on the dangerous path of burning quickly through his capital. There was nothing to be done; the industry that benefited the entrepreneur for so long came crumbling down in a few years; all his reputation, experience, and hard work, and all his attempts to rescue his business were in vain. The entrepreneur kept on going to his office early every morning as it was his habit, not to work (no one came knocking on his door anymore), but rather to contemplate the state in which his career ended. Whatever was left from the entrepreneur's capital was spent on his children finishing their education. Luckily, these children were grateful and, in return, took care of their parents as soon as they started working.

The grocer also suddenly went through the unexpected. The city he lived nearby witnessed spectacular growth! What was a dilapidated suburb housing poor city workers became an integral part of the city itself. His building became an integral part of the main city. Real estate prices

---

267 His family was now long used to it after all and everybody took that for granted.

surged, doubling every two to three years. The third brother, the least educated, the least hard working, and the least intelligent, became a multi-millionaire in a span of few years. One could say that the third brother did something very smart in hindsight; he never sold any of the flats in his building despite the numerous offers he got. "What do I need the money for?", he used to say, "The small profits I am making from the grocery store and the rent coming in every month are more than enough for my wife and me to live comfortably. Plus my children are now old enough to take care of themselves."

And so the intelligent, shrewd, retired, and well-relaxed brother suddenly woke up as if from a dream. He realised that all his planning and cunning, and all his studies and manipulative tactics, came to little at the end. Yes he was comfortable; yes he had a pension and an estate; yes he earned interest on his money; but he was by nature always competitive, dirty competitive if you see our meaning, and the idea of this underdog brother passing him by miles of wealth made him despise his own fortune as if it was nothing and spend the rest of his life living in anger… The entrepreneur was happy for his brother but could not get himself to snap out of the shock of having lost his small empire so quickly.

This is a story of how cunning, intelligence, hard-work, entrepreneurship, moral professional behaviour, immoral opportunistic ways, and most of what one could consider as key ingredients of material success, all added up to very little in front of pure passive luck. And should we choose to measure luck in other non-monetary terms (e.g. discoveries, fame), we are confident that the reader can find many similarly ironic stories that apply. It is also a story of how Success or Failure is never final, and how Success can change hands sometimes very quickly.

697. Success is the achievement of personal or collective objectives independently from the process of achievement, the reasons behind the objectives, or the moral status of such an achievement. Success is a measure of reality against pre-stated objectives regardless of the personal qualities of those achieving them. In

The Ingredients of Success

other words, in talking about Success, it is the end that matters, not the means nor the process.

698. Success is therefore an empty concept if not attached to Morality.

699. Nevertheless, our societies attach a great deal to the notion of Success. Many of us strive for Success. People spend enormous amounts of energy and time, sacrifice things that they often regret later on[268], all for the idea of succeeding or getting somewhere. While a large part of such an effort is worthy of respect, with the exception of sacrificing family and relationships, the reality is that most of us, including the writer, started doing it so young and so conditioned by mainstream thinking that we never really got the chance to think about Success deeply, objectively, and scientifically. The truth is that many of the great minds and successful people themselves may never have paused to assess objectively the odds of their life and career choices.

700. Biology greatly rewards Success:

    a. Success can enhance our chances of survival, and our biology is greatly tilted towards better survivorship.

    b. We all experience a rush of dopamine when our effort is rewarded with success. And the dopamine rush is greatly enjoyable and can be addictive.

    c. Success reinforces our self-esteem and self-confidence, and in the process increases our capabilities to realise greater achievements than what we would normally seek without it.

    d. Even Success drives a greater urge to reproduce. Many studies show that male animals at the lower end of the hierarchy tend to want to procreate less than dominant males in the pack. Failure can stifle sexual drive in many animals.

701. Societies attach a great perception to achieving Success, and

---

[268] E.g. relationships, families, or a certain lifestyle.

many societies are intransigent with Failure independently from context. *Under the light of Success, everything can appear wise, right, smart, and powerful; under the light of Failure, everything can appear weak, naive, idiotic, and wrong.* Sacrifices seem justifiable under Success and futile under Failure, regardless of the reasons behind Success or Failure; this is at least the most common view.

702. All great disturbers in the social sphere are by definition individuals who go against the average and are, as such, *almost always* considered at first as a nuisance to stability, or even as renegades to hunt down. What makes them eventually different? What makes them become icons of a new generation or field? It is Success, purely and simply. These individuals only acquire the status of respected disturbers when their ideas take hold of a critical mass of people. Many great disturbers started by living on the margin as much as any other people living on the margin today. We invite the reader to think about creators of great religions, revolutionaries, politicians, movie writers, creative designers, architects, musicians, and many painters.

703. Ideas in the social sphere will often sound and look naive when they fail, and great and insightful when they succeed, even if the conditions of Success and Failure have very little to do with the merits of the ideas themselves.

704. **We cannot but vehemently disagree with this common view of Success and Failure.**

705. Success is important, as Action is important for Humans as we have stated, and Success corresponds to a particular achievement through Action. Success and Failure can be a form of experimental validation, and we know from the chapter on Knowledge that experimental validation is necessary for knowledge development.

706. But Success is nothing without Morality and without giving due attention to the complicated and inter-related nature of things. Ambition towards succeeding is one of the greatest drivers of human progress and should not be stifled. But the almost

saintly view of Success by societies is a root cause for much post-rationalisation of historical events.

707. In particular, the perception of Success needs to be commensurate with:

    a. The difficulty of succeeding *within the context* of the environment the individual or the group undertaking action is operating in.

        i. For example, becoming a millionaire today is more easy than fifty years ago by the simple fact of money inflation, and becoming a millionaire is more easy if you are born in a well to-do family than in a poor family.

    b. The properties or characteristics bestowed on the person (group) who is (are) succeeding in comparison with the achievement realised. Life gives each one of us different tools, advantages, and disadvantages, and each does his/her best with the tools given.

        i. It is already a great feat to be able to complete the Ironman Triathlon[269]; how much of an achievement and success it is to be able to complete it in time when you are suffering from the Lou Gehrig's disease, a terminal illness that attacks the muscles! Jon Blais is a great example of real success and an overcoming of adversity towards excellence.

    c. The role Luck plays in Success over other ingredients.

        i. Winning the lottery is less of a success and more of a statistical rarity.

708. But what does really drive Success? Can we engineer a situation where Success is more likely? Or is Success purely random? How

---

[269] An Ironman Triathlon has to be fully completed within a 17-hour time period including 2.4 miles of swimming, 112 miles of cycling, and a full marathon, in this order non-stop.

can we repeat a certain pattern of Success? And what is the correlation between Success and Intelligence, Success and Hard Work, or Success and Ethics? These are some of the important questions to ask about Success before we rush to lay a judgment on it or dedicate our life to its pursuit.

As with the name given to the chapter, we shall state four key ingredients of Success.

Luck

"As a rule, the man who first thinks of a new idea is so much ahead of his time that every one thinks him silly, so that he remains obscure and is soon forgotten. Then, gradually, the world becomes ready for the idea, and the man who proclaims it at the fortunate moment gets all the credit. So it was, for example, with Darwin; poor Lord Monboddo was a laughing-stock." Bertrand Russell, *History of Western Philosophy*.

709. With Luck we can overcome almost anything, and without it all our efforts can seem futile and to no good-end.

Malcolm Gladwell's *Outliers* is full of great illustrations of the role of Luck in Success; Nassim Taleb's *Fooled by Randomness* is another interesting source on the subject. We will not endeavour here to add more examples to what was already given by many; their examples more than suffice.

710. Appreciating the role of Luck in the outcome of things is not to demean the success of anyone; other factors do play their role, as we will see below. However, Luck can be so extreme in some cases[270] and its consequences more clearly seen. Moreover, it is always present in everything we do. Our existence itself is a result of Luck.

711. Luck can express itself in different ways in contributing to Success.

   a. Good luck can be a one-time event leading to great success as in the case of inheriting great wealth or winning the

---

[270] As in the case of hereditary situations or someone discovering oil, gold, or a treasure under her/his land.

The Ingredients of Success

lottery, and good luck can be found in the accumulation of several positive circumstances, the combination of which is very rare, as with the proliferation of Life on our planet or the spread of religions.

b. Similarly, bad luck can manifest itself in Failure in one singular event, as is the case with the extinction of dinosaurs, or in the accumulation of several negative circumstances, the combination of which is very rare, as with the collapse of financial systems or the fallout of one civilisation for the benefit of another.

712. We call Luck as key ingredient of Success when a circumstance, a combination of circumstances, an event, or a combination of events, is indispensable determinant of a particular success, and the statistical probability of this determinant is low to extremely low. Naturally, there is some room for differences in interpretation in how far we go back in looking for this indispensable determinant[271], and where we put the threshold of 'low' probability. Nevertheless, most of us have a decent idea of Luck when expressed as such.

713. At the collective level, Luck and circumstances play an important role in the genius of a country, city, or community. The best example in History would be that of Athens. What fantastic achievements and legacy Athens has realised for mankind, it has done them in less than one hundred years with a population of less than a quarter million, including females and slaves who played little intellectual role at the time! Nowhere else, ever, in the history of Humanity, such a productivity was feasible in such a short timespan, and with so few people. Luck and circumstances, including the wins over Darius and Xerxes, played an enormous role in the Athenian history. There were naturally also certain

---

271 For example, for someone to win the lottery, she has to be living first, and Life itself has luck as key determinant. Naturally, when we say that the person who won the lottery is lucky, we are not referring to the luck of her being a living being, but the more narrow luck of having purchased the ticket that turned to be the winning one in the draw.

conditions proper to Athens itself that led to such an explosion of creativity; the role Pericles played was, for example, key to the overall stability of the city.

714. Of course, whenever such examples are given, some retort to ridiculous theories of race superiority; as we know, such theories are pure rubbish. Greeks used to think that they are racially superior to the barbarians. If that was the case indeed, their intellectual superiority should have persisted well beyond the Middle Ages. Many other populations at different times in History fell into the same trap of deriving some convoluted theories of racial superiority from Success. Athenians suffered later multiple defeats and humiliations.

    a. Success through Luck can make people try to attribute it to other more worthy or self-flattering reasons; and the gain of status from Success makes for this post-rationalisation easier. Specific social and cultural conditions can play an enormous role in creativity and productivity, but these are the product of History, circumstances, and interaction, and not only of certain common DNA traits.

715. The sad reality is that it is never admitted out loud enough that you can sometimes work three times as hard as somebody else to find yourself failing. There is nothing wrong in failure; it is actually where you learn the most. But that is not how society views things[272]. What is wrong is society's general perception of Failure and Success, even if Success is due to plain simple dumb luck.

716. But are there any fields of Thought and Action where Luck cannot play any role in Success? Surely in Science for example, Success has more to do with experimental or intellectual demonstration than mass adoption, which should be less driven by Luck and circumstances. Unfortunately, even Science does not escape Luck when it comes to Success. Bertrand Russell's example of Lord Monboddo at the beginning of the chapter is a good illustration.

---

[272] At least in most countries; some parts of the United States are a notable exception.

The Ingredients of Success

It is not enough in Science to be right or demonstrate something as right; it is equally important to be able to share your work easily within the scientific community and have scientists pay due attention to it. This may be easier in our current age of fast and global communication, but in past times, it was not an easy feat. Many great works went unnoticed for a long time before obtaining due merit, and many great historical works of Science may still be completely unknown to us.

   a. Boltzmann was ignored by many in the scientific community during his lifetime and drove himself to death; the value of his work was rightfully understood only after his death, and his work on Entropy is today central to Physics.

   b. When Girolamo Cardano first talked about the square root of negative numbers, he was laughed at; today complex numbers have their distinct branch in Mathematics.

717. As we have seen from Deeds vs. Thoughts and the Influence of the Environment, both Action and the Environment are great contributors to intellectual productivity, discovery, and innovation. For all these reasons, even what seems to be a field with its distinct approach to Success like Science cannot fully escape Luck and its manifestation.

718. Luck can express itself in the readiness of the society to accept what is stated. Many political and religious thinkers' claim-to-fame is a result of a rare coincidence of social readiness and the innovative ideas put forward by these thinkers. Part of Locke's great heritage is due to the social readiness of Britain for his liberal ideas; so is the case with Marx and Socialism.

719. Luck does not only possess the quality of making men great in their time but also in posterity, whether they were great or not in their own time. Many great innovators and discoverers did not receive the credit they deserve till much later after their death. It could be easily suspected that there are many great men that walked this Earth doing great things that we do not know of because of lack of historical remains, some systematic eradication

of legacy by a historic enemy, or usurpation by somebody else. How many times in History, the original credit for an idea or a victory was given to the wrong person?

    a. Plato is famous among the Greeks not because of the accuracy of what he said, or the size of his legacy, and not because he was smarter or wiser than other philosophers of his time; it is mainly because we discovered and inherited his writings more so than that of the others (such as Heraclitus or other thinkers from Antiquity of whom we probably do not know much). Socrates did not write and if it was not for Plato and Xenophon, Socrates would not enjoy the historic status he currently has.

720. By restoring Luck to its proper place in Success, we are not inviting anyone to succumb to laziness by concluding that everything is due to Luck, so it is not worth putting any extra effort in anything. If we take the easy way out, then we are almost guaranteed to fail, and in this case, we have only ourselves to blame for failure. It is a different thing psychologically to fail due to bad luck than to fail because of laziness. Doing the latter and attributing it to bad luck amounts to hypocrisy.

721. Even if Luck commands an important role, repetition and perseverance sometimes play statistically in favour of those who continuously try without despairing.

    a. If I have a 5% chance of winning from a draw and I try only two times and give up, I might not get very far. However, if I try thirty times, I have a higher chance of succeeding, provided that the winning from one successful draw more than offsets the cost of trying thirty times. This is the fundamental *modus operandi* of several industries including Venture Capital and the movie industry.

    b. In business schools, students are often taught the notion of 'sunk cost': if you have incurred certain costs on a project and it fails, do not get too attached to what you have incurred, consider it sunk, and move on. While these notions can be valid under some circumstances, they can equally be very unproductive under different conditions. Most entrepreneurs would not exist today if this rule always applied. If a movie producer gives up after a couple of unsuccessful movies, then no new production houses can ever come up unless they strike it well from the very beginning.

722. Perseverance is one of the ways we turn Luck in our favour.

723. Ultimately, common sense should prevail in deciding whether it makes sense to persevere or not. And perseverance and motivation are hard work, physically and psychologically. It is rare to be able to withstand punches and persevere, and it is even more rare to know when to persevere and when not. Common Sense and Hard Work are the next two ingredients of Success we shall discuss.

Common Sense (which is not that common)

724. Common Sense is a difficult term to define; yet some of what is usually attributed to it by our common understanding is often a necessary ingredient of Success in many fields.

725. Common Sense is not necessarily about being intelligent in the narrow sense of the word. Being gifted in calculus does not necessarily guarantee Common Sense; having a strong memory or a great capacity for analysis is not fundamental for Common Sense.

726. Common Sense can be in part innate but also in a great way learned and improved with influence, education, and experience. Common Sense is less innate than Intelligence even if some individuals are more naturally predisposed to have it. We cannot rely on training alone to make someone good in sophisticated calculus, but we can rely on exposure and education to instil Common Sense in most people.

727. We sometimes refer to people as being 'practical' or 'street smart' when we think about Common Sense. We have yet to see a successful businessman, politician, or manager of some sort who does not enjoy a good deal of Common Sense. It seems that in the

field of Politics and Business, Common Sense is more important than pure Intelligence.

728. Wisdom and maturity are loosely part of Common Sense. This does not necessarily mean that the older one is, the more Common Sense she enjoys. Some can be younger and with greater Common Sense than older individuals; natural predispositions and the amount of experience to which one has been exposed can make a younger individual wiser than what her age might normally indicate.

729. Part of Common Sense is to be conscious of and minimise contradictions in reference to some of the human contradictions we have previously discussed. Although such contradictions are almost impossible to fully eradicate, people with Common Sense typically exhibit a much lower degree of self-contradiction. This is what maturity, at least in part, is also about.

    a. For example, teens are known to be more contradictory than more mature people, that is on average; it is part of their learning process to be as such as the latest behavioural and cognitive research on the subject shows.

    b. Some people also like to talk about focus to illustrate the point made here. Successful people have a strong sense of focus.

730. A strong sense of focus requires certain immunity against daily emotional gyrations. People with Common Sense tend to exhibit greater emotional stability and consciousness in the face of difficulties and challenges. They have more often the big picture in mind and change objectives less frequently than others.

731. In a world where uncertainty and statistical noise abound, the clarity and consistency of mind is often an important ingredient of Success. People with Common Sense are not naive about the world and its complexity; they are often acutely aware of the difficulties on the road to Success.

732. What we call today Emotional Intelligence could be more closely associated with Common Sense than with Intelligence itself.

The Ingredients of Success

Emotional Intelligence is about understanding and being able to detect, interpret, and take into account the emotional part of individuals (including oneself) as well as that of groups. It is also about using such emotional capabilities to one's benefit. A wise person is more aware of her own emotions and the emotions of others.

733. Self-Control is an important psychological characteristic and is shown to constitute an important part of the human cognitive capability. The ability for Self-Control, especially over long periods of time or in the face of many nuisances, is not the same across all individuals. And Self-Control requires energy to maintain it as much as any cognitive or physical effort[273].

734. Common Sense is also about being aware of one's own failings and weaknesses. While it is sometimes difficult to change every aspect of one's character, it is more important to recognise one's weaknesses and avoid situations where such failings can be determinant.

   a. Napoleon was famous for his acute awareness of his failings and strong points; he was greatly aware of himself and was known to work hard on them.

735. A successful leader knows how to complement himself with the right people; he knows where his weaknesses are and what he needs for Success; and he looks for what he needs in the individuals with whom he surrounds himself.

   a. Jack Welch[274], and his famous style of management, has more to do in our opinion with Common Sense and Emotional Intelligence than Intelligence in the more traditional sense. Welch made his job to select

---

273 In the process of Self-Control, our nervous system consumes glucose and other fast-burning energy nutrients in order to maintain a high level of awareness and control, which depletes with time and with the increase of outside nuisances.

274 The charismatic Chairman and CEO of General Electric who oversaw the transformation and great success of the company for a period of twenty years ending in 2001.

Reflections on Fundamental Matters

the right people, train them, incentivise them properly, set the broader management guidelines, and let each perform accordingly. He did not care as much about understanding the technicalities of a jet propeller or medical equipment.

736. Even when Common Sense is not a key cause of initial success (such as in situations of Luck), it can be an important ingredient in preserving what was achieved. Preserving Success can require a different tool-kit than acquiring it, and Common Sense often plays an important role in that. We are thinking about Risk Management in particular here.

737. Proper risk management is usually more of the realm of Common Sense, maturity, and balance than traditional intelligence.

    a. It is no surprise then that, on average, older people are more balanced in terms of risk taking.

    b. LTCM[275] did not blow up because of lack of intelligence; it was because of a lax view about risk management. An intelligent person can analyse a bell curve and combinations of bell curves to great detail; but only a wise man can caution himself from falling in love with his own mathematics and admit that life is often more complicated and tricky than what it seems through our mathematical theories.

738. Admittedly, not all fields require as much Common Sense for Success as the world of human social, political, and commercial affairs. Creative and scientific success may not require Common Sense, wisdom, or maturity as much as that of social, political, or commercial affairs. A strike of genius in these fields usually goes against the prevailing wisdom. No new theories would have been developed if every one attached a sacred importance to Common Sense.

---

275 Long Term Capital Management L.P., the famous hedge fund formed by some of the best minds in the finance industry, which after years of success, crumbled from magnified losses through excessive financial leverage in 1998 triggered by Russia defaulting on its debt.

The Ingredients of Success

   a. Painters and singers do not require as much Common Sense to achieve their success as business leaders.

   b. Some individual sports do not require too much Common Sense either. However, team sports are a different story; in any team activity, there are often social elements that favour the use of Common Sense.

739. Common Sense (as almost anything in excess really) can lead to negative effects in terms of prejudice as well as intellectual and creative ossification. However, if one goes deeper into the history of genius creations, it is seldom an absence of Common Sense that results in great work; it is usually great *imagination* coupled with still some form of Common Sense and Intelligence that allow for great realisations. After all, part of Common Sense is to admit that intuition and common prejudice can be wrong.

Hard Work

740. If there is one common strong trait among successful individuals, it would not be a personality trait, a certain level of intelligence, a certain education, or a number of years of experience; it would be the ability to work hard, consistently; the possession of a high level of energy that keeps the successful individuals going, even when the odds are against them. It is well noticeable that good leaders and good managers have an unusually high level of energy. This level of energy should not be mistaken with a specific personality trait, such as being outspoken; someone can have a high level of energy and yet be introvert or even shy.

741. The best description we could find for Hard Work is to persevere in work towards well-defined coherent objectives despite difficulty and serious obstacles. Hard Work would not be possible without objectives that draw serious resistance. Hard Work helps weed out those who desire Success the easy way.

742. This does not mean that all hard-workers will always find Success; unfortunately life has its share of unfairness in that way. But very often, Hard Work is a necessary ingredient of Success even if it is

Reflections on Fundamental Matters

not a sufficient one. The only ingredient that can compensate for lack of Hard Work is Luck.

743. Hard Work is required to build something, to achieve a goal, or to change oneself for the better. It is also required to preserve that which was achieved or acquired. Usually, it is easier to lose something or destroy it rather than gain it or preserve it.

   a. People who are exposed to the investment world know that more than any other: you can spend your life accumulating gains, and in a few rash movements, some oversight in terms of risk control, deliberate or not, or due to an unpredictable paradigm shift, lose much or all of what was accumulated. Equally, poker players know that all too well. In the statistical jargon, we talk about 'negative skewness': there can be more positive events than negative ones, but when the negative ones do take place, they tend to be more intense, sometimes extremely intense, in a way that leaves most people in denial at first.

744. Acquiring or mastering a talent or a sport, building a monument or a system that stands the test of time, inventing, and discovering, are all activities that have a certain level of trial-and-error in them. Human knowledge, craft, and artistic capabilities are based on repetitions till individuals reach a level where all the learning from the repetitive tasks becomes automatic and efficient. We talk then about intuitive knowledge and about experience.

   a. Even muscles act the same way. It takes much less muscle energy to ski or to run at the tenth time than at the first or second time. In biological terms, muscles get used to the motions, consume less energy, and act more automatically (with the help of the brain of course). Think about how fast and seamlessly you type on your keyboard now compared to when you first started typing.

745. Some individuals may have more condensed experiences than

The Ingredients of Success

others, and innate abilities continue to play an important role[276]. But it is rather extremely rare that skills, intelligence, and abilities manifest themselves fully without the process of trial-and-error; trials and errors filter out many possible mistakes and condition us favourably.

746. In any endeavour of long-enough time, one is often faced with headwinds and moments of doubt. Internal individual or collective energy is greatly needed in such times. Some people talk about an internal belief in something, in oneself, or in others that keeps them going. Others refer to it as 'edge', 'drive', internal fire, or in the old Chinese parlance the 'ch'i'[277].

747. Conditions never remain indefinitely favourable. Success is never final; life goes on and challenges re-emerge. Maintaining an advantage requires as much Hard Work as creating it. Maintaining a good reputation, fame, or market share; preserving a certain glory, a monument, a military advantage, or acquired peace, are all examples of situations where continuous Hard Work is required. And more often than not, such hard work goes unnoticed–the competitive advantage is taken for granted by the outside world.

748. Some of the most thankless jobs are those that correspond to maintaining or preserving Success. We are wired to pay more attention to Change, to the increase and the decrease in wealth, Success, or Power. We like to think that when things do not change fast enough, then no real effort is being spent. The reality cannot be more different.

    a. We never pay attention to the work of peacekeepers or stability keepers (e.g. secret service, police, fire fighters, military, security personnel, bodyguards); we only blame them when things go bad and take them for granted when things are quiet and unchanging.

    b. In the life of a new enterprise, the original entrepreneurs,

---

[276] No man will beat a springbok running, even with all the training at our current possession.

[277] Which (loosely) refers to the vital force within every living being.

often but not always, pass the baton of management to new individuals more experienced in preserving that which was acquired. Even when the creators do not leave, they at least bring on board a new set of talents experienced in preserving value. Corporate history is full of stories of companies that shot up and then shot back down simply because the same management remained in place, and what applied in an environment of creation did not apply in an environment of preservation.

749. Hard Work is not necessarily synonymous with continuous suffering. Hard workers mostly find pleasure in the doing. Most successful individuals deeply enjoy what they are doing; some even admit that they would do what they have done again even if the material benefit was less. Hard workers do not necessarily fantasise constantly about Success; they are more driven by a certain great desire for perfection in what they do, by deep conviction in a certain idea, or love of a certain activity; Success becomes a by-product of this attitude.

"But man is a frivolous and unseemly creature and perhaps, like a chess player, he loves only the process of achieving his goal, and not the goal itself. [...] this incessant process of achieving [...] in life itself, and not particularly in the goal [...]" Dostoevsky, *Notes From Underground*.

Natural Gift

750. Natural Gift includes high Intelligence; developed Intuition; Power of Imagination; Artistic Abilities; and Physical Abilities. What falls from Natural Gift under Common Sense and Emotional Intelligence was already treated, and there are admittedly overlaps between the two ingredients.

751. Natural Gift increases the potential for Success but never guarantees it on its own. Some types of Success cannot be realised without a necessary Natural Gift. Mozart, Dali, Einstein, and Michael Jordan, all had natural abilities that allowed them to reach the success they realised; their natural abilities alone were

not sufficient, but without them they would not have reached the greatness they ultimately found.

752. However, Natural Gift can be overly emphasised by our societies at the expense of other ingredients of Success. And some natural gifts can actually play a rather negative role when it comes to achievement in particular situations.

753. One of the biggest fallacies in our societies is to equate Intelligence[278], and any Natural Gift in general, with Success. Typically, all parents love to hear that their child has a high Intelligence Quotient ("IQ"); parents equate a high IQ with the promise of future success. Intelligence is considered as rare as a diamond. Children themselves while getting high grades in class equate this with the promise of a bright distinguished future. No one is undermining the value of schooling or the importance of making it successfully through the educational system here. *What we are rather targeting is the fallacy engrained in almost every child, and in almost all societies, that being the best at school or having a high IQ is somehow a promise of guaranteed success in the future.* This instilled belief can actually be detrimental to the children that succumb to it over the long run; it can even come to be destructive to their persona and experience as they walk down the road of professional and social life. A quick survey of members of high IQ societies can easily show that most high IQ individuals remain unknown, and many can lead a rather modest or average life. And there is nothing wrong with that! It would be interesting to do a census of the IQ of top politicians and business leaders anywhere in the world and compare it to the average IQ in any high IQ society; the results are likely to surprise us.

754. Even in Science, probably the purest realm of Intelligence, it

---

[278] Obviously before delving too much into this subject, a definition of Intelligence is due. What is meant by Intelligence here is the more traditional definition of the term: great innate processing abilities of the type that make someone good in Science. It excludes on purpose Emotional Intelligence but can include literary and artistic intelligence, as well as exceptional memory (visual, acoustic or other).

is not always the smartest that come up with best theories or discoveries. Einstein had a high IQ, but it is quite far from being the highest[279]; yet his General Relativity Theory is one the most ground-breaking in the whole history of Science. We find it rather funny that the image of Einstein is often equated with the highest form of intelligence in popular culture; it shows a common misconception on the subject of Intelligence and Success. Popular culture assumes that because what Einstein produced is great then he *must* be of the highest possible intelligence. Einstein himself did not necessarily think himself to be the smartest, and it was not out of false modesty. This fact does not take anything away from the greatness of Albert Einstein, on the contrary. Feynman had also a non-exceptional IQ, and he made great contributions to Quantum Physics.

755. Intelligence is a great gift given at birth, and it is a necessary tool in many cases, but it should never be misconstrued as the necessary and *sufficient* condition of Success.

   a. In actuality, too high of an intelligence can be as much of a hindrance as an asset in many circumstances. Life requires decision-making under uncertainty where often analytical intelligence alone is not enough. If existence were only about powerful analytical capacity, then powerful computers alone would suffice.

756. Natural Gift interacts with the environment and predicting what this interaction will result in is very tricky.

   a. A genius with great musical abilities born in a hunter-gatherer society is less likely to go as far as one who is born in a culturally-tuned Austria.

   b. If an individual was born a slave in the southern United States two hundred years ago, his great natural physical strength would have allowed him to be at best a slave fighter, with almost certain eventual death, while today the

---

[279] Einstein's IQ is traditionally put at 160 vs. the 180-220 range for exceptionally rare geniuses.

The Ingredients of Success

outcome of the interaction between his physical abilities and the environment might lead to genuine greatness.

    c. Being too smart around a king in the Middle Ages was not a guarantee of Success but rather of certain eventual death.

757. Power is rarely in the hands of the most naturally gifted, and human nature is often jealous and/or insecure of those who have a great natural gift. Be it intelligence, beauty, or physical strength, they all in their own ways create unwanted animosities that can become real hindrances to the individual enjoying them.

758. Importantly, success in risky endeavours almost always necessitates, whether consciously or unconsciously, a form of blind belief given the large number of variables that can come into play. The more intelligent one is, the less likely she is to deeply hold blind beliefs.

    a. Armed with a generally valid set of ideas and aspirations, the innovator embarks on attempting to realise his/her aspirations with perseverance. It is usually Luck and circumstances that help translate ideas and aspirations into Success. Many good ideas and aspirations, very valid ones, fail miserably despite all the perseverance, out of bad circumstances (to usually work again at some other point in History). And it is only when Success is realised that the innovator's ideas and aspirations gain a credo-like status. Yet and again, in many fields, and at different points in time, the same scenario repeats itself.

759. If one has to continuously keep in mind the conditions required for Success that are out of one's hands; the fact that one's own ideas can have unintended consequences that no one can foresee; the naivety of purpose from a philosophical point of view; human nature and all the like, we fail to see how many people can ultimately take risk, attempt to innovate, or bring about change.

760. Blind belief[280] can be dangerous, but in seeking Success it can have definite benefits. Belief in eventual success is very similar to the kind of hope, and sometimes naivety, youth hold about their capacity to change and impact the world around them, essential for exerting their identity and acquiring a positive approach to life, without which no change coming from youth is possible. Youth hope is indispensable from a survivorship and identity development point of view, even if the odds are often against the change.

761. In attempting to draw a synthesis on Success and its drivers, we can say that Luck is primary over all other ingredients. Without Luck, nothing is easy, and with it everything becomes possible. As for the hierarchy between the other ingredients (Common Sense, Hard Work, and Natural Gift), the relative importance of each seems to depend on the subject matter we are considering, albeit Hard Work seems to be almost always present.

   a. Common Sense seems more important than Hard Work and Natural Gift in Business and Commerce.
   b. In Science, Hard Work and Natural Gift are at least at par and probably more important than Common Sense.
   c. In Sports, Natural Gift is key, but it does not express itself fully without Hard Work and Luck.

762. Luck is in reality present at least in two and a half out of the four mentioned above. There is Luck itself as an ingredient, Luck is present in Natural Gift with which we are born and do not get to choose, and Luck is partially present in Common Sense. Common Sense can be nurtured; some are born with it, others gain it with time if they are exposed to the right environment, but in both such scenarios, Luck again plays a key role.

763. We are therefore left with Hard Work only as the almost pure ingredient under our control[281]. What each one of us can really

---

280 Some might prefer to substitute it by the word Hope.

281 And that is even questionable as some people are capable of enduring longer hours or tougher physical conditions than others thanks to particular DNA traits that they inherit by Luck.

The Ingredients of Success

do is to give her greatest effort and try to draw the best from the tools, internal and external, Life has given her. This way she earns her self-respect and gains her personal integrity regardless of the outcome. The outcome, whether positive or negative, becomes as much of a fact of life as the weather or winning the lottery. When one has earned her self-respect through Hard Work and internal honesty, the outcome becomes less important, provided of course that material needs for the beloved ones (such as family) and oneself are met to a decent level.

764. Our relatively small human scale and the interactive nature of things make us consider Success and Failure with a lot of perspective.

    a. No Success or Failure is final.

    b. No Success or Failure is guaranteed by some magical ingredients.

    c. Success can bias the objective reality, particularly because societies can be irrational about Success and Failure. The status acquired through Success is not always a fair one.

    d. All Success is relative to our human scale, which is negligible in the face of the Universe.

765. What should we do differently then when it comes to succeeding or failing? What is more important than doing things differently is actually changing the way we assess Success and Failure, whether in our own life or that of others, and how we feel about various outcomes and achievements in our life.

    a. We ask the reader to pay attention to how many good singing voices there are out there who will never have the chance to be globally recognised for a whole host of reasons; how many people born in Africa who could be great business men or great leaders if given the means but will never see any of that happening because they are simply born in the wrong place and time.

Reflections on Fundamental Matters

We would like to finish this chapter with two stories of early success and aborted potential. Admittedly, these are two preferred stories of the writer coming from the world of mathematics, and the crucial part Luck has played in us, Humanity, losing on great opportunities. These are two stories of great missed opportunities, of successes aborted too early.

766. Should we wish to talk about universal geniuses, about minds of extreme and powerful rarity, two names in the world of mathematics could be given: Evariste Galois and Srinivasa Ramanujan. And yet probably few of the readers have heard of these names. Many readers may know Gauss, Newton, or Leibniz, but only few, outside the world of mathematicians themselves, generally know of these two names. The reason, simply, is bad luck. Galois and Ramanujan exhibited the kind of genius that could be found in Pascal, Gauss, Euler, Hilbert or Poincaré, started to produce great work, but disappeared too early for rather foolish reasons, and therefore failed to make enough of a mark on History in comparison with others.

> a. Evariste Galois is an example of raw mathematical genius for the large part wasted between a series of unlucky academic circumstances, young enthusiasm for the politics of his days, and an explosive character. Galois was born in 1811 in the suburbs of Paris, started to exhibit strong interest in mathematics at the age of 14, was self-taught, and managed to solve a long-standing problem of polynomial equations at the age of 18. Evariste Galois' approach laid the foundations for the theory known today by his name, the Galois Theory, which is instrumental in Group Theory. Galois failed twice the entry exam to *Ecole Polytechnique*, the most prestigious French school for mathematics at his time. The first time his knowledge was too advanced in some branches of mathematics while lacking in others; the second time, a year later, the same year where he made his major discovery, he simply exhibited too much of the characteristics of a

The Ingredients of Success

genius[282] and an explosive personality which alienated his examiners. In his short lifespan, Galois attempted to publish several times, but his succinct and obscure style stood in the way of the clarity of explanation required in the academic world. Many of the great mathematical minds of his days have seen his work (Cauchy, Fourier, Poisson); some understood it, others not really, while some found the style obscure. Worst, the young and reckless Galois immersed himself in the politics of his days and the turmoil of the French July Revolution. He took part in the fighting and managed to eventually get himself locked in the Bastille. He got out of the Bastille only to die at the age of 21 in a duel over a girl as the rumour goes. In three to four years of mathematical productivity mixed with politics and fighting, the young Galois has managed to leave an astounding and innovative mathematical legacy; for the students of mathematics, it is rather well known how tedious and difficult the Galois Theory is. We invite the reader to take a minute and imagine what Galois would have achieved in a different political time and with the right academic tutorship from a young age. His coming to fame never happened during his time through the combination of rather silly circumstances, academic idiosyncrasies, and his immature character.

b. There is probably no more beautiful example of natural mathematical genius than that of Srinivasa Ramanujan. There might be another Ramanujan out there in the world today of whom we are not even aware, in Bangladesh, India, or Africa, someone similar to him looking for luck and the proper conditions for her genius to blossom. Ramanujan was born in 1887 to a modest family in India. He exhibited very high intelligence from a young age and showed an insatiable appetite for mathematics, far more

---

282 Too quick and succinct in his solutions, making major leaps which takes the normal mathematician a much longer time to understand.

advanced than what the environment he was born in was capable of satisfying. Ramanujan developed his own ways of solving complex mathematical problems and went on re-demonstrating several mathematical theorems. As he grew up, Ramanujan was known to only be interested in mathematics, particularly Arithmetic and Number Theory, and hence failed most other subjects, which caused him to lose his scholarship. Ramanujan lived in extreme poverty, and his claim for greatness was therefore looking very slim had mathematicians from his home region of Madras not discovered him. These mathematicians then introduced his work to British colleagues. The feedback from Britain was similar to that Galois received[283]: there were holes and leaps in his work, but there was also an exceptional ability and a great taste for mathematics. Ramanujan's work particularly interested G.H. Hardy who took him under his wings; Ramanujan found in Hardy the sympathetic mathematical professional he desperately needed. Ramanujan sent about 120 theorems he came up with in his first two letters to Hardy! After some difficult convincing, the young Indian made his way to England to work under Hardy. He was however always frail and, away from home, he eventually contracted tuberculosis in England and was diagnosed with major vitamin deficiencies. He passed away back home at the age of thirty-two.

Here is a story from Hardy about Ramanujan: "I remember once going to see him when he was ill at Putney. I had ridden in taxi-cab No. 1729, and remarked that the number [...] seemed to me rather a dull one, and that I hoped it was not an unfavourable omen. "No," he replied, "it is a very interesting number; it is the smallest number expressible as the sum of two cubes in two different ways." " $1729 = 1^3 + 12^3 = 9^3 + 10^3$... This is the man Ramanujan was.

---

[283] Which is common for those who have not been through the traditional academic curriculum.

The Ingredients of Success

Again, we invite the reader to think about what would have happened to Ramanujan had he not been 'salvaged' by Indian mathematicians and introduced to Hardy. And we invite the reader to also think about how much more Ramanujan could have produced had he not died prematurely from lack of nutrition and disease. This is the role Luck plays in the life of a genius. A genius is never known as such without Luck.

767. Helvetius once said of Shakespeare, "If Shakespeare had been, like his father, always a dealer in wool; if his imprudence had not obliged him to quit his commerce, and his country; if he had not associated with libertines, and stole deer from the park of a nobleman; had not been pursued for the theft, and obliged to take refuge in London; engage in a company of actors; and, at last, disgusted with being an indifferent performer, he had not turned author; the prudent Shakespeare had never been the celebrated Shakespeare; and whatever ability he might have acquired in the trade of wool, his name would never have reflected a lustre on England."

768. We invite the reader to listen to successful people and their wisdom; but we invite the reader to listen more to people who have failed; and to listen even more to the successful individuals who openly acknowledge the role Luck played in their success. More importantly, we invite the reader to read the history of people on both sides of Success and Failure and draw her own conclusions. Everything in History looks more special under the light of a successful result.

"[...] for the idea was by no means so stupid as it seems now that it has failed... (Everything seems stupid when it fails.)" Dostoevsky, *Crime and Punishment*.

Epilogue

Some of the readers, including maybe people accustomed to academic writings, might be disappointed by now by the lack of one comprehensive thesis in this book. After all, the purpose of any non-fictional and non-historical book of the kind written here, probably in the opinion of many, is to provide one strong view, theory, or insight on a particular, definite subject. The conclusion is typically clear and directing in its nature. Obviously, we do not mean to say that all such books are alike; however, it is a common human need and curiosity to seek definite concluding answers, a shout of victory, or a great discovery at the end of a book. There will be no such thing here. If there is any conclusion that one might draw from all that was written, it would actually be the non-conclusive nature of what is around us; the non-conclusive nature of us; and the immense complexity and inter-relation between things, living and inert, of Thought and of Action. How could it be otherwise? Finality and purpose are great human needs: reaching a full explanation for everything around us, including us; knowing clearly this from that; obtaining control over all that is around us; being so sure of one's opinions and perfect reasoning; or at least thinking and believing that this final human state is possible. Aside from the fact that such finality is a mere illusion, could we really imagine a world where a final human state of understanding and believing is possible? How would we live in such a world, and how can we express our individuality in such a state? We are not necessarily advocating an attitude of nihilism or complete scepticism in this book; we use 'necessarily' on purpose to indicate that forms of nihilism or scepticism can very well find themselves in most of the above but are far from being the only two attitudes that can be comprised by what was written here.

One of the criticisms towards this essay could be its eclectic nature. This writing has addressed a wide array of topics while pulling resources from varying disciplines and experiences. It might not be deep enough on some subjects for some, while it might be too deep for others. The multi-disciplinary approach is intended of course. It is curious how sometimes great minds get so taken by their own subject of speciality that they make very common mistakes or seem too naive in other areas. And if they do so, it is not that difficult for us to do the same in our own daily lives. It was once said that a physicist of renown had two regular visitors, a small cat and a big cat (he used to have affinity for cats). The cats used to scratch at his door for permission to enter every day. The physicist could not keep the door continuously open, and he was getting annoyed from all the scratching and from having to frequently interrupt his work in order to let the cats in. One day, the physicist decided to create holes in the door for the cats to enter freely. He made two holes, a big hole for the big cat and a small hole for the small cat… This essay aims at trying to restore some of this lost balance and, by doing so, illustrates the complexity and plurality of approach towards everything around us. An effort was made in order not to go too deep into each and every subject while providing enough elements for those who wish to go deeper into any particular area. The conclusions, however, remain more or less the same. As for the requirement of specialisation in every subject that was treated here, we unfortunately know of no man who is a deep specialist in all of the subjects of this essay combined. If there is such an exceptional human being, it is really a shame that he or she has not written on all of those subjects combined, or the writer might not have come to know of him/her —any omission by the writer is not intended.

The essay can also be accused of being contradictory on some points. As it attempts to draw the best from different areas and various experiences, it may end up with some recommendations on one subject going against recommendations on another. Let us take few examples. Moderation is stated as being one of the Key Values to adopt, while in The Ingredients of Success, Hard Work and Perseverance to improve the odds in luck-dependent situations are highlighted; this on face value could be contradictory—Perseverance at some level opposed to Moderation at the other. We put forward the Absurd as an intrinsic quality of our existence, and then we go later on into more practical topics that might seem banal in view of the Absurd, such as economic or political systems. We talk about the importance of free choice in Ethics after having highlighted the Influence of the Environment and the strong interconnection between things. We mention Herodotus to show how chances rule men, then we cite Keynes to highlight the power of human ideas in shaping future generations. We can continue long as such, and we are confident that there are many more subtle and contradictory elements we continue to miss. There are answers to such apparent contradictions, some of which are present in the essay itself. We shall not repeat things here; in actuality, repetition is not justifiable. These contradictions are sometimes valid and constitute an innate part of things. Some paradigms work well at some level while failing miserably at other levels; they can do well over a certain timespan and become obsolete or ludicrous afterwards. This is inherent to the reality of our existence, and there is no way we know of to escape it. A sceptic can go on doubting everything and mocking everything, but in reality she will run into trouble if she starts doubting her own doubt. This is far from meaning that everything is always contradictory and doubtful; positivism at some level is possible. We would not have been flying planes, discovered that we are cousins with other animals, or known of the history of our universe without positivism, and that is a reality that cannot be disputed.

Maybe the essay is not scholastic enough for some. The language in it is too simple and straightforward at instances to think that the notions behind are simple and straightforward; it can often seem too much like plain speaking. We generally assume that someone who treats subjects such as Philosophy or Metaphysics ought to talk and write pedantically. This, for one, is a critique I fully rejoice in and is entirely intended. The writer is a great believer in the simplicity of language coupled with coherence and accuracy of reasoning over pedantic and academic jargon that gives a complete false sense of knowledge or wisdom. Much bad metaphysics, philosophy, economy, and politics have plagued the world because of this blind love for pedantic rhetoric. The most complicated of problems can be treated with simple accurate language as attested by Mathematics. It does not mean that the result is simple, or that the reasoning is simple; some mathematical problems can be terribly daunting, and proofs can take years to recheck even by the most qualified among us. However, the language behind is simple and non-pedantic, and it is less subject to misinterpretation and confusion. Other readers, likely from a different background, could mock what I have just said in this paragraph. They might have found some of the language used (maybe on subjects such as Knowledge) completely confusing and with a touch of 'show-off'. I apologise for that–I have tried my best to stay away from such traps, but the nature of some of the topics themselves requires a minimum of technicality. I am confident that more simplicity can be achieved in some areas than what I have been able to realise.

A final word: this book is intended to open the mind to the subtleties of Reality and not to strengthen any charlatans who live from any intellectual difficulty or uncertainty and infest us with all sorts of baseless and unnecessary beliefs and prejudices. There is power, wisdom, and civility in realising what we know and what we do not know, what we can know and what we cannot know. We all need to make our peace with this and keep moving forward regardless of our predispositions and wishes.

Appendix:
Objections to the First Premise

769. One can object to what we stated as a First Premise as follows, "Admitting that there are no different 'substances' in the fundamental sense, how can we classify things like Space, Time, and some of what was previously called Universals in Philosophy, including Mathematics? Clearly, we cannot argue that Time or the integer 1 are of the same fundamental nature as a photon!"

While such an objection might seem plausible to common sense, it actually appears much weaker when broken down analytically. We will treat Space-Time, Mathematics, and Universals sequentially.

 a. Space and Time are what we can call *relations*. Relations are an important concept of reality that was often mystified or over-looked. If the Universe is nothing more than a bundle of events, then Space and Time are nothing more than our accounting of the relations between events. By definition, relations cannot exist without events, and whenever we talk about more than one event, we need to be able to distinguish between these multiple events, and this is not possible without relations (unless each event is of a different substance or nature, which is something we have already rejected).

 This is even more important if we consider that events

interact, as interaction does require relations to be meaningful. If we maintain the notion of events of the central premise and leave out interaction, we end-up with a Leibniz-like view of the Universe: an enormous or infinite number of events with no interaction. This cannot be logically refuted; however, philosophers have moved away from such an idea centuries ago. Moreover, if we consider 'no-interaction' to be simply part of the set of all possible interactions, then the Cartesian view of the Universe becomes one of the set of views resulting from the central premise of *events-interactions* alongside infinity of others. Which of these views is the correct one from this infinite set is yet to be determined.

b. How about Numbers or Mathematics more generally? The full answer is very technical and long, but we can mention here some key highlights. From the work of logicians starting at the end of the 19th century, we know today that all of Mathematics can be fundamentally broken down analytically into words, yes simple words[284]. This was the chief work of Frege, *Principia Mathematica*, and a lot of great mathematical work following them. Put simply, Mathematics is simply complicated compositions of words and signs, and the two are not fundamentally of a different nature. Now how about words and signs? What is their nature? If we can answer that, we can equally understand the nature of Mathematics. We can say, without raising too many objections, that words and signs are results of our cognitive structures, simply of our brain structures. This should not be surprising; it is like saying that thinking is a result of our brain structures. And what is a brain or brain structure other than a particular bundle of events 'thinking' about other bundles of events?

---

284 Words in the general sense that includes signs and letters; we can also replace words by a more simple binary code as in the case of computing.

c. Defining Universals[285] or Ideas as notions transcending the physical world and subsisting in a spaceless and timeless realm is equally meaningless. If Time is a relation, then talking about something outside the relation is obviously a meaningless sentence. It is important to realise that with language we can compose sentences and combine words sometimes in ways that initially give the impression of meaning when, in reality, they turn out to be as meaningless as saying, "Space is outside Time." The better approach to understanding Universals is again in our mental structures. The creation of Universals is no different, but naturally much more subtle and complicated, than a topographic algorithm which, when examining a certain surface, is capable of discerning certain shapes on it and naming them. Universals are the results of the algorithm (our mental structures) and the input data (information feeding our mental structures). Associations of names and shapes are then perpetuated through a form of *Cultural Evolution*[286] and consequently obtain the status of Universals.

770. We should mention that some of the most modern scientific theories still consider Space and Time to be mere receptacles[287] in which particles of matter roam. Quantum Mechanics, which are of great worth, are among such theories. However, these theories are far from being capable of explaining the behaviour of the Universe and its origin without complementing them with Relativity, in which Space and Time are mere relations and substitutable to each other. This sort of apparent contradiction is not surprising to anyone familiar with Physics, nor does it

---

285 Such as 'redness' for colour or 'justice'.

286 Cultural Evolution refers to the transmission of certain traits through societal influence from generation to generation rather than by the means of genetic transmission. It is a much faster pace of evolution. For example, we call a cat today a cat because the generation before us called it as such and so on and so forth.

287 The way Newton imagined them to be.

constitute a justification for rejecting its teachings. The eclectic nature of our understanding of the laws of the Universe is not new, and work is continuously done to reconcile discrepancies at the 'boundaries' between theories that otherwise work extremely well in their designated scope. This is not only present in Physics but in all Natural Sciences, and major discoveries usually take place when reconciliations at the boundaries are achieved.

771. A second objection could be stated as follows, "If we consider that there actually are no events but one single total Event, then would we still need to talk about relations or interactions?" This objection is in line of what some of the monists, pantheists, or Buddhists could argue. Spinoza and Hegel have used arguments of similar nature.

    In actuality, talking about a Whole or about different parts of the same nature interacting is not fundamentally different; it is simply a matter of taste and semantics. A piece of sand looked at with a normal eye appears as one unit, whereas through a microscope it has a completely different granular look. Nothing changes in the grain of sand when we describe it using the first view and then the second, only the way we look at it and interpret it. The trouble with some of the monists is that they attempt to force only one holistic view without admitting the possibility of the other. Both views, holistic and analytical, can essentially be the same without contradiction.

772. A third and final objection we will treat here is the one that says that there must be a *cause* to all of this. After all, these events cannot have come to be from nothing. How is it that everything comes to be, gets influenced, and gets created all from within itself? There must be something outside it of a different nature that constitutes a Necessary Cause or a First Cause.

    These arguments are again examples of the cognitive mistakes previously discussed. Causality is one of the ways with which we comprehend the world around us. When we present ourselves with arguments like this one, what we are essentially doing is generalising Causality as much as we can to the Universe.

Without elaborating on Causality too much, we can state that Causality is nowhere explicit in Natural Laws as we know them, and it is effectively a cognitive shortcut to understanding things. Additionally, although it seems strange to our common sense, things can get created in the Universe out of 'nothing' as we are increasingly discovering from Quantum Mechanics. For a detailing on this, the reader can refer to the treatment of the fourth disillusionment of On Knowledge and Truth – Historical Disillusionments.

We are therefore left to examine the reasons behind our subjective need of a necessary cause, which we find to be largely cognitive and addressed in the Second Premise.

Additional Notes and Bibliography

Preface

1. "Laziness and cowardice are the reasons why such a large proportion of men, even when nature has long emancipated them from alien guidance (*naturaliter maiorennes*), nevertheless gladly remain immature for life." *An Answer to the Question: "What is Enlightenment?",* Immanuel Kant, (Konigsberg, 1784).

2. *Ethics, Demonstrated in Geometrical Order,* Benedictus de Spinoza, (1677).

3. *Tractatus Logico-Philosophicus,* Ludwig Wittgenstein, (1921).

Putting Things in Context

4. *Philosophical Investigations,* Ludwig Wittgenstein, trans. G.E.M. Anscombe, P.M.S. Hacker and Joachim Schulte (West Sussex: Wiley-Blackwell, 2009). First published in 1953.

On What Is Around Us and What Is In Us

Epigraphs

5. "[...] I may venture [...]" *A Treatise of Human Nature, Section VI, Of Personal Identity,* David Hume, (1739).

6. "No aboriginal stuff [...]" *Does 'Consciousness' Exist?*, William James (1904), First published in *Journal of Philosophy, Psychology, and Scientific Methods*, 1, 477-491.

7. "Believing, with Max Weber, [...]" *The Interpretation of Cultures: Selected Essays*, Clifford Geertz, (New York: Basic Books, 1973), p.5.

Interaction and Reflexivity

8. "Identifying randomness [...]" *Critical Mass: how one thing leads to another,* Philip Ball, (UK: Arrow Book, 2005), p.94.

9. "Take me as an example [...]" *The Audacity of Hope: Thoughts on Reclaiming the American Dream*, Barack Obama, (New York: Crown, 2006), p. 191.

10. "There are three kinds of lies [...]", *Chapters from My Autobiography*, Mark Twain, (1906).

On Knowledge and Truth

Epigraphs

11. "Be not astonished [...]" *Short Treatise on God, Man & His Wellbeing*, Benedictus de Spinoza, trans. Abraham Wolf (London: A. & C. Black, 1910).

12. "The fate of our times [...]" *Wissenschaft als Beruf, Science as a Vocation*, Max Weber (Munich, 1917).

13. *Bouvard et Pécuchet,* Gustave Flaubert, (1881).

14. "Imagination is more important [...]" *Cosmic Religion: With Other Opinions and Aphorisms,* Albert Einstein, (1931), p. 97.

15. "[...] not entertaining [...]" *An Essay Concerning Human Understanding*, John Locke, (1690).

16. "[...] the most essential characteristic [...]" *Portraits from Memory and*

Other Essays, Bertrand Russell, (New York: Simon & Schuster, 1956), p. 153.

17. "Plurality should not be assumed without necessity." *Ordinatio,* William of Ockham, (c. 1321 to 1325).

18. "All determination is negation" from *"omnis determinatio est negatio",* Letter to J. Jellis, Benedictus de Spinoza, (1674), as later translated by Georg Wilhelm Friedrich Hegel.

Deeds vs. Thoughts

Epigraph

19. "Dans l'attachement [...]" *Le Mythe de Sisyphe,* Albert Camus (Gallimard, 1942), édition *folio essais* p. 22-23.

20. *Thinking Fast and Slow,* Daniel Kahneman, (New York: Farrar, Straus and Giroux, 2011).

21. "[...] a large proportion of our positive activities [...]" *The General Theory of Employment, Interest and Money,* Chap. 12 Section 7, John Maynard Keynes, (UK: Palgrave Macmillan, 1936).

22. " [...] he who is deceived [...]" *On the Fame of the Athenians,* Plutarch.

23. "You are a man [...]" *Crime and Punishment,* Fyodor Dostoyevsky, (Lexington, USA: Maestro Publishing Group, 2011), p. 248-249.

24. *Animal Farm,* George Orwell (London: Secker and Warburg, 1945).

The Absurd

Epigraphs

25. "A simple, decent [...]" *Stages on Life's Way,* Søren Kierkegaard, trans. Howard V. Hong and Edna H. Hong, (New Jersey: Princeton University Press, 1988), p. 163-164.

26. " Il n'y a qu'un problème [...]" *Le Mythe de Sisyphe,* Albert Camus (Gallimard, 1942), édition *folio essais* p. 17.

Everything Changes (almost)

Epigraphs

27. "Spiritual unhealthniness [...]" *Ethics, Demonstrated in Geometrical Order,* Part V, Prop. XX Notes, Benedictus de Spinoza, (1677).

28. "I am weary [...]" *On Democracy, Revolution, and Society,* Alexis de Tocqueville, (London: The University of Chicago Press, 1980), p. 267.

29. "We must all obey [...]" Letter to Sir Hercules Langrishe, Edmund Burke, (1792).

30. " [...] un absolu [...]" *La Pensée et le Mouvant,* Henri Bergson (Paris: PUF, 1998), p. 181.

On the Characteristics of Life

Epigraphs

31. "[...] the main intention of nature [...]" *Two Treatise on Government,* John Locke, (1689).

32. "No virtue [...]" *Ethics, Demonstrated in Geometrical Order,* Part IV, Prop. XXII, Benedictus de Spinoza, (1677).

33. "Only through [...]" *Die Künstler (The Artists),* Johann Christoph Friedrich von Schiller, (1789).

The Influence of the Environment

Epigraphs

34. "[...] understand that men are the subjects and not the rulers of

their accidents." *The Histories*, Herodotus, Book VII Ch. 49, (Pax Librorium 2010), trans. A.D. Godley.

35. "The emerging field of epigenetics [...]" *Zoobiquity*, Barbara Natterson-Horowitz & Kathryn Bowers, (New York: Alfred A. Knopf, 2012), p. 106.

36. "L'existence précède l'essence" *L'existentialisme est un humanisme*, Jean-Paul Sartre (Paris: Nagel, 1946).

37. "During the journey [...]" *Human, All too Human*, Friedrich Nietzsche, (Cambridge: Cambridge University Press, 1986), trans. R.J. Hollingdale, Prop. 206.

38. "[...] un homme, véritablement [...]" *Mémorial de Sainte-Hélène*, Comte de Las Cases (1828), p.302.

39. *Behavioral study of obedience*, Stanley Milgram (University of Yale), The Journal of Abnormal and Social Psychology, Vol 67(4), Oct 1963, 371-378.

On Human Contradictions

Epigraphs

40. "Plusieurs choses certaines [...]" *Pensées*, Blaise Pascal, (edition 1671).

41. "Never mind [...]" *The History of Western Philosophy*, Bertrand Russell, (New York: Simon & Schuster), p.260. First Published in London by George Allen & Unwin Ltd (1946).

42. *Der Steppenwolf*, Herman Hesse, First Published in Germany by S. Fischer Verlag (1927). English Version first published in the United Kingdom by Martin Secker in 1929.

43. *The End of History and the Last Man*, Yoshihiro Francis Fukuyama, (New York: Free Press, 1992).

44. *Leben des Galilei* (Life of Galileo), Bertolt Brecht, first premier in 1943.

45. "Man needs one thing [...]" *Notes from Underground,* Fyodor Dostoyevsky, (USA: W.W. Norton & Company, 2001), p. 19, trans. Michael R. Katz.

46. "[...] people knowingly [...]" *Notes from Underground,* Fyodor Dostoyevsky, (USA: W.W. Norton & Company, 2001), p. 15, trans. Michael R. Katz.

On Ethics

Epigraphs

47. "We are building [...]" Cardinal Joseph Ratzinger (later on Benedictus XVI) in April 18, 2005 homily, Vatican Basilica.

48. "The most important [...]" Albert Einstein in a reply letter to a minister of a church in Brooklyn, New York, USA (November 20, 1950).

49. "I do not understand [...]" Winston Churchill as Secretary of State at the War Office of Great Britain in 1919, in reply to a Royal Air Force command in Cairo in relation to the use of chemical weapons against disobeying Arabs.

50. "When the leaders [...]" *Reflections on the Revolution in France,* Edmund Burke, (New York: Oxford University Press, 2009), p. 247.

51. "It is what Herman Hesse referred to as the sphere of the bourgeoisie [...]" in reference to *Der Steppenwolf,* Herman Hesse, First Published in Germany by S. Fischer Verlag (1927). English Version first published in the United Kingdom by Martin Secker in 1929.

On Religions

Epigraphs

52. "God has no religion." *Re-statements of Christian doctrine: in twenty-five sermons,* Sermon X, Henry Whitney Bellows, (1860).

53. "[...] a religion is [...]" *The Interpretation of Cultures: selected essays,* Clifford Geertz, (New York: Basic Books, 1973), p.90.

54. "Une société sans religion [...]" *Napoléon : ses Opinons et Jugements sur les hommes et sur les choses,* M. Damas-Hinard (1838), p.390.

55. "[...] la religion [...] rattache au ciel [...]" *Opinions de Napoléon,* Privat Joseph Claramond Pelet de La Lozère (1833), p.223.

56. *Clash of Civilizations,* Samuel P. Huntington, (1996).

57. *Les Identités Meurtrières* (In the Name of Identity: Violence and the Need to Belong), Amin Maalouf, (Paris: Grasset, 1998).

58. "I think, therefore I am", "Cogito ergo sum", "Je pense, donc je suis", *Discours sur la Méthode,* René Descartes, (1637).

On Political and Economic Systems

Epigraphs

59. "[...] the greatest of penalties [...]" *The Republic,* Book I Section 347, Plato, trans. Allan Bloom, (1968).

60. "[...] the ideas of economists [...]" *The General Theory of Employment, Interest and Money,* Chap. 24 Section 5, John Maynard Keynes, (UK: Palgrave Macmillan, 1936).

61. "The political problem of mankind [...]" *Liberalism and Labour,* John Maynard Keynes, (Speech and then article, 1926).

Power: a Key Paradigm of Living Beings

Epigraph

62. "[...] the fundamental concept in social science [...]" *Power,* Bertrand Russell, (Routledge Classics 2004), p.4. First Published in London by George Allen & Unwin Ltd (1938).

63. "[...] almost everything that we call [...]" *Beyond Good and Evil,*

Friedrich Nietzsche, (Cambridge: Cambridge University Press, 2002), trans. Judith Norman, Prop. 229.

The Ingredients of Success

Epigraphs

64. "Ce qui vient au monde [...]" *Fureur et Mystère*, René Char, (1948).

65. "Knowledge may give weight [...]" *Letters Written by the Late Right Honourable Philip Dormer Stanhope, Earl of Chesterfield, to His Son, Philip Stanhope, Esq.*, (London: Mrs. Eugina Stanhope, 1800).

66. "As a rule, the man who first thinks [...]", *History of Western Philosophy*, Bertrand Russell, (New York: Simon & Schuster), p.624. First Published in London by George Allen & Unwin Ltd (1946).

67. *Outliers*, Malcolm Gladwell, (New York: Little, Brown and Company, 2008).

68. *Fooled by Randomness*, Nassim Nicholas Taleb, (New York: Random House, 2001).

69. "But man is a frivolous [...]" *Notes From Underground*, Fyodor Dostoyevsky, (USA: W.W. Norton & Company, 2001), p. 24, trans. Michael R. Katz.

70. "I remember once going [...]" *Collected Papers of Srinivasa Ramanujan*, (Cambridge, UK: Cambridge University Press, 1927).

71. "If Shakespeare had been [...]" *A Treatise on Man, His Intellectual Faculties and His Education*, Claude-Adrien Helvétius, trans. W. Hooper, M.D., (London, 1777).

72. "[...] for the idea was by no means [...]" *Crime and Punishment*, Fyodor Dostoyevsky, (Lexington, USA: Maestro Publishing Group, 2011), p. 372.

INDEX

A

Abductive Reasoning | 69
Africa | 10, 243, 245, 326, 332, 423, 425
Agnosticism | 345
Albert the Engineer (the story) | 225
Alexander the Great | 5, 15, 114, 332, 335
Analytical Philosophy/ Approach | 69, 71, 88, 120, 122, 433
  Principia Mathematica | 434
  Vienna Circle | 88, 123
Anarchism | 59, 86, 364
Anaximander | 81
Anicca | 179
Anthropology | 292
  Symbolic | 329
A priori | 29-31, 101, 107, 214, 289, 309
Arab(s) | 15, 62, 114
  Spring | 387
Aristotle | 59, 77, 78, 86, 87, 112, 395
  Golden Mean | 320
Athens, Antiquity | 15, 360, 375, 407
Atomists, the | 130
Austria | 420
Austro-Hungarian Empire | 33

B

Baal | 332
Baal-Hadad | 338
Babylon | 6, 335
Bach, Johann Sebastian | 335
Bacteria | 43, 182, 196, 202, 230
Balkans | 33
Bangladesh | 425
Barbarians | 6, 283, 375, 385, 408
Beliefs | 91, 101, 104, 107, 110, 162, 281
  False Beliefs | 274
  Religion | 345
Bellows, Henry Whitney | 321
Benedictus XVI, Pope | 285
Bergson, Henri | 78, 181, 198
  Elan Vital | 179, 180
Beritus | 6
Bible | 322, 344
  New Testament | 312
  Old Testament | 134, 317
Big Bang Theory | 7, 389
Bill of Rights | 8
Blais, Jon | 405
Bolshevik | 8, 33, 147, 355
Boltzmann, Ludwig | 409
Bosnia-Herzegovina | 33
Bouvard et Pécuchet | 66
Bowers, Kathryn | 223

Brazil | 9
Britain, Great. See United Kingdom
Bronze Age | 4
Brothers (the story) | 402
Buddha | 5, 14, 339
Buddhism | 179, 326, 343, 436
Buffet, Warren | 58, 241
Burke, Edmund | 173, 294
Butterfly Effect | 41, 62
Byzantium | 114, 244, 321, 322, 375

C

Cambrian Explosion | 2
Camus, Albert | 125, 153, 158, 171, 306
Carbon chemistry | 201
Cartesians. See Descartes
Carthage | 5, 6
Categorical Imperative | 295, 297
Categorisation | 23, 29, 122
　Categories | 23, 30, 102
　Naming | 28
Causality | 27, 28, 31, 34, 35, 70, 83,
　102, 162, 302, 436, 437
Cedars | 184
Chaos | 178, 214, 290, 353, 364, 369
Chaos Theory | 7, 39, 268
Char, René | 397
Chavez, Hugo | 388
China | 6, 7, 9, 16, 48, 113, 114, 194,
　233, 238, 242, 288, 355, 363,
　368, 375, 381, 382, 383
Christianity | 14, 17, 78, 79, 131, 194,
　213, 217, 250, 253, 268, 313,
　317, 321, 322, 326, 332, 335,
　336, 338, 343, 345, 384, 391
Churchill, Winston | 275, 291
Circularity | 162, 179, 187
Civilisation | 54, 116, 173, 210, 278,
　283, 373, 385
Climatology | 184, 220
Cognitive Dissonance | 231
Cold War | 368, 382, 392
Columbus, Christopher | 16
Common Sense | 415

Communism | 8, 59, 77, 86, 144, 147,
　148, 336, 355, 363, 368
Compassion | 215, 296, 309, 380
Confucianism | 327
Confucius | 5
Consciousness | 18, 23, 67, 80, 100,
　101, 149, 203, 226, 234, 283, 315
Consequentialism | 292, 299
Conservation of Natural Habitats | 247
Conservatism | 86, 189, 355
Constantine (Emperor) | 339
Constantine (the story) | 325
Contemplation | 78, 131, 132, 133, 178
Credit Bubble | 256
Critical Knowledge | 71, 72, 73, 76
Crusades | 7
Cultural Evolution | 273, 277, 331, 333,
　435
Culture (Religion) | 336
Cyber War | 382
Cynicism | 10, 117, 124, 213, 215, 216,
　218

D

D'Alembert, Jean le Rond | 319
Darwin, Charles | 7, 80, 406
　Darwinian Evolution | 19, 172, 184,
　268, 269, 273, 277, 278, 283,
　319, 391
Das Kapital | 77
Davies, Donald | 373
Deduction, Deductive Reasoning | 5,
　69, 71, 72, 78, 88, 92, 94, 95,
　136, 144
De Gaulle, Charles | 144, 270
Democracy | 228, 229, 356
Deng Xiaoping | 114
Descartes, René | 39, 56, 114, 129
　Cartesian Philosophy | 128, 434
Desire (as concept) | 12, 60, 171, 213,
　214, 230, 239, 252, 367, 370,
　386, 393, 415, 418
　Conflicting | 355, 364
Diderot, Denis | 319

Dostoevsky, Fyodor | 147, 270, 345, 418, 427
Dukkha | 179
Dynamic Systems | 41, 46, 48, 53, 198

E

Earl of Chesterfield, 4th | 397
Ecole Polytechnique | 424
Edward VIII | 270
Einstein, Albert | 7, 13, 70, 74, 285, 418, 420
Elan Vital. See Bergson
Emotions (as concept) | 96, 136, 149, 211, 235, 237, 296, 331, 384
  Emotional Intelligence | 412, 413
  In Morality | 295, 296
  In Religion | 330
Empedocles | 5, 81
Emperor Penguins | 205
Empiricism, Empirical Knowledge | 69, 76, 78, 92, 93, 94, 105, 115, 123, 130, 165
Energy Security | 245
England | 15, 426
English Civil War | 8
Entente Cordiale | 194
Entropy | 174, 178, 197
Essence | 23, 38, 99, 122, 175, 178, 226, 301
Eugenics | 137, 275, 291
Euro | 257, 258
Europe | 7, 8, 15, 59, 140, 150, 194, 210, 229, 233, 238, 255, 257, 258, 291, 305, 315, 332, 334, 355, 372, 385, 387, 395
European Union | 257, 259, 361, 375
Evolution. See Darwin, Charles
Existentialism | 127, 139, 143, 345

F

Falsification. See Popper
Famine | 243
Fear | 59, 130, 141, 151, 210, 236, 237, 239, 251, 255, 318, 323, 358, 360, 363, 364, 379, 384, 385, 386, 387, 389, 391, 393, 395
First Cause | 83, 436
Foie gras | 254
Founding Fathers (of the United States) | 17, 290
France | 8, 15, 17, 33, 48, 121, 140, 144, 190, 194, 229, 243, 270, 291, 313, 333, 335, 355, 363, 368, 370, 381, 424, 425
Franklin D. Roosevelt | 388
Free Will | 44, 45, 81, 83, 162, 230, 286, 306
Frege, Friedrich Ludwig Gottlob | 434
French Revolution | 8, 333, 335, 368
Freud, Sigmund | 7, 82, 86, 269

G

Galileo | 7, 73, 114, 253, 267
Galois, Evariste | 424
  Galois Theory | 424
Geertz, Clifford | 26, 321
Genghis Khan | 7, 17
Genome Project | 7
Geology | 184, 319
Germany | 15, 33, 52, 87, 88, 114, 140, 194, 207, 223, 229, 258, 267, 290, 335, 382
Girolamo Cardano | 409
Gladwell, Malcolm | 406
Globalisation | 38, 56, 61, 226, 259, 391
Glorious Revolution | 8, 368
Gödel, Kurt | 123
Great Depression | 257
Great Recession | 114
Greece | 15, 81, 257
  Antiquity | 5, 6, 10, 59, 75, 76, 86, 114, 115, 131, 178, 335, 339, 356, 408, 410
Grotius, Hugo | 210, 392

H

Hamsa | 339
Hard Work | 418

Hegel, Georg Wilhelm Friedrich | 86, 267, 436
  Dialectical Approach | 87
  Hegelian Philosophy | 39, 101, 268
Heraclitus | 173, 176, 178, 180, 260, 275, 410
Herodotus | 223
Hesse, Herman | 207, 250, 304
Hinduism | 207, 326, 334, 337
Hobbes, Thomas | 12, 212
Holy Roman Empire | 7
Homer | 5
Honesty, Integrity | 143, 315, 423
Hume, David | 21, 70, 162
  Humean Philosophy | 25, 31, 70
Huntington, Samuel | 334

I

Idealism | 86, 87, 88, 267, 358
India | 9, 14, 113, 242, 243, 356, 381, 425
Individualism, Individuality | 56, 115, 133, 138, 159, 259, 270, 299, 365, 429
Individuality | 159, 161. See Individualism
Indonesia | 9, 242, 245, 356
Induction | 69, 70, 71, 73, 93
Industrial Revolution | 113, 115, 212, 217
Instincts | 100, 102, 118, 204, 208, 213, 267, 282, 283, 296, 298
Instrumentalism | 95
Intelligence Quotient (IQ) | 419, 420
Internet | 8, 38, 56, 89, 116, 259, 354, 363, 373, 391, 401
Intuition | 31, 71, 82, 90, 96, 123, 127, 132, 136, 163, 172, 175, 179, 181, 203, 204, 209, 296, 328, 344, 391, 411, 418
  Counter- | 281, 415
Ionians (Greeks) | 5, 15
Irrationality. See Rationality
Islam | 7, 14, 15, 194, 265, 283, 323, 332, 335, 337, 338

Italy | 16, 33, 253, 257, 291

J

Jacob (the story) | 323
James, William | 21
Japan | 9, 16, 53, 113, 190, 191, 382
Jefferson, Thomas | 290
Jessica (the story) | 324
Jesus | 14, 217, 322, 323, 324, 335
John F. Kennedy | 388
Jordan, Michael | 418
Judaism | 5, 14, 17
Justinian (Emperor) | 339

K

Kafka, Franz | 103
Kahneman, Daniel | 129
Kant, Immanuel | ix, 28, 86, 88, 286, 297
Keynesianism | 351
Keynes, John Maynard | 146, 347
  Keynesianism | 52, 53
Kierkegaard, Søren | 153, 162, 168, 343, 345
Kim Yong-il | 388
Kurd(s) | 15, 291

L

Laissez-faire | 41, 53
Language | 67, 100, 120, 435
Laozi | 5
La Terreur | 229, 313. See French Revolution
Laws of Probability | 41
Leibniz, Gottfried Wilhelm von | 207, 215, 424, 434
Liberalism | 7, 189, 259, 355, 367, 370, 391
Libertarianism | 52, 53, 351
Lincoln, Abraham | 314
Little Boy (the story) | 378
Locke, John | 90, 195, 210, 409
Logical Models | 101, 136, 188
Lord Monboddo | 406, 408

LTCM (Long Term Capital Management L.P) | 414
Luck | 411

M

Maalouf, Amin | 334
Mamluks | 7
Mammals | 3, 4, 81, 127, 128, 183, 205, 237, 276
Marcus Aurelius | 314
Marx, Karl | 8, 77, 88, 268, 409
   Dialectical Materialism | 77, 87, 268
   Marxism | 137
Materialism. See Marx
Maxwell, James Clerk | 7, 12
Mediterranean | 6, 87, 206, 288
Memory | 27, 28, 29, 98
Mesopotamia | 335, 338, 340
Metaphysics | 79, 88, 120, 121, 213, 326, 327, 329, 333, 339, 341, 342, 346, 432
Micro-organisms | 202, 379
Middle Ages | 11, 79, 194, 290, 313, 333, 384, 408, 421
Middle East | 15, 194, 288, 332, 339, 356
Milgram Experiment | 236
Moderation | 312, 320, 366, 368, 430
Modesty | 19, 50, 89, 117, 159, 221, 222, 276, 278, 317
Mongol(s) | 15, 17, 114, 375
Monkey & Koala (the story) | 155
Monogamy | 209, 264, 265
Mozart, Wolfgang Amadeus | 335, 418
Muslim Empire | 10

N

Naming. See Categorisation
Napoléon Bonaparte | 15, 17, 48, 114, 229, 234, 321, 413
NATO, North Atlantic Treaty Organization | 371

Natterson-Horowitz, Barbara | 223
Natural Gift | 422
Natural Law (Legal) | 209, 210, 212
Natural Sciences | 35, 69, 73, 74, 110, 119, 132, 436
Natural State | 210
Nature vs. Nurture | 232
Necessary Cause | 436
Neoplatonism | 131
Nepal | 14
Newton, Isaac Sir | 7, 39, 103, 424
New World | 6, 7, 113, 114, 145, 217
Nietzsche, Friedrich | 88, 215, 227, 269, 289, 383
Nihilism | 158, 166, 167, 429
Nous | 99, 131

O

Obesity | 209, 239
Optimism | 113, 114, 146, 207, 216, 255, 266, 313, 431
Orwell, George | 147, 148

P

Paleocene-Eocene Junction | 219
Pascal, Blaise | 118, 249, 325
Pascale (the story) | 325
Penny Wise Pound Foolish (the story) | 192
Perpetual Flux | 21, 178, 180
Persia | 5, 6, 15, 206, 335
Perspectivism | 159, 289
Pharaohs | 4, 260, 387
Phase Transition | 45, 46, 61, 62
Phoenicia | 6, 332
Plato | 77, 86, 87, 128, 130, 213, 347, 410
   World of Ideas | 128
Plutarch | 146
Poincaré, Henri | 13
Politics | 184, 187, 189, 192, 194, 210, 218, 220, 228, 229, 236, 241,

249, 256, 257, 263, 270, 285,
287, 288, 291, 294, 299, 306,
307, 312, 313, 316, 317, 320,
324, 328, 331, 332, 337, 341,
375, 378, 380, 384, 389, 390,
392, 395, 412, 414, 419, 424,
425, 431, 432
Polyandry | 264
Polygamy | 265
Polygyny | 264, 265
Popper, Karl | 70, 123
   Falsification | 72, 88, 117, 123
Posidonius | 179
Positivism. See Optimism
Principle of Parsimony | 95, 110, 145
Protagoras | 103
Pythagoras, Pythagoreans | 5, 131, 338

Q

Quantum Mechanics/Physics | 7, 40,
43, 46, 84, 94, 107, 163, 182,
420, 435, 437
   Quantum Fluctuations | 85

R

Ramanujan, Srinivasa | 424, 425, 427
Ramayana | 345
Randomness | 10, 31, 40, 41, 138, 149,
214, 293
Rationality | 72, 79, 82, 96, 118, 136,
168, 282, 283, 295, 296, 297,
308, 331, 344, 345
   Breakdown | 119, 165, 345
   Ir- | 168
Redwoods | 184
Reflexivity | 37, 38, 42, 47, 88, 101, 278,
279, 353
Reformation | 7, 56, 229, 317, 345, 391
Relativity, General | 29, 74, 94, 111,
176, 187, 420, 435
Relativity, Special | 13
Renaissance | 6, 78, 112, 114, 115, 194,
217, 339, 391
Reproduction | 2, 102, 177, 182, 197,
198, 199, 202, 204, 206, 208,
211, 230, 296, 298, 334, 403
Roman Empire | 5, 6, 332, 339
Romantic Movement | 86, 168, 210,
218, 282, 295
Rousseau, Jean-Jacques | 118, 131, 210,
218
   Confessions | 12
Russell, Bertrand | 88, 90, 97, 226, 269,
377, 406, 408
Russia | 33, 381

S

Saint Augustine | 6, 12, 15, 78
Saint Paul | 14, 15, 250
Saint Thomas Aquinas | 78
Saladin | 7, 15
Sarajevo | 33
Sartre, Jean-Paul | 226, 235
Scepticism | 53, 117, 124, 313, 429, 431
Schiller, Johann Christoph Friedrich
von | 221
Schopenhauer, Arthur | 88, 207, 215,
267
Self-Control | 413
Self-Esteem | 59, 133, 190, 231, 240,
252, 260, 267, 270, 359, 367, 403
Self-Preservation | 102, 298
Senecca | 249
Serbia | 33
Sex | 262
Sexually Transmitted Diseases (STDs)
| 230
Sheep (the story) | 349
Singularities of Reason | 119, 165
Smith, Adam | 12
Snub-Nosed Monkeys | 205
Socialism | 8, 86, 351, 355, 370, 409
Sophists, the | 103, 215
Space Program | 8, 244, 361
Spain | 16, 257, 291
Sparta, Antiquity | 15, 375, 408
Speculative Knowledge | 71, 74, 75,
76, 78
Speculator (the story) | 75

Spinoza, Benedictus de | 17, 65, 124, 137, 173, 195, 436
Standard Model Theory | 389
Stoicism | 130, 249, 319
   Zeno | 6
Survival | 58, 80, 96, 132, 134, 139, 150, 157, 163, 165, 205, 211, 214, 217, 230, 235, 251, 254, 267, 269, 277, 283, 297, 331, 386, 403
   Of the Fittest | 76
Symbols (Religion) | 339

T

Taleb, Nassim Nicholas | 406
Taoism | 5, 207
Tardigrade | 205
Tarek (the story) | 323
Tax | 52, 191, 220, 223, 244, 257, 360, 370
Thermodynamics | 7, 12, 39, 40, 178
Tolkien, J.R.R. | 210
Tortoise | 183
Trading | 75
Treaty of Berlin | 33
Treaty of Versailles | 34, 140
Triple Alliance | 33
Turkey | 15
Turkmenistan | 15
Turk(s) | 15, 114, 283

U

Umayyads | 15
Unconscious | 82, 96, 98, 136, 234, 235, 269, 384, 388, 391. See Subconscious
United Kingdom | 8, 33, 86, 88, 140, 190, 194, 210, 249, 257, 291, 368, 372, 381, 409, 426
United Nations | 339, 381
United States, the | 17, 33, 86, 131, 194, 230, 244, 257, 305, 355, 356, 357, 370, 372, 381, 382, 383, 395, 408, 420

Universal Declaration of Human Rights | 8, 307
Universals (Philosophy) | 433, 435
Universe | 1, 19, 24, 40, 84, 182, 185, 197, 214, 433
Utilitarianism | 295, 299, 305, 308, 320, 345

V

Value | 161
   Creation | 371, 373
   Preservation | 371
   Transfer | 371, 373
Vienna Circle. See Analytical Philosophy/ Approach
Vietnam | 194
Voltaire
   Candide | 255

W

Washington, George | 17
Western (Civilisation) | 9, 48, 78, 86, 87, 114, 130, 140, 206, 288, 291, 320
Wikipedia | 319, 371
Will to Exist | 82, 204, 205, 217, 267
Wittgenstein, Ludwig | 88, 268
   Philosophical Investigations | 13
World Wars | 33

Y

Yugoslavia | 33

Z

Zeitgeist Movement | 11
Zeus | 332

JOHN H.T. FRANCIS is an intellectual and a writer. He is particularly preoccupied with the continued intellectual and social challenges of the modern man despite the remarkable human advances in many fields over the past few centuries. John H.T. Francis uses a multi-disciplinary approach to his thinking, equally relying on disciplines as diverse as Philosophy, Science, Social Sciences, and History. He does not shy away from asking the necessary questions while attempting to draw new elements of answers from various fields in a comprehensive and as coherent as possible manner. In doing so, he highlights the intricate and yet beautiful nature of existence and of the human mind. John H.T. Francis does not believe in the primacy of one field of thought or action over the other, the primacy of one human culture or society over the other, or in a fundamental difference of the human condition and psyche across cultures and ages.

John H.T. Francis has an academic background in Science, Engineering, and Business/Economics, as well as geographically and professionally diverse experiences. He currently combines with his writings a career of entrepreneurship.